MODELS OF ECONOMIC AND POLITICAL GROWTH IN NEPAL

MODELS OF ECONOMIC AND POLITICAL GROWTH IN NEPAL

Keshab Bhattarai
Lecturer in Economics
The University of Hull U.K.

SERIALS PUBLICATIONS
NEW DELHI (INDIA)

First Published - 2007

ISBN: 978-81-8387-109-9

Published by

SERIALS PUBLICATIONS
4830/24, Prahlad Street, Ansari Road
Darya Ganj, New Delhi-110002 (India)
Phone : 23245225. Fax : 91-11-23272135
E-mail: serials@satyam.net.in

CONTENTS

FOREWORDS FOR PART I

Nepal went through series of conflicts and troubles in last 60 years. These were caused by lack of clarity and implementation of growth and redistribution policies aimed at reducing poverty. Non-cooperation among competing political and economic forces has brought Nepal into crisis and growth disaster. The major reason for conflict was the short-sighted horizon of these players who try to maximise their own current share on GDP taking its size as constant over time. It has discouraged productive economic activities and transfer of better technology and knowledge and resources from abroad with dangerous consequences to the economy. With elimination of absolute monarchy and an agreement between the SPA and the Maoists on November 7, 2006 Nepal has entered into a new phase.

An effort is made in this book to analyse the origin of current crises, consequences and solutions using the political economy and dynamic general equilibrium framework. First part presents the current problems in political economy of Nepal and suggests models that are applicatble for solving the current crises taking account of structural realities of the Nepalese economy. The first chapter briefly introduces on a dynamic multishousehold general equilibrium model that is suitable for analysis of growth and income distribution. The more extensive form of this model is contained in the second part. The chapter two is an update on the Nepalese political situation after the 19 days revolution in April 2006 which has brought both political parties led by SPA (seven party alliances) and Maoists to the forefront of Nepalese politics. It expresses frustration on slow progress in creating consensus on economic growth in the context of the more than 8 per cent growth rates achieved by Nepal's giant neighbours China and India. It warns Nepalese politicians not to ignore the more important task of igniting the growth process and request them to be more assertive and decisive for things that matter for the people. The next chapter analyses the political economy game using a Nash bargaining framework for the political eocnomy of Nepal before the April 2006 revolution. It captures the situation that evolved after the beginning of the Moists insurgency, particularly since the Royal massacre in 2001 that had brought Nepal into a civil war. This article was written well before the agreement of understanding between the alliance of seven political parties (SPA) and the Maoists in New Dehli in India in November 2005. It presented solutions of the problem in terms of 10 points, which have been realistic up to a large extent. Then I write a brief note on how human capital led development strategy can be implemented to uplift the lives of millions in Nepal if the state provides subsidies on education and provide environments in which individuals could be motivated towards realising full potential taking a case of myself which I know and has worked in realising the realistic dreams one can have even if grown up in low-income families of Nepal. The second part is more objective analysis of the Nepalese economy based on the skills that I had learnt during my PhD studies in Northeastern and while working closely with my Professors in the US. This part first focuses on assessing the the financial sector and reporting a dynamic general equilibrium model for the Nepalese economy built around 1995 benchmarked to input-output table of Nepal and applied for analyses of economic growth, capital accumulation, investment and redistribution of income among households.

This book is result of my research work that I have conducted since I left Nepal for my PhD studies to the USA in 1991. Articles in the first part were written very recently while working as Lecturer in economics of the University of Hull. The chapters in second part originate in my PhD thesis from the Northeastern University Boston USA. Some of the contents are published as working papers or as journal article but this is the first time I have kept everything in one place for comprehensive presentation of my views on models applicable to the Nepalese economy. My research in other issues that include tax, trade, economic growth, enemployment, labour market, poverty and redistribution and bargaining and strategic choices that I did in Universities of Warwick and Hull are reported in my Economic Theory and Models: Derivations, Computations and Applications.

I would be happy if ideas expressed in this book can give some idea about the analysis on the nature of problems and analysis required for peaceful solutions to the years old colflict and new way of thinking for growth and redistribution oriented Nepal in coming years.

I dedicate this book to millions of Nepalese whose welfare and development form the subject of analysis, to my family Prem, Santosh, Manorama, to mother Harimaya, to sisters Basundhara and Manu and their families, to brothers Kedar, Bishnu and to all my friends and relatives from Batase, Devghat, Kathmandu, Varanasi, Nepalese government, ISS, Northeastern, Warwick, Ontario and Hull and for eternal peace of more than 50 people including my father Harikrishna who were close to me and have completed journey of life and left this world since my childhood in mid 1960s. I accept full responsibity for any omissions and errors.

PART - I

POLITICAL ECONOMY MODELS OF NEPAL

1

AN INTTODUCTION TO ECONOMIC MODEL FOR NEW NEPAL

The SPA government and Maoists singed a peace deal on November 8th, 2006 after about two years of 12 point agreement reached between them in New Delhi and about seven months of the peaceful revolution in which millions people came to the street to eliminate the absolute monarchy who had snatched powers away from them. This agreement has given an opportunity to end the decade old conflict that took more than 13000 lives and made all political forces focus in a sort of "build new Nepal contract" reflecting true aspirations of all those people though full realisation of this dream is yet to be seen as the attention so far has focused more on procedural matters rather than substantive ones. This is a time to think about more scientific approach to economic policy making that brings faster growth and redistributes resources balancing the interest of workers, industrialists, business men and professionals involved in nation building. It requires bold policy decisions looking with a long term vision and interest of the people. It is important that the major political forces, that have adopted multi-party parliamentary democracy, committed to the fundamental human rights and economic upliftment of all people particularly the Nepali Congress (NC), Maoists Party (M) and Communist Party of Nepal (CPN) agree on basic model of the economy so that there is a smooth and uninterrupted continuation of development activities no matter whichever of these parties remains in the power rather than repeating the age old rivalry and rebellion created among them by the corrupt feudal system with a policy of divide and rule and leaving them in cut throat competition for power without any regards to other players in the game. Many think that the current peace deal is historic and Nepal has shown strengths for a cooperative solution of conflict and this cooperation should continue for developing comparative advantages of its economy in very competitive global economy. True democracy, at the local, regional and national level among all parties and public institutions guarantees such commitment mechanism where decisions are based on logical and defendable criteria. In a democratic culture people expect healthy debates on issues and policies of national importance among ruling and opposition parties. Decisions need to be taken based on more scientific analysis of facts and figures and informed reasoning.

Such practice creates a national environment where people start thinking and solving their problems on their own with unhindered freedom of expression and economic activities and disciplined in choices by their resource constraints. Political stability obtained by balancing opportunities and constraints of all players in the game is essential for raising the rates of growth of employment, output, capital stock, investment that are instrumental in improving the living standards of majority of people and alleviation of poverty. This is the context for a multi-household multi-sectoral dynamic general equilibrium model for policy analysis presented in this chapter. It will be very brief introduction here as it needs to be expanded and explored further to make it more comprehensive and more accurate. The focus of this model is on redistribution and growth that summarise the aspirations of all parties and people.

ECONOMIC POLICY MODEL OF NEW NEPAL FOR ANALYSIS OF GROWTH AND REDISTRIBUTION

Poverty reduction strategy requires a thorough appreciation of the production as well as the consumption sides of the economy and the structure of the markets, government and the foreign sectors. This section aims to present a simple multi-household multi-sectoral computable dynamic general equilibrium model in which the government uses taxes and spending strategy to alleviate poverty. It is possible to evaluate the life time welfare of households and the impacts of public policy in redistribution of income over time using this framework.

This model of Nepal consist of households grouped in ten categories, $h_1 \ldots h_{10}$, ranked according to their income status from poorest to the richest, firms grouped in nine different sectors $i_1 \ldots i_9$, a government that collects taxes from labour and capital income and on use of inputs and on household income and imposes tariffs on trade with the rest of the world sector. The growth of the economy and distribution of income among households depend on the capital accumulation process and growth rate of productivity of labour force.

It is impossible to have an explicit analytical solution for a big model like this. Therefore numerical technique is used to solve the model. Household preferences and technology of firms are similar to those in Bhattarai (1997) and contained in part II of this book.

$$\text{Max } U_0^h = \sum_{t=0}^{\infty} \beta^t U_t^h \left(C_t^h, l_t^h\right)$$

Subject to

$$\sum_{t=0}^{\infty} R_t^{-1}\left[P_t(1+t^{vc})C_t^h + w_t(1-t_t)l_t^h\right] = \sum_{t=0}^{\infty}\left[(1-t_t)w_t L_t^h + (1-t_k)r_t K_t^h + TR_t^h\right]$$

where C_t^h, l_t^h and L_t^h are respectively composite consumption, leisure and labour supplies of household h in period t, $R_t^{-1} = \prod_{s=0}^{t} 1/(1+r_s)$ is a discount factor; r_s represents the real interest rate on assets at time s; t^{vc} is value added tax on consumption, t^l is labour income taxes, and K_t^h is the composite consumption, which is composed of sectoral consumption goods, P_t is the price of composite consumption (which is based on goods' prices), i.e. $P_t = \vartheta \prod_{i=1}^{n} \alpha_i p_{i,t}^{\alpha_i}$, and $C_t^h = \prod_{i=1}^{n} C_{i,t}^{\alpha_i^h}$.

Industries of the economy are represented by firms that combine both capital and labour input in production and supply of goods and services to the market.

$$\Pi_{j,t}^{y} = [((1-\delta_i^e)PD_{i,t}^{\frac{\sigma_y - 1}{\sigma_y}} + \delta_i^e PE_{i,t}^{\frac{\sigma_y - 1}{\sigma_y}})]^{\frac{1}{\sigma_y - 1}} - \theta_i^v PY_{j,t}^v - \theta_i^d \sum_i a_{i,j}^d P_{i,t}$$

where: $\Pi_{j,t}^{y}$ is the unit profit of activity in sector *j; $PE_{j,t}$* is the export price of good *j* $PD_{j,t}$ is the domestic price of good *j;* $PY_{j,t}^{v}$ is the price of value added per unit of output in activity *j; s_y* is a transformation elasticity parameter; $P_{i,t}$ is the price of final goods used as intermediate goods; δ_j^e is the share parameter for exports in total production; θ_j^v is the share of costs paid to labour and capital; θ_j^d is the cost share of domestic intermediate inputs; $a_{i,j}^d$ are input-output coefficients for domestic supply of intermediate goods.

This is an open economy model in which goods produced at home and foreign countries are considered close substitutes following the Armington assumption, popular in the applied general equilibrium literature and the production process is given by a nested production and trade functions.

Figure 1
Structure of Production and Trade in the Dynamic Multi-household Models

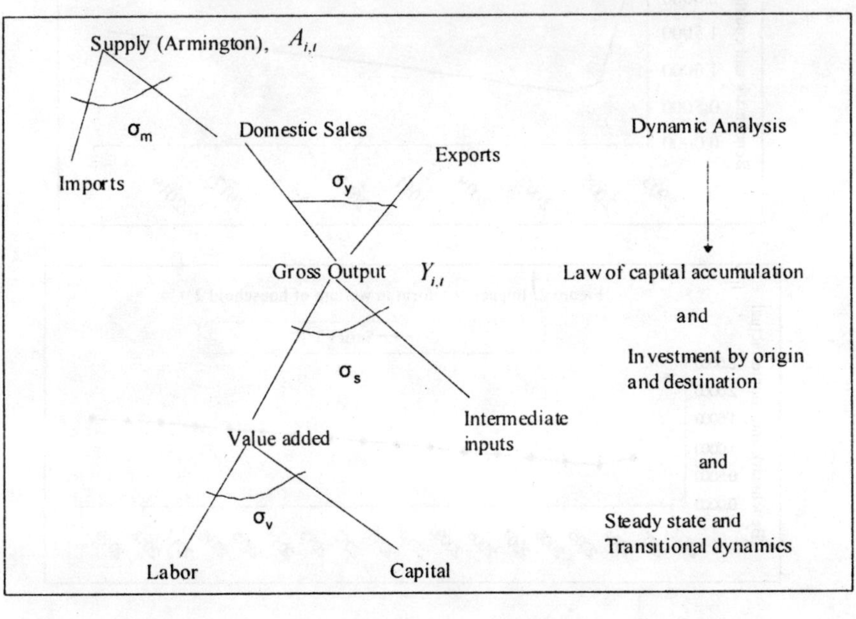

The households pay taxes to the government and government returns part of this income to the poor households and spends rest of it to provide public services.

$$REV_t = \sum_{i,h} t_i^k r_t K_{i,t} + \sum_i t_i^{vc} P_{i,t} C_{i,t}^h + \sum_i t_i^{vg} P_{i,t} G_{i,t} + \sum_i t_i^{vk} P_{i,t} I_{i,t} + \sum_{i,h} t_l w LS_t^h + \sum_i t_i^m PM_{i,t} M_{i,t} + \sum_i t_i^p P_{i,t} GY_{i,t} \quad (25)$$

where REV_t is total government revenue and t_i^k is a composite tax rate on capital income from sector I, t_l^{vc} is the *ad valorem* tax rate on final consumption by households, t_i^{vg} is that on public consumption and t_i^{vk} is the ad valorem tax rate on investment, t_l is the tax rate on labour income of the household, t_i^p is the tax on production, and t_i^m is the tariff on imports.

The steady equilibrium growth path of the economy is determined in terms of the interest rate, discount factor and relative prices of goods and factors in which the excess demand for goods and factors are eliminated and resource balance condition holds for the whole economy, each household, the government and rest of the world sectors in each period and over the model horizon. It also shows how the income of each type of household evolves over time as a function of the relative prices of goods and share of households in income (Figure 2). Government policies and transfers can alter this equilibrium.

Figure 2
Redistribution Impacts of Policy Reforms in the Nepal Model

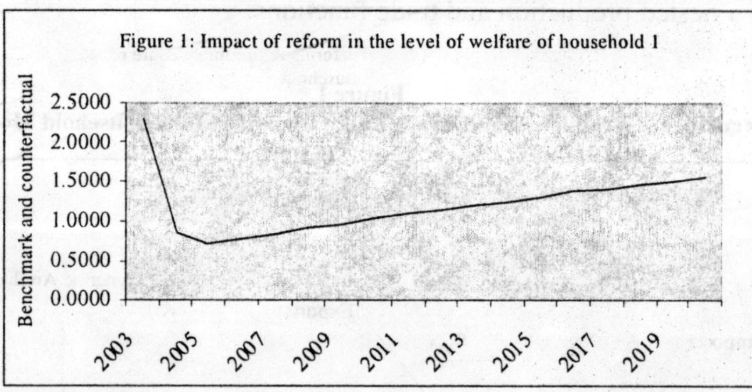

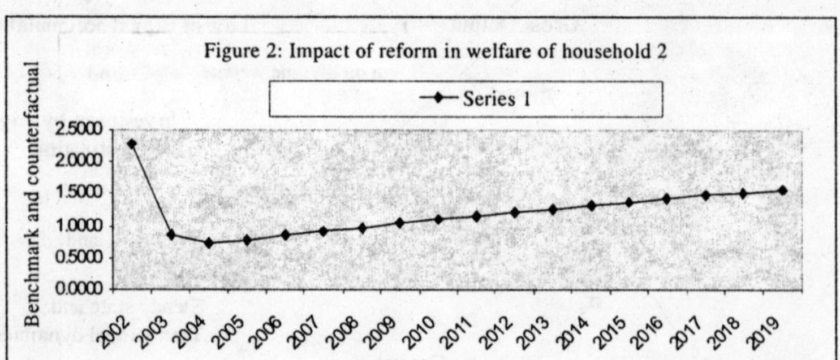

Figure 3: Impact of reform in lifetime welfare of household 3

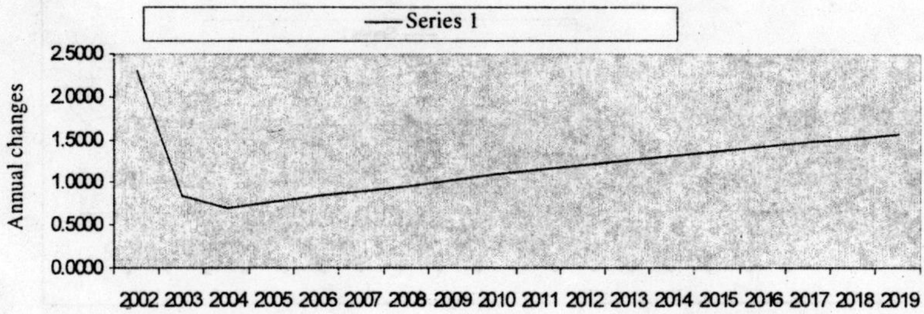

Figure 4: Impact of reforms in lifetime welfare of household 4

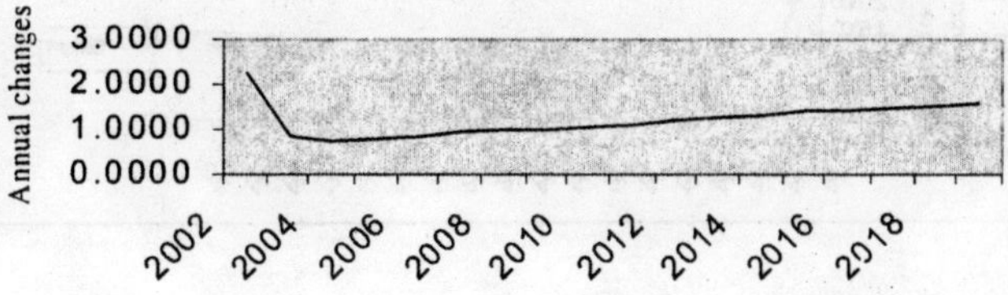

Figure 5: Impact of reforms in lifetime welfare of household 5

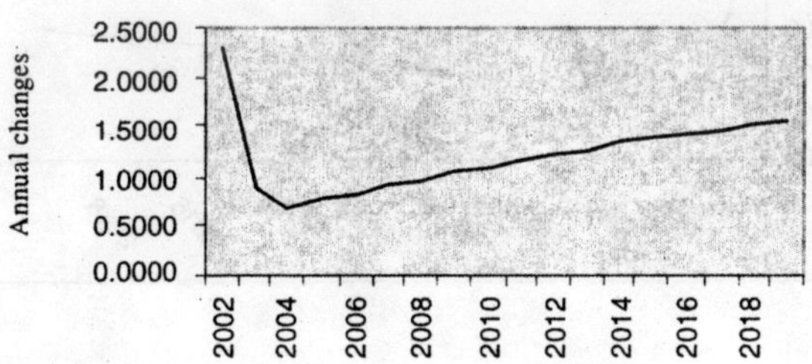

Figure 6: Impact of reform on lifetime welfare of household 6

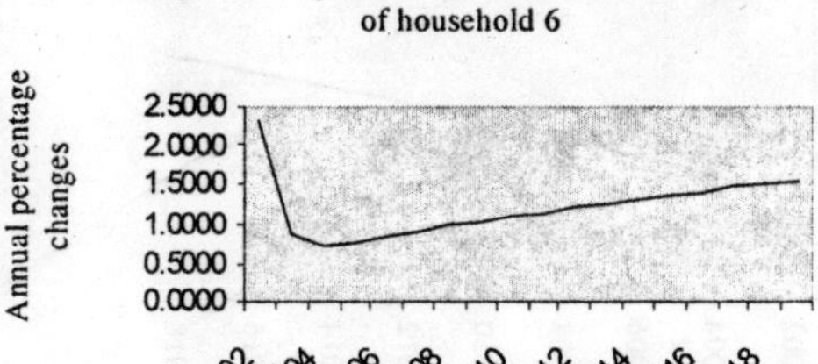

Figure 7: Impact of reforms on lifetime welfare of household 7

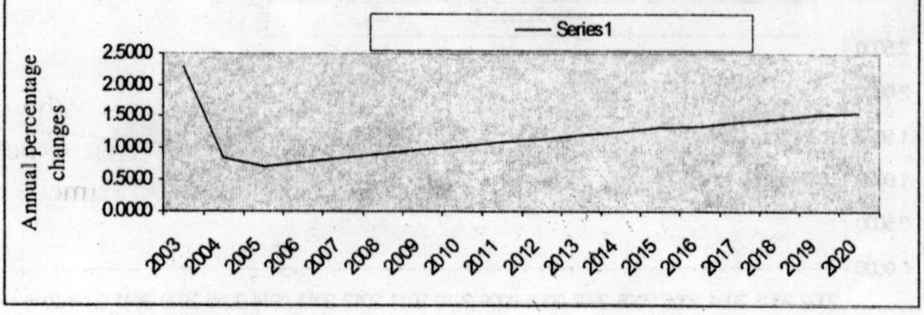

Figure 8: Impact of reform on lifetime welfare of household 8

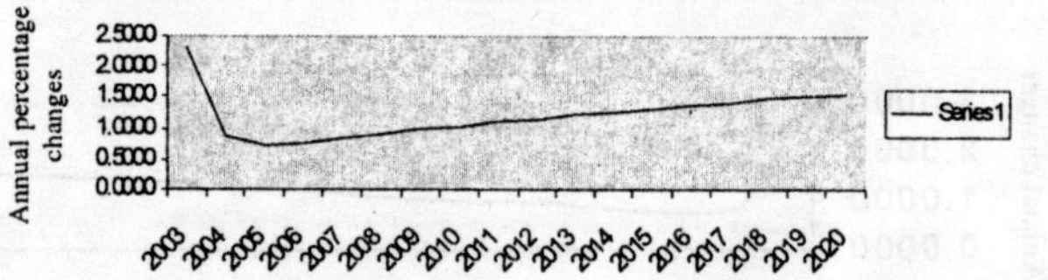

Figure 9: Impact of reforms on lifetime welfare of household 9

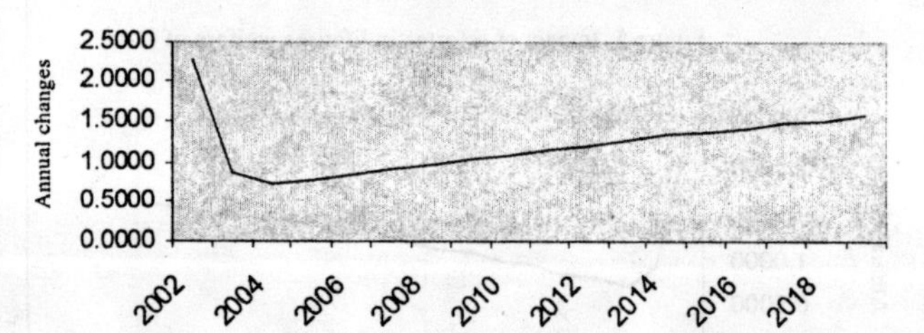

Figure 10: Impact of reforms in lifetime welfare of household 10

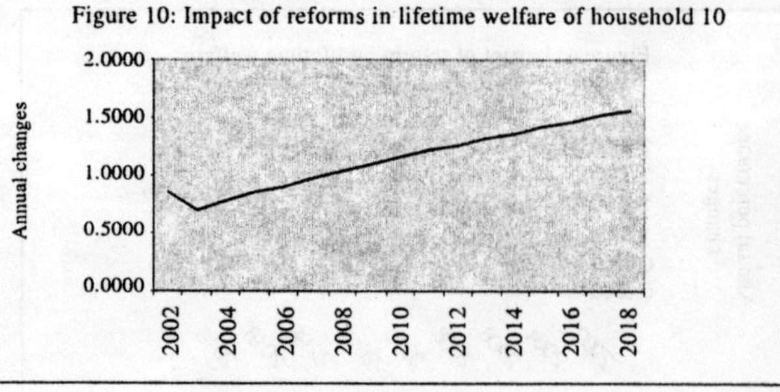

BENCHMARKING AND CALIBRATION OF THE MODEL

The micro-consistency in the model is obtained by making the demand and supply sides balance for each sector in an input-output table maintaining zero profit in equilibrium, balancing the income of households to consumption plus saving, and matching total investment to total savings by the households. The sectoral composition of consumption by households are approximated by the net of tax and transfer income of households that are assumed to remain same across all goods until the more accurate data becomes available. In addition economic survey data is used for the estimates of the distribution of wage, interest rate and transfer income for households.

Key Parameters of the Model

Elasticity of substitution between labour and capital	3.0
Elasticity of substitution between labour and leisure	1.5
Elasticity of substitution consumption and leisure	0.5
growth rate of output	0.02
Benchmark interest rate	0.05
rate of depreciation	0.07
Elasticity of intertemporal substitution	1.1
Elasticity in government consumption	1.0

In my knowledge this is the first applied dynamic general equilibrium model of the Nepal with the dynamics and multisectoral structure contained in the social accounting matrix of the economy as given by the Input Output Tables for Nepal as following:

POLICY SCENARIOS

The income redistribution effect in the model occurs through the differentiated tax rates of household income, value added taxes on consumption of goods and services, labour income tax and capital income tax rates. All these tax experiments should constrain the amount of revenue and find the best optimal rates of taxes given that revenue requirement.

In the above benchmark labour and capital input taxes are replaced by uniform rates of 0.3 and 0.2 in the counterfactual scenarios. Model solutions show how these reforms affect the distribution of income and welfare among households. Results are presented briefly in the following diagrams.

All these model scenarios arise from growing economies that are distorted by taxes in the benchmark and which are removed under the counterfactual scenarios. Tax reform though important seems to have not very significant impact in developing country like Nepal which requires more investment in human capital and physical infrastructure. Piecemeal and patchy reforms will not be able to generate substantial growth according to aspirations of people by introducing measures that make markets more competitive. These results thought yet preliminary take account of wide ranging income and substitution effects through out the markets. Various other scenarios are under consideration and will be investigated further.

Nine Sector Input/Output Table for 1999/00 at Producer's Price (In Million Rs.)

	Agri.	Manuf.	Chem	Metal	Gaselw	Hotel	Transp	Finance	SocServ	Sub-Total	Pcon	Gcon	Prfxinv	Gfxinv	Stock	Exp	Sub-Total	Total Output
Agr.	8694.1	16788.6	544.5	1778.5	0.0	193.6	0.1	18.8	16.6	28034.81	103889.36	0.00	538.38	0.00	44488.77	1942.67	150859.18	178893.99
Manuf	1985.1	6550.4	35.8	1457.0	9.9	211.4	46.9	171.6	2127.4	12595.40	72038.15	0.00	53.43	13.87	-29004.69	30752.80	73853.55	86448.95
Chem	3730.4	22.3	684.3	419.0	15.4	27.0	16.5	0.0	84.0	4998.92	3232.07	0.00	0.00	0.00	-4586.43	3696.72	2342.36	7341.28
Metal	900.1	87.8	25.0	13336.2	36.3	59.3	31.4	437.5	615.4	15529.01	10412.16	0.00	37756.71	25478.72	3741.50	9814.43	87203.52	102732.52
Gaselw	10.4	612.1	34.1	316.1	118.8	310.3	62.4	80.5	112.8	1657.32	1684.16	0.00	0.00	0.00	4823.23	0.00	6507.39	8164.71
Hotel	3195.0	4104.7	244.2	3335.4	84.2	4507.7	6841.8	746.8	1797.6	24857.42	20952.98	0.00	484.95	146.78	10552.47	14347.44	46484.62	71342.04
Transp	4805.3	6582.2	407.5	4566.2	103.8	4284.7	4506.1	666.8	2501.5	28424.08	15808.88	0.00	784.96	237.51	9603.27	6924.96	33359.59	61783.67
Finance	8294.7	4279.1	253.9	3062.6	1143.2	2902.2	6340.7	1383.3	1009.8	28669.54	9576.25	0.00	0.00	0.00	3043.02	0.00	12619.27	41288.80
SocServ	164.5	367.8	21.4	4204.3	20.0	404.4	146.2	449.7	1429.3	7207.70	7007.13	34579.00	0.00	0.00	-14416.39	21441.02	48610.76	55818.46
Domestic Input Purchase	31779.50	39394.95	2250.70	32475.37	1531.57	12900.59	17992.05	3954.98	9694.48	151974.19	244601.13	34579.00	39618.43	25876.89	28244.76	88920.03	461840.24	613814.43
intimp	2147.48	14982.69	2190.90	19674.26	677.08	14673.06	14050.97	408.48	11881.46	80686.38	36282.38	0.00	4179.00	468.00	0.00	0.00	40929.38	121615.76
Total Inter Input	33926.98	54377.64	4441.60	52149.63	2208.65	27573.64	32043.03	4363.46	21575.94	232660.57	280883.52	34579.00	43797.43	26344.89	28244.76	88920.03	502769.62	735430.19
Wages	46202.74	4516.98	221.65	20382.06	801.44	5274.29	11652.75	14234.58	29221.74	132508.23	0.00	0.00	0.00	0.00	0.00	0.00	0.00	132508.23
Depr	1721.62	1092.75	107.44	1784.01	717.71	1472.39	7482.37	1070.36	68.71	15517.36	0.00	0.00	0.00	0.00	0.00	0.00	0.00	15517.36
Indtx	244.01	6097.31	1278.38	6664.20	61.06	659.39	459.64	6.35	218.52	15688.86	7063.48	0.00	813.57	91.11	0.00	1240.97	9209.14	24898.00
capital	96798.64	20364.28	1292.22	21752.61	4375.85	36362.32	10145.88	21614.06	4733.55	217439.41	0.00	0.00	0.00	0.00	0.00	0.00	0.00	217439.41
Value Added	144967.01	32071.31	2899.68	50582.89	5956.06	43768.39	29740.64	36925.35	34242.52	381153.86	7063.48	0.00	813.57	91.11	0.00	1240.97	9209.14	390363.00
Grand Total	178893.99	86448.95	7341.28	102732.52	8164.71	71342.04	61783.67	41288.80	55818.46	613814.43	287947.00	34579.00	44611.00	26436.00	28244.76	90161.00	511978.76	1125793.19

Reference: Adapted from from 25 sector input-output model of Nepal received from the NPC Secretariate, Kathmandu (cortesy Pushpa Shakya)..

This chapter draws on my following works on economic models of Nepal:

- Consequences of April 2006 Revolutionary Changes In Nepal: Continuation Of Nepalese Dilemma Indian Journal of Business and Economics.
- Political Economy of Conflict, Cooperation And Economic Growth: Nepalese Dilemma, forthcoming, Indian Journal of Business and Economics.
- Welfare and distributi`onal Impacts of financial liberalisation in a developing economy: Lessons from a forward looking CGE model of Nepal, Working Paper no. 7, Hull Advances in Policy Economics Research Papers.
- Financial Deepening and Economic Development in Nepal: A Forward Looking CGE Model with Financial Intermediation, Ph.D. dissertation Northeastern University, Boston, Massachussetts.
- *Need of Overhaul of the Planning Commission of Nepal, the Rising Nepal, Aug. 14, 1991.*
- The Role of Foreign Aid in Economic Development of Nepal: A Multi-sectoral Modeling of the Nepalese Economy, M.A. dissertation, Institute of Social Studies, Hague, Netherlands, 1990.
- Analysis of Nepalese Laws on Cheating, Institute of Law, Kathmandu, 1988.
- Review of Personnel Administration Law of Nepal, Institute of Law, Kathmandu, 1987.
- A Country Back-ground paper on Economic Policy of Nepal, prepared for the Consultative Committee of GATT, and the Columbo Plan, National Planning Commission, Nepal, 1988.
- Analysis of Income and Expenditure System of Tamghas: A Village Profile, Department of Economics, Tribhuvan University, Kathmandu, Nepal, 1984.

2

CONSEQUENCES OF APRIL 2006[1] REVOLUTIONARY CHANGES IN NEPAL: CONTINUATION OF NEPALESE DILEMMA[2]

BACKGROUND[3]

Millions of people came to the streets throughout the country and supported successfully and univocally the call for protests against the absolute King made by the coalition of alliance of seven political parties and the Maoists and international community as a whole ultimately to terminate the absolute monarchy for a fundamental transformation and peace and prosperity of political economy in Nepal. Subsequent progress on realising those goals of reform has remained not only slow but also waning the confidence people had put on politicians. Given the depth of poverty and lack of commitment mechanism in the political process whether the equilibrium emerging from these events will be stable and bring Nepal to the rapid path of economic growth like her giant neighbours China and India is questionable. The speedy economic growth can only be a mantra of the political economy that can satisfy people and modernise the economy to fulfil the more realistic aspirations of all Nepalese people.

King relinquished all powers that he had snatched away from them a year earlier by reinstating the House of Representatives (HOR) on the eve of 20th day of protest on April 25. At least 21 of pro-democracy protestors died and thousands

1. This article has appeared in the Indian Journal of Economics & Business, Vol. 5, No.2, (2006): 273-282.

2. This article is an update on the bargaining and coalition model of the political economy of Nepal presented in Bhattarai (2005) that analysed the conflict that has turned Nepal in a civil war among elites led by the King, workers organised under various political parties and rebels mobilised by Maoists that had taken lives of more than 13000 people and terrorised all others. Unfolding events show that predictions made there on potential coalitions and emerging solutions to end the conflict and in itiate the process of growth and alleviation of poverty to avoid a permanent crisis becoming true to a large extent.

3. I very much appreciate my brothers Kedar Bhattarai in Kathmandu for painfully gathering survey information for the empirical part of this paper and for Bishnu Bhattarai in Boston for some discussions on the formulation of questionnaire and my mother Hari Maya Bhattarai, Sisters Manu Maya Bhattarai and Basundhara Khanal and millions of Nepalese people for invaluable inspiration for this study. All errors and omissions are my own.

became injured from bullets and buttons of army and police in various parts of country. This peaceful revolution effectively has eliminated the role of the King in Nepalese politics and has brought the united political forces, alliance of seven political parties (SPA) and the CPN-Maoists as their allies in the movement at the forefront of running the national affairs of Nepal.

CONSEQUENCES

Many events of historic importance are unfolding dramatically since the reinstatement of the HOR. Nepal had never seen such a rapid change in political circumstances. The HOR immediately terminated all executive, judicial and legislative powers vested in the King by a popular proclamation on May 19, 2006, annulled all acts or ordinances that were introduced to suppress people's movement and to raise Kings absolute power or to punish and terminate rebels who were declared as the terrorists in his regime. This move brought the King completely out of the parliament and transferred all those powers to the House of Representatives, which is in process of forming a constituent assembly to draft a new people centred constitution. A special enquiry commission, effectively a peoples' court, was constituted to punish all guilty people who tried to crush the popular movement. The SPA welcomed Maoists formally to enter into the main-stream of Nepalese politics by removing the "terrorist" label put on them by the previous government. It then initiated a dialogue with the Maoists to solve the decade old conflict by accepting the 25 point code of conduct on May 26 that basically focused on creating mutual trusts between the SPA and Maoists on the principle of peaceful coexistence to create a conflict free environment in Nepal. These codes of conduct made rooms for eight point agreement at a formal summit meeting between the Prime Minister Koirala and Maoist leader Prachanda on June 16 which basically is reinstatement of 12 point agreement between the SPA and the Maoists concluded in New Delhi on November 22, 2005. It was aimed to end the conflict and restore the peace and order in Nepal through some very historic steps including the dissolution of the reinstated parliament and forming an all party interim government including the Maoists in good spirit of conducting a free and fair election of the constituent assembly that will draft a new constitution reflecting the ambitions and desires of all Nepalese people as expressed in the peoples movement within a year, putting armies of both sides under control and preferably subjecting them to supervision and monitoring by a commonly agreed international agency such as the UN. This constitution is to be for the Republic of Nepal and many think that it will terminate the royal institution altogether including the ceremonial role for the King.

Despite such movements and national agreements there is still a long way to bring Nepal into a stable and functional democracy that is focused on developing all round potentials of Nepalese people and that brings higher rate of economic growth as achieved by China and India, two of her economically, geographically and demographically giant neighbours. Political mind set is still struggling to resolve the armed conflict and has not yet been able to grasp the importance of economic factors for success of a modern Nepal but rather concentrated in political front. Neither the revolution nor the parties have yet truly addressed the age old weaknesses of the Nepalese society such as the mentality of corruption, distrust, conspiracy for short term gains and uncritical acceptance of earnings acquired through corrupted means at the social level, individualism rather than institutionalism. All political parties have enough of the mutual distrusts, lack of sufficient homework and over concentration on negative criticism to disrupt any good initiative.

The constitution is important but the main agenda and the urgent priority of Nepal is elimination of poverty and economic development. It may be called by different names such as removal of capitalist class or rule of proletariats or elimination of traitors or counter-revolutionaries. All essentially aim for provision of "Dal-Bhat_Duku (bread and butter)" for common people to be realistic to Nepalese situation. Wasting too much time just to frame a constitution forgetting economic realities will be an imprudent use of resources. Nepal has already seen five different constitutions (1947, 1951, 1960, 1961 and 1990). None of these had set economic growth as the major national objective. If the power comes from people why should that take so long time to accept in letter and spirit that people are sovereign and they are the sources of all power? In fact the basis of agreement between the Maoists and the SPA was "democracy, peace, prosperity, social advancement and a free and sovereign Nepal is the chief wish of all Nepalese".

As they delay on delivering the promises, it is natural to ask about the motives of these political parties based on their characteristics and differences with each other and identify whether the emerging equilibrium is stable or not. Looking at the above points of similarities and difference it becomes clear that there would be little difference between the SPA and Maoists once the latter renounces arms and relinquish violence and threat as the means of achieving political objectives. They all want political power. In the feudal culture of Nepal disability to deal with corruption had been a major problem for all other parties in the SPA. There is not enough evidence to state effectively whether Maoists will be able to terminate corruption and create free and fair society after they enter into the main stream.

AMBITION FOR GROWTH

It is more urgent to revive the faith of entrepreneurs, investors and business communities by sweeping reforms of the education system, labour and financial markets, mobilisation of water or other natural resources, creation of physical and economic infrastructure, removing red-tape and making the private sector an active partner in the process of economic growth. Making reward for productivity and raising the opportunity cost of time for more than 50 per cent of effectively unemployed is vital step for economic growth. These cannot happen unless the economic growth is the major focus of the constitution and all political forces in the country.

Why cannot Nepal start a really free school system up to the high schools? Why cannot it institute student loans to college and university level students?

Similarities and Differences between the SPA and the Maoists

Seven Party Alliance (SPA)	*Communist Party of Nepal (Maoists)*
1. An alliance of all major political forces, leftists, centrists and rightists, which have been in power in several occasions. They speak different languages of ideology about democracy, equality and nationalism and about the redistribution and on economic and individual freedom but are essentially same in practice.	1. A party that believes in armed struggle to achieve political means. It has used terrorism and violence and threats to fight against the parliamentary system. Motivated by the revisions of Mao of Marxist-Leninist ideas of class struggle, supremacy of the proletariats, mass participation, and strict party discipline.
2. Terminate absolute monarchy – though leaves some room for the constituent assembly to decide whether to keep a ceremonial king.	2. It aims to create a Republic of Nepal by terminating monarchy.
3. They accept role of market to allocate resources, adopt socialist policies by spending on education and health and leaving industries for the private sectors.	3. It has a very vague idea on how to operate economic policies. Accepts role of market for allocating resources but does not focus on central planning as found in many communist societies but motivated by some obscure ideas of self-sufficiency and industrialisation. Its economic statements are contradictory and not well thought out. Yet to come up with a model.
4. They are accepted by the international community as true representatives of the Nepalese society.	4. It does not have widespread support from the international community until they relinquish arms, violent means to achieve political objectives.
5. Has developed internal democracy in the party to some extent but have not done enough to punish the corrupt officials.	5. Very little known about the internal democracy of the party but has supported by committed party members.
6. Not efficient for implementing ideas in practice and mobilising masses for achieving economic and social objectives.	6. Efficient in running the gorilla wars but whether it will be efficient in running the economy is questionable.
7. No clear focus on economic growth.	7. Speaks the communist language to express ideas on economics and politics.
8. Each of them has been inefficient in the past in implementing ideas in practice when they had a chance.	
9. This is a loose association of seven parties each with ambition to power.	

Why cannot it establish world class universities in mountains and hills using rapid changes in communication technology? Why cannot it focus on manpower development policies that let opportunities for all to develop their full potentials and creative abilities? Why should not it create environments for talented individuals, both the Nepalese and foreigners, to work in Nepal with appropriate reforms in the labour market? Why should not it develop tourism more systematically by making Nepalese Himalayas topmost international standard in holiday destinations? Why should not it focus on developing vast potential hydro electricity for running industries? Why should not it promote the environment for transfer of technology from more advanced neighbours and other developed countries? Why should not it make rules and regulations clearly so that people start thinking that it is the original ideas and thoughts that count most in developing their prospects rather than copying foreign and obsolete ideas? Why should not it start developing financial and other sectors in which Nepal has comparative advantages with more focus on economic growth and creating employment. These are the real concerns that took millions of people to the streets. Delivering them efficiently will make the peaceful revolution and transition of April 2006 memorable and long lasting one.

REASONS FOR ROYAL PLIGHT

Kings were always suspicious of popular freedom. That was no exception to Gyanendra who came to power after Royal massacre in 2001. Imposing direct rule and being obstinate to continue it by promoting sycophantism and coteries of royalists, King made people angrier and became bitter enemy of political parties as well as of the Maoists. His feudal characteristics and attempts to eliminate true political forces by military forces in effect created an appropriate background for talk and understanding and alliance between the political parties with popular support and the Maoists with armed guerrillas and militias all over the country. Political parties had mass support and Maoists had Peoples Liberation Army (PLA), combination of these two was enough to counter Kings' forces and other state machinery under his control. Understandably an agreement was struck taking best out of two forces to fight against and terminate the autocrat monarch and bring democracy, peace and advancement in the country. This initiative formally known as the 12 point agreement was signed between the SPA and Maoists on Nov 22, 2005, mainly aimed to bring permanent peace and advancement by replacing the absolute monarchy by absolute democracy and ending the armed conflicts from Maoists. This agreement in some sense made parties and Maoist to re-evaluate their strengths and weakness in a realistic manner and form a working relation for the cause of absolute democracy by a "storm of nationwide protests" with a strong commitment to basic human rights and freedoms for people and commitment to multiparty democracy with reinstatement of the parliament.

People wholeheartedly supported the movements initiated by the SPA. They were convinced that the King did not have had good intentions for the Nepalese people on February 1, 2005 when he dissolved the existing parliament and took over the direct control of the government. They thought that his initial justification of take-over of power due to disability of political parties to solve the insurgency problem and appeal for international cooperation to solve the armed conflicts was simply an illusion and deceitful means to keep him in power for long. His promises to restore multiparty democracy after uprooting the Maoists using military force was simply ill intentioned and ill motivated and less than one year of his direct rule only angered all political forces. As the time went by many people as well as all international community that supported good cause for Nepalese people also became convinced that Kings' only intention was to strengthen the absolute monarchy. Peace, law and order situation became worse, public became frustrated and angered and went totally to protest against him. Kings' supporters could not even find candidates for the election of local bodies that was boycotted by major political parties.

With mines and bombs planted by rebels and sabotages and curfews and tear gases, bullets and buttons used to control demonstrations called by parties becoming a daily routine in all parts of the country, people could not have peace of mind and normal life. They were not able to use their personal and economic freedom and were terrified even to do their daily businesses. It was not safe to go from one part of the country to another. Economy was crippled by recurrent strikes, fights and violence and demonstrations. It brought widespread frustration nationwide. Economy was paralysed and the country was in crisis.

The incident of conspiracy and distrust as seen in the royal massacre of 2001 had reduced the respect and dignity of King among people. He neither had real direct experience on the acuteness of the problem of massive poverty and toils and troubles of millions of people nor a tactic to manage the state affairs efficiently. He could not imagine that people could come into street in millions all over the country as he did not have true respect for their opinions. He simply wasted the opportunity of reforming Nepal that historical circumstances had given to him and failed to create an environment for peace and growth. He was compelled to give all his powers to people due to his ego-centric selfish handling of state affairs and by isolating himself from the people by relying on regressive and incompetent royalist forces that had proved incapable and inefficient in 1960s and 1990s.

PEOPLE'S CONSTITUTION

Constitution essentially is a contract between the citizen and state. It is an arrangement by which people rule themselves by means of elected representatives who make rules and regulations that establish rights and duties in several matters for a smooth functioning of society. The United Kingdom has an unwritten constitution that is built upon the historic documents on rights of people such as the Magna Carta (1215 AD). In recent years written constitution started with American Declaration of Independence (1776) which basically adopted the principle of no taxation without representation. Then the French Revolution (1789), which established a republic based of liberty, equality and fraternity. The socialist constitution goes back to the October revolution (1917) in which Russian Bolshevik party tried to form a state of proletariats based on Marxist-Leninists ideology of elimination of bourgeoisie and success of workers' party that was followed in China by the Chinese communist party which was later revised by the Mao-Tse Tung. Decolonisation of many Asian and African and Latin American countries in 1940s and 1950s has given further importance to the system of written constitution based on adult suffrage and fundamental human rights and clear statement of the aims and objectives of the political and economic system of a nation (see Hoar Roger Sherman (1917), Chih-Mai Chen (1947), Gooch Robert K. (1947), Wallace D.D. (1951), Houn Franklin W. (1954), Kawai Kazuo (1955), Gangal S.C. (1962), Packenham Robert A. (1964) Peacock Alan T and Charles E Rowley (1972), Weisskopf Thomas E. (1975) Walder Andrew G. (1987), Tideman Nicolaus (1994), Valensise Marina (1988), Haggard Stephen and Chung-In Moon (1990), Lutz Donald S. (1994) Hein Laura E. (1994) Acemoglu (2001)). The major aspect of any constitution is its preamble that sets the aims and objectives of a nation, formal procedure of representation in legislature, formation of executive body such as the councils of ministers and arrangement of a supreme court, statement of procedures of how each of these shall work in practice and provision for exceptional circumstances.

A good constitution alone does not automatically provide a true democracy as Haun (1954) rightly states that the Chinese constitution is the most democratic in the world but in practice China has very limited democracy, every representative basically rubber-stamps the decision of the party. The United Kingdom does not have a written constitution but it is one of the most democratic countries in the world. A long constitution does not necessarily mean that it is good one rather than a short one. American constitution is the shortest but the most complete and thriving constitution in the world, despite being the longest one, the Indian constitution is not free of constitutional problems that reoccur from time to time.

The major contribution that a constitution can make is to set up a democratic culture, an institution that teaches citizens to respect each other and learn from each other and that makes them active energetic and result oriented performers in already very competitive global economy.

REFERENCES

Acemoglu Daren (2001), A Theory of Political Transitions, *the American Economic Review*, 91:4:938-963.

Bhattarai K. (2005), Political Economy of Conflict, Cooperation and Economic Growth: Nepalese Dilemma, mimio, *University of Hull*, May.

Chih-Mai Chen (1947), The Post-War Government of China, *the Journal of Politics*, 9:4:503-521.

Gangal S.C. (1962), An Approach to Indian Federalism, *Political Science Quarterly*, 77:2:248-253.

Gooch Robert K. (1947), Recent Constitution-Making in France, the *American Political Science Review*, 41:3:429-446.

Haggard Stephen and Chung-In Moon (1990) Institutions and Economic Policy: Theory and a Korean Case Study, *World Politics*, 42:2:210-237.

Hoar Roger Sherman (1917), Constitutional Conventions, the *American Political Science Review*, 11:3:519-528.

Houn Franklin W. (1954), The Draft Constitution of Communist China, *Pacific Affairs*, 27:4:319-337.

Hein Laura E. (1994), In Search of Peace and Democracy: Japanese Economic Debate in Political Context, the *Journal of Asian Studies*, 53:3:752-778.

Kay J.A. (1990), Tax Policy: A Survey, the *Economic Journal*, 100:399:18-75.

Kawai Kazuo (1955), Sovereignty and Democracy in the Japanese Constitution, the *American Political Science Review*, 49:3:663-572.

Lutz Donald S. (1994), Towards a Theory of Constitutions Amendment, the *American Political Science Review*, 88:2:355-370.

Packenham Robert A. (1964), Approaches to the Study of Political Development, *World Politics*, 17:1:108-120.

Peacock Alan T. and Charles E. Rowley (1972), Pareto Optimality and the Political Economy of Liberalism, the *Journal of Political Economy*, 80:3:1: 476-490.

Tideman Nicolaus (1994), Capacities and Limits of Democracy, the *American Economic Review*, 44:2:AEA proceeding 106 convention, 349-352.

Valensise Marina (1988), The French Constitution in Pre-Revolutionary Debate, the *Journal of Modern History*, 60:Supplement: Rethinking French Politics in 1788, S22-S57.

Wallace D.D. (1951), The Indian Constitution of 1949, the *Journal of Politics*, 13:2:269-275.

Weisskopf Thomas E. (1975), China and India: Contrasting Experiences in Economic Development, the American Economic Review, 66:2: Papers and Proceedings 87th Annual meeting, 356-364.

Walder Andrew G. (1987), Actually Existing Maoism, the *Australian Journal of Chinese Affairs*, 18:155-166.

Various issues of Kantipur, a daily newspaper, see *http://www.kantipuronline.com.*

3

POLITICAL ECONOMY OF CONFLICT, COOPERATION AND ECONOMIC GROWTH: NEPALESE DILEMMA[1]

INTRODUCTION

Conflict among feudal factors led by the King, working people in trade and industry led by political parties, marginal, poverty trapped people threatened and mobilised by Maoist rebels in Nepal creates a very unproductive environment where investors and entrepreneurs do not get any productive opportunity. Non-cooperation among competing political and economic forces has brought Nepal into crisis and growth disaster. The major reason for conflict is short-sighted horizon of these players who try to maximise their own current share on GDP taking its size as constant over time. It has discouraged productive economic activities and transfer of better technology and knowledge and resources from abroad with dangerous consequences to the economy. A solution is offered here in terms of a contract in more objective and specific growth oriented rules that bound each of them to the policy initiatives in which each of these groups has incentive to stick for peace and prosperity and for adoption and use of knowledge and technology for growth.

Capital, labour and technology have been central factors in determining the rate of economic growth in the classical, neo-classical and endogenous models of economic growth. Both theoretical and empirical studies abound on how these variables impact on economic growth and why these growth rates vary from one country to another even if they have similar rates of saving, endowment and growth rates of labour, and the level of technology[2]. These models rely on competitive markets where factors are paid according to their marginal productivities. Very little discussion is found in the literature, however, on how conflicts among various economic agents in the economy reduce the rates of economic growth as seen in growth disaster countries and how the cooperation among them can generate spectacular rates of growth in growth miracle countries over time. Persistence of conflicts and violence paralyses markets and stops investment and production activities and creates economic crises. It destroys existing infrastructure and prevents creation of new ones. Why big economies are able to control such violence but small ones not? This paper aims to analyse the role of conflict and cooperation in economic growth with the help of a simple game-theoretic model and illustrates its application using the Nepalese dilemma on impacts of conflict on economic retardation and prospect of cooperation on growth. Section two introduces a political economy model[3] to analyse the effects of conflicts and cooperation in economic growth. The political economy structure of Nepal is presented in section three with further analysis of solution on the conflict in section four. The conclusion of the study and recommendations along with references are given in the last section. Appendix contains graphical representation of the model of conflict and growth, sample structure and summary for empirical support of the model, salient features of the Nepalese economy in comparison to her South Asian neighbours.

POLITICAL ECONOMY MODEL OF CONFLICT AND COOPERATION

Take a developing economy that produces Y amount of total output in each year using labour, capital and technology inputs. This Y includes both private (C) and public (G) commodities and services. The government fails to provide private goods as it does not know preferences of households and technology of firms and market fails to provide public goods because of positive and negative externalities in consumption and productions. Public goods including education and health are under supplied, neither market nor the government can provide sufficiently and efficiently. Public sector goods (G) are provided by tax revenue (T) and the consumption C equals the output net of taxes (Y-T). This economy is inhibited by N number of people in total and $n1$, $n2$ or $n3$ numbers in three different groups each with distinct positions and roles in the economy with consumption $c1$, $c2$ or $c3$ and public goods $g1$, $g2$ or $g3$ and corresponding utility levels U1 (c1, g1), U2 (c2, g2) and U3 (c3, g3) respectively. Questions such as who should decide the level of tax, $T=\{T1, T2, T3\}$, and how it should be collected and how should G be allocated among the sections of communities, $G=\{g1, g2, g3\}$, are the major sources of political disagreements and conflict among power contenders. Some arrangements and allocations are growth enhancing and others are growth retarding. In fact inequality in the distribution of public goods according to the need of people and insecurity of personal freedom and protection of property rights to tax payers is the major issue of conflict.

At the higher level of echelon there are $n1$ number the elites, feudal landlords or hereditary rulers. Their wealth and power more owes to their hereditary status, assets or claims than to their competence, creativity and productive contribution to the economy. Members of this group, through well knit connections and favour, often take the whole of the state machinery as their own private property despite themselves being an insignificant minority of population. Workers and rebel, who do not really have an access to this machinery perceive that this group is parasite that sucks their blood and takes a large share of the Y because of administrative or property rights they have established on resources of the economy and protected by laws and regulations they promulgated over generations using their dominance on state machinery. In many instances these rulers protect their position in the society through loyal armies or military and clever strategic networks spread throughout the economy. Kings at the centre and feudal landlords or tribal lords at the local level represent these groups. This group uses this political power and connections to oppress opponents and to secure economic gains. They enjoy more both of private luxury goods as well as public goods. Power is proportional to the size of army and amount of defence goods which are funded by the tax revenue mainly raised from the income of workers.

Then there are *n2* numbers of middle class working people that make the majority of population. They are self-employed as farmers, entrepreneurs or traders; a small fraction of them work in service sectors; others work for organised political parties. Politically members of this group are influenced by ideas of democracy, freedom and individual liberties; economically they are keen to achieve more by using their talents and capabilities on the basis of a fair playing field in their trades; socially they communicate to each other through media, newspapers, journals, conferences, mass-meetings and rallies. A significant diversity and heterogeneity among them appears due to economic, ethnic, religious and cultural backgrounds. They are divided on the basis of their origin or profession and are individually very vulnerable to whims of rulers though collectively they belong to the most powerful economic group in the economy. Since they are divided on the basis of their origins, believes, professions or personal interests, coordination among them is very difficult. Rulers take advantage of this fact and keep a policy that divides them and makes them even weaker by making them play against each other using subtle tactics of pecuniary or political favours. It is in their interest to make this group economically and morally corrupt and weaker to challenge rulers' hereditary claims to the power.

Then there are *n3* numbers of people who have been economically marginalised, lack decent jobs or occupation and have been struggling to meet their basic needs. They have little education or professional skills or property to be economically self-dependent. They face serious income uncertainty and are struggling to meet their basic needs problems. Because of these weak economic reasons, people in this group can easily be mobilised by radicals for a little payment of money for their livelihood. Such marginalisation occurs for several reasons. First one relates to declining inheritance of family property. In a traditional economy and family system each successive generation climbs down the property ladder more often than climbing up. Upon the death of a property holder parent, his/her property is divided equally among children. Thus hereditary property diminishes in each generation according to the number of children in the family. Secondly, they have growing burden of debts incurred for purchasing food, clothes, medicine for activities for survival or for social activities such as weddings or funerals. It is possible that a child in such family is born in debt, grows in debt and dies leaving more debt to its children. They never recover from it and cannot invest in any human capital enhancing activities. Thirdly, children of little educated parents have harder time to get a decent opportunity of education; they drop out in early stage of education cycle and do not have necessary qualifications to compete for jobs and professions in a modern sector. There is very little learning in family setting as none of the parents of such children are likely to happen to be educated. Fourth, they spend more on feasts and festivals whenever they have some savings and have very little collateral to borrow from formal financial sectors. Fifth they hardly have anything to sale except their labour. A significant number of them are found squatting to public lands for a long time without any entitlement or property right to their house or gardens. This puts down their morale, bargaining power and collateral position in the market. Sixth, the state is often not able to provide public goods including education, health and job insurance to poor who remain very insecure and vulnerable through out their lives.

The global economy impacts this economy through trade and flows of capital, ideas and technology. The benefits of these links flow according to the economic powers of these groups, elites benefit the most from international contacts than people in the working group. Part of their activities involves maintaining good external contacts for economic or personal reasons. The marginal group hardly have any access to these international factors.

Division of Income and Power

The level of growth and development of this economy depends on interactions among these groups. In an ideal and egalitarian society share of income for each group depends on the relative proportion in their population such as $s_i = \frac{n_i}{n_1 + n_2 + n_3} Y$ where i = 1..3, s_i denotes the share of income Y for group i which is in proportion to their size in population $\frac{n_i}{n_1 + n_2 + n_3}$, where $Y = Y_1 + Y_2 + Y_3$ and $C_1 = C_2 = C_3$ and $g_1 = g_2 = g_3$. The real economy, that has evolved over hundred of years, since this primordial society, is far from this ideal scenario. The rulers have used opportunity of tax and spend on public goods to alter their own shares as manifested in their palaces and buildings, lands and business and entitlements from state provisions. The dynamic factors originating from economic relations have distorted the distribution as there has been a tendency among the ruling group to accumulate more economic resources and take ownership of new sources of economic growth as the utility of each group depends on income that they get, which further depends on the degree of concentration of the political power.

How does economic power relate to the political power? In democracy each citizen of a country, even with unequal endowments, should have equal political power, $P_i = \frac{1}{N}$ for a population size of N, which they can use to make collective choices[4]. However, an individual vote would not take its meaning unless it is expressed collectively $P = \sum_{i}^{N} p_i$ where P is the total power and N is the total size of population. There is no society in the world where all individuals have the same opinion on any one issue. Therefore this power is often clustered around the groups of individuals with same or similar opinions. In the context of above analysis with three groups in a developing economy each specific group has its utility function that it tries to maximise, $Ui = P_i$ where P_i represents the political power it commands from individuals subscribing to views and ideas that this of group represent. When the power is normalised to one, $\sum_{i=1}^{3} P_i = 1$, then it becomes important to know how this power is distributed among various contesting groups in the economy. Economic growth is enhanced when this power is used efficiently through a social contract that has consent of each section of the society. Misuse of power causes conflict and retardation.

There is a constant struggle in the division of power between elites, workers and paupers. As an increase in the power of one group reduces power of another group, each of them continuously tries to increase its own power. People become more rational with more education and are ready to challenge any source of power that are not directly linked to votes of common people. Real support for the aims and objectives of a group is the real source of powers, which can be increased or reduced by force or coercion for sometime until the fundamentals are realised. At any point of time there is an efficient power sharing bargaining solution that maximises the social objective function subject to the unit power constraint. Maximising a social welfare function with arguments of power for each group of the economy $W = P_1 P_2 P_3$ subject to the power constraint $U = P_1 + P_2 + P_3$ can generate optimal distribution of power among sections. In a real situation each group has a reservation or threshold level of power, represented by the numbers of votes of committed followers, which it is available to that group in any circumstances. The amount of additional part of support fluctuates depending on circumstances of the economy and is closely monitored. Each of them to tries to increase power if an opportunity exists. If this reservation power or the disagreement point in power-sharing agreement is added to the above problem, the efficient solution is obtained by maximum Nash product $W = (P_1 - d_1)\, P_2 - d_2)$ $(P_3 - d_3)$ subject to power constraint where represent the disagreement point as illustrated in diagram 1.

Further, in a three party situation with Elites (E), Workers (W) and Rebels (R) there are six possible coalitions: three absolute power singletons, $\{E\}$, $\{W\}$ and $\{R\}$; two intermediate coalitions $\{E, W\}$ and $\{E, R\}$; and one grand coalition $\{E, W, R\}$. In a winner takes all arrangement the singleton prevails whenever one of the above group manages to win others. When any one particular party cannot clearly win majority votes, two or all of them can form a coalition on the basis of power-sharing agreement. Such agreements tend to be very unstable as each of the coalition partners has an incentive to deviate from the agreement realistically or unrealistically in aspiration of control over all power. The grand coalition is more a theoretical possibility rather than a practical solution. If this can assure

Diagram 1
Efficient and Inefficient Bargaining Solutions

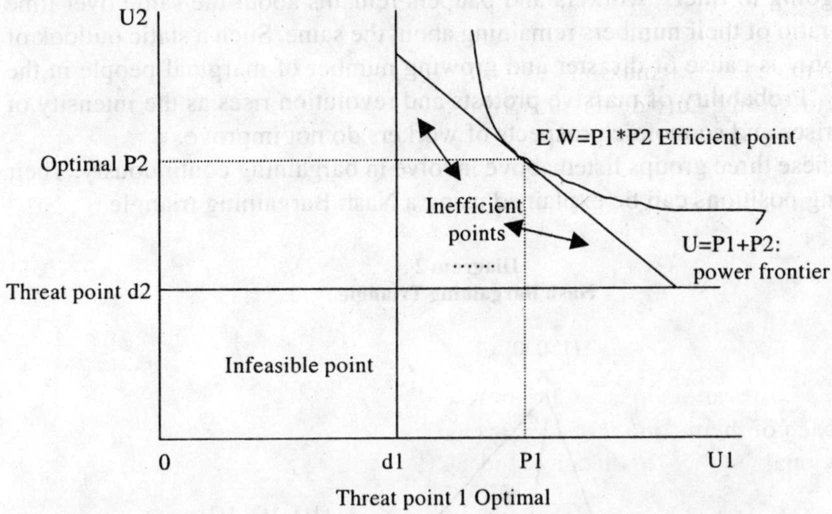

political stability, that can be very vital for achieving the higher rate of economic growth.

Role of Conflicts and Cooperation in the Growth Process

There were very little differences between rulers and common people in the agricultural society. Such differences tend to grow with the development of industry and commerce which not only opens new opportunities but also creates new base of taxes. The gap in the living standards of people between the rulers and the common people rises continuously. This further intensifies the desire of the ruling group to remain in power and increase its economic strengths by investing in securities, insurances and new businesses that would further expand their power. Reforms in such system are unavoidable for a stable and growing economy. Democracies have produced better solution for dynamic economies than communism (Schumpeter (1942) Downs (1957), Myrdal (1982), Sen (1983), Perkins (1994), Przeworski and Limongi (1993), Huber et. al (1993), Shleifer and Treisman (2005), Gunning (1986), Wintrobe (1998), Morris (2001), Paldam (2002), Verwimp (2003), McMillan and Zoido (2005)). Working people are the real producers of goods and services in the economy. They are often not free to carry out their ideas in actions independently but have to solicit for permits, licences to carry business and pay taxes to rules to be able to conduct their business. Decisions of rulers can either promote their business or harm their business depending on incentive structure that it generates.

One can think of two different scenarios for conflict and cooperation in this economy as presented in Figures 1 in the appendix. The conflict scenario in part A at the end takes a static and dull view of the economy in which size of economy is considered to be fixed. Each group struggles to maximize its share from this constant share. The balance of low income trapped economy means the share of income going to rulers, workers and paupers remains about the same over time with the ratio of their numbers remaining about the same. Such a static outlook of an economy is cause of disaster and growing number of marginal people in the economy. Probability of massive protests and revolution rises as the intensity of poverty rises and economic prospects of workers do not improve.

All these three groups listed above involve in bargaining continuously. Their bargaining positions can be explained using a Nash Bargaining triangle.

Diagram 2
Nash Bargaining Triangle

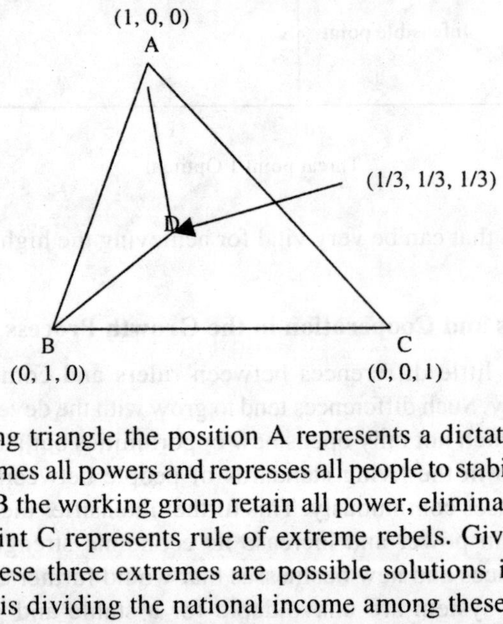

In this bargaining triangle the position A represents a dictatorial position of the ruler, which assumes all powers and represses all people to stabilise and increase his power. At point B the working group retain all power, eliminate the traditional power of Kings. Point C represents rule of extreme rebels. Given the nature of economy non of these three extremes are possible solutions in itself and the bargaining solution is dividing the national income among these three groups as shown by point D. Once such bargain is struck it would be optimal to establish a set of rules that binds each party and let economy move from scenarios A to scenario B in Figure 1 in the appendix. Whether this solution is stable one depends on the gap between the expected outcome and the bargaining result achieved by each party. It is more likely that bargained contracts are broken by one or another party demanding a revision on the contract made earlier according to the new situation. Emergence of new sectors of economy, beginning of new organisations and opportunities, several other reasons may cause such contract to be violated. One group may become stronger than another group to warrant more share in the bargain. Possibility of continuous conflict deters stability of the economy and productive activities.

The far sighted scenario (Figure 1 part B) offers a better solution. Here fundamentals of markets hold, there is some link between the marginal productivity of workers and their remunerations. Entrepreneurs are encouraged to start new businesses and take advantage of latest available technology. Such economy opens opportunities for paupers to upgrade themselves to belong to the working group through means of education and training. It also appeals to elites who join hands with the working group rather than being idle rent-seekers as in the static world. Both these factors raise the proportion of the middle group people relative to those of rulers and paupers.

Diagram 3
Growth of Income and Transition to a Steady economy with Coordination

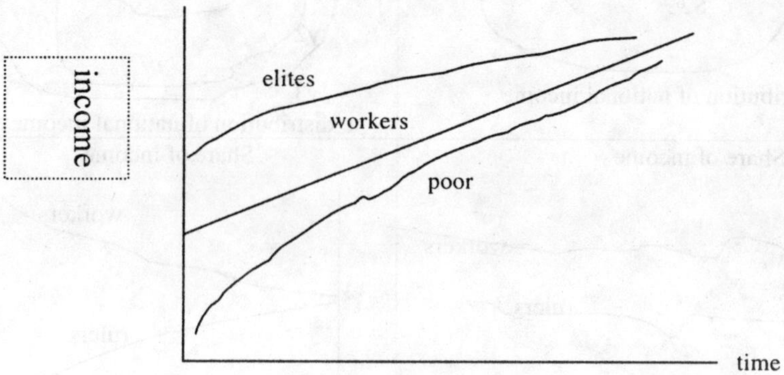

The nature of the solution should look like something as presented in Diagram 3. This solution is not automatic. It may take one generation or two to transform the structure of economy and relative position of these three groups as shown in this diagram. It is possible to achieve this by putting reasonable rates of taxes on the income of rulers and property owners to raise revenue that can be used to finance on education and skill of children from the poor income group along with reforms regarding their fair access to employment and other economic opportunities.

There is more pessimistic dynamic version of the solution to the above game which shows a continuous deterioration of the economy. Permanent conflicts, chaos, and lack of law and order situation due to continued terror and violence in which infrastructure and properties are destroyed, morality and creativeness of investors is harassed. There is massive capital flight and emigration. Such economy is trapped into a vicious circle of poverty.

STRUCTURE OF POLITICAL ECONOMY OF NEPAL

Nepal is one of the poorest countries in the world; 60 per cent of its people live in absolute poverty, below the subsistence level. Power contenders are King, political parties and Maoist rebels representing elites, workers and marginal groups as presented in the model outlined in section two. The political conflict has affected prospects of growth in Nepal as in many other developing economies of Asia, Africa, Caribbean and Latin American economies (see figures 2-5 in the appendix).

Figure 1
Short and Far-sighted view of growth and development dynamics in an economy

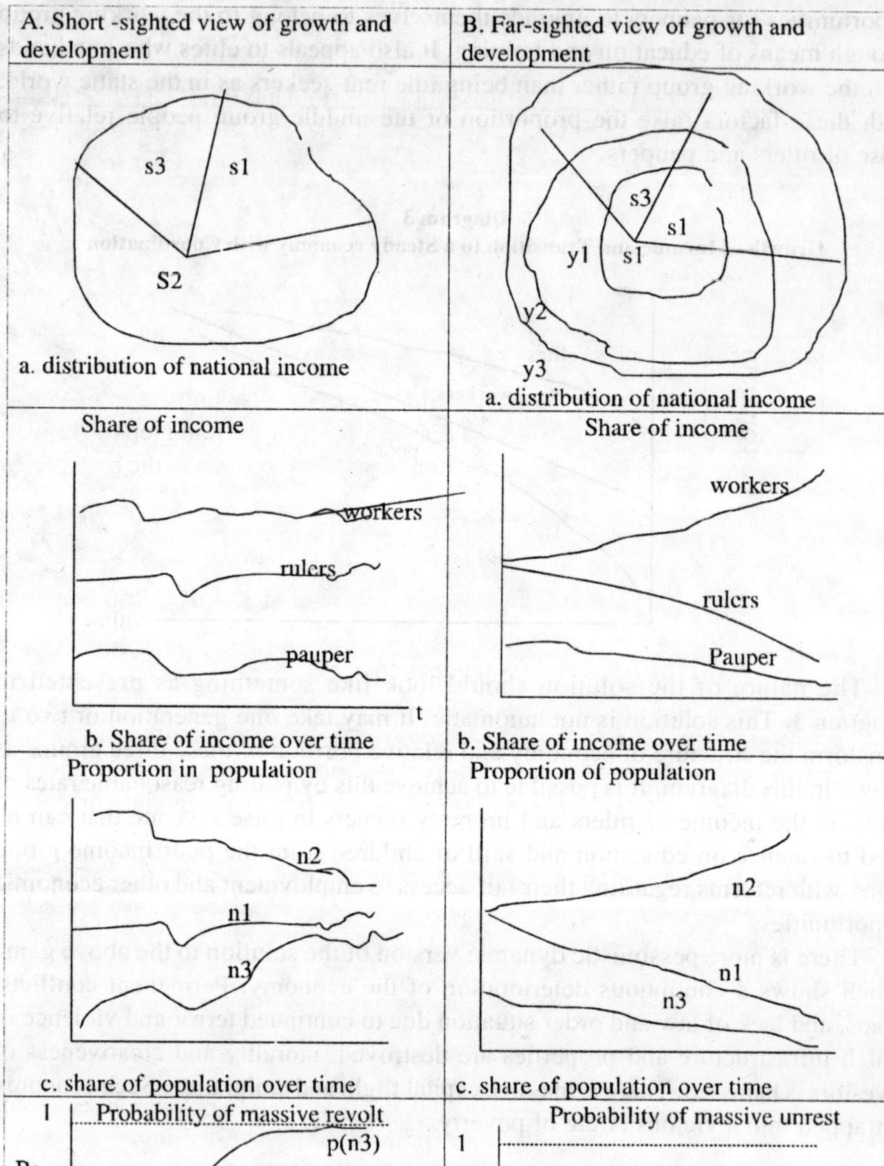

King is interested in maintaining the status quo along with his hereditary power, various political parties have plans and programmes for growth but squabble each other in forming and operating the government and the Maoists are committed to establish a dictatorship of proletariats by eliminating class enemies that include both King and workers running the political parties and have coerced the marginal poor people to join their army for violence and terror in the process of peoples War. An account of each of these elements is given below in order to apply the bargaining model stated in the above section.

The King

King has remained a dominant political power ever since the creation of modern state of Nepal but many people hate the traditional and hereditary nature of King and think that to be a major reason for backwardness of the economy. It is true that about 200 years ago then King P. N. Shah unified this country from 22 and 24 kingdoms scattered in the Western and Eastern parts of current Nepal. He was a popular King because he directed and fought wars with soldiers in the battle fields. Despite being popular in his brevity in war he was less farsighted in setting the hereditary rules by which the eldest son of a King would automatically access on the throne upon his demise. Hereditary King does not have do be aware of real aspirations, problems , objectives and constraints of common people as he neither has experience of tough competition in business or entrepreneurship nor has enough knowledge of recent technologies or ideas that can promote economic growth. Such rulers have made the Kingship very unpopular among people. Because of his vested interests in maintaining traditional values and culture that has divided the Nepalese society by casts, ethnicity, economic classes and made them uncritical and subjugated secondary citizens, his ability to be a role model for coming generation is limited. He misused more of this power than used it for productive purposes. This was part of the reason why Ranas were able to relegate them to status of dummy Kings during 104 years of tyrant and autocratic rules during a period of Industrial revolution in the West. Kings came in forefront of Nepalese politics after Ranas relinquished power under the pressure of democratic movements in 1951. Despite that King has not learnt enough lessons and continues betraying people whenever any opportunity arises in which he could have made a difference in the lives of the common people. King has never shown any real initiative for a free, fair and liberalised democratic system and prosperous economy. He is happier in concentrating all powers in him and maintaining a status quo regarding freedom and democracy. He enjoys more a dictatorial regime and absolute power rather than a democratic regime. The history of Nepal is full of stories on conspiracy and assassinations in the Royal family as the Royal massacre of 2001 is very recent in the memory of many people around the world. The glories of kings in ancient India and Nepal are just myths as far as their relevance in concerned in solving economic problem of current time. The King is simply a dictator who assumes power because of the royal military. Various political events since 1950s such as seizure of elected multi-party government in 1960 and

Figure 2
Levels of Income and Size of Government under Kingship, Democracy and Rebels

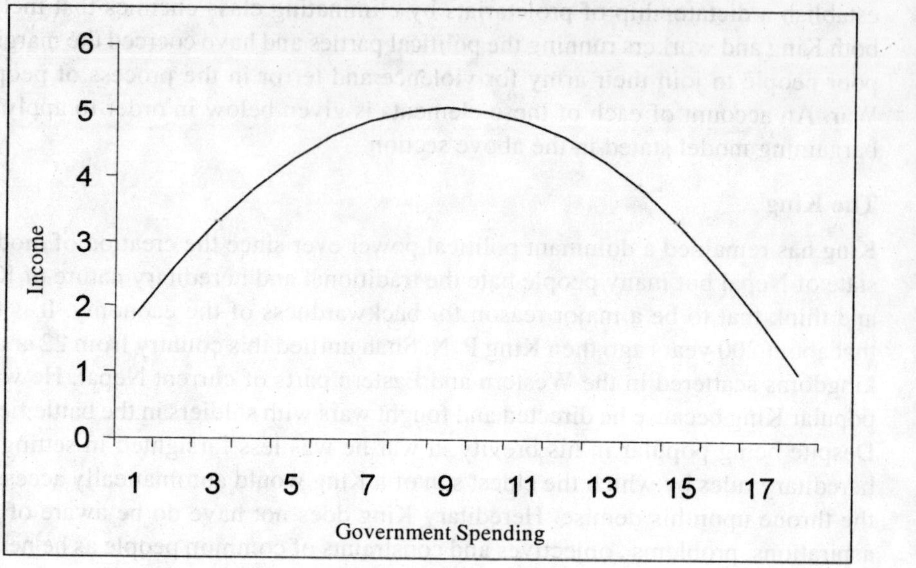

Figure 3
Growth of Output, investment and tax ratios, inflation, exchange rate, trade ratio and population growth rate in Nepal

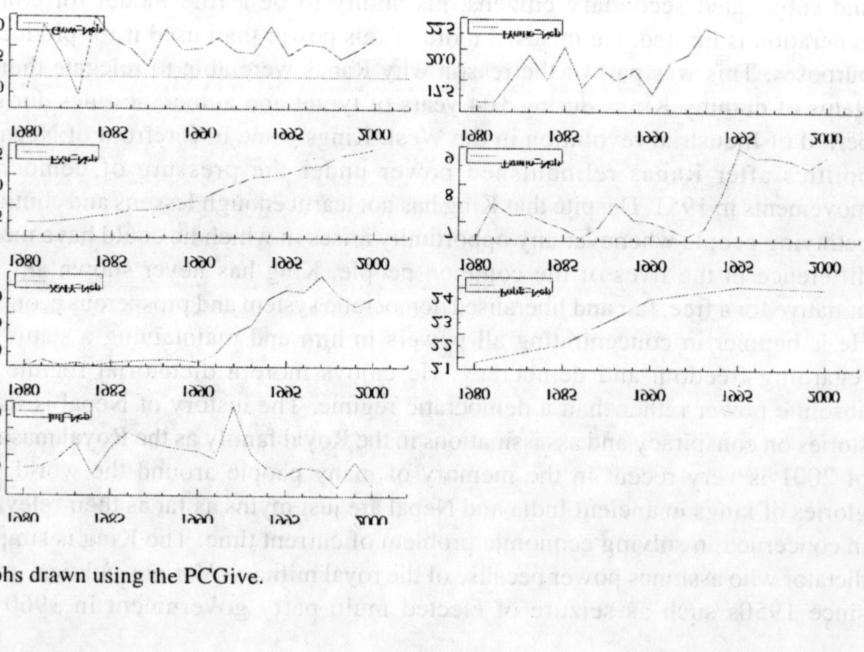

Graphs drawn using the PCGive.

Figure 4

Growth, investment, tax and inflation in South Asia

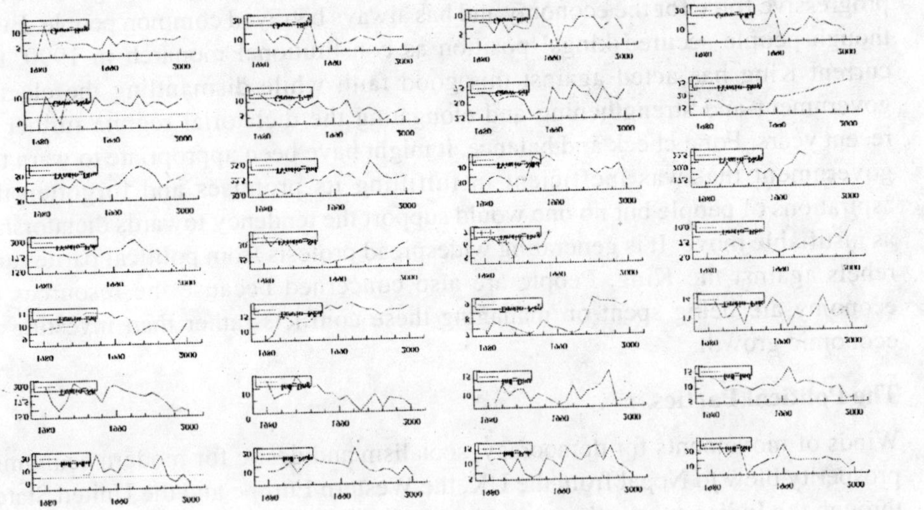

Graphs drawn using the PCGive.

Figure 5

Exchange rate, trade ratio and population growth rate in South Asia

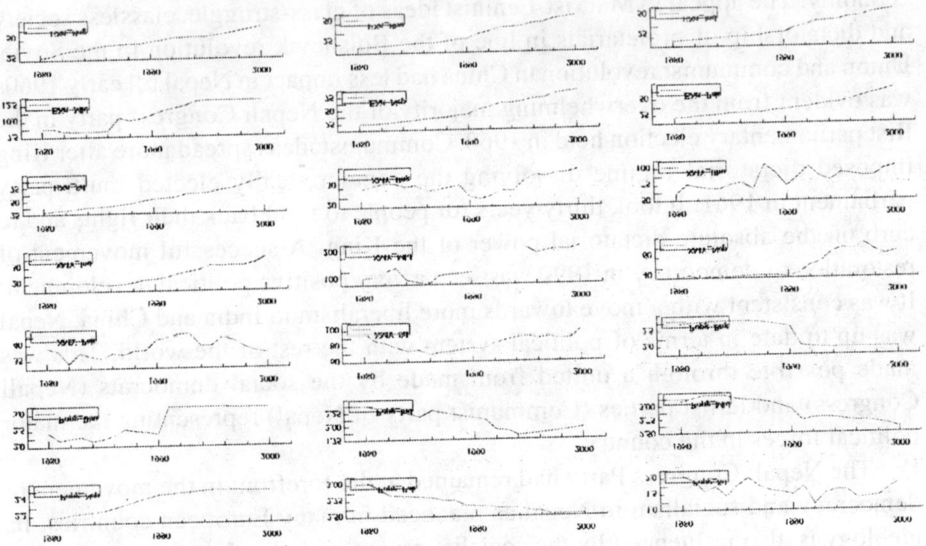

Graphs drawn using the PCGive.

imposition of authoritarian Panchayat regime from 1960 to 1990, re-instalment of dictatorial regime with dissolution of elected parliament and government in 2002 and 2005 are clear evidences for this assertion. Kingship is a regressive not progressive force for the economy and has always betrayed common people. Even though people secured kings' position as constitutional monarch in 1990, the current King has acted against this good faith while dismantling the elected government and strengthening and elongating the dictatorial regime further in recent years. For a check and balance, it might have been appropriate to warn the government that was inefficient in fulfilling its promises and forgotten the aspirations of people but no one would support the tendency towards dictatorship as justifiable move. It is generating widespread protests from political parties and rebels against the King. People are also concerned because the resources of economy are being spent on managing these conflicts rather than investing in economic growth.

The Political Parties

Winds of movements for democracy, socialism and desire for modern economic prosperity blew to Nepal from the UK, the Western Europe and the United States through the Indian subcontinent during the time of the movement of freedom and independence in South Asia in 1940s. Ideas of a constitution that guarantees individual freedom and defines state machinery with a clear division of power among legislature, executive and judiciary; has provision of regular free and fair election of representatives in all levels of the government; makes the bureaucracy responsible to elected officials came along with greater emphasis on individual freedom and property rights for a free, open and liberal society and a growing economy. The appeal to Marxist-Leninist ideas of class-struggle, classless society and dictatorship of proletariats in line of the Bolshevik revolution in the Soviet Union and communist revolution in China had less impact in Nepal till early 1960s was evident from the overwhelming majority of the Nepali Congress party in the first parliamentary election held in 1960. Communist ideas spread more after King imposed dictatorial regime dissolving the democratically elected multi-party parliament in 1961. It took thirty years for people to fight back their rights and to curb on the absolute dictatorial power of the King. A successful movement of restoration of democracy in 1990 was seen a very positive political development. It was consistent with a move towards more liberalism in India and China. Nepal was up to date in terms of political system with the rest of the world. This was made possible through a united front made by the social democrats (Nepali Congress) and leftist parties (Communist party of Nepal) representing the major political forces in the country.

The Nepali Congress Party had remained at the forefront in the movement of democracy and socialism in Nepal as practiced in many European countries. Its ideology is also influenced by the socialist groups of India. It was started by BP Koirala in late 1940s and has remained one of the strongest party through-out the democratic movement in Nepal, has support of liberal minded people and professionals and has remained continuously in direct conflict with Kings regarding the supremacy of elected parliament over monarchy. The influence of the Communist Party (Marxist-Leninist) increased during the Kings' dictatorial regime between 1960 and 1990. Initially the King had used them strategically to counterbalance the growing power of the Congress party. Communists did not hesitate to compromise to remain themselves under the King though he was their topmost class enemy under the communist ideology. In terms of ideology the Congress party was committed more towards the liberalism and democracy than the Communist Party. For an outsider there seems to be a little difference between them as both of them have accepted constitutional monarchy and were aspiring for a socialist economy. This apparent contradiction in the main group of Nepalese communists who participated in the process of multi-party democracy with a constitutional monarch has given a rise to the more extreme leftist parties such as Nepal Peasants and Workers' Party (NMKP) and the deadliest Nepalese Maoist party of rebels after 1990. There are other minor parties representing the interests of ethnic groups such as Sadbhavana and rightist royal elements such as Nepal Rastriya Prajatantra Party. Though each of above parties claim to represent farmers, traders, entrepreneurs, employees of public and private sectors and other people in the working group at national, district and village levels, the Nepali Congress Party and the Communist Party of Nepal (CPN-UML) were the prominent ones in terms of influence and the two main contenders of political power in the parliamentary democracy that started in 1990.

The government of the Nepali Congress had taken good initiatives to reform economic policies after it came to power in the beginning of 1990s winning the general election under the multi-party system. For internal stability, prices were stabilised adopting careful balance in the budget deficit by introducing VAT to broaden the tax base, exchange rates were left to the market, trades and financial sector were liberalised and made more competitive; system of licences and quota was dismantled and Nepal became a member of WTO, more expenditure was allocated to the education and health sectors, many public enterprises were sold to the private sector to enhance efficiency. The basic needs including provision of drinking water and electricity were among the top priority and there were policies for balanced development of communication and transportation networks. Despite these measures these parties promised a lot for reducing poverty but achieved very little. Problem further increased because of increase in corruption and lack of discipline in many politicians and distorted economic decisions and raised concerns from the opposition and rebels. No party could hang on to power continuously. The Communist Party and the party of royalists have also formed their own or the coalition government in the parliament when the Congress lost its majority in 1996.

It is clear that none of the parties have been able to retain their clean and clear image in front of the people. Each of them has suffered from the lack of discipline within their organisation and in government and has used power for corruption and malpractices. They have forgotten the promises they made to the people in the election once they were in office and busy in the power struggle. Though there had been some progress in liberalisation of the economy, in education, health and transportation sectors, the poor growth record shows that these parties did not make enough efforts for growth and investment in the economy; their focus was more on distribution rather than in economic growth. They were weaker in implementation and were more corrupt than people in the Congress government. Despite these weaknesses, the freedom of expression and liberty that the system provided to common people had given an open environment in which people could think about their future. These economic and individual freedoms were taken away when the King snatched people's power in 2002.

Maoists

The Maoist ideology entered in Nepal during King's dictatorial regime between 1960 and 1990; the policy of playing against India with China and vice-versa might have attracted some development aids manifested in roads or transportation networks from China but they came along with the Maoist ideology. Despite theoretical contradiction communists strategically accepted King as their leader and strengthened their organisation while following rules set by the absolute monarch. This was the genesis the Maoist movement and radical rebels in Nepal though it is true that Mao himself was not clear what the Maoism stood for. The Chinese Communist Party has already abandoned this ideology as early as mid 1970s. It is an irony that while the Maoism has been discarded as an ideology in the mainland China with its swift transition to the more efficient market system with property rights and individual freedom on economic activities resulting in unprecedented rates of economic growth, the Moaist rebels are becoming stronger and more effective in creating violence and terror in the name of so called Peoples War in Nepal. In principle Maoism was revision on the Soviet model of Marxist-Leninist and Stalinist ideas and was a cult that preached "equality, opposition of bureaucratism and corruption, an idealisation of frugal lifestyles, a denial of individual selfishness and devotion to the public good, a demand for mass participation in political administration, championing of mass criticism and the rights to rebel, and a theory how a new ruling class emerges within the Party" (Walder (1987)). It is said that this cult creates "a paranoid view of political world among its followers by branding as traitor for someone who has insufficient enthusiasm in the worship of Mao, a mentality that encourage the treatment of enemies as non-humans subjectable to any form of humiliation or torture, a notion of democracy that enforces slavish conformity to a single dictator." In Nepal such extreme Maoist party was formed under the freedom of expression and organisation provided by the Constitution of Nepal of 1990. It had six (out of 235) parliamentarians in the first parliament and all of them committed to protest the parliamentary system from inside the parliament. They boycotted the second general election in 1996 and started Peoples War using any means of terrorism. They have formed a parallel government, looted arms and ammunitions from military barracks, killed people and created fears and tensions in the minds of people. They destabilised the whole system and created confusion and uncertainty among common people including entrepreneurs, traders and business people. They have strongholds in remote poverty belts of Nepal and mobilised the marginal groups massively for terror activities. More than 13000 people have been killed in last 10 years because of the violence and terror created by Maoists and brought the country to a bloody civil war. Peaceful country of Buddha has become very frightening war zone, full of explosions, riots and attacks. This conflict has reduced the rates of investment and saving and economic growth in Nepal. It seems that it is not possible to solve current impasse without bringing Maoists into the mainstream of the political economy of Nepal. More failure in bargaining means more violence and more terror.

NEPALESE DILEMMA: CONFLICT RESOLUTION AND COOPERATION FOR GROWTH

Nepal is in conflict and crises because of inherent contradiction among three political economic forces mentioned in the previous section. King wants to increase his power, political parties want to form their own governments but have proved incompetent while they had an opportunity to do so, and Maoists want to eliminate both of them and create their own state. Conflicts and growing internal tensions have reduced investment and other economic activities, deterred donors to continue developmental activities in Nepal and frightened tourists from visiting Nepal. It has created hatred among people and demoralised investors and created sense of fear among consumers and producers. Cumulative effect of all these political disagreement is leading to a civil war and permanent crises. It is urgent to sort out his problem before any initiative for long run growth. How can a bargaining model be applied successfully to solve this problem? If there is no agreement among these three, this economy will further face a situation of dynamic deterioration. Nepal will be left permanently in poverty and crises. Entrepreneurs and skilled workers will abandon the country, science and technology will not reach out there, it will not benefit from the rapid space of globalisation, it will remain isolated and a basket case of poverty. Any solution that does not satisfy each of these parties is bound to fail. Application of force and coercion may suppress the situation for a while but the problem will rise again.

It is clear from above analysis that King (K), parties (P) and rebels (R) do not have ability to run the government own their own. The singletons $\{K\}$, $\{P\}$ and $\{R\}$ are not feasible solutions, politically, economically or socially; two intermediate coalitions $\{K, P\}$ and $\{K,R\}$ have been tried out and failed; and one grand coalition $\{K,P,R\}$ seems the only solution that has not been put in practice efficiently. As stated in section two at any time there is an efficient bargaining solution for such strategic economic problem where parties maximise their social objective function subject to the unit power constraint (Max $W = P_1 P_2 P_3$ subject to $U = P_1 + P_2 + P_3$ as given in section 2). If this reservation power or the disagreement point in power-sharing agreement is added to the above problem the efficient solution is obtained by maximum Nash product $W = (P_1 - d_1)(P_2 - d_2)(P_3 - d_3)$ subject to power constraint $U = P_1 + P_2 + P_3$ where d_i represent the disagreement point. In a two party case solution looks like in diagram 4.

Returning to three-pronged Nepalese dilemma each party is pivotal for the bargaining solution. King should understand that returning to absolute monarchy is inconsistent with democracy and for the growth of the economy and be satisfied with the titular position as practiced in the many of the western democracies including Britain, Denmark and Spain. Political parties should put economic growth in top priority and adopt efficient and prudent policies taking a view of long horizon. Maoists should reconsider not to introduce failed ideology in Nepal if they are really concerned about uplifting the lives of marginal and poor people taking lessons from the failure of communism and move towards market based allocations and greater democracy and socialism both in Russia and China (Walder (1987), Perkins (1994), Shleifer and Treisman (2005)). The grand coalition that all agree will be one which can come with a solution, at least in the long run in which, $c_1 + g_1 = c_2 + g_2 = c_3 + g_3$ where each have prospects of having equal sum of private and public consumption. This can occur only when the tax revenues from the high income group pays for the public goods of low income groups. The solutions of this bargaining problem may be summarised in terms of following points.

Diagram 4
Efficient and Inefficient Bargaining Solutions

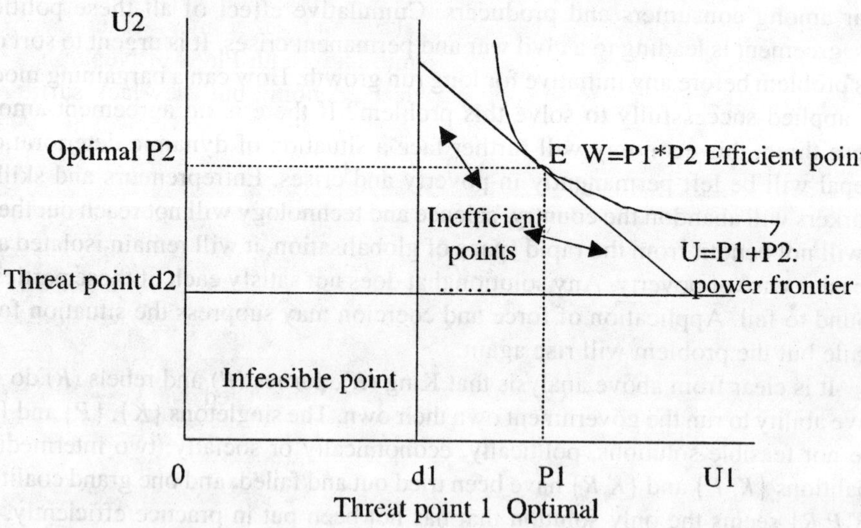

(a) Make "a grow Nepal contract" and put growth as the first objective of the political economic system. Put a system that promotes economic growth and remove features that are harmful for economic growth. Make sure that fruits of growth are distributed more evenly among people.

(b) The parliament should decide a tax rate on income of the King and he should pay these taxes without any hesitation. The King should not be treated more than an ordinary citizen for tax purposes and he should be elected but not hereditary. If King does not heed to people's demand he should be overthrown and his land and palaces should be used for starting schools and universities to educate children from the poor background.

(c) Political parties should run their organisations in true spirit of democracy and have a system of punishing corrupt party officials according to amount of such corruption. Any citizen should be able to make a case against such corruption.

(d) Extra resources should be channelled for education, health care, job security of the marginal groups. Maoists should abandon their arms as well as the violence and terror as a means of achieving their political objectives. They should not threaten common people.

(e) The nation should give each citizen an equal starting point by means of education and training and let their creativity and productivity prosper according to their abilities through competitive system and elimination of corruption.

(f) Each party should respect the fundamental human rights and individual freedom. It should commit itself to establish the rule of law, strengthen laws for property rights, establish liberal system of tax and transfer, ensure transparency in use of public funds and system of eliminating corruptions.

Cooperative solution can improve the situation significantly and let economy to move on the path of prosperity. The Ninth and Tenth Plans of Nepal in NPC (1997, 2002) contain details on the Nepalese economy but they lack sufficient analytical structure required by the challenge of the time. To my knowledge Bhattarai (2000) goes one step towards detailed economic modelling of the Nepalese economy taking account of the structure details of demand, supply and production and trade sides of economy. Acharya (2000) suggests measures necessary to institutional set up for a parliamentary democracy suitable to Nepal. Panday's (1999) points regarding implementations of plans and Hutt's (2005) on recent problems are noteworthy.

The international community can contribute significantly in solving this conflict on the basis of collective experiences that has been accumulated over years in solving these types of problems around the globe. Many lessons can be learnt from the experience of democratic struggles and transformation in many of the Western countries in the past and Eastern countries in recent years, and particularly on how the adult franchise and the market economy can offer better solutions for growth, technical progress and redistribution than by authoritative regimes.

EMPIRICAL SUPPORT FOR THE ABOVE MODEL

A strategic random sampling survey on opinions of Nepalese male and female belonging to various age groups, living in different parts of country and working in cross sections of occupations was conducted during the period between January to March 2006. They were asked to express their opinions about how the existing conflict among the political parties, King, and Maoists had affected their lives, how these problems should be solved and express their believes on which one of them would be able to solve these problems. They also were asked to express their ranking of various factors hindering growth of Nepal, what were the major problems of each of above political forces. The structure of sample and the responses are as reported in Tables 1 and 2.

Table 1
Structure of Random Strategic Sampling on Conflict, Cooperation and Growth in Nepal

Geographic Area	*Sample*	*Age Group*	*Sample*	*Gender*	*Sample*
Tanahun	73	Below 20	34	Male	146
Chitwan	46	20-29	72	Female	84
Kathmandu	22	30-39	44	Total	230
Nawalparasi	36	40-49	45		
Morang	3	50-59	20		
Sunsari	7	60-69	11		
Kaski	6	70-79	4		
Gorkha	4	80-89	0		
Others	33				
Total	230		230		

Ethnicity of respondents	*Sample*	*Educational Background*	*Sample*	*Profession*	*Sample*
Brahmin	113	Masters	41	Teaching	44
Chhetri	26	Diploma	62	Student	81
Newar	17	Intermediate	40	Business	20
Magar	17	S.L.C.	38	Farmer	26
Guring	13	High School	8	Housewife	17
Rai	5	Primary	15	Government Employee	21
Others	39	Illiterate	14	University Teacher	5
		PhD	8	Other	16
		Other	4		
Total	230		230		230

Sample represented opinions of people from 26 out of 75 districts in Nepal, though the sample was more clustered in Tanahun (32%), Chitwan (20%), Nawalparasi (15.7%) and Kathmandu (9.6%). Out of 230 people surveyed 63 per cent were males. These people represented 26 ethnic groups though mainly dominated by Brahmin and Chhetri (61%). Respondents were quite educated by Nepalese standards.

Majority of people reported their daily activities to be seriously affected by the conflict and the major way out of this crisis was a political dialogue (64%) rather than absolute monarchy (17%) or people's republic (11.3%). Corruption (45%), political conflict (27%) and poverty (12%) were pointed to be major obstacles to economic growth. Personal ambition of political leaders (56%), lack of the internal democracy (24%) and coordination were major weaknesses of political parties, while the ambition to retain the absolute power (39%), lack of understanding of the problem (27 %) was considered King's problem. Another 31 per cent thought that he did not know what he was doing. Most respondents were critical of violent means of Maoists and they accused them for unreasonable vision.

Table 2
Summary of Answers from the Strategic Sampling on Conflict, Cooperation and Growth in Nepal

How do you think this problem should be solved?	
(a) by dialogue among parties and democracy	146
(b) abolition of monarch	39
(c) People's republic as proposed by Maoists	27
(d) absolute monarchy	18
Why is not Nepal growing? (1 least)	
(a) Corruption	104
(b) Low investment	2
(c) Political conflict	62
(d) Lack of ideas and technology adoption	17
(e) Poverty	27
(f) Low education	17
(g) fewer health facilities	
(h) communication and transportation	
(i) inefficient market	

Contd...

What is the problem with political parties?	
(a) lack of internal democracy	54
(b) personal ambition	129
(c) lack of coordination	46
What is problem with the King?	
(a) lacks understanding	63
(b) does not know what he is doing	77
(c) ambition to retain absolute monarchy	89
What is the problem with Maoists?	
(a) violent means	117
(b) unreasonable vision	113
Do you own any property?	
House	115
Land 36	
Stocks	7
Bank deposits	24
None	24

CONCLUSION

Conflict among feudal factors led by the King, working people in trade and industry led by political parties, marginal, poverty trapped people threatened and mobilised by Maoist rebels has created a very unproductive environment where investors and entrepreneurs do not get any productive opportunity. Non-cooperation among competing political and economic forces has brought Nepal into crisis and a growth disaster. The major reason for conflict is short-sighted horizon of these players with constant sum view who try to maximise their own current share on GDP® taking its size as a constant. It has discouraged productive economic activities and transfer of better technology and knowledge and resources from abroad with dangerous consequences to the economy. A solution is offered here in terms of a contract in more objectives and specific growth oriented rules that bounds each of them to the policy rules in which each of these groups has incentive to stick for peace and prosperity, adoption and use of knowledge and technology for growth. This is possible if they take a more optimistic grow-Nepal strategy to maximise the growth rate of the economy.

NOTES

1. The first draft of this paper was prepared on May 2005 and then revised with field survey on opinions of people about the crises in February 2006. I very much appreciate my brothers Kedar Bhattarai in Kathmanud for painfully gathering survey information for the empirical part of this paper and for Bishnu Bhattarai in Boston for some discussions on the formulation of questionnaire and my mother Hari Maya Bhattarai, Sisters Manu Maya Bhattarai and Basundhara Khanal and millions of Nepalese people for invaluable inspiration for this study. All errors and omissions are my own.
2. See Ramsey (1928), Harrod (1939), Domar (1947), Solow (1956), Cass (1965), Koopmans (1965), Lucas (1988), Romer (1989) for theories and Madison (1991) Mankiw, Romer and Weale (1992), Barro and Sala-i-Martin (1995), Temple (1999), Bhattarai (2004) for empirical studies.
3. See Gunning (1986), Bardhan (1997), Easterly (2001) for studies on riots and ethnic conflicts and Schumpeter (1942), Myrdal (1982), Sen (1983), Przeworski and Limongi (1993), Wittman (1989), Easterly (2001), Virwimp (2003) on models of development and democracy and Mehrling (1986), Besley and Coate (2003), Maskin and Tirole (2004) for models of political economy.
4. Such political power can mitigate the inequality caused by the market. In evolution of the election system with one person one vote were behind the adoption of the social democratic system by majority of Western economies, as their economies industrialised in the last century and adoption of general welfare system in the second half of the 20th century.

REFERENCES

Acharya NH (2000), *Naya Nepalko Prastavana* (Proposal for New Nepal), Kathmandu Nepal.

Bardhan P. (1997), Methods and Madness: A Political Economy Analysis of Ethnic Conflicts in less Developed Countries, World Development, 25:1381-1398.

Besley T. and S. Coate (2003), Sources of Inefficiency in a Representative Democracy: A Dynamic Analysis, *American Economic Review*, 88:1:139-156.

Bhattarai K.R. (2004), Economic Growth: Models and Global Evidence, Research Memorandum, University of Hull.

Bhattarai K.R. (2000), Welfare and Distributional Impacts of Financial Liberalisation in a Developing Economy: Lessons from a Forward Looking CGE Model of Nepal, Working Paper no. 7, Hull Advances in Policy Economics Research Papers.

Downs A. (1957), *Economic Theory of Democracy*, Harper and Row, New York.

Easterly W. (2001), The Elusive Quest for Growth: Economists' Adventure and Misadventures in the Tropics, MIT press, MA.

Gunning P. J. (1986), An Economic Approach to Riot Analysis, *Public Choice*, 13:31-47.

Huber E. D. Rueschemeyer and J. D. Stephens (1993) The Impact of Economic Development on Democracy, *Journal of Economic Perspective*, 7:3:71-85.

Hutt M. (2005), Nepal and Bhutan: Two Kings, Two Features, Asian Survey, XLV:1:83-87, Jan/Feb.

Maskin E. and J. Tirole (2004), The Politician and the Judge: Accountability in Government, *American Economic Review*, 94:4: 1034-1054.

McMillan J. and P. Zoido (2005) How to Subvert Democracy: Montesinos in Peru, *Journal of Economic Perspective*, 18:4:69-92.

Mehrling P. G. (1986), A Classical Model of the Class Struggle: A Game-Theoretic *Approach, Journal of Political Economy*, 94:6:1280-1303.

Morris S. (2001), Political Correctness, *Journal of Political Economy*, 109:2:231-65.

Myrdal G. (1982), Asian Drama: An Inquiry Into the Poverty of Nations, Kalyani Publishers, New Dehli.

National Planning Commission (1997 and 2002), The Ninth and Tenth Plans of Nepal, Kathmandu, Nepal.

Paldam M. (2002), The Cross Country Pattern of Corruption: Economics, Culture and the Seasaw Dynamics, *European Journal of Political Economy*, 18:215-240.

Panday D. R. (1999), Nepal's Failed Development: Reflection on the Mission and the Maladies, Kathmandu, Nepal.

Perkins D. (1994), Completing China's Move to the Market, *Journal of Economic Perspective*, 8:2:23-46.

Przeworski A. and F. Limongi (1993), Political Regimes and Economic Growth, *Journal of Economic Perspective*, 7:3:51-69.

Schumpeter J. (1942), Capitalism, Socialism and Democracy, Harper.

Sen A. K. (1983), Development: which way now? *Economic Journal*, 93:372-745-62.

Shleifer A. and D. Treisman (2005), A Normal Country: Russia After Communism, *Journal of Economic Perspective*, 19:1:151-174.

Verwimp P. (2003), The Political Economy of Coffee, Dictatorship and Genocide, *European Journal of Political Economy*, 19:161-181.

Walder A. G. (1987), Actually Existing Maoism, *Australian Journal of Chinese Affairs*, 18:155-166 July.

Wintrobe A. (1988), *The Political Economy of Dictatorship*, Cambridge University Press.

Wittman D. (1989), Why Democracies Produce Efficient Results? *Journal of Political Eocnomy*, December 97:6:1395-426.

4

HOW DID INVESTMENT IN HUMAN CAPITAL HELP ME TO GROW?

Overwhelming majority of Nepalese individuals are poor and want to transform their lives so that they can afford basic human needs: food, clothing, shelter, health, education and security. While clever ones and those with good family background have been able to make this happen, any marginal people without adequate means for education and training or starting a real business remain trapped in poverty through out the life. It is almost impossible for poor boys or girls born from parents without any education to get some education necessary for advancement. I would like to illustrate the idea of how good opportunities of education and hard individual efforts built on character and skills help transform such society in one generation. I illustrate this with an example from my own life in forty five years of life span from 1961 to 2006 as I know this is surrounded with unique set of economic circumstances that matter for economic growth of a developing nation like Nepal.

An old saying states that a good education generates politeness and skills in an individual which makes that person a good candidate for jobs. These jobs raise earnings and more earning brings happiness in life for that person and the society. This type of lifecycle model if applied to each individual in the country raises the skill, knowledge, thinking and earning powers of individuals and bring higher rate of growth of the economy and better distribution of income. There can be no doubt that human capital can be instrumental in the process of economic growth in Nepal.

My journey for education and personal development starts from a very humble background in rural hills of Western Nepal. None of my parents had any education; they hardly knew how to read and write the Nepali language. I moved for education first from my own village Batase to then a remote town Devghat with my uncle when I was eight years old and then to Kathmandu when I was eleven, out of Kathmandu valley when I was 18. Full of family and national responsibilities in prevailing circumstances of the country my family life has taught me many things. I was a responsible friend, son, brother or a guardian. In jobs I was a banker, educationist and a development official and had to travel to many parts of Nepal from 1979 to 1988. My first jet trip abroad was essentially a reward for my good grades in MA in Economics the result of hard efforts despite difficult circumstances. It came when I was 28 for an overseas MA degree in the ISS Hague, Netherlands. This further opened my opportunities as I was admitted for a PhD in economics at Northeastern starting from September 1991. I completed the PhD and got an opportunity for a post doctoral research in the University of Warwick from 1996 to 1999 and then am teaching economics as a Lecturer in economics in the University Hull. Actions that I had chosen in my life were successively targeted towards getting enlightenment through learning, knowing the world and fulfilling the personal, family, national and global responsibility simultaneously.

There was no systematic planning for this journey; it came as a rational response to various situations, circumstances and opportunities that became available from time to time and cooperation and good wishes of many people at home and abroad. After years of hard efforts I was able to get higher education and well respected jobs in higher education system in the United States and United Kingdom. I had also helped to some extent to transform lives of my brothers and sisters leading the way for education. As I believe my story is helpful for a creative thinking about the growth and redistribution process in Nepal, I like to expand it a bit further in this chapter.

EARLY CHILDHOOD AND PRIMARY EDUCATION

Majority of people in Nepal live in rural areas. I also have very fond memories of growing in the Batase-Myagde hills in the middle of the Tanahun district of Nepal in 1960s. Naturally it is a very beautiful place with panoramic view of Himalayan ranges which turn golden with the morning sunrise and evening sunlight. Full of rituals and festivities the farmers in the village lived peacefully with clear and bright sun on the day and unhindered vision of stars and moon at night. The village where I grew up was self-contained and culturally rich; households cared each other in time of need and had a system of mutual cooperation and respect. They had happy summer seasons with cultivation of corn and maize and many other types of grains and vegetables in dry sloppy lands and rice plant in irrigable fields of Myagde valley. Occasional storms, hails and rains could shatter their lives but everything recovered itself after some time. Farmers were busy in every season either in cultivation or taking care of their live stocks or family or village festivities. Many of them hardly knew anything in the world beyond the horizon of mountains they could see from their home. Transportation was by foot or in the back of horses for rich ones. Communication was limited in the form of person to person contacts as there were no radios, telephones, TV or newspaper. Most people were illiterate and except a few pundits who managed to spend few years in the learning centres like Kashi-Varanasi or Haridwar in India. This village had very primitive methods of health care: herbs, soups and roots. People spent days working in their fields, gathering woods from forests or grazing animals in common lands and fetching waters from down the hill and valleys. Society was divided in caste system that was quite rigid and full of taboo such as a Brahmin adult touching

Damai or Kami needed to be purified by rinsing pure waters on them. Brainy works belonged to upper casts and menial works to the lower casts, the so called division of classes according to works as mentioned in Manusmriti. Basically this was a feudal system, the landlord with a dominant position in society as they owned the means of production. Brahmins, Ksyatriyas and Business men had more land and economic resources and the lower caste people had to depend on them for their survival. Brahmins worked with brains, Kshatriyas with their muscle power, Vaishyas busy in business and Shudras serving other three classes. Iron law of wages prevailed, workers used to get wages that would be enough to sustain their lives. This was also time of internal migration. After the successful implementation of malaria eradication programme people had been moving from the top of the hills to the bottom of hills or valleys that had easy access to water. Many farmers even were moving away to inner Tarai regions of Chitwan and Nawalparasi which still had more unclaimed and fertiles lands still to be cultivated. Many others went to India to work in army, police or as manual workers temporarily and brought some hard cash back that they could spend on essential goods. This process intensified as the road transport network opened in 1970s in the form of Kathmandu-Pokhara-Butwal-Narayngadh-Mugling highways.

My parents belonged to Brahmin family who had inherited lands from forefathers that would produce enough food for the year and even with some surplus remaining to sell or give away in the time of dry seasons for those in need in 1960s but with growth of family and deterioration of productivity it was not quite enough in late 1970s. I remember my father, Harikrishna Bhattarai (alias Bhageerath Upadhyay) as a very gentle and honest man and full of love for the family. He was virtually an orphan and his elder brother did not bother to put him in traditional school and rather discouraged while he was trying to do himself. He did not know much tactics needed for living successfully in the village. Therefore he fled from home to India in his teens in 1930s and was even confiscated of a few pennies by his elder brother Kul Prasad who chased him out in Bhimad. He then followed a traveller towards India but had to take his own way after they reached a junction in Nautanwa. Not knowing where to go he went to cow farm in UP in India and spent several years. Then he met someone from Nepal going to a job in Calcutta. He followed him and managed to enrol himself in Armed Police forces around 1935. The World War II was lurking in the horizon and the British India Government was looking for more recruits. After spending few years in this new job he was able to go back to Nepal in paid holidays. He had married my mother when he was 27 years old and she was just of nine around 1942. After marriage he again went back to India remained in India for more than forty years. He retired from the Armed Police Service in Calcutta in a pension in 1978 which he could enjoy just for about eight years but has left a lifelong entitlement of widow pension to my mother which she still draws from the Pension Branch of the Indian Embassy in Kathmandu. My mother had joined him in Calcutta for five years and had got my sister and me there. They returned to Nepal with me and my elder sister in 1963. After that my father remained in India and we grew up in Batase hills. I remember writing letter from home as dictated by my mother to him ever since I knew how write a letter. It would have taken more than twelve hours of walk to post such letter. We used to walk a whole day just to post a letter at the nearest post office that was in Damuali- now a very vibrating town in the confluence of Seti and Madi rivers which has remained the headquarter of Tanahun since 1967. We remember our father coming home only once in two years for one or two months with some chocolates and nice clothes and leave some money for the family for the time until his next return.

My two other elder uncles, Diwakar and Kul Prasad were revered in the village as pundits (learned men) and involved in priestly duties and reading spiritual texts Rudris-Vedas. I did not see my grand-parents either from my father's side or from my mother'. This was not unusual because of lower life expectancy of villagers and late marriage of my father. In absence of my father at home we were somehow in the guardianship of these uncles though my mother was quite a strong lady to run the house on her own. Our neighbourhood remained a very lively place and every person in the village knew us and took us with some respect. I particularly remember Suyel family our next door neighbour in Batase with 100s of goats, 4-5 buffaloes, pair oxen and hens and a tiny house full of people. Suyel Dai was active, energetic and very pleasant farmer. He used to help us search a buffalo for milking whenever we did not have one. He used to plough some of our lands for growing maize or dry land rice or millets just for a good meal. That was extra-ordinary support for which they would get invited in feasts and festivals in the season. This is how priestly class had impressed others to make work for them. My mother Harimaya (alias Anumaya) took the responsibility of running the house very well. She maintained the house and brought up me, my two sisters and two brothers though she barely could read and write in Nepali.

My parents tell me story that I was born in Calcutta and brought to Tanahun Nepal when I was 18 months old. They had very hard journey back home at that time and had to walk seven eight days in rains and sun in summer to get up to Batase hills from Bhairahawa with me and my elder sister in their laps. They arrived at Bhairahawa in two days from Calcutta but could not get a plane to Pokhara. This town had an ordinary airport with grassy runways. A plane could land only when land was dry. They waited for a plane to Pokhara for seven days but were deceived by the weather. Every day was bright but rained heavily at night and made the ground wet and inappropriate for landing or take off. Thus they had no choice but to walk for another seven days to reach Batase.

We still belonged to the big joint family dominated by Kul Prasad uncle the oldest of the two other brothers of my father who was the youngest son of Bhawani Shanker and Damayanti–my grand parents. He stayed few days with the whole family and left my mother and us with them. As there were many children in a tiny house our mother reminds us how she had to struggle with other family members for very minor things until my father came next time and the two brothers got separated and divided their ancestral properties into two halves making each family to be free of interference of another.

For thirty years from 1930 to 1965 it seems that my father earned hard cash in India and brought it back and gave it to uncle Kul Prasad who managed to buy more lands with this and other earnings that he was able to collect. By the standard of an average villager we had got reasonable amount of land asset though that was scattered into several pieces here and there. After the division my mother could not cultivate all the lands that we had and gave on the basis of share cropping. Earnings from these lands were enough about for our survival. I remember harvesting seasons when our yards were full of maize, rice and straws and when we used to play on top of them in the childhood. In addition to cultivation we had some live stocks as we regularly used to have a buffalo for milks. We helped mother in collecting grasses, woods, household chores and many other cultivation activities.

The system of school education was just starting in those years. My elder sister Basundhara born in 1958 was three years older than me. She had some schooling in Calcutta and studied up to fourth grade from the Koldada primary school which was about one-hour walk west along the hills from our house in Batase. We had many friends from the village such as Kal Bahadur, Krishna Bahadur, Man Bahadur, Bharat, Raja, Biswaraj, Bhaviraj, Tham Bahadur, Yam Bahadur, Basante, Kulhari, Kedar and many others. These were classmates, playmates and we were relatively free to go around common grounds for play, particularly in the winter when we lands were free of any crops. In school we remember chanting the national songs in the morning keeping fit ourselves in lines in the morning before the school started and in the evening when the school was about to dismiss for the day. Every child used to read loud and this could be heard from far away. The first and second graders chanted ka kha, ga, ka ka, ki, kee the Nepalese alphabets and consonants and English letters ABCD or the multiplication tables from 1 to 10 or as up 20 or the short stories. Among others things I remember swimming in a pond that would collect muddy water from pouring rains during summer time. We even used to go to collect woods, bundle of grasses from the local forest, to fetch waters from the well or to graze animals in common grazing lands to help out our parents. We used to have many trips to sewers or blacksmiths and see local dances or Bhajans or Puja where villages sacrificed goats or he buffallos and shared out their meat among themselves. This happy schooling did not last long for as my sister had to go through arranged marriage when she was just 12 years old upon consultation of our Diwakar uncle who under taboo of age old tradition of Manusmriti that ruled that girls should be married before their first menarche. That virtually put an end to her education that she regrets forever. Similarly my father and uncles wanted me to study traditional religious texts and so they also discontinued me from the regular school after I was in the third grade. I was given a sacred thread when I was six years old with a Gayatri Mantra from Faguram dai of Rising in a Bratavandha ceremony. Then I was put in traditional Chandi-Rudri and Karmakand track of education. I remember of going from one elderly person to another on a take-a-lesson-as-you-meet basis of Chandi, Rudri and Veda. Girls were not allowed to read these texts and reading these religious texts was considered privileges of only Brahmin boys.

I hardly knew any meaning in any of those lessons, I suspect even those who taught hardly knew their meaning-as I discovered from my study of Sanskrit later on. I used to meet uncle Diwakar or my cousins Kalidas, Basudev, Murari and Thirthraj while they were grazing their animals in forests or common grazing lands. Uncle Diwakar was very orthodox; he did not do many things for religious reasons. For instance he prohibited wearing any sewn clothes but had to weare only "Kachhad" or Lagauti. At some point he would even not drink a pipe water, it had to be from a natural well or a stream. I also remember being in temporary open air school in local Chautaris with Pashupati, Ganapati, Chhatraraj and Budho Master (old teacher). Usually these schools would run only in good seasons and would dismiss immediately when it rained. Neither my parents nor my uncles had any clue about the objectives of modern education system. This was not unnatural for that time given the fact that this village was completely isolated from the rest of the world as there were not even radios to listen to news, no roads or motor vehicles nor any electricity. Having a petro-max or lantern was really a big thing. Villagers had to walk seven days to take one tin of Kerosene and satchel of salt from Butwal or Narayngadh to rich to Kathmandu for official business. Machines or mills were not even heard off. Things have changed dramatically since the road opened in 1970s.

Our family became bigger in 1970s. Sister Manu was born in 1969, brother Bishnu in 1973 and Kedar in 1979. My Father retired from his job in India in 1978 and lived for another eight years though that seemed to be the most difficult period of his life because of health problems. My mother had caught epilepsy which must have gone unnoticed for many years and became very acute in 1977-78. It would have taken her life had I not brought her for treatment with Dr. Bishnu Prasad in Kathmandu in 1977, the only doctor in the country who had EEG machine required for treating epilepsy. I was 17 years old when my father retired and returned for good to Nepal in 1978 and away in Sanskrit hostel in Kathmandu doing my studies.

Initially these family problems did not disturb me and I was doing well in my studies. I had topped Nepal in Intermediate level exam in Sanskrit in 1977. I used to go back home in Batase with full of respect and feelings towards my three very young siblings Manu, Bishnu and baby Kedar and two ailing sick parents. We were still in top of Batase hills while almost all of our relatives had managed to migrate to Magde valley. Life in hills was becoming increasingly difficult. It would take about one hour to fetch a jug of water from a well or a tap down the hill for my mother and almost a day to fetch a bundle of woods from the forest. Because of massive deforestations it was becoming harder to find fodder and woods in vicinity and would require longer trips for each coming year. Despite some money that my father had earned in Calcutta the problems of our home was getting worse around 1978. I could not help seeing not a breakfast made until later afternoon, up to two or three o'clock.

Married off in early childhood my elder sister did very hard work for the joint family in Tarkudanda –Kotre; from her 13 to 20 years of age and had migrated to Tilakpur in Nawal Parasi around 1978 with her joint family and was virtually left isolated and alone there as my brother-in-law Jhalak had married another girl. He himself was spending time in doing jobs as a teacher or a leprosy supervisor in the United Mission to Nepal's programme and could not even go home when Kranti was being born in 1978. My mother sent me to meet her with a tin full of ghee and other gifts that she had prepared from Batase. It was possible to take a bus from Dhayere to Narayanghat and from Narayangadh to Bardghat and then walk to Bhutaha on the way to Tilakpur. I took a wrong turn and went towards the Gandak barrage instead and could reach to my sister only next day after a lot of inquiries about Tilakpur. Kranti was born and six days old when I reached their home. It was nice to see how the India had tapped water from Gandak for irrigation to various parts of UP and Bihar but was a bit of tour of rural Tarai though it was not planed as a part of my trip.

GURUKUL IN DEVGHAT AND SANKRIT EDUCATION

When I was about nine years old uncle Diwakar was suggesting me to go to Haridwar in India for studies with senior cousins Dhundiraj, Narayan and Murari. I might have gone with them had my mama (uncle) Shri Krishna who already been there and studied up to Purba Madhyama stopped for it. He thought that was not appropriate for me at that time. He took me instead to Shadang Ved Vidyalaya in Devghat where he was a primary teacher of Nepal government since in 1969. I remember walking up and down of hills, mountains and valleys and very dangerous sloppy passes of Sukhaura, Saranghat and Kafaldanda and dense forests in the foothills of Tarai continuously for three days in the summer of 1970. I saw settlements in varieties of environmental conditions before reaching Devghat. The 108 Galeshwar Baba was very exemplary Sadhu who had earned reputations for being a very strong character for a long time ever since he came down from Baglung and settled himself in a little hut just above the confluence of Saptgandaki and Kali rivers. He had built a tiny Shiva temple by the side of his hut. Every student in this school was required to chant five chapters of Rudri in the evening and morning prayers before doing regular lessons of Laghu Sidhant Kaumudi – the Sanskrit grammar, the Vedas and the Hitopadesha. Friends like Sacchidananda, Navajaj, Indu, Bishnu Prasad, Kulshekhar, Kirtinidhi, Loknath, Rishi, Ekraj, Baral and Buddhilal were class and kithchen mates. We used to get up early in the morning, learn swimming in the Kali or Sapta Gandaki, pray and do some yoga in the temple, cook, eat, and wash dishes before returning to studies. We collected woods, made fire and did hawans in the Yagyshala. We got rice vegetables and lentils from the Galeshwar Baba and got some alms from pilgrims from time to time. This place had plenty of fruits like guava, mangos, pineapple and like that which we could pluck and eat. We also grew some vegetable of our own yards of the school. Annual festival of Maghe sankranti when many people came to Devghat and with some big boats in the Sapta Gandak river was interesting day. Rivers would be swollen out of proportion during rainy time and very interesting to see trees, animals and woods flown over the swollen rivers and the fisherman trying to catch them though sometimes they were swept away by the river by the mighty current of the swollen river. The continuous sound of these rivers would be very natural in summer time. I spent about two years in that school. Then some old teacher who came for pilgrimage suggested me that I would do better in Rani Pokhari Sanskrit High School in Kathmandu. I returned home and prepared for a journey to Kathmandu, a mysterious land beyond my imagination up to that time.

I remember my first journey with my uncle Shri Krishna going to Kathmandu in the winter of 1973 via the Prithvi highway that was just under construction with the Chinese Aid. We took pick up trucks breaking the 100 miles long journey in several parts that took us 14 to 15 hours. This road was much appreciated for engineering than the Hetauda raod that went from the summit of Shiv Bhanjyan but it was still under construction and there were many dangerous parts that could have rolling stones, mud or woods. Anyhow we reached Kathmandu around 10 in the night. Bright lights of Kathmandu made me feel that to be an amazing place. I had never seen bright light in that scale. Such bright city light has not left me ever since.

We met Narahari, Chudamani and Surya Mohan in the Sanskrit hostel and stayed there that night. They brought me to a restaurant for dinner. This was the first time I had eaten in a restaurant with some hesitation as it was considered impure and prohibited for a Brahmin boy to eat in a restaurant. It was in fact taken as a necessary first step of modernization of habit and attitude towards new developments. I lived with Sharada Dhakal nephew of Narahari Acharya under his recommendation. I enrolled in and started studying in nineth grage in the Sankrit School. I used to walk from Pakanajol to Ranipokhari via Chhetrapati and Asan every morning. My parents paid about Rs. 3500 for my living costs from 1973 to1975. I studied very hard in school and was able to get full scholarship in the Teendhara Sanskrit Hostel after two years. Once in the hostel I studied very hard for the School Leaving Exam (Purba Madhama: see appendix 1 for subject studied) that I passed with very a good grade and highest average marks from the School for 1976. I continued to the certificate level and completed that in 1977 and the Diploma level in 1981. Thus I stayed in Sanskrit hostel from 1975 to 1981, from the 10th grade to till I completed Diploma (Shastree) level from the Balmiki Vidhyapeeth. This was the most important period of my education in which I had opportunity to build foundations of my studies and character of hard work. This hostel was established in 1900 and had place for 108 well motivated Brahmin students. Though Bir Shamsher had opened this hostel thinking that education of traditional Sanskrit would be favourable for maintaining autocratic rules of Rana family, the awareness brought by modern education proved quite opposite. This hostel in fact was able to produce many freedom fighters and revolutionaries in Nepal.

It had a little library with books in Nepali, Sanskrit, Hindi and English. Particularly it had a close link with the liberal democratic thinking that liberated Indian continent in 1947 and removed the 104 years old autocratic rule of Rana family in Nepal. It contained plenty of resources in ancient Sanskrit literature, its legends, religion of so called 64 knowledge and wisdom and philosophy. It also contained books of politics, economics and geography, history of revolution, American independence, democratic system in Great Britain and Europe and Marxism and communist propaganda after the Bolshevik revolution in Russia. I studied many of them and participated in literary and oratory contests. I did quite a bit of Yoga and studied economics together with Sanskrit. I was able to earn cash scholarship of 7000 Rupees for being the topmost student in the class in 1977. I bought books with that money and continued my study of modern process of economic growth and development and developed keen interest in Economics.

I used to go home in Batase hills once a year in Dashain since 1973; it was becoming easier year by year as the roads were becoming smooth and regular and would now take only about seven hours for 164 kilometers. After spending my holidays I packed my little bag with some books, rotis or beaten rice that represented love and care from my mother. I remember her tearful eyes every time while she was sending me off to Kathmandu. She never had time to come to see me in Kathmandu as she was busy in bringing up Manu and Bishnu and maintaining house and serving the buffalo for milk. I finished intermediate level in 1977 with Merit (see Appendix 2 for the lists of subjects studied in the Sanskrit Institute). It took one extra year for diploma because the King Birendra's government had closed colleges and hostels in the wake of movement for Restoration of Democracy and Multi Party System. I supported movement for change and participated in some of the rallies but I was more inclined for my spiritual studies than in politics and had keen interest in solving the mystery of life. I used to teach Yoga for workers in the Industrial Disstrict in Patan or attend Yoga sessions organised by some scholars who came to Kathmandu from India for short periods.

My father retired in 1978 after 39 years of service for the West Bengal government in India and came back home in Batase. Despite being of very tender and honest heart he we aturally weak and old and did not want to get involved in dirty tricks of villages and found harder living here than in India. With more siblings growing up and depletion of natural resources like forest the life in Batase in 1978 was much more difficult than in 1968. Most of our relatives had already moved down the valley but our family was unable to build a house or take any bold decision about the migration. Because of worries my mother had developed serious epilepsy and its attack became much stronger as time passed by. Many villagers had seen her falling in ponds while carrying bundles of grasses or woods. My father had got diabetes and could not quite adjust to cold Nepali climate after more than forty years of his service in India. With younger siblings Manu, Bishnu and Kedar and worries of elder sister Basundhara the family problem was becoming more complex. It touched me quite seriously even though I was still a young boy of 19 years old and just doing well in my diploma.

In one fine morning when I had just returned meeting my elder sister who had just given birth to Kranti in Bhutaha Chapi in the jungles of Nawal Parasi, where she had migrated along with many of her relatives from Kotre- Tarkudanda my uncle Diwakar and another pundit of his acquaintance Mr. Umanath Kaphle from Sange- Harkhapur came with a proposal of marriage of still 15 year old daughter. So far I had hated married life and wanted a total salvation – to be a completely liberated person. In contrast my Sanskrit education had taught me to treat parents and young sibling as gods. I wanted to help them in difficult time and after a long process of thought I decided to sacrifice my hunger for knowledge and salvation to help my parents by marrying this young girl Prem in anticipation that she would assist in solving difficult problem in my family. However, it was novice for me not to think that this girl was also a human being she also needed to go to school though apparently her parents already had discontinued her education for some reason. She had no idea of what his father was doing when he brought me to his home to see her. I should have warned Umanath for such a proposal but the mind does not work properly when one is in pressure or in a difficult situation and nor I had a proper advice. One thing I thought when accepting the proposal was to get children and give continuation to this wonderful creation from my side. Fortunately that has happened with Manorama and Santosh two wonderful children with us, who seem to be doing well in their studies wherever they go with me – Kathmandu, Boston or UK.

People who Helped me to Come out of Village

My uncle Shri Krishna was a primary school teacher of the Nepalese government and was posted in Devghat in1969 after he returned from completing Purba Madhyama from Haridwar in India, he says from the Chetan Jyoti Sanskrit Vidyalaya, school run by hermits. He was born in 1941 and had primary school from Rishithum Primary in Dahung. He was 18 he had lived with my parents in Calcutta for sometime in early 1959 an 1960 and was in search of a job but then went to Haridwar to study when my father and his friends suggested him that a person like him should spend time in studying. He completed five grade from Hardwar, eighth grade from Badrinath and Purb Madhyama (school leaving exam) from Hardwar. He was brought from India to get married in Kaflethok, which he regrets very much. He was a man of ideas but after getting married got bogged down to the family life. He saw good prospect of migrating to Tarai. He bought some plots of land in Devghat in 1971 which later on turned to be very valuable as a bridge was built over the Sapta Gandaki river linking Chitwan to Tanahun. That place has become very much a centre of pilgrimage in last 30 years with a Sankrit College, high schools and smooth roads and communication networks. He got three daughters Permila, Shanta, Kamala and son Ganga Hari. He sold some of the land in Devghat to buy a plot and build a cottage in Bharatpur, where his family lives at the moment. This is at the right of the edge of Narayangardh city and Bharatpur College. It is irony that none of his children could excel in education beyond school level despite being so close to education centres and despite my uncle putting great value in education. Perhaps this is partly because of conflict and tensions in their relationship or the nature of their marriage. He retired from the teaching job in 2000 and virtually has become a Sanyasi since then. Now he is working as a secretary in a religious trust in Haridwar, the same old place where he had had his education. Shri Krishna uncle has been close to me and had given some important and valuable lessons in my early childhood that I will remember through out my life. He brought me along with him to Devghat before the bridge was built and enrolled me at Ved-Vedanga School where I studied Veda, Rudri, Hitopadesha, some algebra and most importantly Laghu Siddhant Kaumudi and some yoga. I used to study in peaceful and quite caves in the Bank of Kali Gandaki and had a very good memory and would not take much time to understand difficult concepts in Sanskrit grammar. After about 18 months of study I had almost finished Kaumudi, took the exam for 8th grade (Madhyama) in which I did quite well. Based on this I went to Kathmandu in the winter of 1970 (on Magh 6, 2030) first time from Jamune with some of my cloths and books in a trunk together with uncle. We had address of ChudaMani and Surya Mohan Kaphle from my mother's side and Narahari Acharya from my father's side who were then senior students in the Sanskrit Hostel. Upon recommendation of Narahari Acharya I stayed with Sharada Dhakal who had finished intermediate in science from Trichandra college and studying for bachelor of science with some hope to find a plan to study abroad. Sharada's father was a scholar of Sanskrit and a doctor of Ayurbed medicine. Therefore he had very good respect to Sanskrit education. Sharada was quite good in mathematics and I took many lessons in Chakravarti algebra and Arithmetic with him and later on he taught us some calculus when I was in Balmiki campus. His colleagues Subir, Vyas and other relatives also naturally became close to me. Other fellows from Tanahun, such as Tej Prasad, Mohan, Indra Mohan and Bhairab lived in the same house. I had good friends in Ranipokhari school like Gyan Chandra, Tanka Prasad, Rameshwor, Ram Prasad, Teertha, Tuka, Modanath, Noreswor, Shanker, Shambhu, Prakas and Purushottam. We used to go to Radio Nepal in Children's programme for recording poems some of which also were broadcasted in the evenings. I used to take part in poem, essay and quiz contests and some games like volleyball and football. I learned riding bicycle going with Tanka in Tundikhel. I stayed with Sharada for about one and half years. I was waiting for an interview for the Sankrit Hostel but it had not yet opened. Kalidas -my cousin who had completed his Shastree from Balmiki in 1969 and was teaching Nepali in Tharpu High School since then - came for a B.Ed. training as a part of teacher training under US funded New Education System. Similarly Laxmi Sharan Ghimire who had been Sanskrit colleges in Brindawan in India and did diploma from Balmiki and had just joined MA in Economics proposed me to stay with him. Three of us then rented a room and moved in Lal Bahadur Jyapu's house that remained in the backside of the Paknajol in the middle of cowli flower fields. Anyway with the help of relatives and friends and financial supports from my parents, Kathmandu had become home away from home though it was a completely unknown place to me before I arrived there.

After staying six months with Kalidas and Laxmi Sharan, I passed the interview for free boarding in the Sanskrit hostel and went to join 108 Brahmin boys who get scholarship for studying Sanskrit but were very wise in pursuing other modern subjects such as economics, politics and literature looking at the prospects for the job market. This hostel started in the time of Bir Samsher around 1900 was funded by income from a religious trust–income from lands in various places. It contained rooms and bedding, rice, ghee and some money to buy vegetables, two pairs of clothes virtually everything a student needs for subsistence and for studies. There was a good library with daily newspapers and magazines, a tutor to help in math and English, indoor and outdoor sports. It was located right at the centre of Kathmandu. Students staying there were required to make satisfactory progress in studies. Any one would be expelled if failed continuously for two years. It had a very good student association styled in a parliamentary democracy system with four blocks sending 16 candidates to the hostel's parliament and one to be elected from the general assembly. These representatives elected presidents and seven ministers. This cabinet organised various creative activities including inviting influential speakers for talk that included critical thinkers, philosophers and political leaders of Nepal. It organised oratory contests, poem contests and would form delegations to university authorities in matters of interest of students. Because of these extra-curricular activities it had been very instrumental in democratic movements in Nepal in the past and possesses importance even at the current period. I remember organizing quiz contests, purchasing books worth more than 10000 rupees while I was president of the committee. There was a very healthy competitive environment which sometimes also erupted in rows and showing off of muscle power.

I took full advantage of benefits and facilities and focused in doing well in studies. I had topped my school in SLC (Purba Madhyama) exam and topped the whole nation in the intermediate exam and was among top two in the country in diploma during the period of six years period that I had spent in this hostel. Foundation of my economics and writing skills was laid on this hostel. Those who studied Sankrit generally can write and speak better Nepali and that puts them in advantageous position in exams for jobs or studies or in real working life later on. One I also served as a member in the editorial board of Arunodaya Journal. Graduates of this school are polite and do not show off but they have quite good understanding of surroundings and what they have to do according to the situation. I had many close friends in the hostel; some were seniors to me like Jayaraj, Narahari, Tekraj, Mohan Timalsina, Mohan, Brataraj, Ram Prasad, Devi, Dilli, Ramhari, Keshav Gautam, Tulsi, Majgainya, two Bishnuharis, Jayaram, Atmaram, Shiva, Tej Prasad, Hari, Badri and others like that were my contemporary like Krishna Gewali, Shanker Aryal, Sagar, Purushottam, Shambhu, Harikrishna, Bharat, Rameshwor, Surya Panthi, Khilnath, Shanker and some junior to me like Ganesh, Kattel, Navraj, Parashuram, Dholraj, Rajendra and so on. This was a very well respected student community. As an economist I think there can be no better investment for national development other than expenses in this type of hostel that teaches disciplines, character and value of education if it is made accessible to wider sections of society rather than only poor Brahmin boys. Sankrit hostel scored highly particularly when the traditional Sankrit education is combined with the modern education of humanities and social sciences. It should incorporate computing, technology and sciences according to the demand of time.

I used to attend political speeches of opposition leaders such as BP Koirala, Ganesh Man Shing, Krishna Prasad Acharya and of few others from communist and Panchayat and was convinced that liberal socialist democratic political system was the way towards national development of a country like Nepal. Listening to BBC news and commentaries has remained one of my regular daily activities since then. This faith in democracy got stronger as the existing regimes spread violence and oppression to maintain exixting autocratic regime. As I practiced more of the Sankrit I got more drowned into its spiritual aspect, particularly after practicing Yoga: Pranayama, Pratyahara, Nididhasan, Dharana, Dhyan and Samadhi as instructed in Patanjali yog philosophy. I used to go with Vidur Guru to various philosophical lectures in Adwaita Vedanta and Geeta around Pashupati. These lectures tried to present the complete picture of Hindu philosophy- mainly focused on relinquishing all temporary and worldly objects for ultimate emancipation and salvation of one's soul. It explains the cycle of life and birth, and how it goes through many gyrations, until ultimately some one becomes completely immersed into the ultimate Truth, Consciousness and Joy. Vidur who also had been in Devghat while I was there in 1970s had Acharya (MA) from TU and had been to Vanaras used to talk highly of the depth of knowledge of Hosmane and Hebbar Sharti Pundits in Sadangh Ved Veedhyapeeth in Varanasi in many branches of Sanskrit. With growing hunger for knowledge and life becoming boring due to the closure of schools and colleges and even the Sanskrit hostel for indefinite period in the wake of multi-party movement in Kathmandu, I decided one fine morning just to head-off to Veranasi without telling anyone about my where about. I took a bus to Birgunj, then a train to Varanashi from Jamsedpur and reached the destination where I wanted to be. Took a rickshaw to bring me to Saptganga Ghat and was able to meet Hebbar and Hosmane and Tilak Shastri in the school. I told about Vidur's appreciation of them and my keen interest for learning in fluent Sanskrit. They immediately enrolled me to their school and even scheduled me for lessons in Brihad Aranyak Upanishads. We chanted Rudri before eating in the Chetra–which provided Roti, subjee and chutney as much as required. I could have stayed life long practicing Sanskrit if I had wanted and was eager to do so until Radhakrishna Guru came from Kathmandu. Many people in my village in Batase had spread a rumour that I was killed and dumped by the military for protesting against the regime. It was not unnatural given my style of leaving, critical attitude and arguments for change in Nepal. I had also participated in those demonstrations. This shocked my parents; my father had just retired and returned home. My other siblings were still very young and small. I was the promising one and had vanished from their eyes forever. Radhakrishna communicated my where about in Kathmandu, then that news spread around and ultimately to my parents, which must have been a great relief for them. They immediately wrote a letter for me, my father had in fact given me permission to stay in Vanaras if I thought that appropriate. I heard latter that Vidur Guru was trying to send scholarship had I decided to stay at Vanarasi though he wrote me in letter with some insights that if I stayed in Vanaras it was possible that I could feel left behind later on. I received letter after some time from Kathmandu and from my home asking me to go back at least once and sort out things even if I wanted to go back to India later on. These letters from home and Kathmandu unsettled me and broke my heart and determination indepth study of all Sanskrit in the most traditional way. I told Hebbar shastri about it who smilingly replied that the same thing had happened with Vidur too. Next day I boarded a train and returned to Nepal. When I reached Batase walking five hours at night from Khairani, my parents could not stop their tears of happiness seeing me again alive. I returned to Kathmandu after a few days.

By the time I returned to Nepal King had declared a referendum and asked people to decide whether to choose multi-party system or stick to the reformed party-less Panchayat system. Bans on political parties were removed. There were open gatherings everywhere in the country from all types of parties, Congress, Communists, Royalists, or by those allied on the criteria of regions, ethnicity, language or culture, social classes. It was possible to see politician speaking openly who were banned and jailed by King Mahendra in 1961. I particularly followed talk by BP, KP and GM three leaders of the Congress party and also participated in activities of Tanahun Tarun Dal led by Ram Chandra. I briefly went to Kalinchowk, high up from Dolakha to practice yoga with Thakur baba whom I had met in Devghat. Fortunately we were able complete our exams and get our diploma that made us eligible to apply to jobs that required graduate level qualification. The referendum took place in May of 1980 in which 45 percent were in favour of multi-party democracy and 50 percent for the Panchayat system. There were stories of vote rigging but all liberal and open mined people had expected verdict in their favour but the election result took them totally surprised. Royalists then ruled till another popular revolution of 1990.

Spiritual Orientation and Hunger for Knowledge

Being a student of Sanskrit I was very much attracted by ideas of Sanskrit scholars particularly its philosophy of Adwait Vedant and Patanjali Yog. In Sanskrit hostel I used to get up at 3 and do yoga exercises for three hours, keep pure (Satwik) diet as sanctioned by scripts and control activities of my mind and body. I did mantras in morning and evening, neti-dhauti-basti-nauli-bhastrika brething routines and would sleep about six hours from 8 in the evening 2 in the morning. I had earned many certificates from extra curricular activities such as oratory contest, essay and poem competitions or volley ball or musical chair contests. I was so focused on the idea of salvation that at some points I would have been seen strange or unique animal to many others in the hostel or the fellows and teachers of the Balmiki campus.

Gurus teaching Sanskrit in the Balmiki campus mostly came from various universities in Varanasi but those teaching economics like Minu or Vinod or Sharada were products of Tribhuvan University. My teachers were in general impressed by my writing and expressions and I was able to secure top most marks almost in any subject both in my intermediate and diploma level exams. I also kept a practical view of education, while I regarded Sankrit highly in terms of introvert knowledge.The competitive world required extrovert knowledge that can be applied to explain economic progress, business and growth and accumulation and development process. It was more urgent for a developing society like Nepal. This brought me close to the world of economics. I choose economics right from the beginning when I started my college we had plenty of theories of economics, mathematics, geometry, statistics and algebra. I studied micro and macro economic theories, economic growth, public finance, international trade and mathematical economics (See appendix 1-3 for detailed lists). I bought top class text books in economics from the scholarship that I had won being the top most student in intermediate level–that included from Samuelson, Handerson and Quant, Shapiro, Aclay , RGD Allen, Stonier and Hague, Eric Roll, Haney, Guide and Rist, James Mill, Hicks, Watson and Kautilya. I had a little library of my own of both economics and Sanskrit books. I also had written two texts at that time, which still should be somewhere in my racks in Kathmandu. Because of my background I did not get sense to publish them. Because of my deep study I was able to pass competitive exams with a top grade. I was second in 16 out of 300 candidates the prestigious examination for Officer Five exam for the Nepal Bank in 1980, 6th among 56 selected from 2000 or so that had appeared in the public service commission examination for the Administrative Service of Nepal. Scholarship from the Nepal Rastra Bank for my MA in economics also had boosted my morale further and I proved that the Sankrit background was complementary to economics with top marks in the MA in economics 1984.

FAMILY RESPONSIBILITY, JOBS, MA ECONOMICS FROM TU AND THE DUTCH SCHOLARSHIP FOR MA IN DEVELOPMENT STUDIES FROM THE ISS, NETHERLANDS

I was in dilemma between studies and taking care of sick parents. As a responsible son I wanted the best care of my sick parents, no one was able to help them than myself at home. Elder sister was married when she was 12 and away. She had problems as her husband had married another girl and put her in terrible trouble though he had lied me about this when I went to ask him in Pokhara about this immediately after hearing the rumour about his second marriage in fear that he might be brought to court for this offence. Manu, Bishnu and Kedar were still very young. As an eldest son I was feeling responsible of taking care of this household despite my keen interest in learning and free boarding in Sanskrit hostel. I got married with Prem in 1979 with a view that she would take some of this burden and make parents happy and give continuation of my world. In retrospect it did not turn out quite like that in all aspects. That had annoyed me a bit but a point I could not do anything about it. I was good in studies but immature to think about the life long problems in a systematic manner. Any how I passed my Bacholors exam in 1981. I had studied economics, mathematics, algebra along with Sanskrit and my writing of Nepali was relatively refined (see appendix 2 for detailed list of modules). I also used to write my economics theory tests and papers in English. I registered for MA in Economics with focus on mathematical economics and econometrics from TU which was becoming of good standard after reforms in the education system over some years. We had mathematical economics, growth and development, micro, quantitiative techniques and economic thought in the first year and public finance, monetary economics, macro, and econometrics in the second year. There were 153 students registered that year but I knew very few of them like Roshan, Sunil, Gyan, Bidur, Prasai, Sanjay, Kaini and we had relatively good faculty for teaching that included Kandel, Mathema, Ligal, Rawal, Gajanand, Chitrakar and Parthiveshwar. I did not have much problem in following text books popular in UK or the USA corresponding to the syllabus that we had. However, I had no peace in my mind from the family side, when I thought of sick parents and siblings at home in Tanahun I seriously felt that I should be doing something for them. This made me apply for a job in the Nepal Bank once I was qualified for it and leave Kathmandu and transfer my studies along with my job to Pokhara so that I could assist my sisters, brothers and take care of parents. I thought it was more important to take care of epilepsy of my mother and the diabetes of my father rather than continuing my study in Kathmandu at that point. Obviously problems in my family were of different nature. Everyone in the family expects a lot from that person who can do some thing. They have no choice though they know that such expectations can put extra pressure on the growing person who is still fighting for hiw own career already very competitive world. Such expectation can drag that person down from competitions. I soon realised that marrying Prem was not enough to solve more complex problems of the family and I had to take active steps on my own. I also had thought about the social problems at that time of the community and initiated a Bhattarai Trusts that would mobilise savings from its members and use collected funds to lend some one who had some economic projects either be it buying a pair of oxen or buffaloes or any other agricultural investment activities. Its members were from Bhattarai families and each member would deposit 5/10 Rupees every month. This trust has grown to a handsome amount in last 15 years and acting a short of bank for Bhattarais in Dhayare.

I stood second in a competitive examination in Nepal Bank. Many MBA and MA had taken that examination I had just a Bachelor degree. Many of them had not been able to pass it. Every one of my friends considered that Officer Five at that Bank was a good job. I took it. I was posted in Pokhara branch and I did not had to give up my MA economics as it was possible to transfer my MA from Kathmandu to PN Campus in Pokhara. Once I was able to rent a room there I took my sister Manu and brother Bishnu for schooling in Pokhara and arranged check up for my fathers' diabetes. Blood-sugar imbalances had caused serious problems in his memory and health. It went for a while. Despite several check ups, hospitals in Pokhara did not have enough equipment; they referred us to go to Kathmandu. I brought my father and mother both to Kathmandu for check up.

One who has been in hospital in Nepal knows how many tests are required for diagnosis and how many days it takes to get a decision form the doctors. We stayed several days and spent some money in Kathmandu but the doctors came to a conclusion that the diabetes had started generating many other complications. They thought that good hospitals in India, such Vellore in South India or the New Delhi Medical Institute might be better places to go for his treatment. It could not be controlled here and would reappear after a short period of respite. We took their advice. I took my parents to the Christian Medical College Vellore in India where both of them were treated quite nicely for about a month and half. The Dhayare-Birgunj-Cacutta-Khatpadi-Vellore journey itself would take about three days. After returning from there they felt that they had recovered quite well for some time. I returned to my job at the Bank and studies upon return from Vellore. We had a good team of friends that included Umesh, Guru Prasad, Yadav, Krishna Mohan, Lekhraj, Bishnu GC, Kamal, Rajaram, Ganesh, Keshav, Madan and Dinesh and Pokhara and good teachers that included Sharma, Dhunghana, Bidari and Maheshwarlal. Work and study and looking after educations of brother and sister and frequent visits to Dhayare home to meet parents made me quite busy. Despite this after some time I thought the job in Bank had a limited scope and I should rather apply for a Section Officer in the government service. It had scope all over Nepal and was preferred job of almost all graduates. Had I completed MA I would have applied to be an instructor in a college but I have not had completed that yet. I was eligible for the Nepal Administrative service, and this was thought more challenging and competitive and many thought that it had more scope than teaching. With these limitations and considerations I took the Public Service Exam for a Section Officer in the Nepal's administrative service from Pokhara and was able to pass both written and oral exams for it in 1984. I resigned from my job at the Bank after staying in Pokhara for about three years. It was my first and a good job. It was close to my home and I did not have to give up my MA studies. I was able to learn and earn together at the same time. It was possible however that I would never have been abroad and be able to earn degrees from abroad if I had not left the Bank at that time.

All 56 newly appointed section officers had to have three months long staff college training from the Nepal Administrative Staff College. Its courses included theories of decision making, planning and programming, problem solving, negotiation skills, field trips, conversation and communication and practical English. I remember friends such as Sharad, Ramesh, Gayatri, Bhuwan, Jyoti, Ganesh, Tilak, Malego, Ganesh, Rajendra, Janak, Uttam, Balkrishna, Sudhir, Rai, Madhav, Kashiraj, Durga, Mohan, Tilakman, Khadka, Narayan, and Koirala. All of them were young and talented individuals. However, it was irony that at the end of training everyone was trying get posted in the most lucrative positions in the government using all approaches they had at the bureaucratic machinery. I neither had any politician nor any administrator in the bureaucracy. I was posted in the Ministry of Education and Culture which was considered relatively dry place by others. I experienced myself why people say this after going there as I was unable to get posted even after two months while I used to be very busy at the bank. There was a sharp contrast between the private and public sectors. It looked like that government jobs like this were essentially welfare provision for educated workforce. For a young energetic person it took some time to understand that being in administration is being able to gossip and show off rather than engage oneself in a productive work. The personnel department was not able to place me at work. Administrators had little concern about the wastage of manpower or about my personal problem. I got worried and asked them to send wherever they could. Then they posted me to the regional education office in Pokhara. That office did not let me stay in Pokhara either. I was rather posted as an Assistant District Education Officer in the Gulmi district. I had never been to Gulmi before. Took the letter and went there on a minibus that rolled over muddy roads via Palpa Batase, Bhirkot, Argali, Ridi, and Daungha with loud noise of Hindi or Nepali songs around those holls and valleys. I had taken two boxes of books in economics and all the text books for grade 1 to grade ten in Nepal with me while I went to Tamghas as Acting District Education Officer of Gulmi. The road to Tamghas only would operate in the dry winter season. One had to walk on foot in the rainy season. In the interval between the departure of Dhundiraj Shastree and arrival of Purna Chandra Paudel as my superior I acted as the District Education Officer for Gulmi. It was good for opportunity for an experience though his was a quite tricky job that needed balancing the work of supervising the work of about 10 inspectors of high, middle and primary schools and monitoring the accounts that handled millions of Rupees that went to all primary middle and secondary schools and had some administrative matters relating staffs that ranged from granting leaves or making sure that the office is open for business for the teachers and people of the entire district or for collection of various statistics required for educational planning. People were very cooperative and everything went smoothly.With raining of the staff college that had equipped me with all sorts of possible techniques required to use in administration. I did not have much difficulty in running this office. It would be a bit embarrassing to a 22 year old young man like me when many teachers who had thought in schools for about 30 to 40 years bowed down with respect though it is understandable as many of these teachers did so to avoid being suppressed by government officials who thought themselves a bit superios despite being servants of the people. Education was a politically sensitive sector, there were places where more liberal ideas dominated and places where the extremists or communists prevailed and places that were dominated by royals and loyalists. Schools were gradually being decentralised making teachers responsible to the school management committee. However, these rights were not properly implemented and there were still cases of corruption and malpractices. There were schools where teachers withdrew salary without teaching anything, there were places where they were not teaching properly, there were places that were struggling to get new schools in the vicinity as the children had to walk two three hours to reach to their schools. The national education system had been implemented in Gulmi for last few years but it still had so many problems.

With some old records available in the office I first made up a map of all schools of the district for comprehensive understanding of the situation and made up a plan to visit various schools accordingly. For my MA degree I also did the National Development Service works in Tamghas for my village profile on the income and expenditure system of Tamghas Panchayat. I collected data on wealth and income in a census of Thamghas and processed the data and did statistical and regression analysis for testing my hypotheses. I did all calculations in a pocket calculator and was able to score very good marks for this work. I visited many schools in the districts and saw at the field level how the new the school system had affected the level of education at the local level. I was enjoying my job but the communication with my family was becoming difficult- I was a bit concerned about how my parents were doing. For this reason I requested the regional officer to get me transferred to an office more approachable from my home. After a year in Gulmi I got transferred to Palpa in 1985. It was easier for me to visit home from there and make follow up check ups required for my parents. I had taken tours of both eastern and western part of Palpa while I was there for about a year and half. Still Palpa was quite a bit far from Tanahun and had communication gap as we did not have any telephone at home and letters would take weeks or months to get across. It took me about two weeks to know that my daughter Manorama was born in January 26, 1986. The relatives, neighbours and grand parents had taken good care of her. She was very cute and bright when I saw her first time. It was not clear when she was coming out and by the time I reached home she was about two weeks old. This was not uncommon in Nepal to have a child born at home and taken care by mothers and grand parents while fathers are far away from home for work.

I still had not finished my MA in economics that I had started in 1981(really in 1983 due to lag in education system). Education system had itself prolonged two years but I also prolonged it for another year for my personal reasons. It was not possible to concentrate in studies in districts where one had many administrative responsibilities. This is the reason why I was struggling hard for a transfer back to Kathmandu.

It was difficult for a village person to know anyone in Kathmandu who would be helpful. Luckily I came to know that we had very distant relation with the pioneer poet of Nepali language Bhanu Bhakta Acharya. His great-grandson, Tirtha Raj Acharya who was father of my friend Gyan Chandra knew Ramesh Jung a high official in the Ministry of Education. He as well as Ramchandra Paudel a senior administrator from Pokhara put some words on behalf of me. After some time I was able to get transferred in Kathmandu upon his recommendation. Once I had a post in the Statistics section of the Ministry I focused my whole attention towards completing MA in economics. This section was a very relaxed place; in a sense jobs like this were in fact welfare for educated Nepalese. No one really bothered about the urgency of statistical research. It proved to be a very good opportunity for preparation of my MA degree. There was a quite veranda with plenty of sunlight in the southern wing of the Kaiser Mahal. I used to register my presence and go to that veranda and study all big economics text-books for the whole day as it was possible to postpone less urgent works of the section. In addition working with statistics was complementary to my econometric skills. I had made my understanding deep enough in all subjects for MA. I had eight subjects and took exam in all of them at once. This strategy in fact worked quite well. I did very well in MA in 1986 by existing standards with overall marks of 77 percent. I would have earned a medal for this achievement had I not postponed exam in the previous years. Around that time something interesting was happening in the statistics section as the personal computer got introduced first time under a funding from the International Education Institute of the US in 1986 with Butterworth as a resident consultant and a number of trainers from UNESCO or IEES visited this section for training staffs in educational statistics. We received some training on how to operate computers and how to do cohort planning of education for the country in order to evaluate the efficiency of the education system and how to compute various growth rates in education sector from a consultant from Holland and Singapore. These were quite interesting.

At this time I was also busy in constructing a house in Balkhu. My superior Prachand was a quite understanding person and was impressed by my achievement in MA. He let me go for tour in various districts of Western Nepal to train field level official on statistical methods used for educational planning. I went to Dang, Salyan, Surkhet, Nepalgunj and Doti in the west, Janakpur, Dharan, Dhankuta, Jhapa and Taplejung in the East in process of conduction training or collection of educational data. I could see various parts of the country. Around the same time, one of our relative Cholakanta from Khairani Tar introduced me to the Tek Bahadur Shrestha at the Food and Agricultural Market Centre in the Ministry of Agriculture whom he had known from the German Agriculture Project in Khaireni Tar. He was associated with No-Frills research consultancy. It happened to be a time that they had got one project regarding evaluation of effectiveness of USAID educational scholarship programme in the development of Nepal. The team included Parthiveshwar Timalsina, Tej Ram Paudel and Tek Bahadur and report of the study had to be made for the USAID. I was hired for the project for processing information and collection of data. I travelled in various parts of Bagmati, Gandaki, Lumbini and Narayani zones in taking filed level interviews of people who had returned from their studies abroad and how they felt about impacts of their education abroad in the national development. We had a roaster of all those who went in foreign training, then selected samples and decided persons to be contacted. We went with a quite a lengthy questionnaire that could take up to one hour for a good interview. It gave an opportunity to talk and know the opinions of many educated people that were involved in various ministries and located at various parts of the country. We stayed about a year in Tek Bahadur's home in Sina Mangal with my sister Manu, Raghu and Bishnu and were partly involved in coaching his little daughters.

We moved to urban Ghetto in Kathmandu Ganeshthan around middle of 1987 as it was closer for Manu to go to Tahachal campus and me to go to the Education

Ministry. I also started tutoring at the Vanasthali boarding school in the morning. This is about this time I sold good cultivable lands in Myagde in anticipation of buying a plot of land in Kathmandu. It was so difficult to buy a plot of land as it was so expensive and we were afraid of cheating. With some information supplied to me by Shri Krishna mama from Chitwan I was able to buy a plot of land in Balkhu. This was the first time we had a piece of asset in Kathmandu valley though it was too little compared what had been sold back home in Tanahun. My mother almost wept seeing the little piece of land that we had bought for what we had sold at the village. After some time I sold more lands in village to gather money so that I could construct a tiny house where we could live in Kathmandu. Rents were becoming increasingly unaffordable and everyone saw good prospects in Kathmandu as it had all facilities including education, health, jobs and contacts. A relaxed atmosphere at the statistics section was good for the time I required for construction of home. Many things were involved in construction, land mapping, residence plan, getting permit from the municipality, contractual agreements, making sure of the availability of construction material such as stones, bricks, woods, rods, cements, concrete, water pipe, electricity line and supervision of construction of the house. Since there were many people in this area like me who resettled from outside the valley it was possible to get some information, advice and help from them. I did all running around with a bike. We ran out of money when house was half constructed. We had already put more than 125000 and still house was not complete. It did not have windows fitted, it did not have plasters, and it did not have any furniture. Still we had something in the Kathmandu valley to call our own and were able to move immediately after we had a shape of house leaving all other details to be worked out at time goes by. Among other things having our own tap of water, electricity and bathroom was quite a feeling of liberation. At least there was no landlord who would complain using too much water to wash our face. This area was settled mostly by people who had just migrated and were committed to make things better for the Balkhu community with inner motor roads, access to drinking water, garbage collection, and Kumari clubs. We had friends such as Rishi, Aryal, Ram and Basu Ojha brothers, Amaresh, Dhakal, Neupane, Dambar, Adhikari, Regmi brothers (Kamal and Mitra), Pathak, Jha and Harendra, Bharatman, Ghimires, Niraulas, Sibakotis, and other Bhattarai's. Adjustment to Kathmandu socially was not that difficult though we were under serious budget constraints.

After the construction of house I decided to move to a place where I would have an opportunity to go abroad for studies. With good qualifications in econometrics and mathematical economics I was able to get transferred in the Economic Analysis Division of the Planning Commission of Nepal which had good reputation for opportunities to go abroad and was then staffed by very well trained young economists of the country that included Shivraj Lohani, DR Khanal, Bharat Pokharel, Pushpa Shakya under the member Dr. Vijaya Bahadur Sing and the Dr. Durgesh Man Singh. Some of them had degrees from abroad. I worked in the basic needs monitoring team of all districts of Lumbini with Chhetra Pratap

Adhikari who was the member of the National Assembly form Tahanuh for a while and got involved in various excercises of national planning in the Division. Among others I remember attending the training in input-output model around the summer of 1988 in which Chris Elbers from Holland had given some lessons. The NPC used to have two three good scholarship every year. I was top in the merit list but selection was discretionary not automatic and not certain as I did not have good contact with administrators. After some internal bureaucratic struggles with some approach from Ram Chandra Paudel and Adhikari to Madhusoodan Dhakal and Prithu Narsingh Rana I won the Dutch government scholarship to study MA in Regional Planning in ISS Hague for 18 months from September 1988 to December 1989. Bharat Pokharel in the section was also in search of opportunities to go abroad and had managed to be selected under the Full Bright programme. Lohani also used to give some advice. Therefore the Economic Analysis Division proved again to be a good place to be abroad given my qualifications in economics and experience in the government. I got confirmation of acceptance and went to Holland on September 11th of 1988. This was my first journey abroad outside India and full of excitement and expectations.

We rented a house as a group that included Keshari Pandit, Govinda Gewali, Tuladhar and Bhim Prasad and MunSinge from Sri Lanka not far from the ISS on the way to the Delft. The scholarship money was quite handsome. Every one had implicit objective of studying very hard for grades and saving some money to bring back home. I should say I was satisfied on these both fronts. I had scored 81 percent in my course works. Being a MA student at ISS meant to be a member of the international community as the students were recruited from all parts of the world. Students in economic policy and planning group included Ateek (Pakistan), Banzi (Tanzania), Bwembya (Zambia), Cheaze Pelaez (Dominican Rep.), Dasanayaka (SriLanka), El Mak (Sudan), Gonzalez Gomez (Peru), Hidayat (Indonesia), Chowdhury (Bangladesh), Eric (Trinidad), Ayylew (Ethopia), Msudi (Tanzania), Mazimba (Zambia), Milnovic (Yogoslavia), Mwabez (Tanzania), Mwampeta (Tanzania), Pizarro (Philippines) Rani Das (Bangladesh), Ten Berge (Surnam), Tofri (Indonesia) Iqbal (Pakistan). We were five from Nepal Adarsha Tuladhar, Govind Gewali, Keshari Pandit, Bhim Bahadur and Bhawana Makey. I was originally in the regional development planning group with Alkirbee (Yeman), Asiimwe (Uganda), Walujadi (Indonesia), Edgar (Mexico), Ma (China), Hossain (Bangladesh), Osman (Sudan), Vesna (Yugoslavia), Mohammed (Ethiopa), Koumakh (Senegal), Xiaocun(China), Aggarwal (India), Shahzad (Pakistan), Sunyoto (Indonesia) Munasinghe (Sri Lanka). It was very good teaching system run by economics team that included George Irvin, Neil Robertson, Sideri, Alarcon, Mark Wytes, Fritz Hannapple, Heemst, FitzGerald, and Karl Jensen. For MSc. dissertation I contacted Chris Elbers in the Free University of Amsterdam and Henry Robbemond had provided a lot of help in computing regional model in FORTRAN. I also had a Dutch family and had been invited to conduct name ceremony by one of the Nepalese family in Voorburg. I had a very successful year at the ISS.

I applied for PhD at Northeastern before I left the ISS. After six seven months of my return from the ISS, I got a letter from Professor Jonathan Haughton, offering me an admission to the PhD in economics. Letter showed possibility of scholarship. I applied for and won the Full Bright Travel grants in Kathmandu which included health insurance, visa fees and a return ticked to Boston. I was able to perform well in the first semester and win the research and teaching scholarships for my PhD. I took dynamic general equilibrium modelling of the Nepalese economy as my topic for my PhD dissertation which was a very challenging project at that time and no one had done dynamic multi-sectoral general equilibrium model. In addition I did graduate level courses from the mathematics and computer science departments. With hard works and help from professors I was able to complete and get a job that further opened my career as a researcher and lecturer in economics in UK.

With continuous hard works in Nepal, Holland, US, Canada and UK I have managed to solve economic problems of my family to some extent. After my father died in December 1986, I made a decision for migration of whole of my family to Kathmandu. We sold off plots of lands scattered in many different places and bought a four anna plot in Balkhu Kathmandu with great difficulty as I did not know any person in the valley. We constructed four rooms for family of eight with great difficulty. We were close to starvation at that point. Things were so bad that my family had to spin wools for living. Still with a job in the Education Ministry and later on in the Planning Commission we were able to survive. Whole family could have been in a great economic pressure had I not been able to win the Dutch Government Fellowship to study in the ISS in Holland where I managed to live in around 350 guilders out of 1400 guilder provided as stipends and saved the rest of it. At the end I got the degree and as well as a handsome amount from the savings made from the scholarship by the Nepalese standards. I brought saved amount back home and could plaster inside the house and was able to purchase another piece of land in the name of my brother Bishnu. I bought land because I was afraid that one day brothers would blame me for selling ancestral property and making them migrate to Kathmandu, particularly if they do not have had something of their own.

My sister Manu Maya passed Intermediate in Education with science and mathematics. She spent some time teaching in a private boarding school in Alapot, a relatively remote village in Kathmandu. Then she passed a primary teachers' examination in Tanahun and was posted in Chhang Dada Primary school, relatively remote place in Tanahun. I remember how we had to argue with local school committee Chairman in time of her appointment. This was a permanent post and was relatively secured with pension. Under the Decentralisation Act of education the Chairman had to issue an appointment to the teacher of a school. Later on she managed to transfer this job to Kathmandu with some approach to then Assistant Education Minister Chhetra Pratap whom I had worked with under the Basic Needs project. After coming to Kathmandu she could continue her bachelors and masters in education with mathematics and science as her prime subjects. She is a Head

Teacher in a public high school in Kathmandu not far from her new residence. She got married to Sita Ram Aryal a veterinary doctor from Gorkha in 1990 after I returned from Holland and before I went to Boston for my PhD. They have got son Saugat and Sunidhi daughter both handsome and beautiful and managed to construct a house in Kalanki and settled down there quite well. Manu is a good example of advantage of investment in education of a girl.

While my elder sister was married when she was 12 years old that discontinued her education, younger sister managed to build her confidence through education. I remember having very difficult negotiations with Jhalak for my elder sisters' problem. When I moved to Kathmandu, he also decided to move there around 1988. With my polite approach he could not reject my proposal for building a house for Basan sister in Balkhu but he insisted that to be nearby where we lived. Basically he wanted to leave her in our responsibility. There was not choice left even for us. She had now three daughters Kranti, Sukriti and Pragati whom Jhalak would not give much attention. I remember many sleepless nights because of Basan sisters' problem but she had no other place than us to explain or complain about her problems. Fortunately the investment made in that house has grown in value and she is now in somewhat easier in economic terms than before as she can rent out one flat and use that money for subsistence. Her life is a bad example of not allowing education for a girl.

Bishnu was my beloved brother and I wanted his proper education and had taken him to Pokhara. When I had no choice but to go to Gulmi in 1985, I decided to keep him in a Siddhartha Vanasthali Boarding School which required about 800 out of 1300 Rupees of my salary at that time. I could keep him there for one year but could not afford that for another year. Therefore we had no choice. Bishnu went back to Min high school Tharpu in Tanahun for his tenth grade and SLC. He managed to pass it first time in 1987 and joined us again for toils and troubles of life in Kathmandu. He also joined intermediate degree in commerce from a private college in Tahachal. In the meantime he started working in day time. He did learn some lessons on the value of hard work after working for a Trekking company in Thamel where his boss was very demanding and made him move a lot in his business with very little payment. When I returned from Holland after my MA degree I had also brought an IBM 86 machine. It had programmes such as spreadsheets word perfect, SPSS and few other basic programmes. I taught Bishnu how to use computer in that machine and later on was able to get a consultancy on data processing from the IIDS in Baneshwore with some approach to Dr Bhesh Bahadur Thapa. Bishnu learned programmes such as SPSS along with me. This skill somehow transformed his life. He did Bachelors of commerce degree while working but went to US in 1997 before taking a viva for his M.Comm. He worked very hard in Boston to get an undergraduate degree from the Bunker Hill College and has graduated with M.Sc in Computer Science from the Fitchberg College in year 2006. After hard work of many years he has been able to get a well paying job matching his skills.

Youngest brother Kedar was luckiest of all in terms of hardship in life. He spent early years of schooling in Gaira, Kilchowk and then in the Banstapur around 1987 and with Manu in Alapot for a year and joined the Laboratory High School when we managed to move to Balkhu. He finished his SLC in the first class in 1995 and went to Boston on my invitation in 1996. He was enrolled in the John Obrien High school in the 11th grade. I did not understand why he dropped himself out in the 12th grade and started working in a shop in the downtown Boston to earn money. After two and half years in Boston he went back to Nepal basically as he did not know how to renew visa to stay but he had very hard time of readjusting to the Nepalese situation once he was exposed to life in Boston. He did higher secondary degree and enrolled himself for a bachelor in computer science which has taken him more time than he expected. He has not been able to recover from the shock of readjustment. It is difficult for me to understand why. Is it because he has been provided with the basic needs at home now with some rental income from the house, widowed pension to my mother on behalf of my father from the Indian Pension Services in Kathmandu? He does not yet have have the determination, purpose and seriousness that myself, Manu, Bishnu have had about education and for personal development. I am very hopeful that it will come after he gets his graduation in the computer science.

Turning to my family life Manorama my daughter was born in January 26, 1986 in Dhayare in Tanahun after we had managed to move down to Myagde valley from the Batase hill. She was just about 10 months old when my father died and about two years old when we moved to Kathmandu. She did nursery in Balku and the Lab school and went to Boston when she was six years old in 1992. She studied in Bawldin, Quincy, Edwards and Latin Schools in Boston from 1992 to 1998. She went back to Nepal in 1998 and studied in the Siddharth Vanasthali for two years. She also had terrible time of readjustment in Nepal. Then she joined me in Hull and did A level from the Wyke College and spent one year of biomedicine degree from the University of Hull. She is now in the fourth year of her medical degree in the University of Aberdeen in Scotland. She is very determined and motivated and independent student and hoping to maintain a record of being the first doctor in the family. Santosh was born on 25th of May 1988 after all our family had moved to Kathmandu in the Children's Hospital. He was three and half when he went to Boston where he studied in Farragut, Quincy and Boston Renaissance before joining the Vanasthanli School for grade six. He studied from 8th grade to GCSC in the Kelvin Hall high in Hull since August 2000 and then did A level from St. Mary's College which is just two minutes away from our home in Hull. He got very good A grades in Mathematics, Physics and Chemistry and has started a four years masters degree in Physics and Math in the University of York. He is determined to be independent and perform well in this. With the student loans both Manoraam and Santosh are hoping to be able to finance their education themselves. Hopefully they will find good jobs at the end of their studies.

Prem could not make much progress in studies because of lack of her primary education and deficiency in learning in the early childhood and family responsibilities after she got married. She was 15 when she had married but could not read and write effectively even the Nepali as normal Children do or as her six sisters Ved Kumari, Shusila, Kamala, Bimala, Shashikala, Sirjana and Bidya had done. Her brother Achyut did B.Ed. and is a head teacher in the Jana Jukta High school in Sange Tanahun. I also had already passed SLC when I was 14. I do not understand why pundit Umanath did not want his first daughter study further. In retrospect I think she should not have married that early though we have had two wonderful children both doing well in their schools. I have lived my life alone myself from when I was nine to when I was 20 and then when I was in Holland and then in Boston and then in UK from 1996 to 2000 but a wife like Prem can make life a lot better. With experience abroad Prem is getting better in managing the household and making the family life much easier.

HOW DID EACH MEMBER OF MY FAMILY BENEFIT FROM MY EDUCATION?

Since there are many members in the family it is important to see how my education has contributed toward making better prospect for each, which will be mentioned here.

Father HariKrishna (alias Bhagirath Bhattarai) Upadhyay: He was born in 1918 during the period of World War I. He was an orphan. His mother Damyanti died when he was two and father BhawaniShanker when he was nine. He was care-taken virtually by his sister-in-law. Pundit Diwakar, his younger brother, had separated from the joint family before he was born. His elder brother Kul Prasad did not take any effort to teach him. Rejected and dejected he left for India in 1931. First spent days as a farm worker herded cow of some wealthy Indian farmer in Uttar Pradesh. One day he met one individual coming from Nepal going to his job in Calcutta. He followed him and managed himself to enrol in the Indian Armed Police Service temporarily around 1935. He told that he even changed his name to Harikrishna Chhetri for a while to make himself attractive for recruitment to then British Indian Government but was allowed to maintain his true name later on. Then he took a permanent job in 1939. He remembered bombs dropping close by him during the World War II and had to work in riots but he never bet anyhone. He had a very good friend Ambar Bahadur Adhikari from Patan who used to meet me in Kathmandu.He kept his job for 39 years and retired with Lance Naik pension in 1978. It took about two years to get his pension Patta to withdraw his pension.

He had married my mother when he was 27 and she was just of 9 in 1945 in Batase at the end of the World War II. He brought my mother only once to Calcutta in 1959 for five years. My elder sister Basundhara (alia Ekadashi) was born in May 1958 and I was born in the December 2, 1961. They brought us back to Batase Tanahun in 1963 when I was just 18 months old. He used to come back in paid holidays for one or two months in every two years since then. Earlier he had to walk several days before reaching home and journey became easier after the construction of East-West and Prithvi highways. My elder sister Manu was born in May 1968, Bishnu was born in January 1973 and Kedar in December 1978. He suffered from diabetes and complex health problems caused by it in last seven eight years of his life, that became particularly became worse after 1983. He managed to buy a plot of land with a small house in Dhayare in 1980 using the money that he had earned in his pension. His health problem became serious and was brought to specialists in Pokhara, Kathmandu and Vellore in India for check up. He would recover for a while but it could never be cured completely. He died in late December of 1987 when he was 68. He was an honest and gentle man. All villagers loved him. All of his three sons were away when he died. Villagers had already taken his dead body to Marenghat in Seti and burned it to ashes that they floated into the river when I reached from Kathmandu after Balkrishna Ghimire came with some emergency news in Samakhushi Kathmandu but did not tell of his sad demise. He virtually spent his entire active life working for Armed Police Service of West Bengal Government but maintained good contacts with his family back home in Nepal and had relatively happy life except his ill health after his retirement. He knew to read and write simple letters to communicate with friends and families and was very good in Hindi songs. He used to lend money to any person who asked for it but many of them cheated hime and never paid that back. He represents the economic problems of many people in Nepal during the period in his life 1918-1978.

Mother Harimaya (alias Anumaya) Bhattarai: She was the elder daughter and one of four children of Purna Chandra and Purnakala Kaphle. Her father was a local pundit in Dhahun-Bhaisekharka, another hill in the north eastern side of Batase. She was born in 1936 and married to my father in 1945 when she was just nine years old. Then she spent another 13 years at home with the family of Kul Prasad uncle and then she decided to follow my father to Calcutta in 1957 when she was 22 years old. She took care of a new born baby whose mother had died in the Hospital while giving him bir for about six months before she got my elder sister Basundhara. She was 23 when she got my sister and 25 when she bore me in 1961. Family background had given her confidence and ability to tackle real problems in life and asked my father to go back to Nepal rather than staying in India- therefore made the family return to Batase in the summer of 1963. She spent another three years in the joint family. When my father got separated from the joint family and divided properties with Kul Prasad uncle in 1966, she took responsibility of running the house. She was active in cultivation and used to keep a buffalo for milk and made us happy in absence of our father. She gave birth to Manu in 1969, to Bishnu in 1973 and to Kedar in 1979. She caught epilepsy after 1973 that shook her confidence and strengths. I took her to hospitals in 1978 in Kathmandu and she has been taking medicine for this since then. This problem got worse through out 1980s. After my father died in 1986, I took her to Kathmandu to live with us in a house built in Balkhu. Gradually her condition became better. She completely recovered from the Epilepsy. She gets widow pensions from my father and gets some rental income from the house. These are sufficient for her living. Her children are grown up and she has seven grand Children and one grand-grand child. Kedar lives with her and my sisters Manu and Basundhara live close by. When I visited in 2004 I made up a thorough check up of her health. She was found to have some diabetes and some blood pressure. Now after the treatment the diabetes has gone and she still takes some medicine for blood pressure. I call her every two weeks from UK and so does Bishnu from the US. She is now one the most senior members of the Bhattarai family of Myagde and gets respect form every one. She is relatively happy and tension free at her old age.

Sisters and Brothers

Basundhara: My elder sister Basundhara was born in 1958 in Calcutta and was three years older than me. I remember going to the Koldanda Primary school with her which must be around 1966-68. We used to read fables together at the dim keroscene lamp every night and Swasthani in the month of Magh. We used to play together at home while mother was away to work in the fields or to fetch water or to collect wood and grasses. She was relatively bright in her studies – as I remember. She still remembered a bit of Bengali from Calcutta and was very pretty in her nice looking dress. However, she has remained victim of the ignorance of my parents of the importance of education in her life. My mother took her out of school so that she could look after Manu while she was away to work. Moreover she was married away to Jhalak in Tarkudanda in 1970 when she was just 12 years old and Jhalak was just 15 and was just in his eight grade. Both of them did not know the meaning of being married at that time. As a married girl had to serve her husbands family, this actually put an end to the process of her education. She had to serve more than 13 people in her new home; she could rarely talk to her husband. I remember visiting her from time to time with some Kasar-Roti (sweets) gifts of from my mother taking bus up to Kotre and then about one hour of walk up to the Tarkudanda. She would obviously be very happy seeing me there. Jhalak passed SLS around 1972 and got posted as a primary teacher in Rising as he did not have enough money to go to a college. Later on he managed to get the education degree from Pokhara. He was relatively bright compared to his brothers and did understood things quite quickly. I did not understand why my father did not support him for his college while I remember tendering his applications for BA in public administration from my pocket and informing him to take exams at the time when I was doing my diploma study from the Balmiki campus. He visited me once there when he admitted to have married another girl. I asked him about how he would treat my sister as it was not customary for married girls to have any other prospects in Nepal. He promised that he would treat her equally but that never happened. He was like a friend to me but he was not happy with my sister as she was not educated. He gave a lot of psychological trouble to terrify her and she would come to us and tell these sufferings which would tear us apart. Sometimes I wonder what he would have done to her if we were not there to speak on behalf of her. I had been to name ceremony their first daughter Kranti in Tilakpur in 1982 with a tin full of ghee from my mother. I lost one complete day as I took a wrong turn from the Bardhghat towards Bhaiselotan as someone directed that it was to that side. I saw the Gandak barrage that time but took another day to find Basan place. I again visited several times to her in Bhutaha as my parents were quite concerned with her well being. She got Pragati in 1985. Later on as I moved to Kathmandu and had started constructing a house in Balkhu, Jhalak also decided to move to Kathmandu. Many Nepalese of our generation wanted to live in Kathmandu as the power was completely centralised, everything had to be done from this place and all education and health facilities were concentrated in this place. We made some understanding in solving Basan Didi's problem that was bothering us. Jhalak wanted to contribute towards building a house for her in close vicinity of where we were staying. Apparently he had made some money from his investments in Pokhara. She moved to Kathmandu and gave birth to Sukriti in 1988 and her small house was constructed in 1989. But because of lack of funding she had to move to a house without any windows but this problems was shorted out as time went buy. Kranti went to Germany with her step sister Pratibha to live with Silvia in Blackforest area of Germany – where she had moved since a terrible event in which Jhalak took poison to finish himself in around 1988. The psychological and economic problems of unhappy marriages were boundless. In 1998 Kranti returned from Germany to live in Nepal. Basan sister was somehow keeping with her three daughters and all of them hated Jhalak for ignoring them and favouring their step family. Kranti had become a Christian while living with Silvia but she was well accepted in the family until she decided to go along with Mandal, a boy from Janakpur side in 2003 who first came to her as a tutor her but fell in love with her. Now she had got a son but there is a rumour that the love has disappeared. Pragati however took her own decision to study nursing in Birgunj and married a boy that she liked. She seems to be doing fine in her home. Sukriti is making effort for her education. In some way they have found their own ways in some sense they still feel rejected and dejected. These all sufferings and shortcoming has to do something with the early marriage and discontinuation of school of my sister Basundhara. Who is to blame? Individuals involved or the society? It should be the ignorance of importance of education of both of them.

Manu: I remember from the moment she was born on the fine morning of Baisak 25, 2025 (May, 1978) as my mother called lovingly to me that she has got a sister for me. She was about two years old when I went to Devghat with uncle Shri Krishna and would meet her only once a year when I went back for Dashain holidays since then. She did her primary schooling in Ghaira, Kilchok about half an hour down from Batase village. She did her middle school in Tharpu. She was very helpful to my mother in household chores through out 1970s. She went with me to Pokhara to study in the Kanya (Girls) High school in 1982 along with Bishnu when I started a job in the Tersapatti branch of the Nepal Bank Limited. She did 8th and 9th grade from that school but had to return back to Dhayare after I went for the Section Officer position of the Government of Nepal in 1984. She passed SLC from Tharpu in 1986. Then again went with me for Intermediate in

Education with science and mathematics from Tahachal campus in 1987. She taught for a while in a local boarding school in Alapot village beyond Sundarijal, a remote place of Kathmandu district, in recommendation of Ganesh my friend from Sankrit hostel. She studied very hard and passed I.Ed. in 1988. In the meantime she took and passed primary school teachers exam in Tanahun and was posted in Chhang primary school and she managed to get it transferred to Kathmandu with some help form Chhetra Pratap who was Assistant Education Minister at that time. She started her B.ED in 1989 and complete successfully in 1991 and completed M.Ed in 1998. She got married to Sita Ram Aryal a veterinary doctor from Gorkha in that year and later had been to Philippines with him for a while on leave from her school when he was doing his masters in 1997. He is now a high level official in the government of Nepal. She had two children and has got a good residence for the family. She has been the Head Teacher of the Jan Vikas High School for last ten years. She is contributing towards the expansion and development of that school in a planned way. Taking math and science and educational skills were instrumental for her career.

Brother 1 Bishnuhari: He was born on January 24, 1973. I had already had been in Devghat for about 18 months then. He grew up in the village as I did and went for Primary school in Gaira Kilchok along with Manu. He was given a thread in Devghat around 1979. I would meet him only briefly when I returned in Dashain holidays. His primary school was terrible. He failed once in grade two and had to repeat a year while I was topping the whole nation in intermediate level at that time. I was very unhappy with this situation. I was also not happy with Manu's progress at that time. This is the reason why I decided to take a job in Nepal Bank and go to Pokhara in 1981 and brought him together with Manu to enrol into schools in Pokhara to keep him on my eyes and educate him properly. He was enrolled in Bar Patan middle school in the sixth grade. With extra coaching in the morning and evening gradually he picked up everything and was able to pass the sixth grade without much problem. He also did up to eighth grade from that school. When I passed the public service commission examination and went for training in Kathmandu, I took him along with me and enrolled him as a day scholar in the Siddharth Vanasthali School. I was hopping to be placed in Kathmandu but that did not happen mainly I had no relatives the administrative or political hierarchy to approach for this in Kathmandu. Ministry of Education posted me to Pokhara and then to Gulmi. As he was in the Vanasthali I decided to live him in boarding for the ninth grade, though this required about 800 out of my meagre 1300 salary. When I came later on I found him weak as well as not making much effort or progress as I expected. So we decided that he should better go to Min high school in Tharpu for his 10th grade that was about 45 minutes walk away from hour home in Dhayare. That option was not bad. He managed to pass the SLC exam from there at the first attempt in 1988. At least that was a great relief. This was a time of great transition in our family. I had decided to migrate everyone to Kathmandu for proper education of all four of us, for my jobs and for health care of my mother. Bishnu then joined the Tahachal campus to study intermediate in commerce. This was a very critical moment in our family. I got the Dutch government scholarship from the National Planning Commission to go to Netherlands from September 1988 as a reward for my very good performance in MA and for more than four years of service in the government. From some help from my friend Bishnu GC he was able to get a helper job in one of the travel agency in Thamel while he was studying for I. Com. The manager of that company gave Bishnu a very hard time after which he resolved to do better in schools. Bishnu completed his I.Com. in 1991. I had brought a PC from Holland with word processing, spreadsheet and other software. I taught Bishnu basic computing skills. Then with some foreign degree I had got an opportunity to work for the IIDS in Baneswore to process the survey data of the general election in 1990. We worked very hard on SPSS coding and tabulated the results as asked by the researchers that included American political scientists such as Leo Rose, Hague and Nepali scholars and politicians like Bhesh Bahadur Thapa, Kul Shekhar Sharma and Baburam Bhattarai. I did not only processed this survey data but also had gone to conduct the election in one of the booths in remote village of Kavre district where the winner happened to be the candidate from the Maoist group. This experience in computer later was basis for Bishnu to find a desktop publishing job in the media document centre Nepal where Jhalak was working for some time since he came to Kathmandu. Jhalak later went for an MBA degree in Philippines but Bishnu continued this job. Manu got married. In the meantime I got an offer for PhD degree from the Economics Department of the Northeastern University. My application of for the Full Bright travel grants was successful and I got a return ticket along with visa and health insurance from the US Education Foundation in Nepal. I went to Boston via Singapore, Tokyo, Los Angles on September 11th 1991 and had got a study leave of three years according to the rules of government of Nepal as I had worked more than five years by that time. Bishnu continued his B.Com. and continued working for DCP. When that was dissolved he got a job in a Forestry Project under the foreign aid from the UK. A little training in computer had done some wonder in his career. I issued invitation letter from the Northeastern when I was about to graduate with PhD in 1996 which was postponed to 1997 because of my delays in submission as I had to settle down in a new job in Warwick. Bishnu had completed everything except viva for his Masters' thesis which he already had submitted when he went to Boston in 1997. My family Manorama, Santosh and Prem were still in Boston. They showed Bishnu and Kedar, who had arrived a bit earlier, around Boston. Because of the unusual circumstances it happened that I was working in Warwick in UK while five of my family members were in Boston. Bishnu did very hard work – as a waiter in restaurants or as a proctor in residence halls. When I visited Boston in 1988 Bishnu leaned how to drive a car and passed both theory and practical exam just in one week. It was quite amazing performance. I remember how difficult it had been for me as I did not have a car and had to request some others to take me to the test. Now I had rented a car for the whole week and had taught various tricky bits and that went quite well with his driving test. He started studying undergraduate degree in Bunker Hill College which he found to be very expensive and taking a toll of his life but got through it in 2003 and then went to Fitchburg State College for M. Sc. in computer science. He graduated with this degree in May 2006. He also has got a 60K job in Accenture Company now. After these all hard works he has managed to get a position that he had wanted. His education has paid for him. Bishnu also has been married with Dianne Augustine, a girl form Pittsburgh. They share an apartment in Belmont and seem to be doing well in the journey of their lives.

Brother 2: Kedar was born in December 1978 and is 17 years younger than me. He was relatively in better position in terms of economic difficulties that we had to face in process of transition. He did primary school in Gaira, Kilchowk up to 4th grade, went to Basantapur school for about six months in 1987 when I was working in the Ministry of Education. Then he went with Manu to Alapot in a local boarding school for about a year to study English. Then started in grade 4 in Laboratory Boarding school 10 minutes away from hour new home in Kathmandu and progressed continuously and passed SLC in the first division in 1996. He took my invitation to attend my graduation in Northeastern in 1996 and stayed there four about two and half years. He might have been better off had he managed to continue in Obrien high school but did only the 11th grade and decided to work instead of studying. He earned some money working for a sub-way in the downtown Boston and went back to Nepal with some money that he managed to earn. He did 11th and 12th grades from a higher secondary school in Kathmandu that was completed in 2000. Then he started a four year BSc. in computer science in 2001. He could not quite complete it in time because of health related reasons especially due to disillusionment of certain girls but has managed to recover from it now and is expecting to clear all and get the degree in 2006. He intends to do an MBA in coming year if he passes this B.Sc. successfully. He has little work experience and did not face much problem as we did but should be more mature after he clears his degree in the computer science.

Uncle ShriKrishna Kaphle: I do not know how he did his primary education from Rishithum near his home in Tanahun but he is described to be a very unsettled boy when he was with my father in Calcutta around 1959. He was about twenty years old then and was suggested to go to study. He went to a Sanskrit school in Hardwar did the fifth grade, then to Badrinath for eight grade and back to Hardwar in the bank of Ganges river for Purba Madhyama which he completed around 1964. Then Atmaram Acharya, my maternal uncle in Beltar, went to bring him to get him married. He could not go back to his studies in India, nor could he do it from Nepal once he was married. He started a job as government primary school teacher around 1967 which he held for about 32 years. He brought me to Devghat in 1969 where he was teaching at that moment. He regarded education highly and regretted himself for not being able to continue it and bogged in family life. He ignited my instincts for education. I had seen him with piles of books of Intermediate like the Hidden Treasure Grammar or Vernacular Nepali. I do not understand why he could not focus on his studies even when he was a primary teacher. It is surprising however that none of his four children could continue education beyond school level. He left Kaflethok, did not have any intimate relation with his brother Benimadhab and his family and migrated to Bharatpur Chitwan. Now he is retired and lives a life like a hermit, and involved in social service activities in India. I am very thankful to him for bringing me to Devghat and to Rani Pokhari Sanskrit high school when my parents did not know how to proceed in my education. Now he is like a true friend to me.

PhD IN ECONOMICS FROM NORTHEASTERN UNIVERSITY IN BOSTON USA FOLLOWED BY FAMILY AND BROTHERS

I was a responsible family man while I started my PhD at Northeastern. I remember the warm send off at the International Airport in Kathmandu where all of family member were present: they included my mother, Bishnu, Kedar, newly migrated Basundhara and Jhalak and Kranti, Pragati and Sukriti newly married couples of my sisters Manu and Sitaram, Raghu Nath and my friend Shaker. This trip was full of anticipation and expectations and in which I had to work hard to be successful. Under the Full Bright travel grant scheme I had a ticket that would bring me to Boston via Bangladesh, Singapore, Tokyo, Los Angles to Boston. Flight from Kathmandu left in the bright afternoon of September 9th 1991 with more than 14 hours of waits in Singapore and the time gaps I arrived in Boston next evening when Boston was completely lit with lights. I did not know anyone in Boston at that time. After immigration clearance I took a taxi for Northeastern which dropped me at the University's quad with my luggage that included a sleeping bag, a large plastic bag full of books, reports and statistical bulletins published from various agencies in Nepal that I thought would be useful for my PhD. I had bought a sleeping bag with me thinking that I might even had to sleep in the street given my meagre budget. It was a welcome week, I asked volunteers how I can adjust for few days until I sorted out my admission and registration. I was recommended to stay at the White Hall for that night where I spent about six nights. I met Ravi Kachalia from Gujarat who also wanted to find a place. We agreed to find a place together and happen to get one in the 65 Burbank Street. I explained my situation next day to Gregory Wassall who was the Director of the Graduate School, whom I had made a called from Nepal from the Ministry of Communication the previous week about my weak financial situation. He seemed to have noted this carefully. They immediately offered me tuition waiver and was assigned to work with Professor Sun Yoo Kim who also recommended me to work for Dean Bade for a project that included a study on the experience of international students at Northeastern. My knowledge of processing data using SPSS at the IDS in Nepal became very useful for that job and I was able to solve my immediate financial problem and concentrate in my studies. I managed to get all As in end of semester exams in December. I spent my Christmas break to finish the project report that I had got from the Dean. Hasnath from BU helped me a bit in reporting. Further I was given Northeastern University teaching and research assistantship (NUTA) for the winter 1992 based on my performance in the first semester which continued for another year as I could maintain my grades. This gave me an opportunity to invite my family from Nepal. Kachalia had moved with his friends and I was alone for a while, but my classmate Bhutta from Baluchistan, Pakistan joined me after a while as we could discuss some subjects together till my family arrived to live with me in August 1992. I remember my friend Anil Shrestha, Hasnath from BU and Juan Lallave (friend I knew from Silvia Chandler in Germany- Jhalak's freind) receiving my family in Boston. Santosh started from grade 1 in Farragut Primary and Manorama from Grade three in Bawldin and I started my second year of PhD and preparation for the comprehensive exams. Miss Sherman was a very lovely teacher of Santosh and Manorama met Yumi Shakya daughter of Subarna Shakya in Bawldin. Both of them did very well in their homeworks and in the schools and would get impressive certificates and pictures at the end the school years. We had good PhD community that included friends like Bang Bang (Indonesia), Hui Pan (China), Somadeep (India), Aud (Thailand), Kazim (Turkey), Mumtaz (Pakistan), Belamune (Tunisia), Fogg (US), Walid and Sharazadeh form Lebanon, Anwiti (India) Ben Zhau (Hong Kong) and good faculty members like Sum, Parente, Haughton, Adams, Brookins, Kim, Alper, Dadkhah, Morrison, Fraumeni, Adams, Alper Gradually we got acquainted to other friends through the Greater Boston Nepali Community (GBNC) such as Niranjan, Shakyas, Shova and Santosh, Ajaya, Ravindra, Brajesh, Parajuli, Anil and Aruna, Manandhar, Binod Shah. Jagadeesh, Ambika, Rajauriya, Sunil, Honda had given some orientation to us while we were there. It is amazing how we all learn survival tricks from each other in time of need.

Manorama and Santosh went to Quincy in downtown from the next year. While I was doing PhD from Northeastern my children were growing and having good schooling in Boston. Only scholarship from the economics department was not enough to pay for rents and maintain the family. I used to do proctoring job like many other students in residence halls and Prem did some part time jobs to support ourselves. I learned driving in an old car that a Professor from Harvard was about to send to the junk yard which we knew from Pravigya regmi who was living with us for few months. Pravigya was son of Devraj Regmi from Palpa whom I had known from the Ministry of Education. Later on Adhikari family with their two daughters Astha and Ekta moved to the street near to us. This way we had some Nepalese community even in Boston. This had made keeping balance between family life and studies much easier.

After two three years Santosh and Manorama were doing very well in school. In process of finding a better school Santosh got into the Renaissance Charter School and Manorama into the Boston Latin. Both were selected on the basis of scores in competitive tests. We had got a subsidised apartment in the 70 Burbank Street which became renovated while we are there and turned from a violent to a very peaceful one. It was in a very convenient location in Boston. Prem used to work part-time as house care assistant for some families and earned something as well. I had opportunity once to invite Nepalese economist in the US such as Dhakal, Mukti, Upadyaya and Bhandari while we were participating in AEA meeting in

1994 in Boston. John Adams was very interested in started a Nepal Research Centre in the Northeastern with some support from Nepal and I had visited PM Girija Koirala in his visit at New York through Dr. Jaya Raj Acharya who was now permanent representative of Nepal to the UN. Jaya Raj latter on came to Northeastern and stayed with us for few days in 1995 when he visited the Harvard University as a fellow in the Centre for International Affairs. I was also keeping in touch with family in Nepal was glad to know that Bishnu was doing well in his B.Com. from Ratna Jyoti campus in Chhetrapati, Kedar from Laboratory high, and Manu from Kirtipur campus and as a teacher in the Jan Vikas Primary School. Those were the first days of email communication between Nepal and the US, I used to get very excited in getting emails from Nepal. I had also started a discussion group in the internet on issues development activities relating to Nepal and developing economies and written and published articles in Samachar Bichar and used to post frequently in Socio-Economics group of Nepal. Study at Northeastern was quite a busy time for me.

I passed all four PhD comprehensive examinations at the first instance; then did some graduate courses in mathematics and computer; then came the time for selecting a topic for PhD dissertation. Until then I had an ambition to go back to Nepal and do better for the country though in one side of my mind I was thinking a topic such as the tax reform proposal of President Clinton or the labour market issues using PUMS data set with Professors Sum and Alper. I also wanted to work on an economic policy model of Nepal for which I had background of working in the Planning Commission of Nepal, regional development model of Elbers with much complex FORTRAN routines that I had learnt at the ISS for my MA and work in the Ministry of Education and the Nepal Bank. I basically was thinking of doing a challenging work that could place me in a job at the end of dissertation. I met a few senior PhD students who were about to finish their PhD. Since I had worked with a CGE model earlier I essentially wanted to work on this. Professor Parente had taught us dynamic one sector models and he was very good in derivations. Professor Bolnick and Haughton worked for HIID and had international links and some experience with CGE models in GAMS. Haughton knew about my previous experience at ISS and my work on a CGE model. I was hoping to get jobs in international organisations such as the World Bank or the IMF after the PhD and thought that more policy oriented work could put me in such jobs. Professor John Adams also encouraged for a Nepalese CGE. For this reason I wanted to work on the Nepal model and in building a dynamic CGE model for Nepal. As I found out soon that there was no multisectora dynamic CGE model till that time except the basic Ramsey model in the GAMS library.

I remember working till late at the Northeastern Economics department to get model running. When it was too difficult I wrote to GAMS Corporation in Washington DC asking whether they could help me on this. They forwarded my request to Professor Thomas F. Rutherford of the University of Colorado, Boulder who provided me very important help in the process of programming and implementation of the model in MPSGE. He invited me to Colorado a number of times to work on this model and introduced me first to Professor Michael Ferris of the University of Wisconsin who provided hints at various point of time including an access to a Sun-computing system in the University of Wisconsin that were used to run many model simulations and then to Professor John Whalley with whom I learnt many professional skills on use of applied general equilibrium technique for economic policy analysis in a real world situation.

I had formally defended my dissertation on March 26, 1996, one week before I started a research position in the University of Warwick in the United Kingdom. The thesis was accepted and I was advised to submit it after some redrafting for the purpose of clarity in exposition. In the process of adjusting to a new place and to a new position even minor re-drafting remained on pending for some time. Meanwhile, economics department of Northeastern was in trouble. Its PhD programme was being suspended from the next intake. This meant downsizing of economics department. Three out of four members of my dissertation committee, Bolnick, Parente and Haugton left the economics department of Northeastern at the end of the Spring quarter of 1996 which made communication with them virtually impossible. This prolonged my graduation. When I found it difficult to obtain a visa to return to the US from London or Ontario I asked Professor John Whalley to become my new supervisor which he accepted in consultation with Professor John Adams at Northeastern.

As I wrote in my acknowledgment then, I owe much to Professor John Whalley of the University of Western Ontario in Canada and University of Warwick in the UK for accepting the role of the primary reader and providing me valuable time and guidance in finishing up this dissertation when the costs of meeting my former committee members became prohibitive. I am equally grateful to Professor John Adams, the Chair, for re-organizing my committee including Professors Whalley and Wassall and encouraging me to submit the final draft as quickly as possible. His long-standing research interest in the economies of South Asia was of great help during my study period at Northeastern. I made my final submission from Canada in winter to graduate in the Summer of 1997. Assistance from Professor Whalley was very critical.

Professor Bruce Bolnick played a very important role as the chair of the dissertation committee until the summer of 1996. I met him in the beginning of Fall 1994 and expressed my idea of incorporating the financial sector in a forward looking CGE model. He encouraged me to accept the challenge of developing a new framework of analysis beyond what could be found from a detailed review of the literature in this area. I am thankful to him for the part he played and for permitting me to be in touch with Professor Rutherford and for all instructions though he opted to be a "virtual member" of the committee when he left for Malawi as a consultant for the Government in October 1996. Before leaving to the University of Pennsylvania Professor Stephen Parente had helped me on the dynamics of the model though he was very skeptical of the large-scale CGE approach for policy analysis. I still did not know the importance of publication for a career in economics. Completing PhD thesis was a major concern.

My interest in developing a good model for policy analysis was born when I was writing an M.A. thesis at the Institute of Social Studies, the Hague, the Netherlands during 1989-90. Then I had an opportunity of external guidance from Chris Elbers at the Free University Amsterdam, who for his PhD was then working on a theory of spatial disaggregation in general equilibrium models with an application to the Nepalese economy. He had been to Nepal to provide a training in the input-output model of Nepalese economy for officials involved in economic planning of Nepal of which I was also a participant as I was working in the Economic Analysis Division of the NPC. In the winter 1993 Professor Jonathan Haughton referred me to Professor Shanta Devarajan and Jeffrey Lewis both of whom redirected me to Timothy Buehrer, then at the Harvard Institute of International Development, who had closely worked with Philipo de Mauro and Maxwell Stamp at the Asian Development Bank, Manila, in developing a Computable General Equilibrium (CGE) model of Nepal. Buehrer provided me the ADB model code and explained some of its applications.

Initially I started implementing the model with application to various labor market issues such as migration, underemployment and human resource development, and interrelationship between the Indian and Nepalese labor markets. Then I realized that for a developing economy such as Nepal, capital rather than labor was the most important binding constraint of long-rung growth and development. I thought the construction of a fully specified dynamic equilibrium model was important to experiment various economic policies in a model economy in place of a sequence of single-period temporary recursive equilibrium structure as used in the ADB model.

I would like to express my gratitude to the Department of Economics, Northeastern University which provided me time and financial support, without which it would have been impossible for a person coming from Batase, Jamune, a remote hill town in Tanahun district in central Nepal, to do this dissertation. Delfin S. Go, at the World Bank, and C.K. Keuschenigg had provided me with their latest research papers on the topic. The IRIS and Federal Reserve Bank of Minneapolis also sent some working papers.

Special thanks to my brother Bishnu Hari Bhattarai in Kathmandu, for painfully collecting various informations on the Nepalese economy and sending it to me. Love from my mother is source of my inspiration. I appreciate Prem, my wife, who was not supported to come out of tradition for her formal education but who enjoyed helping me all the time. Last but not the least, I appreciate the patience of my daughter, Manorama, and my son, Santosh, who were getting little attention from me during my study period. Much of my time was spent doing research while they were going through their elementary education. I am indebted to all other people who helped at various stages of this dissertation.

My economic situation had improved a bit by the end of this dissertation. I had my children studying in Boston schools, Prem had got exposure to the life in the USA, my two brothers had come to Boston for education, Manu in Kathmandu had established herself well. Basundhara didi also had better condition than before.

Though each of them still had some challenge in the wake of this transition. The psychological burden migration decision to make family move from Dhayare to Kathamandu was gradually easing off as I had got an opportunity to get a paying job in the Western world in a prestigious university like Warwick. My family still remembers my little dance when I had got a job with Whalley in early 1996. My own education had opened door for all my siblings and for myself. How did I met expectations of the project and how it impacted my decisions and activities later is the subject of next section.

RESEARCH WORKS AND LECTURESHIP IN UNIVERSITIES OF WARWICK AND HULL: HIGHER EDUCATION IN THE UNITED KINGDOM

I did not know real importance of academic writing and publishing until I worked in the University of Warwick as Research Associate with Professor Whalley[1]. He was one of the great economists with more 300 publications at the same time he was also so polite and concerned about the issues that mattered to me. I was busy in building a static and dynamic multisectoral and multi-asset applied general equilibrium tax models under the ESRC project on dynamic general equilibrium modelling of the UK economy using modelling skills that I had learnt in my PhD works particularly with Professor Rutherford in the University of Colorado in USA who had recommended me for this job. I frequently visited Whalley in the Western Ontario and presented a paper on the redistribution effects of transfers in University of Ontario and in the TAPE conference in Denmark and division of the gains in trade in service network in the Economic Policy Research Unit (EPRU) in Denmark and NBER summer meeting in Boston in 1998. Earlier I had gone to GAMS modelling workshops run by Professor Rutherford twice in Denmark and twice in Colorado in 1997. Whalley also introduced me to Carlo Perroni, now Professor in Economics in Warwick and to modelling team made of Graham Siddorn, Bill McKnie and Ambroise in the Inland Revenue. He was a very learned economist and had very intuitive understanding of many economic problems and was rigorous and thorough in checking the results of general equilibrium models. He would quickly understand whether any results made sense or not and would make several counter questions. His research area spanned from public finance, development economics, international trade and environment and was consulting many governments around the world. I particularly learned public finance and trade modelling while working with him. This along with my background in dynamic general equilibrium model and econometrics had expanded the set of tools that I can use for research and teaching in economics. Warwick economics department had many world class faculty members doing very important research and used to organise conferences and seminars in economics. The project that I was working was under the consortium of Macro Economic Modelling Bureau organised under Professor Kenneth Wallis and thus I had some what close links with Keith Church, Peter Mitchel, Mark Crawling, Reinhard and Rudi Douvan who were working in the Bureau. I was located next to Whalley's room in the

Economics Department with Lisandro Abrego who had MSc. from Boston University and was doing PhD from Warwick was working in an environmental project with Carlo and John. We were basically working in the applied equilibrium modelling using GAMS and I was hired for my experience in MPSGE. Besides that I had found all faculty members including Arulampalam, Marcus Miller, Jeremy Smith, Sayantan Ghosal, Amrita, Leigh Zhang, Jeff Round, Neil Rankin, Myrna Wooders and staff very friendly during my stay in Warwick. I had plenty of opportunity to participate in conferences and seminars organised frequently and join various events including the weekly football matches among the staff.

I had bought a house in Chappelfields near Earlsdon on Coventry with a mortgage of £29000 pounds in August 1996 in anticipation of bringing whole familty to my work. That loan was offered against my annual income of £18500 from the Warwick University, this was very surprising to me given my experience of building a house in Kathmandu. It gave me a feeling of how smooth was the financial market in UK. I was not able to bring my family when I wanted. As a Nepalese citizen, I did not get visa from London to go to Boston from the US Embassy and they asked me go back to Kathmandu for it. This was becoming very costly and inconvenient. Later on I tried this from Toronto while visiting Professor Whalley in the research trip it was impossible even then. In addition my job at Warwick was under a contract for a period of three years. Kedar and Bishnu two of my brothers had joined with my family there in 1996. I was able to get visa from Kathmandu in April 1997 and visited family during the summer but I could not get everyone move with me as my job situation was still uncertain. Kedar had started 11th grade in O'brian high and Bishnu wanted to start a college quite soon. I could not take any decision in an uncertain environment until my job market situation got settled. Every final year PhD candidates should go through such decisions. I thought my best strategy was just to work very hard and get most out of the research position that I have had and prepare myself for an academic job to be able to take care of family responsibility leaving things to the nature to take care itself until I was able to do so. This strategy worked to some extent though it was very hard decision upon reflection.

I left the University of Warwick at the end of my contract period in September 1999 and accepted a Lectureship in Economics position in the University of Hull. I remember attending an interview which included Professors David Richardson, Donald Woodward, Richard Green, Dr. Jonathan Atkins and Dr. Trotter. This department included faculties from economics and economic history. They offered me a job and I found myself teaching macroeconomics, econometrics and economic modelling at undergraduate and post graduate levels as well as supervising research projects in B.Sc., M.Sc. and PhD levels. I also was offered £5000 grant from the Faculty of Social Science to further my research. In addition I spent a lot of time in drafting papers and submitting them to refereed journals and presenting papers in national and international conferences. Professor Whalley helped me to get articles published in the Emperical Economics, Economics Letters and book volumes Econometric Modelling and Applications from Cambrigde, Contributions to Economic Analysis from Elsevier- North-Holland and Advances in Public Economics from Spring Verlag. I went to University of British Columbia with Gainluigi Pelloni to present the dynamic general equilibrium paper to the Canadian Economic Association Conference 2000. I did quite good research in the summer of 2000. Economics had good research standing in the Research Assessment Exercise of 2001 in which I had four papers produced as a part of work in the ESRC project in Warwick. My family who had been to Nepal since 1998 joined me in Hull in August 2000. We bought a house at 68 Auckland avenue in May 2001. Santosh went to Kelvin high in eight grade and Manorama started A level at Wyke college. We also bought a car and took a tour of whole UK in the summer of 2001 camping in many places. During the term time I had found teaching a bit challenging as I tended to pitch at higher level and covered a bit more than students liked. We had good friendship among colleagues with six GTAs and 21 faculty members. The economic history section joined the History department in 2001 and economics was contemplated for a while to remain separate and eventually joined the Business School in 2003. Economics colleagues Tapan Biswas, Mike Ryan, Chris Hammond, Steve Trotter and Jon Atkins came here before me, Mike Nolan, Anthony Dnes and Raymond Swaray joined latter on. Richard Green, Chris Tsoukis, Jo McHardy, Simon Vicary, Juan Paz-Farrel have left for other universities, Pikoulakis and Sue Palfreman got retired. I have supervised PhD works of Naveed, Francesco, Armah, Panahi, Okyere, Negm and Sloan and examined dissertations of Quin Fu, Basil, and Mustafa and supervised more than 32 M.Sc dissertations and hundreds of undergraduate level independent studies and dissertations (see appendix 4 of this chapter). I have made applications to large research grants to the ESRC and part of the Hull team in the consortium of Supergen project from the ESRC. Working in a team that includes Bright, Tucker, Wang, Thyles, Miller, Gregory, Jose, Dwiwidi, Common, Reid, Benson, Chandra from Marketing, Business, Management, Human Resources, Accounting and Finance or Logistics besides economics is fun and economics group has been able to get 12th best rank in the country on teaching as published in the Guardian Newspaper on May 2, 2006.

I liked Britain and took British citizenship in May 15, 2003 in order to fulfil my dreams for academic excellence. It enabled me for more interaction with groups of economists from all around the world. I have been to Public Economic Theory Conference in China to present a paper in economic growth at global level in 2004, to Canberra Australia to present a paper in unemployment and inflation in OECD economies, to Japan to present a paper on 123 model of the UK economy and to casino Italy to present a paper on Keynesian macroeconomic models, to Berlin in Germany for unemployment and inflation paper, to Belgium to present the tax model of the UK economy to USA to participate in the American Economic Association annual meeting in San Diego in 2004, Pensylvania in 2005 and in Boston in 2006, in Vienna for the European Economic Association Conference in 2006 and to Marselle France for the public economic theory conference. Once Prem, Manorama and Santosh also had British citizenship we took a ferry from Hull to Rotterdam in Netherlands and drove to Amsterdam, Brussels and Bruise in the Easter of 2006. I have been to Ghana in Africa, and am planning to go to Bombay, Brazil, Moscow, Turkey and Spain next year. I am member about ten professional organisations in economics that include Royal Economic Society, Econometric Society, Public Economics Society, European Economic Society, American Economic Association, International Input-Output Association, EcoMod, and International Atlantic Economic Society, GAMS and OXmetrics modelling networks. I use my research in teaching and supervision of students. My teaching constitutes of papers that I have done over years and many others available in the literature. Perhaps a better example of this can be given in terms of number of articles included in a recent hand-out book that I used for supervising dissertations and independent studies as following:

1. Consumption, Investment and Financial Intermediation in Ramsey Models, Applied Financial Economics Letters, Applied Financial Economics Letters 1(6), 1-5. pp. 3-13.
2. Macroeconomic Impacts of Consumption and Income Taxes: A General equilibrium Analysis, Research Memorandum no. 41 Business School, University of Hull. pp. 14-39.
3. Multi-Sectoral Multi-Household General Equilibrium Tax Model: an Application, Problems and Perspectives in Management, 3/2004. pp. 40-74.
4. Efficiency and Factor Reallocation Effects and Marginal Excess Burden of Taxes in the UK Economy, European Research Studies, 2003, v. 6, iss. 3-4, pp. 177-205. pp. 75.
5. Welfare Impacts of Equal-Yield Tax Experiment in the UK Economy, forthcoming in Applied Economics. pp. 105.
6. Multi-household dynamic general equilibrium analysis of poverty and income redistribution pp. 141.
7. Political Economy of Conflict and Growth: Nepalese Dilemma, forthcoming IJEB. pp. 165.
8. Keynesian Models of macroeconomic policy (Casino conference) pp. 198.
9. Interest Determination Rule four UK and Other Four Major Industrial Economies a Research Memorandum no. 42 Business School, University of Hull. pp. 236.
10. Economic Growth: Models and Global Evidence, Research Memorandum no. Business School, University of Hull. pp. 262.
11. Unemployment and inflation in OECD economies pp. 306.
12. Determinants of Waged and Labour Supply in the UK, Hull Economics Research Paper no. 277 accepted for publication in the European Research Studies. pp. 354.
13. Wage dynamics in the UK pp. 379.
14. Discreteness and the Welfare Cost of Labour Supply Tax Distortions, International Economic Review 44:3:1117-1133, August 2003 pp. 390.

15. Division and Size of Gains from Liberalization of Trade in Services, Review of International Economics, 14:3:348-361. Bhattarai K. and J. Whalley (2006) pp. 419.
16. Welfare Gains to UK from a Global Free Trade, the European Research Studies, Vol. IV, Issue 3-4, 2001. pp. 444.
17. Redistribution Effects of Transfers, National Bureau of Economic Research, Working Paper no. 6281. Bhattarai K. and J. Whalley. pp. 487.
18. Welfare and distributional Impacts of financial liberalisation in a developing economy: Lessons from a forward looking CGE model of Nepal, Working Paper no. 7, Hull Advances in Policy Economics Research Papers. pp. 519.
19. General Equilibrium Modelling of UK Tax Policy in S. Holly and M Weale (eds.) Econometric Modelling: Techniques and Applications, pp. 69-93, the Cambridge University Press, 2000, (with J. Whalley). pp. 570.
20. Role of Heterogeneity of Labour Demand in Tax Incidence Analysis in Baldev Raj and R. Boadway (Eds.) Advances on Public Economics, pp.47-69, Physica-Verlag, 2000. and Empirical Economics, 24:4, 1999, pp.599-620 (with J. Whalley). pp. 605.
21. On some properties of a trade closure widely used in numerical modelling, Economic Letters, 62 no. 1 1999, pp. 13-21, (with M Ghosh and J Whalley) pp. 631.
22. More on Trade Closure in L Raut and G Ranis (eds.) Trade, Growth and Development: Essays in Honour of Professor T. N. Srinivasan, Contribution to Economic Analysis 242, Elsevier, NorthHolland 1999. (With M Ghosh and J Whalley). pp. 646-664.

Details on my teaching since the time of my years in Northeastern are included in the appendix 3. I was in fact in full fledged teaching position after coming to Hull University in 1999 when I was of 38 years old though I had started my career when I was just 20 years old in 1981. I have spent 10 years of working life in Nepal; recent 10 years in the UK and middle sever years at Northeastern in the US. Thus I have worked about 26 years so far in different roles as a lecturer, researcher, teacher, educator, tutor and administrator and made migration decisions from Batase hills to Dhayare, then to Kathmandu the capital city of Nepal then to the US and then permanently to the UK. As a result of this experience I have accumulated some useful knowledge which I am going to put in a series of books. My book projects for the next year include (1) A General Equilibrium Tax Model of The UK Economy (2) Economic Models For Nepalese Economy 3) Economic Theory and Models: Derivations, Computations And Applications (4) Research Methods For Economists (5) Microeconomics: Theory and Applications (6) Macroeconomics: Theory and Applications (7) Econometrics: Theory and Applications. This idea has emerged from my work in Hull in last seven years of which this section is a part.

From the experience so far it is possible for me to think about myself about various important issues that need research at the global level and do presentation of those ideas in various international conferences. For instance a conference plan (see appendix 5 of this chapter) that I have made for the coming year would have been unimaginable about ten years ago given my situation at that time. This is what I call the result of continuous efforts for education and using support available for academic progress. This keeps me busy at my work for the greater welfare of the global society as I have fulfilled my responsibility to some extent toward my family and to the nation where I was born and brought up. It is good that the hard effort in education has brought me close to the professional colleagues who have been advancing the boundaries of knowledge that matter for the improvement of human welfare in this planet.

The Hull Business School where I work now was established in 1999 at the time I joined the University of Hull. Ever since economics joined the Business School I have taken route of research for teaching to advance my career and school also has helped me in doing this up to some extent. I am mainly involved in supervising research work of students both at undergraduate and post graduate levels (see appendix 4 and 5). This School is expanding very rapidly and becoming a very large institution with many departments such as Accounting and Finance, Economics, Business, Human Resources, Marketing, Management and giving high priority to attain international excellence in teaching and research and an integral part of the University and Hull community. It is a great place for academic achievement. I am free to work on problems of my choice.

What is Next?

At this point I feel that more I write there is more to be written. These expereicnes could be analysed from more than one agle. The complicated struggle for higher education and livelihood presented above became much longer than that I had expected. It might be shorter for Manorama and Santosh or people of new generation who have got a clear focus from the very beginning. Once again I feel like a free person the one that I was when I was about at my sixteen Siblings as well as my children have grown up to a point that they can take care of themselves. Prem is with me will remain till the end of this journey. I should be looking a path for liberation and salvation. Now I believe salvation would come from the contribution that I can make for a better global society starting from the work place where I am. First I need to understand the view points of all learned people of current generation. That is why I am taking membership of all professional organisations in economics and doing hard work to understand how economists use their knowledge and understanding to transform this world around us. I am inclined to commit myself for productive writing that can make us understand the reality of world and change this for betterment of human kind that can be in Nepal or in UK or Europe or US; universal. That is the reason why I like my job at the university. I have plenty of things to think about and work for many years to come, to understand and explain true self of myself and the world around us. In twenty years time from now on I will be an old man and this task will shift to people who come next.

Appendix 1
Degrees from Nepal, Subject Studies, and Results

Degree and Institution	*Year*	*Subjects*	*Grade*	*Overall Marks*	*Overall Percent*
SLC (PM)- SLC Board Nepal (2032)	1975-1976	Sanskrit Literature, Philosophy, essays and translation, Elementary Nepali, Arithmetic, Panchayat, Sanskrit Grammar I and II, Nepali Literature, Civics and Commercial Geography	II	520/900	57.8
SLC (Supplement) SLC Board (2033)	1977	English Prose, Poetry and Literature and Essays, Grammar and Composition	Pass	87/200	43.5
Certificate in Sanskrit Tribhuvan University, Institute of Sanskrit Balmiki Campus (2035)	1977 1978	Principles of Economics, Economic Theory, Trade, Algebra, Trigonometry and Geometry, Nepalese Economics, Sanskrit Grammar I-IV, International English, Basic Spoken English, Reading and composition, Logics, Introduction of Nepal, Public Finance, Stories, Drama, Lyrics,	Merit	624/900 130/200	68.4
Diploma in Sanskrit Tribhuvan University, Institute of Sanskrit Balmiki Campus (2035)	1978 1979	Principles of Economics, Economic Theory I and II, Public Finance, Mathematics and Statistics Economic System Planning and Growth, Nepalese Economics, Contemporary English, Sanskrit Grammar I-V, Prose-Poetry-Essays, Philosophy and Religion, English for Stories and Prose	Merit	631.9/800 130/200	74.3
English Conversation II	1978	English Language Institute, American Cultural Centre, Kathmandu Nepal	Prize	Successful	
MA in Economics Tribhuvan University, Kirtipur Kathmandu and PN Campus Pokhara	1981-1984	Theory of Economic Analysis (Micro and Thought), Quantitative Techniques, Economic Development and Planning, Mathematical Economics, Economic Analysis (Macro and Welfare), Monetary Theory and Policy, Public Economics and Policy, Econometrics, National Development Service	First Division	698/900	77.5
Bachelor of Law– Private Institute of Law, Tribhuvan University, Nepal	1985 1986 1988	Legal Theory and Interpretation, Constitution Law, Public International Law, English, Moot Court, Alternative English, General Fiscal Law, Company and Corporation Law, Criminal Law and Evidence, International Institution and Human Rights, Seminar, Legal System Planning and Public Finance, History of England, Political Thought, Compulsory English, Nepali, International Trade Law, Taxation Law, Procedural Law, Contract and Law of Property, Hindu Jurisprudence and Nepali Legal History, Internship and Court Practice, Banking and Negotiable Instruments, Criminology.	Second	380/650 343/650 209/400 Total 982/1800	54.8

Appendix 2
Degrees from US and European Institutions, Subject Studies, and Results

Level and Institution	*Year*	*Subjects*	*Grade*	*Overall Marks*	*Overall Per cent*
PhD in Economics–Northeastern University Boston, Mass. USA	1991 to 1997	Micro Theory I, Macro Theory I, Economics of Manpower Planning, Micro Theory II, Macro Theory II, Development Planning Seminar, Mathematics for Economists, Labor Economics, Econmetrics II, Public Finance Theory, International Trade, PhD Research Seminar I and II, Human Resource Development, Readings in Economics, Cross Section Analysis, Probability I Optimisation, Statistics, Analysis of Algorithm, Algorithm and Data Structure C++ Lab	QPA 3.169	83 Credit Hours Quality points 262.999	PhD in Economics
MA in Development Studies–ISS Hague, Netherlands	Sept1989 to Dec1990	Econometrics, National Accounting, Development Theories, Macroeconomic Analysis, Industrialisation and Development Strategy, International Economics of Development, Quantitative Analysis of Development, Quantitative Models of Policy and Planning, Principles of Socio Economics Models, Introduction to Multi-Sectoral Models, Internationalization of Production and Policy Options, Internationalisation of Finance in the Developing Countries, International Primary Commodity Markets: Modelling for Policy Analysis, Historic Development in International Relations, National Economic Development, States, Government and Development Agencies, Culture Ideology and Development	B	Course Mark 81.51% Synthesizing papers 85% Research Paper 65.50%	76.44
Member Omicron Delta Epsilon	Life Long	For outstanding performance in Economics			

Appendix 3
My Experience in the Higher Education Sector in the United Kingdom

	Graduate Teaching Assistant: Department of Economics, Northeastern			*Lecturer in Economics, Department of Economics, University of Hull, since 1991*			*Lecturer in Economics, Business School, University of Hull, since 1991*	
1992	Econometric Analysis	MA/ PhD	1999	Macroeconomic theory and policy for MSc.	MSc	2003	Economic Forecasting	MSc
	Mathematical Economics	MA/ PhD		Econometrics	BSc/Msc		Economics Modelling	BSc
	Statistics and Statistical Inference	MA/ PhD		Intermediate consumer theory	BSc		Research methods	BSc
	Micro and Macro Economics	MA/ PhD		Supervision of MSC. dissertations in economics	MSc		Independent study	Bsc
1993	Econometric Analysis	MA/ PhD		Examination of PhD in Econometrics	PhD		Undergraduate dissertations	BSc
	Mathematical Economics	MA/ PhD		Macroeconomic Analysis	BSc		Supervision of MSc. dissertations in economics	MSc
	Statistics and Statistical Inference	MA/ PhD	2000	Macroeconomic theory and policy for MSc.	MSc		Supervision and Examination of PhD in Economics	
	Micro and Macro Economics	MA/ PhD		Econometrics	BSc/Msc	2004	Economic Forecasting	MSc
	Lecturer in Economics, University College, Northeastern University			Macroeconomic analysis	BSc		Economics Modelling	BSc
1994	Principles of Economics I	BA		Intermediate consumer theory	MSc		Research methods	BSc/BA
	Principles of Economics II	BA		Microeconomics	PhD		Independent study	Bsc
	Principles of Economics III	BA		Supervision of MSC. dissertations in economics	BSc		Undergraduate dissertations	BSc
	Growth and Development Economics	BA		Supervision and Examination of PhD in Economics			Supervision of MSc. dissertations in economics	MSc
1995	Principles of Economics I	BA	2001	Macroeconomic theory and policy for MSc.	MSc		Supervision and Examination of PhD in Economics	
	Principles of Economics II	BA		Econometrics	BSc/Msc		Supervision of post graduate Supermen Modelling project	
	Principles of Economics III	BA		Macroeconomic analysis	BSc	2005	Economic Forecasting	MSc
	Growth and Development Economics	BA		Intermediate consumer theory	BSc		Economics Modelling	BSc

1996-1999	**Research Fellow/Associate in the University of Warwick**			Microeconomics	BSc		Research methods	BSc/BA
	Dynamic general equilibrium analysis of UK economy			Supervision of MSc. dissertations in economics	BSc		Independent study	Bsc
	Chapter in Econometric Modelling Techniques and Applications			Supervision and Examination of PhD in Economics			Undergraduate dissertations	BSc
	Three NBER working papers		2002	Macroeconomic theory and policy for MSc.	MSc		Supervision of MSc. dissertations in economics	MSc
	Article in Empirical Economics Journal			Econometrics	BSc		Supervision and Examination of PhD in Economics	
	Chapter in Advanced Public Finance, Spring Verlag			Macroeconomic analysis	BSc		Supervision of post graduate Supergen Modelling project	
	Redistribution and transfer paper			Intermediate consumer theory	Bsc	2006	Economic Forecasting	MSc
	Seven reports to ESRC and collaboration with Inland Revenue			Macroeconomic Themes	BSc		Economics Modelling	BSc
	Six international presentations			Supervision of MSc. dissertations in economics	MSc		Research methods	BSc/BA
	An article in Economic Letters			Supervision and Examination of PhD in Economics			Independent study	Bsc
	A chapter in North-Holland Economic Contribution series						Undergraduate dissertations	BSc
	Department of Economics; University of Warwick						Supervision of MSc. dissertations in economics	MSc
1998	Research methods in economics	MSc/MA/PhD					Supervision and Examination of PhD in Economics	
	Examination of PhD dissertation						Supervision of post graduate Supergen Modelling project	

Appendix 4
Supervision of Research Projects of Student in the University of Hull

Ph. D. Supervision (Current)

1. Mark K. Arhmah "Econometric and General Equilibrium Analysis of Exchange Rate in Developing Economies".
2. Emmanuel Okyere "Macroeconomic Economic Policy Rules, Economic Growth and Development".
3. Hoessein Panahi with Richard Green "Geographic Proximity and Economic Growth".
4. Andrew Sloan Heterogeneous inflation dynamics of the UK regions and EU states: an attempt to explain with Hybrid New Keynesian Models.
5. Seham Negm Trade and Economic Growth in Egypt.

General equilibrium modelling of the UK economy for Supergen project Team: Dr. Milton Yago, Dr. Jon Atkins, Dr. Steve Trotter, Professor Richard Green.

Ph.D. Dissertations supervised/Examined

1. Francesco D. Bispham (2006) "Panel-Cointegration and Unit Roots and Efficiency of Asymptotic Estimators".
2. Naveed Hassan Naqvi (2003) "The Relationship Between Private and Public Capital and Impact on Economic Growth: The Case of Pakistan".
3. Hamad El-Nil Gadain Mustafa (2002) "Aspects of Sudanese Trade: 1970-1992".
4. Basil Morris Jones (2001) "Growth, Convergence, and Economic Integration in West Africa".
5. Qiang Fu (2000) "Bayesian Multivariate Time Series Models for Forecasting European Macroeconomic Series".

M.Sc.(Econ) Dissertations Supervised

1. Daniel Shaw (2006) Gains to William Morrison after its takeover of Safeways Supermarket.
2. Edwin Beecrof (2006) When and Whether it would be appropriate for Britain to join the Euro.
3. Yu Bo (2006) Nonperforming loans to China's banks.
4. Haibin Fang (2006) Is universal banking system applicable to China?
5. Singapore Join venture in construction business.
6. HongKong Prospects for fast food Deli restaurant in Hong Kong.
7. Bahrein Impact of Bahrainisation the labour market.
8. Eric Does advertisement by drug companies affect prescriptions by doctors.
9. Hong Ruiling (2005) The impact of fiscal policy on international trade in China.
10. Ukwuani Valentine Chijioke (2005) Macroeconomic effects of fiscal policy in Nigeria: a development dynamics in under-developed market economies.
11. Marian Antoieta Mina Manriquz (2005) Analysis of the efficiency of the refining industry in Mexico through the maximization of revenues.
12. Lamber Amewu Kwakudua (2005) The impact of fiscal, monetary and exchange rate policies on output in Ghana.
13. Ying Qiu (2005) To be globalised or not to be globalised: can developing countries benefit from globalisation?
14. Li Chu Pan (2004) A case study of the integrated marketing communication model and competitive strategy analysis in the home shopping industry.

15. Ten Ge (2004) Can we control the economic fluctuations? An investigation in the UK Business Cycles.
16. Segunda Kyamy (2004) How can oil revenues be used to alleviate poverty in sub-Saharan Africa region?
17. Ying Xu (2004) Growth and inequality of income distribution: the case of China and India.
18. Qi Xin (2003) The Relation Between Inward FDI and China's Regional Economic Growth.
19. Gorden Newlove Asamoah(2003) The Impact of Financial Sector Reform on Saving, Investment and Growth of Gross Domestic Product in Ghana.
20. Charles Godfred Ackah (2003) Financial Development and Economic Growth: the Case of Ghana.
21. Zhou Li (2003) Capital Flow and Economic Growth in China.
22. Emmanuel Okyere (2003) Financing Economic Development with Special Reference to Ghana.
23. Issac K. Nyamekye (2003) Transmission mechanism of monetary policy with Special.
24. Pei Pei Goh (2002) The 1997 Asian Financial Crisis: Its Impact, Causes and Lessons.
25. Roland Yawo Getor (2002) Contribution of Human Capital to Economic Growth: A Panel Evidence.
26. Patricia Pinamang Acheampong (2002) Does Inflation Promote Economic Growth?: Evidence from Ghana.
27. Xiangfeng Li (2002) Impact of Devaluation on Chinas Trade with the US: Is There Any Evidence of J-Curve?
28. Farrukh Sajjad (2002) Evaluation of Tax Reform Using an Applied Multisectoral General Equilibrium Model for Pakistan.
29. Jeniffer Nalugonda (2002) The Trade-off Between Inflation and Unemployment: Evidence from the UK.
30. Mark Kojo Armah (2001) The Impact of Exchange Rate in the Balance of Payment in Ghana.
31. Joseph Roseveare Mills-Dadson (2001) The Effect of Monetary Policy in Output in Ghana.
32. Benjamin Tettey Dabrah(2000) The Effect of Exchange Rate Changes in Ghana.

Independent Study 2006

Name of student	Topics for independent study
1. Ali, Ayesha	Temporary and Permanent income and consumption
2. Atabekyan Honhannes	Unemployment problem under the Blair Government
3. Chen, Xueting	Fund management in China
4. Cheung, Ming Kei	Oil prices
5. Clara Ohakim	Pension funds in Nigeria and KPMG
6. Craig, Smith	Economic growth in European countries
7. Daniel Christle	Labour market reforms in Great Britain
8. Huang, Jue	Unemployment and inflation by UK regions
9. Katrin Bonger	Unemployment among lone parents in UK
10. Ling, Bradley	Poverty trap and distribution of assets in UK
11. Lynn Pfetzing	Youth unemployment in Great Britain
12. Mok, Wai	Minimum wages

13.	Neal, John	Impact of oil prices in transportation
14.	Olagbaju, Ropo	Mass merger in Nigerian commercial banks
15.	Pacey, William	Congetion in Transport networks
16.	Runnall, Christine	Fair trade
17.	Wang, Lu	Impact of exchange rate policy in Chinese economy
18.	Wang, Tao	Export similarity index
19.	Xin, Yifei	Exchange rate and trade in China

Independent Study 2005

1.	Neil Atherton		Rise of of internet firm and Interest rate: case study of Dixon
2.	Craig	Barlow	Natural rate of unemployment in UK and China
3.	James	Dutton	Economic growth in Ireland and UK
4.	Miroslav	Halamka	Flat tax
5.	Benjamin	Hardie	Economic Development: North-South divide and trends
6.	Richard	Hepworth	Are wages currently enjoyed by today's footballers sustainable in the long run?
7.	Nicholas	Holland	Life cycle model and labour supply
8.	Mayowa	Koku	Oil price and OPEC
9.	Lu	Jin	Foreign direct investment and growth in China
10.	James	Killerby	House price fluctuations
11.	David	Land	Top- up tuition fees
12.	Craig	MacBeath	Benefit system: incapacity benefits
13.	Evangeline	Karanja	Is free education Kenya leading to development?
14.	Idu	Onumonu	Effect of national debt on developing economies
15.	Claire	Pack	oil or house prices
16.	Sarah	Purdom	Should the UK join the EU by 2010?
17.	Rui	Qiu	How the oil price affects the Chinese economy?
18.	Jonothan	Spencer	Why does poverty still exists in 21st century Britain?
19.	Suet	To	Benefit of CEPA agreement to Hong Kong economy
20.	James	Verdegem	Oil prices, are we paying too much?
21.	Yu	Wang	Export in China, or impact Disney in HK
22.	Kristian	Wawryka	Economic determinants of foreign aid
23.	Hubert	Wirkus	Internal and external consequences of the US budget deficit
24.	Ye	Zhang	Economics of Spam
25.	Yuxiang	Zhang	Appreciation of RMB: lessons and consequences
26.	Charles	Jeffery	Ethanol: future source of energy
27.	Heather	Roberts	Is park and ride better than congestion charges?
28.	Christopher	Morris	Case for appropriate toll on M6
29.	Bo	Hu	Success or failure of privatization of railways in UK
30.	Svapna	Narayandas	Employment effect of IT sector in India

31. Thi Nguyen Has taxes on cigarettes reduces its consumption and related diseases?
32. Ting Xie Influence of China's exchange rate devaluation
33. Alex Murtgatroyd Football ticket prices-a look at supply and demand price and price discrimination
34. Daniel Russell Phillips curve, inflation and unemployment
35. Ka Ngan The impact of the increasing oil price on the UK economy
36. Zhi Qi Market analysis of the coal industry
37. Joseph Johnson Economic problem of developing countries
38. Hao Zhang China and WTO
39. Cheng Yi Merger and acquisition
40. Lu Lei Merger and acquisition
41. Steven Mulligan M & A: Halifax and Bank of Scotland
42. Eugenio Cruz Oil industry - the potential for west Aprican oil

Independent Study 2004

1. Fan Sheng Nie The market segmentation in China's stock market
2. Habblett Vikki Pension crises in the UK
3. Chen Jing Non-performing loans in China's financial markets: Reforms of ICBC?
4. Baeumol Christoph The Impact of Basel agreement in the allocation of credit
5. Gerstner David Comparative study of Privatisation of Railways in Germany and the UK •
6. Song Duan Duan Assessing whether foreign investment in Chinese Auto Industry is a good investment opportunity and with a profitable future
7. Cosette Pncet Why Economics Policy works better in UK than in France ?
8. Roth Daniela Comparison of the monetary policy of the ECB and the Bank of England and compare their
9. Riley Suzanne Retirement age and unemployment among youth in the UK
10. Dunning Thomas Is China's fast rate of economic growth sustainable in the next few years ?
11. Schmitz Annette How does the Iraq War affect the British Economy and which companies benefit from it?
12. Wang Simin Determinants of student accommodation rents in Hull , investigation of the hypothesis of university bias
13. Flintham Garry Impact of new technology in production and supply
14. Qian Jing Tax rates in UK wage earners and their labour supply
15. Wang Xin How can UK keep low unemployment rate compared to France and Germany?
16. Norton Laurie Impact of Steel Industry in Maritime Industry
17. Smith Peter How the budget deficit affected the UK economy in last 20 years?
18. Li Zhen What are the impacts of tax reform in China?

19. Irwan HJ Rashid Mohammad Kwon Diversification problem faced by oil exporting countries
20. Hashin Mohammad Is competition necessarily beneficial to consumers?
21. Sharma Adrian Examination of potential economic and financial effects a ban on smoking in all public places in the city of Hull
22. Shaw DaniaL How has the capital intensive technology affected the social welfare in South Korea?
23. Swiecka Diana Is electrical money going to replace traditional methods of payment?
24. Wang Xin How can UK keep low unemployment rate compared to France and Germany?
25. Yif Lau Gin How the policy taken by the Chinese government affect allocation of growth fund?
26. Yuxin Yang Toll for cars in the Shenda the highway between Shenngyang to Daliang in China
27. Sethi Sumit Will China be the biggest economy by 2020?
28. Li Jayne Ka Yee Consequences of fluctuations in oil price in 2004 in the US
29. Kelvin Lau Effect of Increase in the oil price on the future of Chinese and the US economy
30. Akhtar Sumera Binte An appraisal of the code of corporate governance in Pakistan
31. Chung Wantai How does "closer economic partnership agreement (CEPA) affect economy of Hong Kong and China?
32. Yang Xiao Evaluation of effects of tariff in Chinese auto industry
33. Ji Shi Xiong The relationship between Chinese exchange rate and international trade
34. Heath David Effects upon revenue of Newcastle United after not qualifying for the Champions' League
35. Cheng Vivienne Lai Chen How innovation influences and is influenced by market structures?
36. Wang Yu Tong Impact of China's accession to WTO?
37. Litherland Ross Merit goods, sea defence in UK
38. Shen Jie Study of profits of HSBC bank
39. Shen Jie Unemployment in the UK
40. Wong Benjamin Effect of migrant labour on unemployment in the UK
41. Munnings Christopher Is the Humber Bridge toll set at appropriate level or should there be toll at all?
42. Anderson Henric Which queue to choose? A Productivity study of Supermarket Operators
43. Beaton Thomas Coastal protection in Hull: a cost benefit analysis
44. Chen Jiahe Role of International Trade in Economic Growth of Japan and the UK

45.	Graham	Rebecca Comparing the actual versus expected growth rate in the UK?
46.	Lau	John How should the NHS services be financed? Should some of it be privatised?
47.	Ling	Deng Analysis of risks and returns in the financial market
48.	Little	Rhys Comparison of economic effects of Gulf War II with Gulf War I in 1991
49.	Markwick	Andrew How much of an effect do higher tax rates have on emigration in the UK?
50.	Munton	John Assessment of foreign direct investment in developing countries
51.	Nguyen	Thung Linh Is junk food tax a solution to the obesity problem?
52.	Ogundepe Altise Aridegbe	Small business failure in developing countries:a focus on Nigeria
53.	Qian	Jing Tax rates in UK wage earners and their labour supply

Undergraduate Dissertations (2006/07)

Johnson JA	Effect of globalisation in Africa: case of Nigeria
Yumi S	Welfare and efficiency effects of trade negotiations
Oronsaye S	National economic empowerment strategy: Nigeria
Hibbert LB	Euro and UK: problems and prospects
Scott E	Coffee and Pub goods: income and substitution effect
Spavin J	Negative externality and economic policy: UK
Stephenson TA	Impact of sports in local and national economy
Veldhoven GL	Substitution and income effects: demand analysis
Betts CL	Determinants of FDI in Premiership clubs
Thomas LW	Role of football industry in UK economy
Kwarteng N	Role of human capital in economic growth: Japan
Griffith EH	Impact of taxes in UK economy
Reynolds P	Oil price, inflation and UK economy
Jack, Skofic	Investment decisions in sport clubs
Busari RA	Analysis on Nigerian stock market

Undergraduate Dissertations (2005/06)

Student Name	Topic of dissertation
Ferguson N	Pollution: global approach – Game theory
Carswell D	USAID: modalities and conditionalities
Foster O	Growth in China: growth model
Faulkner K	Smoking ban in pubs and business: public policy-Survey
Ford C	Reasons for Crime
Wilkinson G	Bilateral, multi-lateral and NGO aid-tied/ distributional impacts on poor
Munton J	Impacts of natural disasters such as Katrina and Tsunami

Azmat S	Economic Growth
Pickering R	Morgages-its modalities, short vs. long run
Browne D	Privatisation in Nigeria: its economic impacts
Anugwon N	Debt relief and market competition in developing economies
Ismail O	Transferability of economic policies from advanced to developing economies

Undergraduate Dissertations (2004/05)

Student Name	**Title**
Chan K	Impact of SARS in Hong Kong and Chinese Economy
Cheng L	Contribution of Economic Reform in China
Clerkin R	Minimum Wage And Economic Development
Beaumont N	Economic and Environmental Cost Facing a multinational company producing a global product
Lincoln D	Empirical Study into the Determinants of House Prices
Padam A	Economic Growth in China
Price L	Impact of Intervention of Community Pharmacist on Cost of Prescription of Medicine by GPs
Sanusi A	Debt Growth in Nigeria: Causes and Consequences
Sanusi T	Impact of Deregulation in Nigerian Oil Sector
Scully P	Rise in the Oil Prices and Growth of Economically Less Developed Economies
Upright S	Trade War Between European Union and the United States
Xiaosong Luan	What can China get from the WTO?
Yang H	Role of International Investment in China's Economic Development
Young A	Sustainable Consumption Patterns by Europeans in 21st Century

Undergraduate Dissertations (2003/04)

Student	Title of Dissertation
Gemma Allenby	Gender Inequality in Wage Rates
Nocola Leivers	Evaluation of Labour Government Policy
David Hogan	Consequences of Migration
Mathew Corricelli	Convergence across the Globe
Michael Mee	Macroeconomic Impacts of Copper Prices
David Cole	Analysis of Convergence
Maxilian Dahan	Impacts of Enron Scandal: Rational expectation
Gaa Wing Lok	Trade and Growth
Shailesh Patel	Impacts of legalising the cannabis
Francis Stone	Analysis of recession using new Keynesian model

Kedar Bhattarai in Kathmandu: Conflict and growth in Nepal

ACKNOWLEDGEMENTS FOR PART II

I had formally defended this dissertation on March 26, 1996, one week before I started a research position in the University of Warwick in the United Kingdom. The thesis was accepted and I was advised to submit it after some redrafting for the purpose of clarity in exposition. In the process of adjusting to a new place and to a new position even minor re-drafting remained on pending for some time. Meanwhile three out of four members of my dissertation committee left the economics department of Northeastern at the end of Spring quarter of 1996 which made communication with them virtually impossible. This prolonged my graduation.

I owe much to Professor John Whalley of the University of Western Ontario in Canada and University of Warwick in the UK for accepting the role of the primary reader and providing me valuable time and guidance in finishing up this dissertation when the costs of meeting my former committee members became prohibitive. I am equally grateful to Professor John Adams, the Chair, for re-organizing my committee and encouraging me to submit the final draft as quickly as possible. His long-standing research interest in the economies of South Asia has been of great help during my study period at Northeastern.

I received very important help from Professor Thomas F. Rutherford of the University of Colorado, Boulder in the process of programming and implementation the model. He introduced me first to Professor Michael Ferris of the University of Wisconsin who provided hints at various point of time including an access to a Sun-computing system in the University of Wisconsin used to run many model simulations and then to Professor John Whalley with whom I am learning many professional skills on using applied general equilibrium technique for economic policy analysis in a real world situation.

Professor Bruce Bolnick played a very important role as the chair of the dissertation committee until the summer of 1996. I met him in the beginning of Fall 1994 and expressed my idea of incorporating the financial sector in a forward looking CGE model. He encouraged me to accept the challenge of developing a new framework of analysis beyond what could be found from a detailed review of the literature in this area. I am thankful to him for the part he played and for permitting me to be in touch with Professor Rutherford and for all instructions though he opted to be a "virtual member" of the committee when he left for Malawi in October 1996. Before leaving to the University of Pennsylvania Professor Stephen Parente had helped me on the dynamics of the model though he was very skeptical of the large-scale CGE approach.

My interest in developing a good model for policy analysis was born when I was writing an M.A. thesis at the Institute of Social Studies, the Hague, the Netherlands during 1989-90. Then I had an opportunity of external guidance from Chris Elbers at the Free University Amsterdam, who, for his Ph.D., was then working on a theory of spatial disaggregation in general equilibrium models with an application to the Nepalese economy. In the winter 1993 Professor Jonathan Haughton referred me to Professor Shanta Devarajan and Jeffrey Lewis both of whom redirected me to Timothy Buehrer, then at the Harvard Institute of International Development, who had closely worked with Philipo de Mauro and Maxwell Stamp at the Asian Development Bank, Manila, in developing a Computable General Equilibrium (CGE) model of Nepal. Buehrer provided me the ADB model and explained some of its applications.

Initially I started implementing the model with application to various labor market issues such as migration, underemployment and human resource development, and interrelationship between the Indian and Nepalese labor markets. Then I realized that for a developing economy such as Nepal, capital rather than labor is the most important binding constraint of long-rung growth and development. I thought the construction of a fully specified dynamic equilibrium model was important to experiment various economic policies in a model economy in place of a sequence of single-period temporary equilibrium model as used in the ADB model.

I would like to express my gratitude to the Department of Economics, Northeastern University which provided me time and financial support, without which it would have been impossible for a person coming from Batase, Jamune, a remote hill town in Tanahun district in central Nepal, to do this dissertation.

My thanks also are due to Delfin S. Go, at the World Bank, and C.K.Keuschenigg, who provided me with their latest research papers on the topic and IRIS and Federal Reserve Bank of Minneapolis for sending some working papers.

Special thanks to my brother Bishnu Hari Bhattarai in Kathmandu, for painfully collecting various information on the Nepalese economy and sending it to me. Love from my mother is source of my inspiration. I appreciate Prem, my wife, who was not supported to come out of tradition for her formal education but who enjoyed helping me all the time. Last but not the least, I appreciate the patience of my daughter, Manorama, and my son, Santosh, who were getting little attention from me during my study period. Much of my time was spent doing research while they were going through their elementary education. I am indebted to all other people who helped at various stages of this dissertation.

Despite all these acknowledgments for various supports for this dissertation, all errors and omissions are my sole responsibility.

PART - II

A DYNAMIC COMPUTABLE GENERAL EQUILIBRIUM MODEL OF THE NEPALESE ECONMY AND ITS APPLICATION

Financial Deepening and Economic Development in Nepal: A Forward Looking CGE Model with Financial Intermediation

5

INTRODUCTION

Contributing to economic development by liberalizing financial markets has been a central theme in policy debate world-wide over the last decade. The major argument advanced in this dissertation is that financial sector reforms in Nepal have released extra resources for investment by improving efficiency in resource allocation, and increased the volume of savings available for productive investment as spending was cut on unproductive assets to meet unseen contingencies in the future. Hence, financial sector liberalization is an important component of overall reform. It also argues that the Nepalese reform process has redistributed income from urban to rural households. Financial liberalization has increased the demand for rural labor to complement added capital stocks in rural-labor intensive sectors. Wage rates for rural labor increase more than that of the urban labor, leading to an increase in their welfare.

Financial sector reforms have their main impacts on the volumes of saving and investment. However, economic theory alone cannot determine the magnitudes of changes in the volume of savings and investment concomitant to such reforms. Whether the volume of saving increases with financial liberalization or not, depends upon whether the income effect from a change in the rate of interest dominates the substitution effect. Saving will increase only if the substitution effect is stronger than the income effect. Thus the effect of financial sector reform on saving is ambiguous. Similarly, financial sector reform is often characterized by an increase in the real interest rate. Standard theory states that when the cost of investment funds increases, the amount of investment is likely to fall. The net effect of the reforms on investment, then, depends upon whether the reallocation of capital after the liberalization can compensate for the effect of an increase in the cost of funds after liberalization.

In Nepal the financial reform process started in mid 1980s and took major shape in 1992 under a new government. Before the 1992 reforms, the Nepalese financial sector was characterized by ceilings on interest rates, credit controls, high reserve requirement, tight regulations on entry and exit of financial institutions, controls on foreign exchange, uncontrolled budgetary deficits and underdeveloped capital markets. The financial repression from all these features resulted in higher transaction costs for borrowers, and often negative rates of interest for savers. High subsidies on credits to selected sectors coexisted with higher interest rates for other sectors. The distortionary effects of repression were wide ranging. Though the reform measures have removed many of the distortionary elements involved debate on efficiency and redistribution effects of further reforms continues.

Prior to liberalization, funds were over-invested in subsidized sectors, while many other sectors remained under-funded. Has reform made the difference? This again is an empirical question. Another debatable issue concerns the welfare effects of financial sector reforms and whether they are positive. If welfare improves, by how much? Is the gain in welfare from reform distributed equally among consumers located in rural and urban areas? It is commonly perceived that urban consumers benefit more from liberalization than rural consumers, as the former have more access to the financial institutions than the later. Is it true? These and several other questions are answered in the thesis.

I consider the economy-wide long-run consequences of financial sector liberalization using a forward-looking multi-sectoral computable general equilibrium (CGE) model of the Nepalese economy with financial intermediation. The model is used to investigate efficiency, redistribution and welfare effects of financial sector reform as the economy evolves. In the model consumers are located in urban and rural areas. Their decisions between saving and consumption are studied under life-cycle behavior. There are 11 producers of goods and services. Investors' decisions regarding the allocation of the capital stock reflect inter-temporal profit maximization. They sell products both in domestic and foreign markets. The government collects revenues from taxes on income, consumption and international trade and spends all of these revenues. The laws of motion of capital and exogenous growth rate of the population determine the growth path of the economy.

The model is applied to study the effects of partial and complete economy wide reforms, as well as piecemeal reforms. A partial reform refers to a 50 percent reduction in the distortionary cost of financial transactions after the reform, while a complete liberalization means the elimination of all distortions across all sectors. Piecemeal liberalization is sector specific.

The major conclusions from the model analyses are the following:

1. By equalizing rates of return across sectors, liberalization insures efficiency in the allocation of resources. Efficiency in resource allocation increases the capital usage in sectors that were more repressed before liberalization. It causes a reduction, or slower growth, of capital use in sectors that used to be subsidized before repression. Ultimately all sectors return to their output and capital use levels on a steady state growth. The expansion in the capital stock allows production to expand accordingly. Output expansion is greater in sectors that were repressed heavily before the liberalization.

2. The benefits of liberalization accrue more to the rural households than to the urban households. Following liberalization rural labor intensive sectors invest more with increased access to financial institutions. More labor is required to complement additional capital. Demand for unskilled labor increases faster than the demand for skilled labor. This means increases in wage rates of rural labor is greater than the increases in the wages rates of the rural labor. Consequently welfare gains of rural households are larger in comparison to the welfare gains of urban households. In this sense, liberalization redistributes income from urban to rural households. The redistribution of welfare occurs by increasing wages of unskilled labor in comparison to the wages of skilled labor.

OBJECTIVES AND SCOPE OF ANALYSIS

The world-wide emphasis on deregulation of financial institutions, privatization of public enterprises and liberalization of economies for the efficient allocation of resources has shifted the attention of policy makers to issues of long-run growth from the issues of stabilization and short-run adjustment (World Bank 1996). Similarly academic economists have tilted their research to develop tools appropriate for analysis of long-run growth rather than for an analysis of stabilization and cyclical adjustment in the short run (Barro and Sala-i-Martin 1995: 9-13). While the development of growth literature in the mainstream macroeconomics during the last decade has been encouraging (Prescott 1986, Sargent 1987, Lucas 1988, Stokey and Lucas 1989, Blanchard and Fisher 1990, Mankiw and Romer 1993, Parente 1994, Parente and Prescott 1993 and 1994), application of these models in policy analysis has not been fully successful owing to the limited institutional structures and scant sectoral details in these models (Leeper and Sims, NBER 1994:81-139). Applied general equilibrium analysis with more disaggregated institutional and sectoral structures started in mid the 1970s (Shoven and Whalley (1973, 1984, 1992), Robinson (1989), Mercenier and Srinivasan (1995)). I find none of the previous studies were applied to study the multi-sectoral impact of financial sector liberalization in a forward-looking modeling framework. The mushrooming new macro models are not adequate to provide satisfactory answers to questions relating to inter-temporal and inter-sectoral interaction resulting from decisions of various economic agents in a realistically disaggregated economy.

The major goal of this dissertation is to analyze the growth, welfare and distribution impacts of financial liberalization policies in Nepal within a framework of a forward-looking multisectoral general equilibrium model. Model will be applied to study the distribution of income among households and inter-sectoral and intrasectoral variation in output, employment and prices following a complete or partial liberalization. I believe that the ability of model to track prices and quantities of a multi-period character in a well decentralized setting, helps one to construct time-consistent policy proposal for an economy.

FINANCIAL SECTOR REFORMS IN NEPAL

The economic liberalization project started during 1992[1] represents a breakthrough towards consistent economic policy-making in Nepal. This was a reform package that included various reforms: on fiscal management, on external trade, on the financial system, on tax system, on industrial policy, privatization of public enterprises, and on institutional and legal frameworks. All these reforms were basically intended to increase the role of market forces in determining the allocation of resources in the economy. Therefore, the reform of the financial system and development of the capital market for more efficient mobilization of domestic resources received a high priority in the package. The reform program was under the initiative of the Eighth Plan (1992-97) prepared by the National Planning Commission and Extended Structural Adjustment Facility of International Monetary Fund (IMF 1992, Dixit 1995a, EIU quarterly report IV 1995, ES, MOF 1995). The political support received by the project was unique[2]. The Nepali Congress (NC) government that came in power after the restoration of democracy in 1991 had a strong political will to reform policy that would create a right background for the long run development of the economy. Development of the financial sector accompanied with a complete liberalization of trade, fiscal reforms and institutional development, was considered a key to the economic reform.

Four factors contributed the initiation of reform: economic compulsion, political will, bureaucratic commitment, and technical know-how (Dixit (1995)). Economic liberalization in Nepal was a compulsion when India started liberalizing its economy in early 1990s. With a long open border to India Nepal did not have a choice. Nepal had to stay in close relation with Indian policies to maintain export competitiveness, to prevent the flight of capital, and to check the flow of unrecorded trade.

There was a strong political will for reform. Leaders were trying to pursue their vision about more prosperous economy and a better society. They were inclined to turn their ideals into objectives and making political effort in order to achieve those objectives. This is reflected in Koirala government's commitment to a sustained economic reform, though his government was defeated in a no-confidence motion in the parliament before this commitment could be translated into a reality.

A group of bureaucrats (Dixit 1995b p. 7) in three super ministries (NPC, NBR, and MOF) were strong advocates of reform though line ministries were hesitant to liberalize their own sectors. The government was able to receive technical know-how of the reform process through the Policy Dialogue Committee constituted under the economic liberalization project[3].

The initial steps taken by the Koirala government in process of policy reform were encouraging. By conventional standards Nepal came a long way during the period 1992 to 1994 in its drive to attain a private sector led competitive market economy.

Nevertheless, there is a long debate in the literature regarding the impact of liberalization in the economy (McKinnon 1973, Shaw 1973, Van Wijnbergen

1982,Taylor 1983, Turtleboom 1991, King and Levine 1993, Pagano 1993, Fry 1995). Nepal cannot be exception. Debate on who gains and who looses in the process of reform intensified and it had major political consequences. The major ones are the defeat of Koirala's government in a no-confidence vote in July 1994 followed by a hung parliament in the general election of November 1994, a six month old minority government under CPN-UML in 1994-95 that called for a general election in a year by dissolving parliament, NC-RPP-NSP coalition since September 1995 after the Supreme Court decreed unconstitutionality of dissolving of parliament. While election manifestos of all major parties promised reforms for a better course for development of the economy and a higher living standard of the common people, the question of division of benefits of liberalization is the major underlying cause of conflict of interest among people and policy makers.

The major argument of this dissertation is that many of the conflicts, mainly related to allocation of resources in the economy, may be resolved if the financial system is allowed to operate in a more competitive environment which delivers resources to an industry according to its productivity and allows optimization of preferences of consumers, producers and distributors with a due consideration of constraints in the economy. It requires an analysis of the functioning of various parts of the economy and a well formulated general equilibrium model can be the right tool for such analysis.

ORGANIZATION OF THE DISSERTATION

Chapter two provides background information on the process of reforms and structures of financial sector in Nepal. A brief review of previous modeling efforts highlights the need for a CGE model of the Nepalese economy in studying wide-ranging impacts of the financial reforms. The general body of modeling literature that shows a link between the financial system and the rest of the economy is reviewed for further references. Chapter three builds on this background information and presents details of a forward-looking CGE model of Nepal suitable for the analysis of financial reforms. It specifies intertemporal problems of consumers, investors and producers subject to relevant constraints over the model horizon. It relates demand and supplies of financial assets resulting from savings of households, investments by firms, government budgets and balance of payments. It defines competitive equilibria and welfare indices in the model economy. Chapter four then describes the organization of data in the form of a social and financial accounting matrix, the calibration of model parameters and elasticities of production, consumption and trade functions. The model is used to analyze the impacts of financial liberalization on the welfare of households, wages of skilled and unskilled workers, rental rates of capital and indices of capital stock and output growth across sectors under various model scenarios in chapter five. Finally, chapter six presents conclusions and an overall summary of this study, and outlines applications and extensions of the basic model for analysis of various other policy issues in the model economy.

NOTES

1. My discussion of economic reform process draw on Dixit's two papers and economic survey 1995, and the Eighth Plan of the National Planning Commission of Nepal.
2. The USAID, World Bank and IMF were involved at various stages in preparation of the liberalization program (see World Bank 1994, IMF 1992 and 1993,Dixit 1995).
3. The Policy Dialogue Committee(PDC) and Business Dialogue Committee (BDC) were two executive committees of economic liberalization project. PDC chaired by a NPC member consisted of secretaries of Finance, Industry, and Commerce Ministries, the Governor of NBR , a representative from BDC and USAID as the members. The BDC was chaired by the Federation of Nepalese Chambers of Commerce and other commodity groups, USAID and PDC.

6

REFORMS AND MODELING OF NEPAL'S FINANCIAL SECTOR

In theory, every reform is worthwhile when gainers can compensate the losers, while it is not so obvious in practice. As I mentioned, in the previous chapter in Nepal's case, the distribution of benefits of reform among the households has been the key underlying reason of the debate for and against financial reform.

In general discussion the success of financial reforms is often measured in terms of numbers of financial institutions, the cost of funds, the volume of savings and investment, assets and liabilities and freedom of financial institutions on the allocation of credits. All these measures are used to ascertain the degree of competition in the financial system freedom before and after the liberalization. General equilibrium analysis goes one step further and quantifies the benefits in terms of changes in welfare of households after liberalization. Welfare is a comprehensive indicator and reflects impacts of such reforms through changes in prices and quantities in goods and factor markets of the economy.

In this chapter I will begin with an assessment of success of financial sector reform in terms of traditional indicators, mentioning that none of the previous modeling exercise on the Nepalese economy focused on financial sector reforms. I refer to a number of either theoretical and empirical models that have tried to incorporate the financial sector in inter-temporal and the general equilibrium framework. Finally, I give a brief account of Nepal's financial system. All discussion in this chapter serve as a background for the discussion of a forward-looking CGE model in the next chapter.

TRADITIONAL INDICATORS ON EARLY IMPACTS OF FINANCIAL SECTOR REFORMS

Financial reform measures are designed to increase the volume of saving and investment over the years. Turtleboom (1991) presents several steps in a sequence of liberalization: restore macro economic equilibrium and restructure or liquidate insolvent financial institutions; introduce indirect instrument of monetary controls with freely determined interest rates, such as treasury bills sold at auction. They ask establish supervisory guidelines regarding loan classification, provisioning for bad debt, interest rate capitalization, capital adequate, and limits on portfolio concentration; increase competition by granting more bank licenses, permitting the entrance of foreign banks, and privatizing government owned banks; and remove interest rate controls and direct credit ceilings.

Repression contains several elements: restriction on entry into banking, often combined with public ownership of major banks; a high reserve requirement on deposits; legal ceilings on bank lending and bank rates; quantitative restriction on allocation of credits; and, restriction on capital transaction with foreigners. Restricted entry into the financial system allows financial institutions to extract monopoly rents. A high reserve requirement permits resources to be transferred to the government. The ceiling on interest rates diverts funds from formal to informal financial institutions or cause capital flight.

Economists have realized that there are preconditions for these financial reforms to become successful. Specifically these conditions are counted as (Montiel 1995:9): the existence of an appropriate legal framework, including well-established property rights and an efficient judicial system; the existence of a financial safety net to avoid liquidity crises; an adequate regulatory framework to prevent collusion and avoid excessive risk taking due to moral hazard; the existence of a potentially successful borrowing class, and fiscal adjustments to the revenue previously lost from repression.

In Nepal, the reform package contained seven measures for the development of the financial system: (1) ease entry restrictions, (2) deregulated interest rates (3) reduce statutory liquidity ratio (4) Finance Company Act 1992 (5) Security Exchange Act 1992 (6) security Exchange Board 1993 (7) Nepal Stock Exchange 1994. The financial reforms were accompanied by reforms in fiscal management, external trade, industrial policy and on institutional and legal frameworks along with emphasis on privatization of public enterprises. The lists policy issues, targets of reforms and problems in Table 2.3, show that the new government believed that the efficiency in the allocation of resources could be maintained in a competitive market economy with price stability and balance in the external sector.

The early impact of financial sector reforms initiated in 1992 were very encouraging. Regulations governing the entry of new financial institutions have been eased. Some specialized financial institutions, such as rural development banks, full-fledged stock exchange, finance and insurance companies started (Table 2.4 in the appendix of this chapter). Establishment of such institutions helped to deepen capital market activities and stock market activities (EIU, 1st Quarter, 1995).

The entry of eight new banks increased competition in process of financial intermediation, resulting in a greater competition in the banking system. Customer service at banking institutions improved considerably. Though the literature states the effect of financial liberalization on saving is ambiguous and many models based on constant relative risk aversion predict that an increase in the real rate of return on capital depresses present consumption in favor of future consumption (King and Levine 1993, Pagano 1993; Romer 1990) the financial reforms led to increase in deposits and lending considerably (section 2.4). From the experience of many developing economies that have adopted liberalization savings ultimately depend upon the intertemporal elasticity of substitution (Montiel 1995).

The deregulation of interest rate was complete by the end of 1993. Banks are now free to set their interest rate on their own. The competition among the financial institutions has lowered the interest rate to the borrowers. The average lending rate had fallen from 21 per cent in FY 1991/92 to 15 per cent in FY 1994/95 (Table 2.5 and 2.6). The spread between deposit and lending rates is declining (Table 2.5). The efficiency in allocation of financial resources has improved. The efficiency gain in 1995 was equal to a 6 per cent (EIU,1st Quarter, 1995).

It should, however, be noted that the structure of interest rates in the formal financial markets is complicated by the structure of assets and liabilities of the financial system. Financial intermediaries do not pay any interest on demand deposits. Interest rates vary among the savings and time deposits. Similarly loan rats vary according to industries and activities. Table 2.5 shows the structure of interest for the period after the financial institutions were free to set their interest rates.

The statutory liquidity ratio is eliminated. Government bonds are sold by means of auction and commercial banks are not compelled to invest on bonds. More credits are flowing to the private sector now than before (Table 2.7). A fourteen per cent reduction in the share of total credit flowing from the commercial banks to the government would not have been possible without the policies that increased freedom of the commercial banks. Financial development was further strengthened by the NC government's commitment on controlling deficit by not financing it through excessive money overdrafts (Economic Survey, 1994:89).

The supervision of the financial institutions has been strengthened further. The capital adequacy norms have been stiffened, loan recovery efforts stepped up, and loss making bank branches are permitted to close down. Provision for bad debts has improved. The privatization of the state owned banks has been initiated.

Foreign currency bank accounts are now permitted. Nepalese exporters can keep 100 per cent of hard-currency export earnings in their bank accounts. Foreign investors in Nepal can fully repatriate dividend and equity capital. Banks have been re-capitalized. Nepal gained Article VIII status under the IMF charter ensuring country's commitment to full convertibility of Nepalese Rs. on the current account. This means more liberalization on external trade. The capital account also has gradually being liberalized.

Liberal financial sector has helped privatization. Private sector activities in the airline, hydro-electricity and communications sectors have increased significantly. Control over the government deficit helped maintaining the stability of price level has been achieved though prices increased by 20 per cent in the 1991. In process of adjustment towards the realities of economy the newly elected government cut many subsidies of public enterprises supplying electricity, water, fertilizers, and consumer goods. Inflation leveled down to a single digit by the second year of reform.

Nepal Stock Exchange has begun to trade on primary and secondary financial assets. About 12 finance companies have been established after the liberalization to compete for the portfolio investment of the households. Since the opening of the Nepal Stock Exchange the volume of public issues have quadrupled from Rs. 53 to Rs. 243 millions , and the performance in FY 1993/94 alone was equivalent to the total amount of issues over the 13 years period governed by the Securities and Exchange Center. According to a report, the investors in the NSE belong to the middle income group, those with monthly income Rs. 5,000-10,000(IRIS, Rajbhandari 1994). Shares were over-subscribed, the average over-subscription was more than five-fold, and the average number of transactions has increased from 5 per day to 90 per day(Dixit 1995:12). Market capitalization has almost tripled.

Despite these encouraging result there are several problem underlying the Nepalese financial system. People have a small saving capacity because of low per capita incomes. There were very few policies to promote savings and productive investment in the economy in the last three decades.

Illiteracy is another major obstacle in developing banking habits. A person who does not know how to write, and uses a finger prints on the banking documents has to trust other people while making deposit and loan contracts. Poor communication facility hinders advertisement of services by the financial institutions. Inadequate transportation facilities create a physical barriers between banks and its customers. Bank transactions take a lot of time. The lack of power supply makes computerization and introduction of modern technology difficult. Flows of funds and information among banks and their branches is very slow.

Problems of adverse selection and moral hazard were present in the banking system in Nepal. The Credit Guarantee Commission would take care of delinquent loans. These problems raised the average lending rates and lowered the average deposit rates paid to depositors. Because of the asymmetric information Nepalese financial intermediaries are very conservative in lending activities. The importance of collateral for the security of a loan and the lengthy paper work prior of disbursement of loans reflects this conservatism.

In spite of early euphoria the capital market of Nepal is still at an early stage in Nepal. Only 79 companies have registered with the Nepal Stock Exchange. Shares of only a few companies, mainly financial institutions, are traded each day. Low volume of transaction in the stock market show that investors are not yet sensitive to the stock market. The volume of transactions is very low as reflected in the market capitalization of companies registered at NEC of Rs. 12, 960 (6.2 per cent of GDP) during the fiscal year 1994/95. This reflects the fact that companies traded in the stock market could not pay a reasonable dividends to the investors. The value of shares traded during 1995 was less than half of one per cent of GDP. There is no noticeable variation in the minimum and maximum values of the transaction as reflected in the NEPSE Index. The NEPSE Index is not yet sensitive to the shocks generated in financial markets all around the world. It is not surprising if one considers the inconvertibility in the capital account.

Lack of experience and inadequate information on the part of corporate management, bankers, debt and equity issuers, financial intermediaries, regulators and government official has led to a distorted capital market. Some companies traded on the stock exchange have not filed financial statement for the past two or three years or are un-audited and unreliable (Dixit 1995). Thus investors do not have more information than rumors and speculations. In addition, Nepal does not have a comprehensive securities and exchange act to insure disclosure obligations, takeovers and mergers and operation of debt instruments. Investors could be easily taken for a ride.

In the absence of political stability continuation of the reform of financial institutions will be very difficult. While the expansionary policy announced by CPN-UML government[1] that ruled for nine months was slightly inconsistent with its commitment for the development of a national capital market, and against reform measures taken by the previous NC government. The coalition government that followed the CPN-UML is fragile to take any firm stand on issues of financial reforms.

Modeling in the following chapter that studies transition from a financial repression to a free market regime incorporates these structural characteristics of Nepal's financial system.

MODELING FINANCIAL SECTOR

All traditional indicators of success of reforms and obstacles to reform are helpful in making qualitative statements about the benefits of reforms. A more thorough analysis requires more precision based on a detailed analysis of behavioral, technological and institutional framework of the economy. This is done using economic models. The section discusses the back-ground literature that I can use while constructing a general equilibrium model for analyzing the financial sector reforms in Nepal.

Modeling of Nepal's Financial Sector

Three categories of model can be found in the literature on Nepalese economy: a simple econometric model used by the government of Nepal, Chris Elbers' multi-regional model for the Nepalese economy and Asian Development Bank's model for Nepal.

A simple econometric model was used in the Eighth Plan (1992-97). From the modeling point, it was considered an improvement over the existing techniques of economic analysis in Nepal (NPC 1992). Earlier the planners used aggregate incremental capital output ratio in spirit of Harrod-Domar model to project resources required by the economy. Given the estimates for total resource requirements and projections of internal resource mobilization for a period under consideration, a resource gap could be projected for the economy which served as a basis to draw up additional measures for resource mobilization including the negotiations for foreign aid. Using time series data of past 20 years, separate functions for consumption, saving, production, investment, imports, exports, public expenditure, revenue and other variables were estimated based on simple OLS regression models (Khanal in ESCAP 1993). Outputs of these models are very unreliable due to incorrect specification of the model equations. It is not unnatural to find lagged values of dependent variable to produce significant R-square and significant coefficients. Time-series econometricians emphasize on stationarity and error corrections for robust analysis of time-series models. These corrections were not done in Nepal's econometric model. Moreover, this model is based on partial equilibrium analysis, and cannot capture the general equilibrium effect of policy actions designed to promote efficiency, growth and welfare over the period. Explicitly it does not consider any role of the financial sector.

Chris Elbers developed a multi-regional multi-sectoral model of Nepalese economy for his Ph. D. dissertation at the Free University of Amsterdam in 1992. This is an ambitious open economy model with seven production sectors and seven regions with transportation networks connecting the north-south regions of eastern, central and western parts of Nepal. It recognizes the optimization behavior of consumers and producers and thus is founded on more rational assumptions than existing model employed by the Planning Commission of Nepal; it derives demands for goods and services from the utility maximizing behavior of consumers. Similarly, supply functions are derived from the profit maximizing behaviors of producers. Budget constraints for consumers and suppliers are explicitly stated and the price mechanism brings equilibrium in the market. This model introduced behavioral analysis of economic agents in economic model of Nepalese economy. This model further opens up a possibility for analysis of different modes of transportation costs on resource allocation processes and their implications for intra-regional, inter-regional and foreign trade in the economy.

Elbers' model is more appropriate for analysis of regional development issues. My concern here is with efficiency and distribution impacts of financial sector liberalization over the period. His model inter-sectoral financial costs and distortionary wedges in a dynamic framework. Adding financial sector in intertemporal framework with a regional structure becomes unnecessarily complicated. Moreover, the enormous information required by the model makes it less applicable for the purpose of immediate policy analysis.

The Buehrer-Philippo (1993) model (ADB model hereafter) refines Maxwell Stamp's work on a general equilibrium model for Nepal prepared for the Asian Development Bank in April 1992. This model disaggregated the Nepalese economy to twelve activity and commodity sectors, three factors[2], two household types[3], two capital account[4], and two rest of the world[5] accounts. It is less ambitious than Elbers' model but more suitable to policy analysis at the macro level.

This model applies the small economy assumption to the Nepalese economy, with imports and exports to Indian and rest of the world markets. This model bring more sectors than in Elbers' model, specifically treatment of tourism, textiles, chemical and capital good sectors as separate sectors seems appropriate given the condition of Nepalese economy. Though more information on behavioral and technological parameters of the model might improve the results, this model can be used for immediate policy analysis even with the limited data available on the Nepalese economy. Calibration of model is based on the social accounting matrix (SAM) of 1990/91.

In this model consumers are assumed to purchase a mix of domestic and imported goods to maximize utility from consumption of imperfectly substitutable domestic and foreign goods. Income of households derives from factor income, transfers and remittances. The firms in the economy supply goods and services with combination of capital, labor, and intermediate inputs to maximize their profits. Likewise consumers and producers decide in the static framework.

A fixed loan or grants from the rest of the world are used to meet any shortfalls in government spending or public and private investment. Such an inflow of resources also balances foreign trade. The model is closed assuming investment to be equal to savings. Savings in turn is determined as a fixed share of household income in spirit standard Keynesian models. The exogenously fixed level of investment is funded by domestic and foreign savings. Foreign saving closes the gap between the gross investment and domestic savings. Part of factor income is paid to governments as taxes. Households consume or save their income. However, consumers' optimization problem is static, not inter-temporal. One cannot analyze the life-cycle hypothesis of consumers behavior in this model.

In the ADB model foreign exchange is also determined endogenously. In the prevailing situation of foreign exchange restrictions, this may be questionable. Similarly the model assumes two transformation functions for each tradable sector, which implies tradable goods are first exported to markets with convertible currency and an intermediate domestic use product. Then these tradable goods are transformed to goods exported to India or domestic output sold domestically. Similarly this model applies two-level nested functions for imports. This implies buyers first decide between domestic and Indian goods and then choose between using the resulting intermediate sale good and imports from the rest of the world. Considering the role of Indian economy, this specification of trade seems appropriate for the Nepalese economy.

Buehrer-Philippo found very small impacts of trade liberalization and implementation the of hydro-power projects in the economy. I argue that this was mainly due to lack of a well specified dynamic specification in their model. The ADB model has a updating dynamics to analyze the impact of policy changes in the economy. Though this is an improvement over the previous two types of models discussed above, lack of forward-looking behavior in this model makes it inappropriate to apply this model for studying long-run steady state behavior and the transitional dynamics of policy changes. Similarly this model does not contain explicit specification of the financial sector. Therefore it is not suitable for analyzing the effects of financial sector policies on aggregate economic activities.

To sum up, I find ADB model a very useful framework which can be improved further to look at multisectoral and inter-temporal analysis of financial sector policies in Nepal. A fully specified forward looking multi-sectoral model developed in this dissertation can be considered an addition to the literature on the Nepalese economy.

An Overview of Other Models with the Financial Sector

Since no model of Nepal addressed financial sector of Nepal directly it is pertinent to have some general idea on theoretical and empirical literature of other economies that explains a link between the financial sector and rest of the economy. For simplicity, I will categorize this discussion one sector models and multi-sectoral models.

Modeling Financial Sector in One Sector Framework

Analysis of the effects of financial development on economic growth depends essentially on the choice of a growth model. In a simple Harrod-Domar model with constant returns to capital, financial conditions influence the growth rate permanently, i.e., more saving translates to more investment and the ouput and incomes are linearly dependent on the volume of investment. McKinnon (1973:59) emphasizes the complementarity between money and physical capital. In his model firms self-finance a lumpy investment project, thus the demand for real money balances is based upon the total expenditure, ratio of investment to total expenditure and the positive rate of real interest. Shaw constructs a monetary model in which money is backed by productive investment loans to the private sector. The larger is the money stock in relation to the level of economic activity, the greater is the extent of financial intermediation between savers and investors through the banking system. Financial intermediaries raise real returns to savers and at the same time lower the real cost to investors by accommodating liquidity preferences, reducing risk through diversification, reaping economies of scale in lending, increasing operational efficiency, and lowering information costs (Fry 1995:28). As most of the investment projects are financed in part with own funds and in part with borrowings, the outside money the hypothesis of McKinnon and the insider-money hypotheses of Shaw are complementary.

In neoclassical growth models production functions are non-linear; diminishing returns to capital will drive the marginal product of capital to a steady state level. Sustained growth is possible if a productive factor, accumulates endogenously, and is not subject to diminishing returns. In the endogenous growth models, such as the A-K model, diminishing returns do not apply to capital, therefore, any improvement in financial sector policies will have a positive effect on economic growth (King and Levine 1993).

Dornbush and Reynoso (1989:2) express reservations about the role of financial liberalization in economic development. They say it is important only when financial instability becomes a dominant force in the economy. Like the foreign trade regime, it probably does not make much difference to the level of per capita GDP unless it is very distorted.

The endogenous growth model provide a new perspective on the role of financial intermediation on economic development. Pagano (1993) illustrates a very simple model in which a reduction in the cost of financial intermediation enhances the growth rate of an economy by reducing the cost of financial intermediation and yielding an increase in the amount of investment. The financial sector policies have level as well as growth effects. A very simple endogenous growth model with financial sector can be illustrated by means of following four equations.

$$Y_t = AK_t \tag{1}$$

$$I_t = K_{t+1} - (1-\delta)K_t \tag{2}$$

$$\phi S_t = I_t \tag{3}$$

$$g = A\frac{I}{Y} - \delta = A\phi s - \delta \tag{4}$$

Here Y is output, A is technology parameter, K is capital stock, I is investment, and S is savings. In the equation (4) g represents a steady state growth rate of the economy, which can be influenced by the proportion of saving funneled to investment, f, the social marginal productivity of capital, A and the private saving rate, s. This equation is derived by substituting (2) into (3), and then using $K_{t+1} = (1+g) K_t$, then by (1) substituting $K_t = Y_t/A_t$ to solve for g in (4).

The efficiency in the financial institutions reduces the wedge between the gross cost of borrowing and the net return on lending, ϕ. The comparative advantage of financial institutions in handling to information regarding the assets and liabilities of agents in financial markets enables them to attract funds from savers. They provide an efficient combination of expected return, risk, and liquidity by reaping economies of scale in financial transactions, information gathering, and portfolio management (Fry 1995:294-95).

At low income levels borrowers have little net worth. This raises monitoring costs and creates a large premium on the external finance necessary to compensate lenders for the cost of monitoring borrowers and enforcing the financial contracts. The high cost of funds raised externally will make external funds prohibitive, so self-finance and informal finance, linked to social relationships dominate in such circumstances. As income grows, borrowers' net worth grows, and legal institutions are strengthened. Reliance on external finance increases. As collateral is limited, substantial monitoring continues to be necessary; therefore commercial banks will be the dominant financial institution. At higher income levels, the net worth of borrowers supports arm's length transactions. Lower monitoring costs permit the emergence of securities markets.

The new economic growth literature highlights the information processing role of financial intermediaries. The endogenous growth models with learning by doing, or intergenerational trade in which a representative consumer, or consumers in overlapping generations are used to study the effect of credit availability. In these models consumers living for two or three periods maximize intertemporal utility with perfect foresight or by state-contingent behavioral rules.

Many of the one sector models that explain the growth effect of the financial sector use overlapping generation models or dynamic programming models (Blanchard and Fisher 1990, ch. 4, 5, 9, 11). Bencivenga and Smith (1991) use an endogenous growth model with overlapping generations and multiple assets to show the conditions under which financial intermediation is growth promoting. A few studies have been done on asymmetric information and its general equilibrium effects. Financial markets involve delivery in future and the future is always uncertain. Financial contracts could be written in terms of state-contingent Arrow-Debreu securities (Arrow 1953, Debreu 1959). Gimenez, Prescott, Fitzerald and Alvarex (1992) introduce an explicit banking sector that intermediates between households and the government sector and use the model to evaluate the welfare effects of alternative monetary arrangements and the effects and desirability of a procyclical interest policy in the U.S. economy. Households are forward-looking in their model. They found that a procyclical real rate of return on government debt neither stabilize the economy nor affects welfare significantly, while the welfare benefits that increase the after-tax real rate of return on household savings are very large.

Greenwood and Jovanovic (1990) explain the Goldsmith-Mackinnon-Shaw (Goldsmith 1969, Mckinnon 1973 and Shaw 1973) view by developing a model that explains endogenous determination between financial intermediation and the rate of economic growth. Greenwood and Jovanovic, and Bencivenga and Smith, show that financial markets reduce the fragmentation of the credit allocation process, permitting more productive use of available funds. These are basically one-sector models.

Cooley and Smith (1991) study saving behavior of agents living in three periods in overlapping generations, where young can labor or invest in human capital, middle aged agents can manage a firm if they have invested while young or supply labor, and old agents can only manage firms if they were educated while they were young. In the absence of financial instruments and a rental market in capital, all agents invest in education when young, work when middle aged, invest in capital, and operate a firm when old. There is no specialization. When financial markets exist, specialization is possible; young agents can invest in education, borrow to put capital in place and then operate a firm in both middle and old age. Agents repeat activities and learning by doing occurs. If financial markets fail, an economy becomes stuck in a low-growth equilibrium.

Azariadis and Smith (1993) investigate how an inflation tax aggravates problems in credit markets and impairs financial intermediation. They find that at moderate rates of inflation the Mundell-Tobin effect (Blanchard and Fisher, 1990 Ch. 10) applies and monetary equilibrium is determinate. Dynamic equilibria display monotone movements over time of output and inflation. At high rates of money creation, the inflation tax on bank deposits encourages households to disintermediate, tightens incentive constraints, and induces banks to ration credit to some borrowers. Credit rationing reverses the Mundell-Tobin effect in the steady state and equilibrium becomes indeterminate, which implies damped endogenous fluctuations in economic aggregates.

Schreft and Smith (1993) consider a monetary growth model along the lines of Diamond (1965) and Diamond and Dybvig (1983). With a government that issues illiquid interest-bearing bonds and liquid, non-interest bearing currency, sufficiently large money creation can generate two non-trivial steady-state equilibria. Banks in one equilibrium hold large amounts of government bonds relative to their holding of capital. Another steady state, with relatively low equilibrium interest rates and a relatively high capital stock, signals the efficient operation of the banking system.

Marcet and Marimon (1992) develop a stochastic growth model with alternative financing opportunities. Jones and Manuelli (1993) show the growth effect of money. Bruno (1993) shows the relationship between inflation and growth by taking account of various shift factors in aggregate demand and aggregate supply. Parente (1994) concludes that the technology adoption decisions of firms and the growth rate of per capita output depend on the efficiency of capital markets.

One sector models reviewed in this sub-section provide some important insights on modeling front but they are not enough to handle the issue that I am investigating. The májor challenge of this dissertation is to incorporate the forward looking dynamics contained in these one-sector models into a broader multi-sectoral and multi-institutional framework and investigate macroeconomic and sectoral impacts of financial liberalization.

Modeling Financial Sector in Multi-Sectoral Framework

The CGE framework is the most appropriate modeling technique for analyzing impacts of inter-sectoral variation in investment cost and effects of financial liberalization over the period. Though CGE modeling became a standard tool of policy analysis between mid 1970 and mid 1980s (Shoven and Whalley, 1984) none of the early CGE models explicitly addressed the efficiency and distribution impact of the financial sector reforms. The explicit general equilibrium modeling of the financial sector started with Tobin (1969), who found that equilibrium in the markets of stocks of assets was conditional upon the assumed values of outputs, incomes, and other flows resulting in a mutually consistent equilibrium of the financial and real sectors. Tobin's analysis was applied to the case of an advanced country. Although the importance of the financial sector's contribution on economic development in developing countries was emphasized by McKinnon and Shaw (1973) their analyses were mostly qualitative and descriptive. A number of applied general equilibrium models that incorporate a financial sector in a multisectoral framework came out in the mid 1980s to analyze structural adjustment in response to severe deficits in foreign capital inflows (Feltenstein 1986; Lewis 1985; Rosensweig and Taylor 1990; Fargeix and Sadoulet 1994). Stabilization programs involved containing the rate of inflation ,adjustment of the interest rates and exchange rates, creating a net inflow of foreign capital and increasing domestic saving in order to maintain an adequate level of investment. The inclusion of a financial sector in the standard real-side CGE was felt necessary. It is surprising that in spite of the emphasis on the financial sector, financial intermediation in an intertemporal framework was hard to build into these models. Formulating a multisectoral model in a dynamic framework was a much more involved task. Algorithms to solve these nested non-linear models were not readily available (Rutherford, 1995).

CGE models with endogenous relative prices and incomes increasingly appeared during 1970, were considered to be great improvements over the input-output or linear programming models of economy with fixed prices and fixed technological coefficients (Dervis, et. al. 1982). These studies did not address financial sector policy questions sufficiently (Robinson 1989, 1991, Shoven and Whalley 1984, Decaluwe and Martens 1988, Devarajan, Lewis and Robinson 1985). The work on CGE models in developed countries has focused on efficiency questions in the framework of neoclassical welfare analysis or so called "triangle counting". Work on developing countries has focused on structural issues relating to tax and trade policies (Robinson 1989). Including detailed microeconomic structures, these models sought to explain the impact of various policy interventions in goods and factor markets and to generate policies relating to fiscal, exchange rate and trade policies in a medium-run framework.

For dynamic analysis, the early CGE models relied on ad hoc updating procedures. Depending on closure rules for investment and saving, these models were either driven by savings if investments adjusted to a given level of savings, or driven by exogenously fixed investment if the deficiencies in saving were met by foreign saving or deficit financing. Over the period, the change in capital stock in the current period equaled either a fixed proportion of income saved or target investment. The new capital stock was then put into the model of the next period to reproduce output with a given technology of production (Dewatripont and Michel 1987). Given these closure rules, capital markets do not function independently. Several implausible labor market closure rules are applied. Some models fix wage rates, leaving unemployment to be determined endogenously. Moreover, inclusion of other important aspects of labor markets such as improvement in skills through education, migration is not possible. These labor market shortcomings have an important bearing on analysis of the financial system, considering the constant elasticity of substitution between labor and capital in these models' production functions.

The first financial sub-model in CGE models starts was Adelman and Robinson's (1978) introduction of markets for loanable funds and for currency that clear at the interest rate and the overall price level (Mercenier and Srinivasan 1994:149). They did not take account of the effect of overall price level on output and employment, nor the real balance effects. Inflation is a purely monetary phenomenon in their model.

The next attempt at a CGE model with a financial sector is Lewis' (1985) model for Turkey. Its focus is on the importance of rigidities in the labor, product, and credit markets in determining the adjustment to external shock. His model does not clearly distinguish between fiscal and monetary policies. The static framework is not very appropriate to study the growth effects of financial intermediation.

Lewis goes one step than the standard CGE models in assuming that wealth takes not only the form of capital stock. Saving may not be directly channeled into purchases of investment goods through a simple intermediation process as assumed in the neoclassical models. Alternatives for storing wealth exist. Wealth is kept in different assets according to the behavioral rules of the portfolio allocation process (Lewis, 1985:19).

Credit markets are segmented in developing countries (Fry 1995). This makes the borrowing rate a weighted average of subsidized and unsubsidized rates. Preferred borrowers have unlimited access to credit at regulated rates, but other borrowers obtain a large proportion of their funds at competitive rates or from unofficial "curb" markets. I modify this to include investment cost index. The cost of funds for the preferred priority sectors is lower and paid by charging higher rates of interest for other sectors.

In contrast to the short run focus in Lewis, I want to concentrate on the long-term function of real financial sector. My model excludes a money demand function and monetization of budgetary and foreign trade deficits. Savings by workers and capitalists are held as increments in financial wealth in form of bank deposits. These banks are in turn subject of monopolistic market structure.

The banking sector intermediates between savers and borrowers. This sector needs to fulfill two requirements in a competitive market. On asset side, the balance sheet of the banking sector, which is composed of total required reserves, subsidized and unsubsidized loans should be equal to the liability side that consists of time deposits, working capital balance of firms and foreign deposits. Second, interest receipts of the banking sector equal factor payments implying zero economic profit for the banking system. In financially repressed economies, the banking sector receipts will not equal payments.

Lewis argues that the banking sector's balance sheet requirement that total assets should equal to total liabilities is equivalent to saying that the total demand for and total supply of credit are being equal. This requirement is in fact, the same as the saving-investment closure in the real sector. This is generally not true in developing economies, particularly in the case of financial repression. Lewis' argument that, starting from any one side the other side can be derived by the Walras' Law, cannot capture the reality of developing economies. Similarly the assertion that the equilibrium real interest rate serves to mediate between supply and demand for capital in the real sector, and that the parallel changes in the real deposit and average borrowing rates serve to bring about stock equilibrium in the banking system, does not hold true in repressed regimes. People save a part of their real incomes. Then they allocate savings among competing assets based on their judgments regarding the returns on such assets. When banks collect deposits from people, they are able to invest in real capital and rent them to production firms. Financial paper is only for convenience in accounting. This is the major reason for our focus on the real side of the financial sector. The equilibrium in the banking sector is guaranteed by the wedge between the lending and deposit rates, which represents the cost of financial intermediation, thus satisfying the zero-profit condition of the banking system.

Another interesting CGE model with a financial sector is discussed by Feltenstein (1986). He considers a disaggregated open economy that is a price-taker for some goods and price-setter for others. An active government produces public goods and pays for its purchases from the tariffs and taxes (on incomes, profits, and sales) that it collects. To finance the deficit, the government issues a combination of bonds and money. Thus bonds, the money supply and the public indebtedness are endogenous to the model. His model includes foreign bonds and generates endogenous capital flows. His model answers several questions: What is the impact on the savings and consumption behavior of the economy if the government changes its output of pubic goods? How will a change in the government's method of financing its deficit change the overall balance of payments? How will a differential change in tax rates affect output and welfare levels through its direct impact on relative prices and What will be the impact upon the economy of an exogenous change in the world price of an imported good? Feltenstein applies his model to Argentina. From the long run point of view, inducing aggregate demand by adopting inflationary finance is not a responsible policy. Long-run policies that do not focus on improvement in the supply side are doomed to failure.

A more ambitious CGE with a financial sector appears in Taylor and Rosensweig (1990). This model applies to Thailand and has a more developed financial sector. The authors claim that this model has successfully solved real-financial general equilibrium relations and can deal with fiscal and monetary questions. There are eight market participants: households, traded and non-traded sector firms, state enterprises, government, central and commercial banks, and the rest of the world. They extend the conventional SAM for detailed financial bookkeeping by linking saving by different participants portfolio changes, producing a financial accounting matrix (FAM). Savings by households are allocated across in physical capital, currency holdings, net deposits with the commercial banks, government securities, and corporate shares. The real and financial sectors are linked by flows of funds and the interest rates on bank loans. Within-period savings flows add to asset and liability stocks to determine the end-of-period portfolio balances. In the long run, however, such complicated portfolio analysis is not very illuminating as there is enough time on the horizon to allocate savings until returns on stocks are equal in each sector.

The financial markets clear through price and quantity adjustment to flows of funds. Adding changes in financial stocks to initial asset and liability holdings so as to generates excess demand equations for end-of-period asset choices. Given the initial portfolio allocation by households, firms, government, banks, and the rest of the world, changes in portfolios during the period are affected by exchange rates and fiscal and monetary policies. This is a model with Keynesian spirit, with unemployment and fixed nominal wages. Expansionist fiscal and monetary policies induce very strong growth. Inflation does not have a detrimental effect on the real side of the economy. Predictions of this model do not match with reality. In reality, non-trivial inflation has detrimental effect on savings, investment and the inflow and outflow of capital (Roubini 1992, Gomme 1991, Monteil 1995).

Another contribution is Easterly (Taylor 1990:269-301) who shows that severe effects on investment will result from an overvalued exchange rate even when financial institutions are allowed to accept deposits in foreign exchange. Overvaluation leads to a current-account deficit and capital flight. He examines the effect of devaluation via real channels and the real level of financial shocks in a dollarized Mexican economy. The impact of a contraction of investment extends to the medium term because of the loss in physical capital formation. This will have to be made up later if the economy is to stay on its long-run growth path. The lesson is not to postpone devaluation. A timely devaluation will induce a portfolio shift away from dollar-dominated assets and reduce dollar external debt. This model shows the futility of systems that attempt to cure capital flight by making available foreign currency instruments in the domestic banking system.

In a special issue of *World Development* (1991) Bourguignon, Branson, and de Melo 1991 present an ad hoc dynamic model a "maquette", or a micro-macro economy- wide simulation model. This further refines the specification of a financial CGE by introducing imperfect adjustment of wages to inflation and expectation formation regarding inflation and devaluation, and allowing one to contrast the short-term and long- term impacts of alternative policies.

Microeconomic optimization in this CGE model is combined with the portfolio allocation according to Tobin (1969) so that growth and distribution are outcome of interaction between expected inflation, the rate of interest, balance of payment conditions, unemployment, the exchange rate, foreign borrowing, and foreign prices of exportable goods; and of endogenous micro variables such as sectoral relative prices and outputs, capacity utilization and changes in assets holdings by firms and households. The interaction among macro and micro variables depends on exogenous policy variables such as government expenditure, the stock of money, the monetization ratio of foreign borrowing by the private sector, nominal exchange rates, tax rates, foreign interest rates, import prices, expected exchange rates, and inflation. Similarly, initial conditions such as the initial level and distribution of liabilities and assets and structural parameters such as elasticities of demand and supply for goods, factors, and assets, determine income and growth.

Bourguignon *et al.* (1991) emphasize three channels through which a stabilization package can have adverse effects on the income distribution: production incentives brought about by changes in the relative prices following changes in tariffs, other taxes, and exchange rate; the change in investment due to changes in asset prices particularly caused by fiscal and monetary tightening; and portfolio shifts due to capital gains and losses in response to changes in asset prices. For a given mix of expenditure reduction, the extent of the relative price rigidities, such as fixed real wages, mark-up pricing, and the extent of factor mobility as denoted by supply elasticity and differences in the consumption expenditure pattern determine long-run distribution pattern resulting from structural adjustment. Even with all these complications, financial intermediation is missing from their model.

Bourguignon, De Melo, and Suwa (1991) explicitly implement the "maquette" model for six developing economies, including Malaysia, Indonesia and Morocco, with explicit derivation of a monetary identity from the national income and balance of payments identities and specification of portfolio choice, goods, factor markets and trade conditions. The model is solved for different policy packages such as devaluation and fiscal restraint, under various closure rules such as fix price, flex price, less-developed financial markets, less open financial markets, a less open foreign trade regime, non-indexed wages and non-markup conditions. The major outcomes of the model are the growth in GDP, the investment ratio, the interest rate, the CPI deflator, the exchange rate, the fiscal deficit ratio, the agricultural terms of trade, the ratio of current account GDP, the poverty gap, and real income per capita. The dynamic structure of the maquette is very preliminary compared to fully forward-looking behavior to be adopted in my model.

Fargeix and Sadoulet (1994) show growth and welfare effects through a transmission between financial and real phenomena, complementarity between public and private investment, dynamics of inflation and wages, investment and capital out-flight and the role of public expenditures on growth though public investment and on household welfare through current expenditure. This model also has a short-run focus and so is not appropriate for long-run analysis.

While the multisectoral and institutional structures contained in these multisectoral models are appropriate to study various policies in a general equilibrium framework, the dynamic structures of these models that explain evolution of the model economy along the steady-state, and deviations of model variables from a steady state due to changes in financial sector policies is still not refined. This is where dynamic CGE literature can borrow techniques developed for long run growth models that have appeared after 1980s.

Forward-Looking CGE Models

All CGE models discussed so far have a very crude dynamic structure. There are very few CGE models that explicitly introduce forward-looking behavior by economic agents. Ramsey (1929) explicitly defined the forward-looking problem in a simple one-sector one-agent model. A forward-looking consumer in the Ramsey model has an infinite horizon and chooses the path of consumption that maximizes the present value of utility given the discounted life-time income. Koopmans (1957), Uzawa (1962,1964),Cass (1965) anlyzed forward-looking problem in framework of optimal growth models while the CGE modeling technique was not yet developed. It took a very long time for forward-looking approach to be incorporated in a multisectoral economic models. Ballard-Fullerton-Shoven-Whalley (1985) handle inter-temporal optimization problem by imposing a steady state condition for evolution of model variables. Their model is applied to evaluate welfare effect of various tax measures in the US economy. Charles Ballard (1984) studies dynamic effect of consumption tax in inter-temporal framework with and without bequest motives. The Goulder and Summers (1989) model of the US economy is another model which incorporates forward-looking behavior in a CGE context. More recently Fullerton and Rogers (1993) have adopted a life-cycle model in order to study dynamic effect of tax reforms in USA. Go (1994) uses Ramsey-type central planners and studies a dynamic general equilibrium framework which examines the sensitivity of investment and growth to external shocks and adjustment policies in the case of the Philippines. Consumers maximize the present discounted values of consumption in a infinite time horizon, and producers maximize the value of the firm. In Go's model the intertemporal preference parameters in the consumption function determine the path of capital stock for future years, and labor supply is assumed to be exogenous. He solves the central planner's problem by combining the intersectoral efficiency in the allocation of resources resulting from a general equilibrium model with the intertemporal efficiency generated from the dynamic optimization of each firm's value and aggregate consumer's utility. Pareto-optimality conditions imply the model solutions to be equivalent to solutions of a general equilibrium model. I improve on Go's structure by incorporating decentralized markets and the financial system.

Devarajan and Go (1995) present the simplest possible general equilibrium model of an open economy in which the decisions of a producer and a consumer are intra- and inter-temporally consistent. Though this is illustrative and simple to learn, actual policy models warrant much more disaggregation. They abstract from considerations of the financial side of the model. Keuschnigg and Kohler (1994) use a multisectoral CGE model with forward-looking investment and saving behavior by overlapping generations for a commercial policy analysis of the Austrian economy. The labor supply decisions in their model are endogenous. Keuschnigg and Kohler (1995) extend their model to analyze the growth effects of trade liberalization. They do not consider financial intermediation.

My model distinguished from other CGE models by explicitly incorporating investment cost index in the multi-sectoral forward-looking behavioral framework which allows us to study the impacts of financial sector reforms over period. It is an addition to the literature as non of the previous models have the specifications of the financial CGE models designed to study the inter-sectoral impact of reduction in the cost of funds.

THE STRUCTURE OF THE NEPAL'S FINANCIAL SYSTEM

With some background on the reform and modeling of financial sector it is pertinent to discuss a bit more on Nepal's financial system. Banks, insurance companies, savings and mutual funds, and stock markets make up a formal financial system of an economy (Fry 1995: 317-352). It is well accepted in the literature that the growth of a formal financial system goes in parallel with the growth of the economic system. The financial system is one of the major determinants of economic development (Goldsmith, 1969). While the funds borrowed from these formal financial institutions, in addition to self-financing at the firm level are a dominant forms of financing in developed economies, this system is found at quite primitive stages in various developing economies (Patrick and Park, 1994). Informal financing comprises a major part of financial system in these economies (Wijnbergen, 1982, 1983). The greater emphasis on privatization and liberalization has brought reform in financial sector to the forefront as a strategy for development (World Bank 1989, 1996). The financial sector limits and relaxes the budget constraints of households, firms, government, and the foreign sectors in the economy. Improvement in the financial system reduces the cost of capital but increases the volume of capital available by enhancing the efficiency of allocation and by inducing more saving by consumers[6].

Though insurance companies, savings and mutual funds and stock markets make a financial system of an economy, banks predominate in the financial sector in the early stages of economic development. In Nepal, deposit mobilization by the banks is about 29 per cent of GDP (ES, 1995 table 1.1 and 7.3). The volume of direct financing in the stocks and bonds through the Nepalese stock market, which started only in 1993, is very small. The value of assets traded during 1995 in the Nepal stock market, equaled less than one per cent of GDP (ES, 1995 p.69). Insurance companies, which trade in risks and uncertainties, are still small in terms of volume of transaction and coverage of business activities. Self-financing is mostly limited to consumption purposes. The informal sector, though important, is fragmented and cannot benefit from the economies of scale that characterize modern financial institutions. These informal financial institutions mostly finance consumption loans, for marriage ceremonies, funerals, feasts, and other kinds of social consumption.

Nepal's financial system consists of formal and informal financial market (Fig 3.1). The institutions in the formal financial markets are created under the law. They have distinct offices and working rules and procedures. The commercial and merchant banks, finance and insurance companies, stock markets, and rural and agricultural development banks operate in the formal financial market. Transactions of these institutions are recorded properly. These institutions mainly serve the credit needs of the corporate and government sector, and of households who are able to transact with these institutions. Most of the formal institutions are located in the urban areas, though a few of them have branches in rural areas with dense settlements.

Neighbors, local money-lenders, extended family acquaintances, agricultural traders and merchants and land-owners constitute the informal financial sector in Nepal. In some places self-help scheme is worked out by the local people for themselves. Borrowing activities of this sector have relatively low default rates compared to those of the formal institutions.). Implicit social support enforces the repayment of loans. Moreover, when borrowers cannot repay, there are other means to satisfy lenders such as a transfer of land or other asset (World Bank, 1994). Most loans in the informal sector are related to use of durable goods by the households, such as buying a buffalo for milk or oxen for plowing. Consumption lending from the local merchant helps obtain supplies of daily necessities.

Information regarding revenues, expenditures and debt financing of the public sector are well documented in the annual economic survey prepared by the Ministry of Finance. However, the revenue, expenditures and financing position of the private sector enterprises are almost non-existent. In many cases record-keeping and accounting practices are poor and almost unknown in rural areas. Often, financial statistics are deliberately manipulated for tax purposes. Over- or under-invoicing to reduce tax burdens is common. The lack of information is more serious in the self-employment sector.

Fig. 2.1
Structure of the Financial System in Nepal

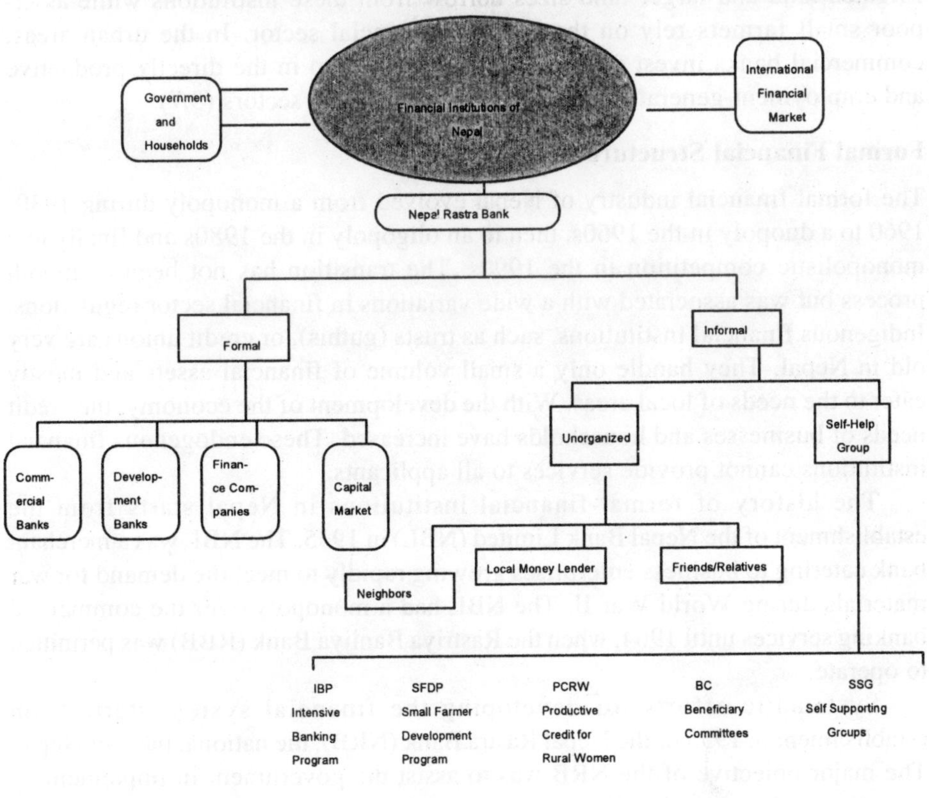

A researcher has to rely on various sources for analysis of the financial sector. Some of these sources are national accounting series and occasional manufacturing sector samples prepared by the Central Bureau of Statistics (CBS), which publishes revenues and costs of various industries. The annual report and quarterly bulletin of the Nepal Rastra Bank (NRB) contain data relating to money and the financial sector. The Agricultural Credit Survey (1969/70) and its review survey (1979/

80) provides flows of credits from institutional and non-institutional sectors. The multi-Purpose Household Survey (NRB,1988) reports consumption, income, savings, and time allocation patterns of households in urban and rural areas. The Farm Management Survey (DFAMS,1986) gives details on the technology of production and use of inputs for farms in Nepal. The annual balance sheets and income statements of financial institutions, public corporations and private enterprises are available. Drawing on these sources, William and Quibria (1988) systematically describe the trends of resource mobilization and financial sector development from 1961 to 1988. They discuss trends in national savings, interest rates, the allocation of funds among different sectors, and the asset and liability structure of the formal financial institutions. Yadav et al (1992) survey rural households and find segmentation of rural financial markets due to the collateral requirement of the formal financial institutions. They found that farmers with irrigated land and larger land sizes borrow from these institutions while asset-poor small farmers rely on the informal financial sector. In the urban areas, commercial banks invest far more in commerce than in the directly productive and employment-generating manufacturing or service sectors (3.7).

Formal Financial Structure

The formal financial industry of Nepal evolved from a monopoly during 1930-1960 to a duopoly in the 1960s, then to an oligopoly in the 1980s and finally to a monopolistic competition in the 1990s. The transition has not been a smooth process but was associated with a wide variations in financial sector regulations. Indigenous financial institutions, such as trusts (guthis), or credit unions are very old in Nepal. They handle only a small volume of financial assets and mostly cater to the needs of local areas. With the development of the economy, the credit needs of businesses and households have increased. These endogenous financial institutions cannot provide services to all applicants.

The history of formal financial institutions in Nepal starts from the establishment of the Nepal Bank Limited (NBL) in 1935. The NBL was a merchant bank catering to business enterprises growing rapidly to meet the demand for war materials during World War II. The NBL had a monopoly over the commercial banking services until 1964, when the Rastriya Banijya Bank (RBB) was permitted to operate.

Systematic efforts for developing the financial system starts from establishment in 1955 of the Nepal Rastra Bank (NRB), the national bank of Nepal. The major objective of the NRB was to assist the government in implementing monetary and financial policy in order to achieve economic stability, liquidity, and a higher rate of economic growth (Nepal Rastra Bank, 1981). The NRB's emphasis has been on developing an efficient and competitive system of financial intermediaries to mobilize internal resources. The banking industry became a duopoly when the RBB opened in 1964. As commercial banks were mostly involved in short-term credits to trade and commerce, there were not any institutions to provide medium and long term credits required by business enterprises, and short-term credits to farmers. The Nepal Industrial Development Corporation (NIDC: 1959) was started to provide medium and long-term credit for private and public enterprises. The Employee Provident Fund (EPF:1963), and Nepal Insurance Corporations (NIC:1968) were started with a focus on the long run. The Agricultural Development Bank (ADB:1963) was established to provide loans to rural areas.

In this early phase of development of financial sector in Nepal, all of the institutions were specialized and had a virtual monopoly in the field of their operation. Following the philosophy of active government, the entry and operation of these financial institutions were heavily regulated. These institutions were guided more by motivations of social services such as providing a cheap credit than by rendering the pure economic services required for growth of the economy. The monopolies in the banking sector affected the efficiency of financial services. Returns on assets were not very high so financial institutions could not prosper and become more innovate.

In the 1980s Nepal Rastra Bank allowed operation of new joint venture banks: Nepal Arab Bank (1984), Nepal Indosuez Bank (1985), and Nepal Grindlays Bank (1985), with an amendment to the Commercial Bank Act in 1984. Though these new banks were expected to bring international banking experience to Nepal and break the monopoly of local banks, the inefficiency in the banking sector continued. In spite of liberalization and deregulation of interest rates and an introduction of an auction system in treasury bills, the behaviors of banks in regard to interest rate on deposits, loans and bonds did not change during early liberalization phase. New banks located in the urban areas introduced more efficient banking practices, they became partners with the existing banks in the oligopolistic banking market in Nepal. The financial needs of the growing private sector were not met efficiently. Even though Mckinnon and Shaw advocated financial sector policy reforms as early as 1973, Nepal was under a repressed structure of financial system until 1984. The Nepal Rastra Bank fixed interest rates which were applicable to all commercial and development banks. It initiated a series of financial sector reforms after the introduction of Structural Adjustment Program in the mid-1980s.

In the process of liberalization the Nepal Rastra Bank fixed the prevailing interest rates on deposits as minima and authorized the commercial banks to offer higher rates until they reached a ceiling up to 1.5 per cent above the rates on saving deposits. Banks did not respond and the interest rate remained the same. Then the ceilings were removed in 1986, but the floors remained. The minimum interest rate on three, six and nine months deposits was 8.5 per cent and 12.5 per cent on a one-year deposit. Banks were allowed to offer higher rates. Again banks stuck with the rates fixed by the central bank. In February 1989, banks were allowed to set their interest rates. The floors also were removed. Banks did not increased interest rates to attract more deposits even though a higher rate of inflation was expected because of a trade and transit impasse with India that created a scarcity of essential goods in Nepal for almost one and a half years.

The NRB further liberalized banking sector in 1992. Conditions for entry into the banking business were relaxed. Then the NRB eliminated statutory liquidity ratio which required all banks to invest a certain share of their assets in government bills (altogether about 25 per cent). The Finance Company Act of 1992 was another move to develop financial institutions. This was further reinforced by the Securities Exchange Act in 1992, that made provisions for setting up Securities Exchange Board and Nepal Stock Exchange that opened its trading floor in January 1994.

The installation of a new democratic government in 1991 pushed financial markets to be more open and transparent. Degree of freedom of financial institutions has been enhanced. Competition in the financial sector has been intensified by the relaxation of rules of entry and exit. Still, the market structure of the financial system shows features of price leadership under a monopolistic competition.

Informal Financial Sector

The informal financial sector, considered as the residual of the financial system in the literature, still plays a very important role in financial dealings in many developing economies (Von Pischke *et al.* 1983). The McKinnon and Shaw theory was followed by modeling of the formal sector by Kapur (1980), Mathiason (1980), Fry (1988), and Polak (1989). Critiques of financial liberalization by Taylor (1983), Wijnbergen (1982, 1983), Stiglitz (1981, 1993) and Bolnick (1982,1988), and Monteil, Agenor and Haque (1993) pointed to the importance of the informal financial sector. Neostructuralists criticize the financial liberalization strategy because the curb market interest rate may go up due to an increase in the real deposit rate in the formal financial institutions. Taylor (1983) assumes an institutionally set wage rate, that inflation is determined by the relative capacity of capitalist and workers, mark-up pricing, and a critical need for imports of raw materials, capital equipment and intermediate goods. Restrictive monetary policy raises the interest rate and devaluation raises the price of imports·producing stagflation. Van Wijnbergen (1982, 1983, 1985) incorporates a curb market in the monetary model, using Tobin-type portfolio behavior for time deposits, currency and direct loans to the business sector through the curb market. He finds that people move from curb market loans into time deposits after a rise in the time deposit rate, so the total supply of funds to the business sector declines. This results because the curb market provides one-for-one intermediation, whereas banks provide only partial intermediation due to reserve requirement.

The debate on the net contribution of financial liberalization in an environment with the informal financial market is not yet settled, and is an issue of empirical investigation.

In Nepal the informal financial services are provided by neighbors, local money-lenders, extended family acquaintances, agricultural traders and merchants and land-owners. For a majority of the population, which is not familiar with rules and regulations and are uncomfortable in reading and writing, both in urban and rural areas, the credit needs are fulfilled by the informal sectors. The contact between the lenders and borrowers are very close in the informal market compared to those in the formal markets. The lenders know the creditworthiness of the borrowers and have some control over their repayment as they can closely monitor the borrowers' financial activities (NRB-APRACA, 1990). This is the reason why the cost of transactions in the informal financial sector is smaller compared to the cost of transaction in the formal financial institutions. In fact, the informal financial sector can reach to the very bottom of the economic system, though by nature the sizes of informal sector loans are very small, individually.

The Agricultural Credit Review Survey (1976/77) reported that 76 per cent of households borrowed from the informal sector. The World Bank (1991) estimates that institutional credit still accounts only about 20 per cent of total borrowing.

The majority of borrowing is from friends and neighbors (Table 2.1) and then from a large informal credit societies that range from debt-bondage to landlords (Kamaiyas in Tarai) to a large scale commercial financing by highly structured self-help groups. According to a report on the mid-term evaluation of the Sixth Plan (NPC, 1992), most people in the Hills area borrowed from their neighbors. The second major sources are private money lenders who account for another 20-25 per cent of the borrowing. Banks count as the major source for some 15-20 per cent of lending. The cooperatives and others were very minor sources of rural credit.

Table 2.1

Sources of Rural Credit in Nepal, 1986

	Mountain	*Hills*	*Tarai*	*Total*
Bank	11.7	18.8	20.6	19.1
Cooperative	0.4	1	2.7	1.4
Neighbor	47.1	48.3	39.5	44.3
Moneylender	24.3	17.4	27.7	22.5
Friends	8.6	6.5	5.8	6.7
others	2.5	2	0.6	1.4

The majority of borrowing by the poor is not for investment purposes, but for consumption (Table 2.2). Yadav (1984) reports that out of total borrowing, small farmers use 60 to 90 per cent for consumption purposes. The interest rates on

Table 2.2

Sources of Rural Credit in Nepal, 1986

	Mountain	*Hills*	*Tarai*	*Total*
Bank	11.7	18.8	20.6	19.1
Cooperative	0.4	1	2.7	1.4
Neighbor	47.1	48.3	39.5	44.3
Moneylender	24.3	17.4	27.7	22.5
Friends	8.6	6.5	5.8	6.7
others	2.5	2	0.6	1.4

these informal loans vary from 30 per cent to 150 per cent (World Bank 1991:47) which is higher than a 15- 20 per cent rate of interest on the loans from the institutional sources.

As is common to many other agriculture dominated developing economies an average villager in Nepal is chronically indebted. Nepal Rastra Bank (NRB, MPBHS 1988) data show that the lower decile of the households are accumulating debt at an unsustainable rate by repaying only a fifth of that they are borrowing. Thus the debts are passed from one generation to another. There is saying ; "a villager is born with debt, grows in debt, and dies with debt". The relation between the debtor and creditor may take various forms. A debt is revolved in a socially homogenous community. In other cases it is recovered by an expropriation of labor, grain or by soliciting political support to the creditor or by a transfer of assets (such as land). In the worst case it may result in bonded labor or forced migration out of the community.

Self-help Groups

Considering the serious problems of rural indebtedness as outlined in the previous section, there has been some effort to develop another source of the rural credit, popularly know as self help groups. APRACA (APRACA 1990:3-5)[7], classified informal self-help groups in Nepal into three different categories: formal , semi-formal and informal. People in these groups are employed as small marginal farmers, land-less laborers, people in low income service sector, low-income craftsmen and artisans, small entrepreneurs, rural women, petty traders and small shop-keepers. The credit needs of these people are fulfilled either by formal sources such as Intensive Banking Program (IBP), Lead Bank Scheme (LBS), Production Credit for Rural Women (PCRW), or Small Farmer's Development Program (SFDP) or by informal sources constituting of local money-lenders, trusts, and informal self-help groups.

Nearly 700 multipurpose rural cooperatives, 33 District Cooperative Unions, and 34 non-agricultural registered cooperatives, popularly known as Sajha, are the main formal self-help groups in rural Nepal. Started in the early fifties by HMG/Nepal these cooperatives are coordinated by the Cooperative Department. These are not sufficient to fulfill the credit needs of the rural population.

The semi-formal self-help groups are not formally registered with any government agency, and are not legal entities in themselves. They are promoted by the banking institutions and other development agencies. These institutions are promoted, organized and supported by formal bodies like banks and extension agencies of the government. The organizational structure, style of functioning, linkage with banks, and other features clearly differentiate them from informal groups. There are four major forms of semi-formal self-help groups.

The first semi-formal self-help group constitutes of Small Farmers Development Program (SFDP). It was launched in the mid-1970s with the aim of assisting small and marginal farmers, land-less laborers and other weaker sections of the society for the purpose of receiving institutional credit. SFDP consists of three types of self-help groups - men's group, mixed groups with men and women, and women's groups. The Agricultural Development Bank (ADB/N) appoints a project officer who acts as a group promoter and organizer. The progress reports on SFDP have been very positive (NPC 1992).

The second type of semi-formal self help group is the Intensive banking Program (IBP). IBP was launched to channel part of the resources of commercial banks to priority sectors, mainly aimed for rural development. Supervised credit for the rural poor and weaker sections of society is a core aspect of the program. Low income families with a per capita income of Rs. 2,511 (in 1990 prices) get credit from banks on a group guarantee basis.

The third type of semi-formal self-help group is Production Credit for Rural Women (PCRW), launched by HMG/N in collaboration with UNICEF and the Intensive Banking Program (IBP) for improving socioeconomic status of women. The officials of PCRW assist rural women to form into groups and to take up various social and income raising activities. They receive support from development wing of various ministries of HMG/N , banks and international donor agencies.

The fourth type of semi-formal self-help group is Beneficiary Committees (User/Consumer Groups). Formed under the Decentralization Act, 2039, and promoted by Village Development Committees in order to operate local development projects Such committees consists of five members elected by the beneficiaries of the project.

The bottom of financial service ladder is made of informal self-help groups. Informal self-help groups are organized for various socio-economic and cultural activities by the people themselves with no intervention from government or semi-government agency such as banks. Some of these groups are traditional based on ethnic relations, neighborhood, or other common interests. Dhikur, Guthi, and irrigation management groups are some examples. Some of these are of more recent origin, created by people (students, teachers, service holders, ex-service men farmers, young women) themselves for activities such as savings and credit, community development, input and product marketing, maintenance of utilities and other community development , socio-economic and cultural activities. It is very difficult to present a quantitative assessment of financial services provided by these informal self-help groups as systematic information on these things are lacking.

ASSETS AND LIABILITIES OF INTERMEDIARIES

The assets and liabilities of Nepalese Banks were approximately equal to $1 billion during 1993. This figure is far below the assets and liabilities of largest banks in the world. The Dai Ichi Kango Bank had $436 billion assets during 1992 (Fortune, Aug., 1992). The absolute size of deposits is not a correct measure of financial deepening in an economy. A better indicator of financial deepening is the ratio of deposits to GDP.

Fig. 2.2

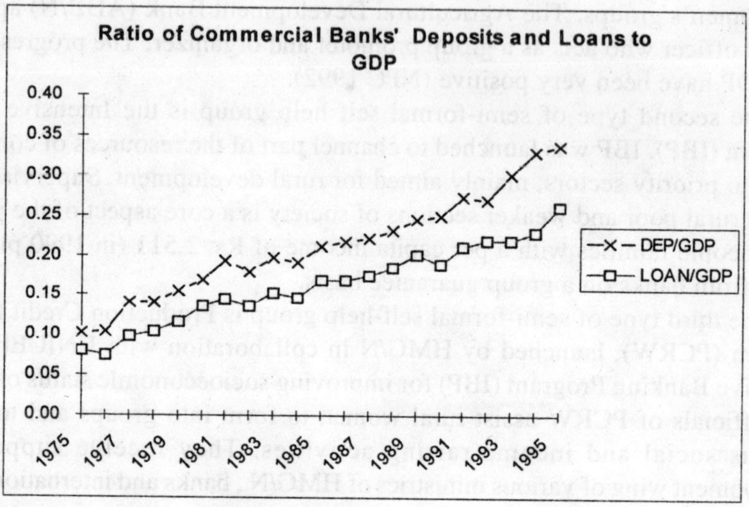

There has been a continuous increase in the ratio of deposits to GDP. This ratio increased at higher rate in the 1970s than in the 1980s.It picked up again during the 1990s. Though real growth rate of total deposits, on average, was about 5 per cent per annum, it was dominated by demand deposits and were erratic during the 1980s. Nepal's banks do not pay interest in demand deposits. The increased proportion of demand deposits in the banking system, therefore is not due to the higher interest rates but can be associated with speculative demand for financial assets due to the financial repression. A high ratio of deficit to GDP, the control of the rate of interest, resulting in a negative real interest rate to lenders, overvaluation of foreign currency, and very high rate of increase in value of real estates, particularly urban lands caused an increase in speculative activities. While the rate of interest in informal sector were around 40 per cent (World Bank, 1992), those in banks were at most 13 per cent, even not enough to compensate for inflation. This explains why commercial banks were not able to increase the proportion of long-term loans despite increase in deposits.

Some explanation is needed why people keep saving money in banks in spite of a negative returns on deposits. Mainly it is the lack of alternative assets such as stock markets or mutual funds. Some monetization occurs with the development of new transportation networks and the development of urban centers. The indivisibility of investment also raises deposits in the banks as people accumulate deposits until they are enough to purchase land, or construct buildings that require a large sum of money.

Figure 2.2 also shows that the ratio of loans to GDP has followed the increase in the ratio of deposits to GDP but not exactly. After maintaining a high liquidity position at around 20 to 30 per cent of total deposits, commercial banks lend rest of the deposits to the private sector, to the government and to public enterprises.

The adverse effect of financial repression becomes obvious if one observes the asset structure of the commercial bank lending, particularly in the overwhelming amount of loans for trading compared to loans made to industries and agriculture (Fig. 2.3). Chart on loan disbursement by financial intermediaries shows in repression banks are very conservative in lending. They lent more to commerce and social purposes than to working capital financing of industrial enterprises. In a predominantly agricultural economy, amount of credits flowing to the agriculture sector is lower even than to the general or social purpose lending.

Fig. 2.3

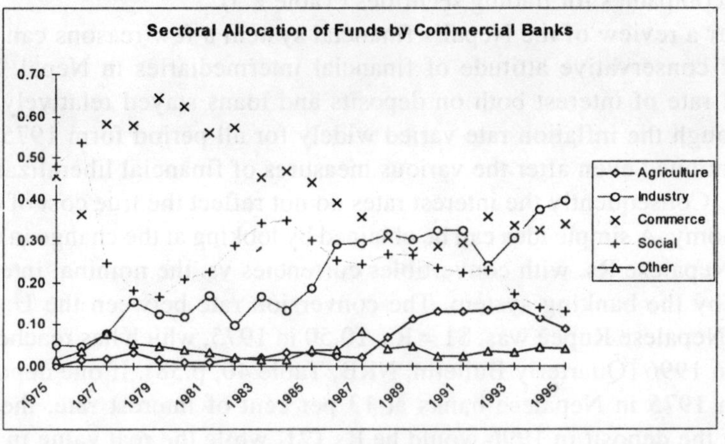

Commercial banks have a dominant position in the formal financial market of Nepal. The loans offered by the non-commercial bank financial institutions (NCBFI), such as the Agricultural Development Bank, Nepal Industrial Development Corporation, and the Employee Provident Fund were increasing up to mid 1980s, have been around 10-12 per cent of total lending form the commercial banks. As a ratio to the GDP, the lending by the NCBFI has remained in the range of 2-3 per cent of GDP.

Fig. 2.4

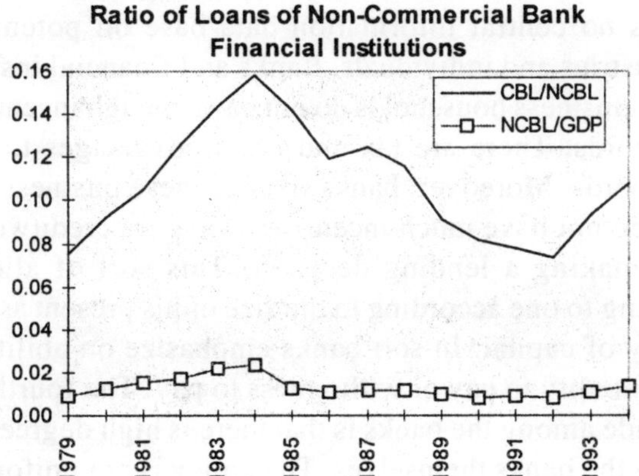

Nepal's secondary capital market is still in an early stage of development though the modern corporate sector had begun more than a half century ago with the establishment of the Nepal Bank Ltd. and Raghu Pati Jute Mills in 1937. The government started issuing bonds in 1964. The security exchange center (SEC) started in 1976 could not push capital market further. It dealt mostly in government bonds until 1984. In spite of its ten years efforts on full-fledged listing of corporate shares, collecting bids and offers on shares, debentures and government bonds, clearing the transactions and disseminating information about the financial and managerial performance of listed companies, the SEC has not be able to list more than 79 companies for trading securities (Table 2.5).

After a review of the Nepal's financial system a few reasons can be found for very conservative attitude of financial intermediaries in Nepal. First, the nominal rate of interest both on deposits and loans stayed relatively constant even though the inflation rate varied widely for all period form 1975 to 1994. This continued even after the various measures of financial liberalization were adopted. Consequently the interest rates do not reflect the true cost of capital in the economy. A simple idea can be obtained by looking at the change in exchange rate of Nepalese Rs. with convertibles currencies vs. the nominal interest rates offered by the banking system. The conversion rate between the U. S. dollar and the Nepalese Rupee was, $1 = Rs. 10.50 in 1975, which has reached to $1 = Rs. 60 in 1996 (Quarterly Bulletin, NRB, Table 40, p.58). If one deposited Rs. 10.50 in 1975 in Nepalese banks at 13 per cent of interest rate, the nominal value of the deposit in 1996 would be Rs.121, while the real value in 1975 Rs. would be Rs. 21. If that person bought a dollar at Rs.10.50 and kept in a foreign account at 5 per cent rate of interest and sold the amount ($2.65) in 1996 can receive Rs. 159.20, and in 1975 prices Rs. 27.7. Second, the average size of loans in Nepal is very small. Except a few big borrowers who take a disproportionately large share of loans flowing from the intermediaries, the majority of borrowers apply for small loans, which are according to the size of their income and business. This in turn means a higher cost of transactions of funds from the banks. Third, there is a high degree of asymmetry of information between lenders and borrowers. There are several reasons for such an information problem. There is no central information data-base on potential customers, business, and industries and individuals. Banks and financial institutions do not share information. Business households do not have enough incentives to disclose their financial records. There are tax and other advantages to not disclosing one's financial records. Moreover, banks finance these business houses against collateral. Banks do not have much incentive to require creditworthiness of the borrowers when making a lending decision. This sort of allocation rule is equivalent to lending to one according to the size of his present asset irrespective of the productivity of capital. In sort banks emphasize on ability to pay at the moment than potentiality to pay or willingness to pay. The fourth reason for the conservative attitude among the banks is that there is high degree of information asymmetry among the banks themselves. The policy is not uniform even among the same categories of financial institutions. The government owns two major commercial banks of Nepal which collect 70 per cent of the deposits. Many other new banks that have entered recently into the markets are completely in the private sector. Given the fact that representatives of the central bank and ministry of finance are appointed in the board of directors of government owned banks, the private sector sees it as unfair competition. From the point of view of private banks, the government owned banks have access to the extra information, or a direct or indirect access to the banking and monetary policy of the economy. On the other hand, the government owned banks argue that they have branches in rural areas and complain that they are rendering social services in the form of collecting deposits and allocating loans to the priority sector even though these activities are not profitable. It is a fact that the size of loans in the rural sector are small and not profitable. Providing banking services in the rural areas is very costly. Moreover, the political influence occurs in loans when banks are owned by the government.

KEY LESSONS

Six key lessons can be drawn from the detailed assessment review of the Nepalese economy and financial sector, and are as follows:

The financial system remained seriously repressed until the mid 1980s. Such repression was characterized by the control on interest rates, exchange rates, a heave reserve requirement on deposits, strong barriers to entry for banks and other financial institutions, artificial limits and stringent rules for rationing credit among various sectors.

The impact of economic liberalization has been instrumental in the growth of formal financial institutions. The number of banks and financial institutions and deposits mobilized from them have increased significantly, the cost of intermediation has been decreased, interest rates have been completely liberalized, an independent capital market has been developed. Still, there are elements of market power in the financial system.

Control on budget deficit and public borrowing have reduced inflation. There have been reforms in the exchange rate system and convertibility of current accounts. These helped to build up the confidence of the investors in the domestic financial system. The cycle of political instability that started from the mid-1994 had a detrimental effect in the growth of financial system. Activities in the capital markets and deposits in the banks have slowed down.

The formal financial industry of Nepal evolved from a monopoly during 1930-1960 to a duopoly in the 1960s, then to an oligopoly in the 1980s and finally to a monopolistic competition in the 1990s. Informal financial sector plays a very important role in rural Nepal. The size of the financial sector is very small in Nepal because of the low level of the income of the people and some inefficient financial policies adopted in the past.

Commercial banks predominate the formal financial system. Loans flowing from the non-commercial bank financial institutions have been around 10 per cent of the total lending from the commercial banks. Capital markets are yet in quite preliminary stage.

The banks set aside 20-25 per cent of the total deposits collected from the customers for liquidity purposes , and lend the remaining to the business and households. A close review of the portfolio of commercial banks in the past show that banks have been conservative in lending. The size of loans flowing to traders and social and general purposes remained about 80 per cent of commercial banking lending until mid 1980s. They are still about 50-60 per cent of total lending of the commercial banks. Consequently, the share of loans flowing to industry and agriculture for the capital formation remained very low.

The informal financial institutions still comprise 70-75 per cent of the credit market in rural Nepal. The cost of funds is very high and most of such credit is spent on consumption and social events. A negligible amount of rural borrowing is spent on investment activity. The informal sector fulfills the credit needs of small households who do not have an easy access to the formal banking sector.

Three categories of model can be found in the literature on Nepalese economy: a simple econometric model used by the government of Nepal, Chris Elbers' multi-regional model for the Nepalese economy and Asian Development Bank's model for Nepal.

A simple econometric techniques though good for forecasting for a very short run do not take account of the general equilibrium effects required for more rigorous analysis of a policy designed to promote economic growth and welfare over the period. Chris Elbers' multi-regional multi-sectoral model and BDB's multi-sectoral models are very useful frameworks of analysis but they lack dynamic specification and analysis of the financial sector. A fully specified forward looking multi-sectoral model developed in this dissertation can be considered an addition to the literature on the Nepalese economy.

A significant body of literature exist on the role of the financial sector in long run growth. The applicability of a particular model for policy analysis depended upon its structure. Models with single representative agent are good study long-run growth but are not appropriate to study income or welfare distribution issues among the households. One sector macro models are not appropriate to answer cross-sectoral impacts of liberalization. One period models are not suitable to study growth and development of an economy. Thus a choice of appropriate modeling environment is very important for policy analysis.

Various CGEs with financial sectors were developed in the late 1980s and early 1990s and show the possibility of general equilibrium analysis with a financial sector. They focus on a relatively short period. The effect of financial sector variables in these models really depends upon the assumptions about the flexibility of wages, exchange rates, and other prices in the economy. In the short run, this is the key issue of debate among macro economists, classical and neo-classical, Keynesian, neo-Keynesian, rational expectations, new classical and new business cycle theories have their own interpretations of transmission mechanisms between the financial sector and the real side of the economy. For the long run opinions of these schools converge as there can be a perfect adjustment in portfolio allocation so that prices, wages, and exchange rates can change as dictated by long-run equilibrium. The contribution of the financial sector in the economy should be channeled through a reduction in the real cost of resources, such as intermediation cost, or elimination of monopoly mark-ups, and equalization of rates of returns across sectors. This is the approach taken in this dissertation. There has been a continuous improvement in theoretical and computational techniques to make studies more realistic. Improvement in computation technology has allowed models to capture more dimensions over time, sector and regions.

NOTES

1. It was a nine point program to banish poverty, hunger and illiteracy by the year 2005. The main points included the construction of local roads and small irrigation projects, supply of pure drinking water, education, literacy, and health facilities; skill-oriented training and employment,; community forestry; rural electrification through minimal hydro-electric projects; and development of small and cottage industries. This also included programs such as build your village yourself subsidies of Rs. 500,000 to each of 4000 villages, old-age stipend to people more than 75 years old; increase of Rs. 300 on allowances of government employees. Altogether, the budget represented a 27 per cent increase in the government budget. The economists were skeptical of government's ability to implement the programs.
2. Urban labor, rural labor, and capital.
3. Urban and rural.
4. Investments and inventories.
5. India and ROW.
6. We emphasize financialization of saving rather than increase in saving as there is a debate on the income and substitution effects of interest rates on saving. Saving may increase only if the substitution effect is larger than the income effect.
7. Asia and Pacific Regional Agricultural Credit Association (APRACA), in a Sixth General Assembly held in Kathmandu, 1986, had emphasized identification of self-help groups, developing and refining linkage models, plans and programs between formal financial institutions and informal groups. Members of APRACA-Nepal are Nepal Rastra Bank (NRB), Agricultural Development Bank (ADB), Agricultural Project Service Center (APROSC), Nepal Bank Limited (NBL) and Rastriya Banijya Bank (RBB).

APPENDICES

Table 2.3
Economic Liberalization Project Nepal (1992-1995): Issues, Targets and Problems

Policy issues	*Target or measures of Reform*	*Problems*
Fiscal Austerity	-Reduction in deficit from 8.75 per cent of GDP to 7.75 -internal borrowing from 2 per cent to 0.5 per cent during the same period -Inflation rate 5 per cent of GDP -Increase in revenue mobilization of 0.5 per cent per year	Populist program of CPN-UML government that ruled for six months
Tax reforms	Simplify tax laws -Self-assessment system (VAT) -confinement of tax brackets in three rates (10,25,35 per cent) -lower property taxes -root out administrative inefficiencies	Ambiguities in tax laws narrow tax baselow elasticityarbitrariness in implementation -tax codes, rules and regulations need to be transparent -maintain edge with neighboring economies
Financial Sector Reforms	-Ease entry restrictions -reduce statutory liquidity ratio -deregulated interest rates -Finance Company Act 1992 -Security Exchange Act 1992 -security Exchange Board 1993 -Nepal Stock Exchange 1994	-a large spread between lending and borrowing -regulatory, monitoring and supervisory role of the central bank -lack of experience of corporate management-representation of central bank in two state-owned banks and not in others -Ownership of stock market by NIDC -lack of comprehensive security acts such as rules on disclosure of information, takeovers, mergers, -surveillance codes on brokers and market maker activities
External trade reforms	-Abolition of dual exchange rate system, 1993 -Permission to open accounts in convertible currencies -elimination of quantitative restrictions (abolition of import auctions) -rationalization of tariff structure (from more than 100 slabs to 6 slabs, peak tariffs reduced from 255 per cent to 110 per cent) -export facilities-duty drawback, bonded warehouse, simpler export documentation	-more detailed understanding of Nepal-India trade relations -parallel markets -understanding of new world trading order -convertibility of capital account -conceptual clarity to the extent of across the board protection

Contd.

Industrial Policy reforms	-simplification of tariff structure -tax-incentives to invest in less developed areas, reinvestment of profits, diversification and privatization, training and research -simplification of registration and licensing proceduresIndustrial Enterprise Act -Foreign Investment and Technology Transfer Act (1992) -All industries opened up for foreign investment that exceed Rs. 20 million of fixed investment -Separate policy for promotion of specific industry such as of airlines in 1991	-one window but many doors, -transparency in procedures, -discretionary authority of officials -minimum investment requirements for foreign investment (Rs. 20 millions) -facilitation of infrastructure, raw materials and credit rather than tax incentives required-complicated industry registration procedure
Reform in Public Enterprises	-sales of assets and business of 3 Pes -selling of company shares of 4 Pes -liquidation of 2 Pes -more flexible pricing policies for PEs remaining in the govt. sector (NEC increased price first by 60 per cent, then by 24 and 38 per cent, Nepal Water Supply Corporation increased charges 100 per cent eliminated agricultural subsidies	-training of workers and managersvery limited-lack of awareness of its importance among policy makers and people
Agricultural reform	-permission to import selected fertilizers by the private sector -deregulation of sugar prices -establishment of Grameen Bikas Banks	
Legal reform	Company Law Contract Law Consumer Protection Law	-inability of government to communicate merits of reform -Broad-based consensus

Source: Dixit (1995) in IRIS Country Report No. 17.

Table 2.4
Major Financial Institutions of Nepal

Central Bank	
Nepal Rastra Bank (NRB,1955)	
Commercial Banks	
Nepal Bank Limited (NB,1935)	Rastriya Banijya Bank Ltd. (NRB, 1964)
Nepal Arab Bank Ltd. (NABIL, 1984)	Grindlay's Nepal Bank Ltd.(1985)
Banque Indosuez Nepal Ltd. (1985)	Himalayan Bank Limited (1993) : A joint venture with Habib Bank of Pakistan
Nepal State Bank of India Ltd. (1994)	Everest Bank Ltd. (1994): A joint venture with Union Bank of India
Nepal Bangladesh Bank Limited (1994)	
Development Banks	
Agricultural Development Bank of Nepal (ADBN, 1963)	Nepal Industrial Development Corporation (NIDC, 1959)
Far Western Grameen Bikas Bank (1994)	Sajha (Agricultural Cooperative)
Mid-western Grameen Bikas Bank (1995)	Eastern Grameen Bikas Bank (1994)
	Western Grameen Bikas Bank (1995)
Other Financial Institutions	
Employees Provident Fund Corporation (EPFC, 1963)	National Insurance Corporation INIC, 1968)
Premier Insurance Company Ltd. (1994)	United Insurance Company Ltd. (1994)
Everest Insurance Company (1994)	People's Finance Ltd. (1994)
Kathmandu Finance Ltd. (1994)	Small Industries Development Corporation (SIDC, 1971)
Industrial Service Center (ISC, 1974)	Credit Guarantee Corporation (CGC, 1974)
Post Office Savings Banks (1982)	Citizens' Investment Fund (1992)
Primary and Secondary Financial Market	
	Nepal Stock Exchange Limited (1994): Replaces Security Exchange Center Ltd. (1976)
NIDC Capital Market,	Nepal Share Market,
National Finance Company,	Citizens' Investment Trust
Mutual Savings Scheme	Stock Brokers (Individuals and registered companies)
Some Special Financial Sector Programs	
Intensive Banking Program	Small Farmer's Development Project
Lead Bank Scheme	Priority Sector Lending
Commercial Banking Analysis and Strategic Study (CBPASS)	Women's Skill Development Project
International Financial Institutions	
Bi-lateral Donars: JICA, GTZ, USAID, SNV, NORAD, SATA, CIDA	Multi-lateral Donars: World Bank, IMF, Asian Development Bank,

Source: Economic Survey 1995 and the daily Kathmandu Post in http://www.nepal-info.com, Janaury 1, 1996.

Table 2.5
Mobilization of Deposits and Real Interest Rates in Nepal

	Ratio of deposits to GDP			*Average Real Interest Rates and Spread*					
	Com. Banks	*Others*	*Total*	*Loans*	*Domestic Deposits*	*financial Spread*	*market Loans rate*	*Foreign Exchange Rate for $*	*Inflation*
1975	7.5	1.1	8.6	15.7	18.7	3.0	2.8	10.50	-0.7
1976	9.2	1.9	11.1	10.3	14.3	4.0	0.8	12.45	2.7
1977	12.3	2.5	14.8	0.8	4.8	4.0	0.8	12.45	11.2
1978	12.8	2.4	15.2	8.5	12.5	4.0	0.8	11.90	3.5
1979	13.1	2.5	15.6	6.2	2.20	4	0.8	11.90	9.8
1980	14.3	2.8	17.1	2.6	-1.40	4	0.8	11.90	13.4
1981	15.2	3.4	18.6	5.6	1.60	4	0.8	11.90	10.4
1982	15.8	3.8	19.6	2.8	-1.70	4.5	0.8	13.10	14.2
1983	18.6	4.3	22.9	11.8	6.30	5.5	1.8	14.40	6.2
1984	17.9	4.4	22.3	12	8.40	3.6	1.8	16.30	4.1
1985	19.2	4.9	24.1	14	-3.40	17.4	1.6	17.60	15.9
1986	20.4	5.3	25.7	2	-0.80	2.8	1.8	21.10	13.3
1987	19.9	5.5	25.4	5	1.50	3.5	3.1	21.80	11
1988	21.7	5.7	27.4	7	6.20	0.8	0.9	23.50	6.3
1989	24.5	6	30.5	12	0.50	11.5	0.9	27.40	11.5
1990	24.1	6.4	30.5	8	2.20	5.8	0.9	29.10	9.8
1991	25.3	7.2	32.5	4	-9.00	13	0.8	42.70	21
1992	27.3	9.4	36.7	4.5	3.60	0.6	0.8	42.60	8.9
1993	28.3	6	34.3	4.1	3.10	1.0	0.8	49.48	8.9

Source: Economic Review, NRB April 1994, p. 24, 39; Quarterly Bulletin for other deposits of 1992, 1993, Economic Survey, '95 Table 1.1 for GDP and p.3 for inflation; Thornton , J. of IMF 1987 in Journal of Dev. Adm. Studies, vol. 9 No. 2 pp. 13-22.

Table 2.6
Structure of Interest Rates after Liberalization (Per cent per annum)

	15-Jul-93	*15-Oct-93*	*15-Jan-94*	*15-Apr-94*	*15-Jul-94*	*15-Oct-94*	*15-Jan-95*
Treasury Bills	10.4	7.3	3.8	5	6.2	6.7	7.1
National Savings certificate	12-15.5	12.15.5	9-15.5	9-15.5	9-15.5	9-15.5	9-15.5
Development Bonds	3-10.5	3-10.5	3-10.5	3-10.5	3-10.5	3-10.5	3-10.5
Refinance Rate	13	11	11	11	11	11	11
NRB Bond Rate	11.2	7.3	3.9	5.1	6.2	6.8	7.1
Deposit Rates							
Saving Deposit	9.0-10	7.0-9.0	7-7.5	7-7.5	7-7.5	7-7.5	7-7.5
Time Deposit							
3 months	9.5-10	6.5-8	6.5-7	6.5-7	5-6.5	5-6.5	5-6.5
6 months	10.0-11.0	7.0-8.5	7.0-7.5	7.0-7.5	6.0-7.5	6.0-7.5	6.0-7.5
1 year	11.5-12	7.75-10	9.0-9.5	9.0-9.5	8.5-9.0	8.5	8.5
2 years and above	12.5-13	10.5	9.5	9.5			
Lending Rates							
Industry	16.0-21.0	15.0-19.0	15.0-18.0	15.0-18.0	13.0-17.0	14.0-17.5	14.0-17.5
Agriculture	16.0-19.0	14.0-17.0	14.0-16.0	14.0-16.0	13.0-15.0	13.0-15.0	13.0-15.0
Export Bills	15.0-12.0	13.0-16.0	13.0-17.0	13.0-17.0	12.0-14.0	12.0-14.0	12.0-14.0
Commercial Loans and Overdrafts	15.0-21.0	15.0-22.0	15.0-19.5	15.0-19.5	13.5-18.0	12.0-19.0	12.0-19.0
Agricultural Development Bank							
To Cooperatives	14.0-18.0	14.0-18.0	14.0-18.0	14.0-16.0	14.0-16.0	12.0-15.0	12.0-15.0
To others	16.0-20.0	16.0-20.0	16.0-18.0	16.0-18.0	16.0-18.0	14.0-17.0	14.0-17.0
Nepal Industrial Dev. Corporation	18.0-19.0	17.0-17.5	16.0-17.0	15.0-16.0	15.0-16.0	15.0-16.0	15.0-16.0

Source: Quarterly Bulletin, Nepal Rastra Bank, Mid-January 1995, p. 30, table 18.

Table 2.7
Allocation of Banking Sector Credit (in %)

	1993	*1994*	*1995*
Government Sector	50.4	43.2	36.7
(a) His Majesty's Government	47.4	40.6	35.1
(b) Non-financial Corporations	3	2.6	1.6
(B) Private Sector	49.6	56.8	63.3
(a) Financial Corporations	1.2	0.9	0.8
(b) Private Sector	48.4	55.9	62.5
Total	100	100	100

Source: Economic Survey, 1995

7

FORWARD-LOOKING CGE MODEL OF NEPAL

This chapter begins with a discussion of three essential equilibrium conditions of standard Arrow-Debreu general equilibrium model that guarantee an efficient allocation of resources in an economy. It is followed by suggested modification in that framework in order to study the effects financial repression on a dynamic multisectoral model, a place for the proposed model in the literature and its details.

In a standard Arrow-Debreu model relative prices guarantee an efficiency of allocation of resources if three classes of equilibrium conditions are satisfied (Mathiesen 1985; Rutherford 1995).

The first class of these conditions relates to the exhaustion of products, or a zero economic profit condition. When markets are perfectly competitive assuming a constant return to scale any firm can enter and exit the market until profits are eliminated, i.e., $-\Pi_j(p) \geq 0$; no producer earns excess profit. This condition can be written compactly as:

$$-\Pi_j(p) = C_j(p) - R_j(p) \qquad \text{(a)}$$

where $\Pi_j(p)$ represents unit profit function in terms of the unit revenue function $R_j(p)$ and unit cost function $C_j(p)$. $R_j(p)$ is the maximum revenue attainable by supplying one unit of output (y_i) at given prices subject to the technological constraints.

$$R_j(p) = \max \sum_i p_i y_i \ \text{ s.t. } g_i(y_i) = 1 \qquad \text{(b)}$$

The unit cost function $C_j(p)$ is the minimum of the cost function to produce one unit of output. $C_j(p)$ represents the minimum cost of producing one unit of output using input combinations.

$$C_j(p) = \min \sum_i p_i x_i \ \text{ s.t. } f_i(x_i) = 1 \qquad \text{(c)}$$

The function $f_i(x_i)$ gives input i required to produce one unit of output.

Thus, when the input and output choices are independent profits in competitive market system, i.e. the differences between the revenue and costs of production, ultimately tends to be zero.

The second condition of the standard Arrow-Debreu framework is that at equilibrium prices and activity levels, the supply of any commodity must balance or exceed demand by consumers. The market clearance is given by

$$\sum_j y_j \frac{\partial \Pi_j(p)}{\partial p_i} + \sum_h \omega_{i,h} \geq \sum_h d_{i,h}(p, M_h) \qquad \text{(d)}$$

The first sum, by Shephard's lemma[1], expresses net supply of goods i by the constant return to scale production sectors, the second sum $\sum_h \omega_{i,h}$ represents the aggregate initial endowment of goods i by households, and the sum on the right hand side represents the aggregate final demand for good i by households given market prices p and household income level M. These demands are derived from the utility maximization conditions subject to the budget constraints faced by the households.

Finally income balance condition states that the value of each agent's income must equal the receipts from factor endowments.

$$M_h = \sum_i p_i \omega_{i,h} \qquad \text{(e)}$$

Assuming non-satiation on the part of utility maximizing consumers, by Walras' law we can state that

$$\sum_i p_i d_{i,h} = M_h = \sum_i p_i \omega_{i,h} \qquad \text{(f)}$$

Aggregating the market clearance conditions using equilibrium prices and the zero profit conditions at the equilibrium activity levels:

$$\sum_j y_j \Pi_j(p) = 0 \qquad \text{(g)}$$

$$y_j \Pi_j(p) = 0 \; \forall_j \qquad \text{(h)}$$

The complementary slackness conditions in an equilibrium are given by:

$$p_i \left(\sum_j y_j \frac{\partial \Pi_j(p)}{\partial pi} + \sum_h \omega_{i,h} - \sum_h d_{i,h}(p, M_h) \right) = 0 \; \forall_i \qquad \text{(i)}$$

This means any commodity with excess supply has an equilibrium price equal to zero. Any commodity that commands a positive price has a balance between aggregate supply and aggregate demand.

Complementary slackness is a feature of equilibrium allocation even though it is not imposed as an equilibrium condition. In equilibrium any production activity operated makes zero economic profit and any activity that makes a negative return is idle (Rutherford 1995).

The Arrow-Debreu specification of CGE approach makes following assumptions in order to guarantee three equilibrium conditions outlined above. First, all factors are fully employed and fully mobile across sectors. Thus unemployment of labor or capital is a short-run phenomenon which will completely adjust in a medium to long-run horizon usually considered in CGE models. Second, demands are homogenous of degree zero in prices such that an unanticipated inflation has no real effects. Third, all sectors are marked by perfect competition among producers. The progress in modeling imperfect competition with CGE framework is still in progress (Mercenier and Srinivasan 1995).

In spite of these limitations use of CGE modeling increasing in policy analysis because of its strength in finding the general equilibrium impact of policies that have economy-wide importance.

SUGGESTED MODIFICATIONS ON THE STANDARD MODEL

The standard Arrow-Debreu economy can be extended over period by incorporating maximization problems of consumers and producers over the period. There are mainly two ways to extend the Arrow-Debreu model over the period. On the demand side, it should incorporate the intertemporal decision of the households. In other words consumers care about the future. Therefore their consumption decision today are affected by their expectation about life time income and preference for the future consumption. Consumer allocate life-time income to maximize the present value of utility either with myopic expectation as in Ballard-Fullerton-Shoven-Whalley (1985) or perfect foresight as in (Ballard 1983), Mann and Rutherford (1991). On the supply side a dynamic economy is characterized by investors' problem over the period. Producers make investment in the sectors that promise higher rate of return. Reallocation of investment continues until the rate of return across the sectors become equal. Thus one may expect capital stock to increase in sectors that generate higher rate of return and shrink in sectors that may not generate attractive returns to investors. Ultimately the demand and supply should be equal in equilibrium. This means returns on investments are linked to the demand for goods by the consumers through channels of income and relative prices of commodities in the market. Sectors with higher relative prices in comparison to the cost of production attract more investment and thus are supplied with greater stock of capital.

The efficient allocation propositions in the Arrow-Debreu economy are based on standard assumptions characterizing a perfectly competitive market, i.e. homogeneity of products, unlimited numbers of consumers and producers in the economy, perfect flow of information, no government intervention either in the supply or the demand side of the economy. There are many ways in which Arrow-Debreu model deviate from the real economy. This dissertation examines the case when the efficiency in the financial intermediation assumed in the Arrow-Debreu economy does not hold. To be more specific, all savings are automatically invested in the Arrow-Debreu economy, which assumes that there is no cost of intermediation while channeling savings from the net savers to the net borrowers in the economy.

In contrast to smooth functioning financial market in the Arrow-Debreu economy it is quite obvious that the financial intermediation takes a certain portion of savings in process of mobilizing savings from lenders to investors. In case of developing economies financial system are subject to various regulations, e.g., control of the interest rate, rules of credit allocation to different sectors, and sections of the community. These regulations, commonly known as the financial repression, cause a deviation between the payment to investors and the cost of investment; i.e. the willingness to buy financial assets by the savers and willingness to sell those assets by the investors. This causes an aggregate inefficiency in the economy that is reflected in higher cost of capital to the investors and lower payments received by the savers. Similarly, rules regarding the allocation of credits across the sectors makes the cost of capital vary from one sector to another. The preferred borrowers get cheap credits and others face a very high cost of capital. Thus the regulations of credit result in inefficiencies at the sectoral level. These two types of inefficiencies that are reflected in a lower amount of investment, slower growth and reduction in welfare in a repressed financial system in comparison to a fully liberalized system. This is an issue I intend to carry further in this dissertation.

Any development in analytical tools rests upon the analytical foundation laid by previous authors. Works done here owe much to three different sources. First, the inter-temporal analysis is influenced by literature on growth and economic development (Cass 1965, Uzawa 1964, Lucas 1988, Go 1993, Mercenier and Michel 1994, Parente 1994, Parente and Prescott 1994, Devarajan and Go 1995). The CGE framework and the benchmarking techniques are referred to (Bolnick 1989, Devarajan, Lewis and Robinson 1991, Shoven and Whalley 1992, Rutherford 1995c, Devarajan and Go 1995). Second, I have used the Mathematical Programming System of General Equilibrium Analysis and the General Algebraic Modeling System (MPSGE/GAMS) (Rutherford, 1994, 1995a ,1995b, 1995c, 1994) to formulate the model programming. It is solved by using the PATH algorithm (Dirkse and Ferris 1994).Third, several features of this model are taken from the Asian Development Bank's (ADB) model developed for the Nepalese economy. The number of households and production sectors and number of goods match with an unpublished version of the ADB model built by Maxwell Stamp in 1992, which was updated by Buehrer-Mauro in 1993. The addition to the dynamics, micro-foundation and treatment of financial sector called for several changes in those models. The solution algorithm and programming techniques used to solve the present model are completely different than the ones used in the ADB model.

The section outline of this chapter is the following. The next section presents differences of current model from other existing models. Then inter-temporal preferences and constraints of the households in the model economy are discussed in section 3.3. Intraperiod equilibrium in goods and factor markets are discussed in section 3.4. This section discusses the process of supply of domestically produced and imported goods in the model economy. It discusses supply of and allocation of skilled (urban) and unskilled (rural) labor, the process of capital formation and the structure of capital stock in the model economy. Then it discusses how the gross output is allocated between domestic markets and exported to India and other economies according transformation technology described the constant elasticity of transformation (CET) functions. On the other side, constant elasticity of substitution (CES) functions are used to describe the imports of goods and services from India and the other economies.

In section 3.5 the demand for goods and services are derived from the intertemporal maximization problem of households and arbitrage condition of producers. It also discusses techniques of calibration in a dynamic model to a steady state equilibrium. The structure of fiscal and balance of payment in the model economy is explained in section 3.6. The role of the financial system is discussed in section 3.7. It includes description of supply of and demands for funds, and allocation of those funds in productive and unproductive uses in a repressed and liberalized regimes of the financial sector and their consequences in the growth rate of the economy. Finally, the competitive economy is defined followed by a brief description on the closure of the model and an evaluation of welfare measure which is crucial in choice of policy alternatives.

RELEVANCE OF THE PROPOSED MODEL

Going beyond a simple static framework of the ADB model this model attempts to analyze issues relating to the economic development of Nepal. This study fills a gap in the CGE modeling literature by analyzing the effects of financial repression in intersectoral framework. More specifically this model differs from the ADB model in the following respects:

Households in this model are forward looking. They maximize the present value of utility by consuming a number of goods. For this they compare intertemporal and intrasectoral trade-offs while allocating their life-time income. The producers, government, and traders influence choices of households in many ways, which affect the prices of goods and services. While the ADB model is essentially a static equilibrium model, all the variables are indexed by time in this model. Interaction among them explains the evolution of economy over the period of analysis under consideration. With stronger micro, dynamics and financial sector, the policy prescription generated by this model may be more consistent in explaining the development and changes in the structural features of the economy.

The ADB model does not consider the role of financial intermediation in the process of capital accumulation. The intertemporal behavior of households and investors in this model allows one to study the evolution of the impact of financial policies in the economy. It can answer micro and macro issues relating to resource mobilization and development in the economy.

Dynamic closure in this model significantly differs from a static closure in the ADB model. This model describes the adjustment along a steady path over the long run and it explains transition dynamics before the economy achieves such a steady state growth path of income, employment and the capital stock.

Various dynamic issues such as migration, effects of inflows and outflows of capital, improvement in human resources can be studied more consistently in this model than in the ADB's sequential updating framework. Bccause of these features this model gives a new soul to the ADB model.

Before presenting the model formally the direct and the indirect effects of financial liberalization in the model economy are summarized, which illustrates, how one can experiment a policy in the model economy.

The households care for the future, and, save a portion of the current income. They also care about the value of their savings. If capital markets guarantee a positive interest on savings, households will make savings. If they believe that the financial system is repressed and therefore keeping deposits in banks erode value of savings, they choose to save in unproductive real assets or foreign assets. The formation of capital, thus, is intimately linked with the households' consumption and saving behavior. While good financial policies promote savings, inappropriate financial policies cause resources to flow out of the system. More specifically, when an economic policy cannot guarantee a safe background for financial savings, then resources flow out to speculative and unproductive uses, such as buying precious metals, purchasing idle urban lands, and to a hoarding of foreign exchanges or securities. Such unproductive uses of savings harm the economy by lowering the investment and hence growth rate of income and retarding. The rate of capital formation will slow down. As discussed in the model, in a limiting case, inappropriate financial policies may reduce the productive investment such that it may not be enough even to cover the allowance of depreciation in the economy. When the gross investment is less than the rate of depreciation economy depresses. Ultimately the welfare of the households diminishes. The proposed model shows that the financial repression leads to a financial shallowing, and hence to a lower economic growth rate of the model economy. It shows that the general equilibrium effect of the credit ceilings intended to promote selected sectors have an adverse effects on income and employment. Such intersectoral effect of financial sector policies is not sufficiently covered in the literature.

The growth models, whether they are classical, neo-classical or endogenous type, base conclusions about the growth rates of economy on a strong proposition that the portion of income not consumed at the current period is automatically turned into an increment of the capital stock. In other words, the amount of investment exactly equals the amount of saving. This assumption is not necessarily valid for the developing economies, where savings can leak out of the economic system in many ways. Whether the amount of net savings translates into investment essentially depends upon the confidence of the people in the policies of the financial sector. If the financial sector cannot promise on preserving the values of financial assets and providing net returns to savers, they prefer to lock-up their investible funds in unproductive real assets. It is not impossible to realize a negative investment in the economy, even though a significant amount of current income may have been saved.

Financial resources used in the most productive sectors lead to a greater amount of capital accumulation. Given that the capital stock per capita is the most critical factor for higher rate of economic growth, financial deepening promoted through liberal policies leads to a capital deepening, hence to a higher rate of economic growth in the model economy.

Consistent financial sector policies require that the real interest rate paid to the saving agents be equal to the rate of time preference of the households, a factor in the marginal rate of substitution between the present and future consumption. Only fully liberalized economies can guarantee that such a match between the intertemporal costs and benefits of savings be equal. The proposed model clarifies this by comparing a fully liberalized economy to a repressed economy.

The general equilibrium models are appropriate tools for studying the indirect effect of financial liberalization. The changes occurring in a sector have a widespread backward and forward linkages in the economy as a whole. Such linkages are often estimated by inter-industry relationships explained in terms of input-output coefficients and investment coefficients. An appropriate structure of capital is very important in order to acquire productive efficiency in an economy. Goods produced by one sector can be used either as investment goods or an intermediate input by other sectors. Thus promotion of investment in one sector, raises the demand for investible goods from other sectors. Any distortion in the allocation of investment among the production sectors, also leads to an inefficient structure of capital stocks in the economy. An efficient composition of capital goods requires an optimal structure of investment, that might result from the rationality of financial institutions. Such a structure of capital goods is possible in the model economy if the investors are permitted to operate freely in reallocating investment until the rate of returns become equal in each sector. Adherence to the principles of competition eliminates any inefficiency that may appear in a monopolistic or an oligopolistic market structure.

Financial deepening also leads to a reduction in the cost of financial transaction in the economy. The reduction in the proportions eaten out by the financial intermediaries means that the spread between the savings and investment narrows down. More resources are released for the investment, which means a higher rate of capital accumulation and a higher rate of growth in the model economy.

The financial liberalization becomes successful in an open economy, which guarantees a free inflow and a free outflow of the capital. Any restriction tend to distort the prices of capital in the domestic markets in comparison to the prices of capital in the external markets. This leads to unproductive speculative activities. In contrast, when the economy is open, prices of capital reflect the true economic cost. Long-term policies become sustainable only when they are based on such natural prices.

Financial deepening is possible only with a control in the government's budget deficit and an economic way of adjustment in the balance of payment account of an economy. A sustainable policy requires that the government spending does not excessively exceed to the government revenues. The balance in the external account of the economy implies that earnings from an expansion of exports pay for most of the imports of capital, intermediate and other commodities. Financial liberalization is impossible unless these is a reasonable discipline on both of these conditions (World Bank 1996).

In the model, period by period static equilibrium is embedded in a completely dynamic equilibrium of households and investors. Households maximize utility by allocating their life time income between consumption and saving over the horizon. Investors maximize the rate of return from investing in projects generating the highest rate of return. The exogenous growth rate of labor force and the cost of capital between the periods drive the growth rate of the economy. The model economy is open for trade with India and the rest of the world. The government collects taxes and spends on public consumption. The basic model can be modified in order to answer specific questions relating to the growth rate of the economy. It also examine cases when savings are channeled to unproductive assets.

The demand and supply equations generated from the optimization of households and firms' maximization problem are presented both in primal form and then in dual forms. Essentially solution of every primal problem has a dual counterpart: primal and duals are two sides of the same coin. While the primal form is more obvious among the economists a dual form is more compact for discussion and development of more complex solution algorithms.

CONSUMERS' INTERTEMPORAL PROBLEM

In the model representative households located in urban and rural areas of the economy solve an intertemporal utility maximization problem to allocate lifetime income over an infinite horizon. Formally, households solve:

$$\text{Max} \sum_{t=0}^{\infty} \beta_t U(C_t^h) \tag{3.1}$$

Subject to

$$\sum_{t=0}^{\infty} P_t C_t^h = \sum_t w_t^h L_t^h + M_o^h \tag{3.2}$$

where β is the rate of time preference, C_t is consumption, P_t is the present value price of the composite consumption good in period t; w_t represents present value of wage rate; L_t represents the supply of labor by a household; and M_o represents all other income including the value of current capital, net transfers from the government and remittances.

We specialize the utility function to be of constant elasticity of substitution type to express the relationship between the current and future consumption[2].

$$U(C_t^h) = \frac{\left(C_t^h\right)^{1-\sigma} - 1}{1-\sigma} \tag{3.3}$$

Here σ is the elasticity of substitution between the present and future consumption. A higher elasticity of substitution in the intertemporal utility function implies a higher degree of consumption smoothing and substitution over time. This is a well defined utility function in the literature used by Ramsey, Frisch, Timbergen, Koopman and many others in growth and development literature.

Given the specification of utility function in equation (3.3) the intertemporal utility maximization problem can be represented by maximization of equation 3.4 subject to the wealth constraints given by equation (3.5) below. The consumers are facing the Ramsey (1928) type problem. Each type of consumer has to decide how much of income s/he should consume at each model period on commodities, $C_{i,t}$, and how much to save in terms of financial assets (FA_t) and unproductive real assets (RA_t), so that the utility could be maximized over the life time, while letting the economy grow at the steady state level after the terminal period.

$$\max U_0^h = \sum_{t=0}^{\infty} \left(\frac{1}{1+\rho}\right)^t \frac{\left[\prod_{i=1}^{11} C_{i,t}^{\alpha_i^h}\right]^{1-\sigma} - 1}{1-\sigma} \tag{3.4}$$

The choice variables in this maximization problem are the amounts of consumption good from sector i to the household of type h. The term $(\frac{1}{1+\rho})$ is the utility discount factor (β_t) of the households. Utility is discounted by consumers' positive and constant rate of time preference ρ for simplicity, though we realize that the rate of time preference may be different for categories of household, particularly when the financial markets are segmented in the economy. There are eleven goods bought by consumers in each period and α_i^h is the share of income spent on i sector good of the household of category h. (See Chapter 4 for details).

The inter-temporal budget constraint, that equates the present value of consumption to the present value of life time income (wealth) takes the following form:

$$\sum_{t=0}^{\infty} R_t^{-1} P_t C_t^h = WH_t^h \tag{3.5}$$

where,

$$R_t^{-1} = \prod_{s=0}^{t-1} \frac{1}{1 + r_s} \tag{3.6}$$

is a discount factor to convert future income in the present value terms; r_s represents the real interest on financial assets; P_t and C_t are vectors of relative prices and composite consumption goods respectively same as in equation (2) above and

WH_h , is the life time wealth of consumer of category h, that can be defined as the following.

$$WH^h = \frac{J_0^h}{1+r_0^c} + \frac{J_1^h}{(1+r_0^c)(1+r_1^c)} + ... + \frac{J_2^h}{\Pi_s^t(1+r_s^c)} + ... = \sum_{t=0}^{\infty} R_t^{-1} * J_t^h \quad (3.7)$$

Where $J_{h,t}$ is disposable household income in period t.

Like consumers investors solve an intertemporal problem. The profit function of investment and the capital stock is the link between the present period and future periods. In the model this link is given by the following system of three equations:

An unit of investment in sector j is composed of investment goods produced by other sectors. Therefore the cost of intermediation is weighted average of the prices of components of investment.

i
$$\prod_{j,t}^{I} = P_{j,t+1}^{k} - \sum_{i} P_{i,t} a_{i,j}^{I} \leq 0 \quad (3.8)$$

here $\prod_{j,t}^{I}$ is profit from one unit of investment, $P_{j,t+1}^{k}$ is the price of capital in period $t+1$, and $a_{i,j}^{I}$ is the investment coefficient matrix. One unit of capital at the start of period 1 generates a rate of return ($r_{j,t}^{k}$) today and delivers 1-δ unit at the start of the subsequent period. The profit function of accumulation of capital stock by the investors is given by the following equation:

ii
$$\prod_{j,t}^{k} = (1-\delta) P_{j,t+1}^{k} + r_{j,t}^{k} - P_{j,t}^{k} \leq 0 \quad (3.9)$$

In a competitive system, the lending rate equals borrowing rate, which is equal to interest on deposits plus the administrative costs. This implies the cost of funds to borrowers is the same as the income received by the savers. When the financial system is repressed there is a spread between the lending and borrowing rates.

The objective of firms in each of twelve production sectors of the economy is to maximize the present value of profit subject to the constraints of production technology.

Subject to technology constraints to be discuss in the following section each firm chooses level of output and employment to maximize the following profit function:

$$\max \sum_{t=0}^{\infty} \beta_t^f \pi_{i,t} = \sum_{i=0}^{\infty} \beta_t^f (P_{i,t} Y_{i,t} - w_{u,t} L_{u,i,t} - w_{r,t} L_{r,i,t} - r_{i,t} K_{i,t} - \sum_i P_{j,t} Z_{i,j,t})$$

(3.10)

Here $P_{i,t}$ represents prices of commodity j, b_t represents the profit discount factor of producers; $Y_{i,t}$ is gross output, $w_{u,t}$ is wage rate for rural labor, $w_{r,t}$ is wage rate for rural labor, $r_{i,t}$ rate of interest in capital, $K_{i,t}$ is the capital use in production, $L_{u,i,t}$ is urban labor used in production, $L_{r,i,t}$ is rural labor, $Z_{i,j,t}$ is intermediate input used in producing $Y_{i,t}$. Assumptions of perfect competition imply that profit for each period equal zero. Therefore β_t are irrelevant for producers problem. Only the investment function is dynamic. The input output coefficients are fixed for a given time, therefore, it represents a fixed cost of production for the firms. The firms take the prices of labor, capital, and intermediate inputs as given, and can vary the amount of labor and capital in order maximize their inter-temporal profits.

Constant returns to scale technology in each period implies zero economic profit in equilibrium. Therefore, the number of firms is not important. We exploit this property in calculation. Incorporation of intertemporal adjustment and installment costs of capital stocks, such as one due to insufficient infrastructure or irregular supplies of essential services and materials, is left for future exercises (see Hayashi 1982, Abel and Blanchard 1983, Stokey and Lucas 1989, and Go and Devarajan 1995).

I postpone the discussion of intertemporal equilibrium conditions until section 3.5 turning now to a discussion of model structure in each period.

INTRATEMPORAL EQUILIBRIUM

The aggregate consumption for period t, is a Cobb-Douglas function of commodities:

$$C_t^h = \left(\prod_{i=1}^{11} C_{i,t}^{\alpha_i^h}\right) \tag{3.11}$$

Thus the utility in each period can be represented as:

$$U_t^h = \frac{\left(\prod_{i=1}^{11} C_{i,t}^{\alpha_i^h}\right)^{1-\sigma} - 1}{1-\sigma} \tag{3.12}$$

Within the model, aggregate demand and capital supplies depend on relative prices between time periods. Holding fixed the quantities, each period is characterized as static equilibrium model in which no sector earns a positive profit, and aggregate supply equals aggregate demand.

In addition of consumers there are government and tourists in each period. Discussion of these two sectors follows the discussion of production technology and trade in section 3.6.

Production Technology and Trade

In each period the supply process in this economy can be explained by ten types of nested production functions as listed below.

1. composite labor from skilled and unskilled labor
2. capital accumulation and capital allocation functions

3. value added function
4. Leontief function between value added and intermediate inputs
5. Constant elasticity of transformation (CET) export function between the Nepalese markets and the other economies
6. Constant elasticity of transformation export (CET) function between domestic sales and exports to India
7. Constant elasticity of substitution (CES) function between domestically supplied goods and imports from India
8. Constant elasticity of substitution (CES) between the Nepal-India market and the other economies
9. Total absorption in the economy
10. Intermediate inputs

Readers are requested to match these steps to the corresponding nodes in Fig. 3.1 which gives a graphical glimpse of the nested structure of production, trade and sales in the model economy. The sectoral subscripts are suppressed here for simplicity. At node 1 the aggregate labor (L) in the economy is composite of the skilled (L_u) and the unskilled (L_r) labor. At node 2 the capital sock of the economy, accumulated by the investment over the period comes from the domestic producers, or are imported from India or the rest of the world. The investment coefficient matrix used in equation 3.8 shows the relationship between the origin and destination of capital goods in the economy. An increase in the investment in one sector leads to increase in demand for investment goods of the other sector as described by the investment coefficient matrix. At node 3 the value added V (GDP at factor cost) is CES function of composite labor and the composite capital. The raw material inputs from other sectors are also required to produce Y commodities in a given sector. At node 10, Z refers to the intermediate demands in the economy. Input-output coefficients show the degree of forward and backward linkages along the various sectors of the economy. In other words, an increase in demand of a particular sector increases input demand from other sectors. At node 4 the gross output of a given sector (Y) thus constitutes of value added (V) and amount sold in the domestic markets to other sectors as intermediate inputs (Z). While the value added or GDP refers to the net output of a sector, the gross output includes intermediate transactions that are used up in process of supplying goods in the economy. The Leontief aggregation of intermediate inputs and value added generates Y.

At node 5 the gross output from each sector can be sold to other economies (E) or to the Nepal-India sector (XE). The allocation between these two markets really depends upon, the terms of trade with other economies, the ratio of prices in the Nepal-India economy to prices to the prices of the goods in other economies. The supply of goods to Nepal-India economy again is divided between domestic sales (NE) and exports to India (IE) at node 6. This again depends on the terms of exports with India or on the ratio prices of commodities in the domestic markets

Fig. 3.1

Nests in Production, Trade and Sales

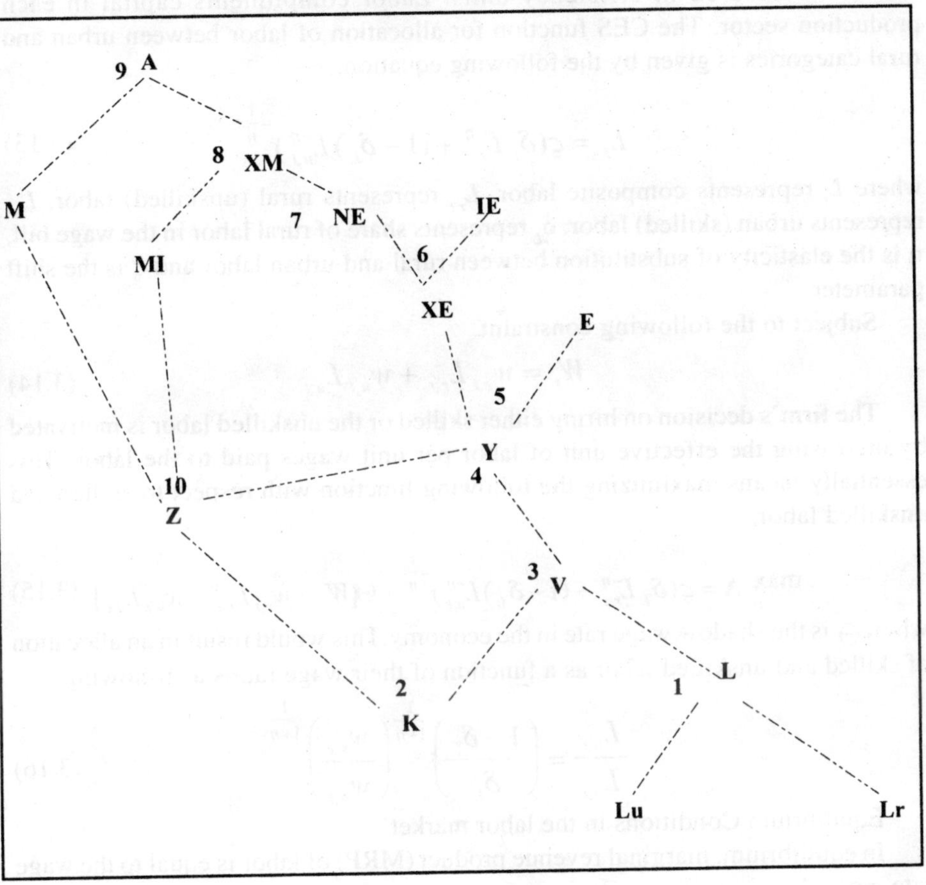

vs. the prices in the Indian markets. A constant elasticity of transformation function is used to separate amounts of domestic sales NE and exports to India, IE. Thus at node 7 NE is the total amount supplied by the domestic producers in the domestic market.

At node 8, the constant elasticity of substitution-Armington (1969) function is used to aggregate imports from India (MI) and domestic sales (NE) to obtain total supply of goods (XM) from the Nepalese and Indian producers to the Nepalese markets. This depends on the terms of imports with India. Then additional goods are imported from other economies (M). At node 9, the CES aggregation of M with XM, gives us a total absorption A in the economy. Terms of trade with other economies determines the amount to be imported from these economies in relation to purchases from the Nepal-India sector. For non-tradable sectors node 7 represents the total supply of commodities in the economy. Now I proceed to a discussion of model equations for each of these nodes in detail.

Labor Market

Labor is measured in efficiency units. Labor compliments capital in each production sector. The CES function for allocation of labor between urban and rural categories is given by the following equation:

$$L_t = \varsigma(\delta_L L_{r,t}^{-\eta} + (1-\delta_L)L_{u,t}^{-\eta})^{-\frac{1}{\eta}} \qquad (3.13)$$

where L_t represents composite labor, $L_{r,t}$ represents rural (unskilled) labor, $L_{u,t}$ represents urban (skilled) labor, δ_L represents share of rural labor in the wage bill, η is the elasticity of substitution between rural and urban labor and ξ is the shift parameter.

Subject to the following constraint.

$$W_t = w_{r,t} L_{r,t} + w_{u,t} L_{u,t} \qquad (3.14)$$

The firm's decision on hiring either skilled or the unskilled labor is motivated by increasing the effective unit of labor per unit wages paid to the labor. This essentially means maximizing the following function with respect to skilled and unskilled labor.

$$\max \ \Lambda = \varsigma(\delta_L L_{r,t}^{-\eta} + (1-\delta_L)L_{u,t}^{-\eta})^{-\frac{1}{\eta}} + \Theta[W_t - w_{r,t} L_{r,t} - w_{u,t} L_{u,t}] \qquad (3.15)$$

where Θ is the shadow wage rate in the economy.This would result in an allocation of skilled and unskilled labor as a function of their wage ratios as following

$$\frac{L_{u,t}}{L_{r,t}} = \left(\frac{1-\delta_L}{\delta_L}\right)^{\frac{1}{1+\eta}} \left(\frac{w_{r,t}}{w_{u,t}}\right)^{\frac{1}{1+\eta}} \qquad (3.16)$$

Equilibrium Conditions in the labor market

In equilibrium, marginal revenue product (MRP) of labor is equal to the wage rate, i.e.

$$w_t^h = \frac{\theta_i^h P_{i,t} Y_{i,t}}{L_t^h} \qquad (3.17)$$

where θ_i^h is the share of income going to labor of category h from the *i*th production sector, $Y_{i,t}$ is the output in sector i.

This also means that the wage rate for a given category of labor will be the same across all sectors in the model economy.

$$w_t^h = \frac{\theta_i^h P_{i,t} Y_{i,t}}{L_i^h} = \frac{\theta_i^h P_{j,t} Y_{j,t}}{L_t^h} \qquad (3.18)$$

In each period, equilibrium supply of labor is equal to the demand for labor.

$$\sum_{i,h} L_{i,t}^h = L_t \qquad (3.19)$$

The effective labor income of household of category h is given by:

$$w_t^h L_t^h = \sum_i w_{i,t}^h L_{i,t}^h = \sum_i \frac{\theta_h^i P_{i,t} Y_{i,t}}{L_{i,t}^h} \quad (3.20)$$

Dual equations of labor market

The demand for labor in sector j is given by:

and, demand for labor is $$L_{j,t} = Y_{j,t} \frac{\partial \Pi_{j,t}^V}{\partial PV_{j,t}} \frac{\partial PV_{j,t}}{\partial PL_{j,t}} \quad (3.21)$$

where $L_{j,t}$ is a composite of rural and urban labor.

Equilibrium in the labor market requires that:

$$\sum_j L_{j,t} \frac{\partial \Pi^L}{\partial PL_t^{LC}} \leq \overline{L}_t \quad (3.22)$$

$\overline{L}_t$ in the above equations is a composite of urban and rural labor. The choice of urban and rural labor by firms is obtained by maximization of the dual profit function in hiring decision.

$$\Pi_{j,t}^L = PL_{j,t} - [(\theta_j^R PL_t^{R^{1-\sigma_v}} + (1-\theta_j^R) PL_t^{u^{1-\sigma_u}})]^{\frac{1}{1-\sigma}} \leq 0 \quad (3.23)$$

where

$PL_{j,t}$ = composite price of labor

$PL_t^{R^{1-\sigma_v}}$ = rural labor

$PL_t^{u^{1-\sigma_u}}$ = urban labor

$$PL_{j,t} = (\theta_j^R PL_t^R + (1-\theta_j^R) PL_t^u)^{\frac{1}{\rho}}$$

θ_j^R is share of rural labor cost to composite price of labor.

Capital Market

Entering capital (K_0) stock is transferred into initial capital stock for the various sectors, $K_{i,0}$, according to a fixed coefficient transformation process. Once the initial capital is allocated among different sectors, $K_{i,t}$, the law of motion of capital in a sector is explained by the following equation.

$$K_{j,t+1} = I_{j,t} + (1-\delta_K) K_{j,t} \quad (3.24)$$

where, $$I_{i,t} = \sum_j a_{i,j,t}^I I_{j,t} \quad (3.25)$$

Net investment demand, $I_{i,t}$, in each sector is the sum of investment by origin. The relationship given by $a^{I}_{i,j,t}$ is called capital coefficient matrix of the economy. This means that an increase in investment demand in a particular sector affects the sales of investment goods in other sector as described by the capital coefficient matrix of the economy. Thus individual firms making total investment plans simultaneously increase the demand for investment goods from other firms as well. The sum of coefficients in a row of the investment matrix maps investment from origin into the investment by destination. Though the coefficients of investment matrix ($a^{I}_{i,j,t}$) in the short run may be considered to be fixed, in the long-run, these coefficients change. One can use row and column operations, RAS, technique to update the investment matrix in order to reflect the changing structure of the capital stock in the economy (see Allen and Gossling 1975, p.3 for listing of various RAS methods).

From iterative substitutions we can solve for the capital stock in any period in terms of investment matrix as following:

$$K_{i,t} = \sum_{s=1}^{t} (1-\delta_{K,t})^{s} K_{i,t-s} + \sum_{s=1} (1-\delta_{K,i})^{s-1} \left[\sum_{j} a^{I}_{i,j,t} \right] \qquad (3.26)$$

We assume that in the terminal period the investment in each sector grows at the rate of the population so that economy can continue along the steady state growth path even after the terminal period as given by the following equation (Rutherford 1995).

$$I_{j,t} = (g + \delta_{K,j}) K_{j,t} \qquad (3.27)$$

g = growth rate of the economy, which equals the growth rate of the labor force in terms of efficiency units, and δ_K = rate of depreciation.

Equilibrium Conditions in Capital Market

In a fully liberalized economy the equilibrium return to capital across the sectors should be equal. The demand for capital in equilibrium can, therefore, be explained in terms of the following law of equi-marginal product of capital across the various sectors of production in the model economy assuming the risk everywhere is the same.

$$r_{j,t} = (1-\theta) P_{j,t} L^{\theta}_{j,t} K^{-\theta}_{j,t} = r_{i,t} = (1-\theta) P_{i,t} L^{\theta}_{i,t} K^{-\theta}_{i,t} \qquad (3.28)$$

Otherwise it would be profitable to transfer funds from a less productive sector to more productive sectors of the economy. This condition is very critical in improving the efficiency of capital market in the economy.

In a competitive economy, the rental cost of capital should be equal to the marginal product of capital and depreciation.

$$r^{k}_{i,t} = r_{i,t} + \delta_{i,t} \qquad (3.29)$$

In repression the cost of capital also includes the markup rate on top of the gross interest.

$$r^k_{i,t} = (1-\tau_j)\cdot r_{i,t} + MK_{i,t} + \delta_{i,t} \tag{3.30}$$

The requirement that the returns on capital be equal across different sectors of the economy is not met in case of a financially repressed economy. The allocation of capital among sectors is not strictly based on differences in productivity but to some other artificial regulations. There are several reasons why rates of return cannot be equalized in a repressed economy. First, there are interest rate ceiling that distort the economy by creating a bias in favor of the current consumption against the future consumption. The potential savers engage in relatively low yielding self-financed projects or unproductive real assets rather than making deposits in the financial institutions. A few lucky borrowers are able to obtain funds at low rates to invest in relatively capital-intensive but unproductive projects. The pool of potential borrowers contain entrepreneurs with low-yielding projects (Fry 1995 Ch. 2). One very simple rule of allocation of capital in such a repressed regime is a rule of inertia. The ratio of investment in sectors i and j is equal to the ratio of capital stock in these sectors in the previous period.

$$\frac{I_{i,t}}{I_{j,t}} = \varpi.\frac{K_{i,t-1}}{K_{j,t-1}} \tag{3.31}$$

Here ϖ the coefficient of inertia for allocation of capital among the sectors.

It follows from this discussion that in such a situation total production can be increased by moving capital from a less productive sector tô more productive sectors. This role of financial liberalization will be studied in the model economy in chapter 5 when applying the model for policy analysis.

On the supply side, the total stock of capital employed by various sectors cannot be greater than overall capital stock of the economy. This overall stock is total of household savings minus the debt outstanding of the government and the accumulation of foreign exchange reserves.

$$\sum_i K_{i,t} = \overline{K}_t = \sum_h FA_t - (\overline{DB_t} + \overline{FR_t}) = \sum_h FA_t - \sum_{t=0}^{\infty}(B_t + \Delta FR_t) = \sum_{t=0}^{\infty}(c_t S_t - \Delta RA_t) - \sum_{t=0}^{\infty}(B_t + \Delta FR_t) \tag{3.32}$$

Here FA is the financial assets of the households, DB is stock of government debt, FR is foreign exchange reserve, B is borrowing each year by the government, RA is the investment in unproductive assets, Δ is the change operator. Accumulation of financial assets, or the capital stock will be larger smaller the size of leakage of savings in unproductive assets.

Dual solution of demand[3] for capital in sector j is given by:

$$K_{j,t} = Y_{j,t}\frac{\partial \Pi^V_{j,t}}{\partial PV_{j,t}}\frac{\partial PV_{j,t}}{\partial PK_{j,t}} \tag{3.33}$$

where $Y_{j,t}$ is activity level; $PK_{j,t}$ is price of capital $PV_{j,t}$ is price of value added.

In addition to equation 3.27 the equilibrium condition in the capital market, as before, requires that

$$\sum_j K_{j,t} = \overline{K}_t \tag{3.34}$$

$\overline{K}_t$ is the aggregate capital stock in the economy, which grow according to the low of motion of capital stock as given by equation 3.26. $\sum_j K_{j,t}$ is the total demand for capital by various sectors of the economy.

In an ideal Arrow-Debreu economy, a zero profit, or arbitrage condition of sector j investment can be represented as:

$$P^k_{j,t+1} = \sum_j P_{i,t} a^I_{i,j} \tag{3.35}$$

When an economy is repressed there is additional distortionary cost $\tau_{j,t}$ on top of the cost of materials required for per unit investment in a given sector. The profit from the investment in a repressed economy is given by:

$$P^k_{j,t+1} = \left(1 + \tau_{j,t}\right) \sum_j P_{i,t} a^I_{i,j} \tag{3.36}$$

where

$\tau_{j,t}$ = per unit wedge between the return to saving and the cost of investment.

$P^k_{j,t+1}$ = present value price of sector j capital at the beginning of next period

$P_{i,t}$ = present value price of sector i commodity at period t

Value Added

Value added, or GDP at factor income, is given by CES function of labor and capital as following.

$$V_{i,t} = [\delta_v L^{\rho_V}_{i,t} + (1-\delta_v) K^{\rho_V}_{i,t}]^{\frac{1}{\rho_V}} \tag{3.37}$$

Similarly an unit profit function of the value added is a CES function of labor and capital and the costs of these inputs (PVj,t). Price of value added is essentially income to the owners of factors of production. Meanwhile they are cost to the employers of those inputs. Unit profit function for operation of value added can be explained in terms of following:

$$\Pi^v_{j,t} = PV_{j,t} - [(\theta^L_j PL^{1-\sigma_v}_{j,t} + (1-\theta^L_j) RK^{u^{1-\sigma v}}_t]^{\frac{1}{1-\sigma}} \leq 0 \tag{3.38}$$

where;

$PV_{j,t}$ unit cost of value added

$PL_{j,t}$ wage rate

RKi,t rental rate of capital

$\Pi^{v}_{j,t}$ unit profit from operation on value added

The price of value added is essentially income to the owners of factors of production. Meanwhile they are cost to the employers of those inputs.

Gross Output

The gross output in each sector can be explained by the nested production function between the value added and the intermediate inputs.

$$Y_{j,t} = V_{j,t} + a_{i,j} Y_{j,t} \tag{3.39}$$

Where Yj,t is the output of sector j in period t, Vj,t is the value added part and $a_{i,j}$ is the intermediate inputs per unit of gross output produced in sector j. The firms operating in tradable sectors sell output in domestic and foreign markets and firms operating on non-tradable sectors sell their output in domestic markets.

Zero profit for sector *j* written in dual form in terms of composite prices of commodities and inputs is the following:

$$\Pi^{y}_{j,t} = [(\theta^{x}_{j} PX^{1+\eta}_{j,t} + (1-\theta^{x}_{j}) PD^{1+\eta}_{j,t})]^{\frac{1}{1+\eta}} - \theta^{v}_{j} PV^{v}_{j} - (1-\theta^{v}_{j}) \sum_{j} a_{i,j} P_{i,t} \leq 0 \tag{3.40}$$

The exact meaning of the symbols of the above profit function are following:

$\Pi^{y}_{j,t}$ unit profit of activity in sector j

$PX_{j,t}$ price of exports

$PD_{j,t}$ price of domestic sales

PV^{v}_{j} price of value added per unit of output in activity j

$P_{i,t}$ price of final goods used as intermediate goods

θ^{x}_{j} share parameter for exports in total production

θ^{v}_{j} share of costs paid to labor and capital

$a_{i,j}$ input output coefficients.

The equation 3.38 is an unit profit function . The profit of operating these firms are given by the difference between the revenue from sales and the cost of supply. The unit revenue function is constant elasticity transformation (CET) composite of unit price of domestic sales and unit price of exports. The unit costs are divided between value-added, i.e. payments to labor and capital, and the unit intermediate input costs.

For clarity of exposition I assume that there are four traders in the model: trader number one and trader number two operating in the export sector and trader number three and trader number four operating in the import sector.

Exports from Nepal to Other Economies

The trader number one in the model buys all of these output and exports them to the other economies (*Ei*) or sells them to the trader number two who operates trading business in the Nepal-India sector ($XE_{i,t}$). The technology of transformation of this fixed commodity between the Nepal-India market and the other economies can be explained in terms of the following constant elasticity of trade equation.

$$Y_{i,t} = \Psi(\gamma_i E_{i,t}^{\chi_i} + (1-\gamma_{i_i})XE_{i,t}^{\chi_i})^{\frac{1}{\chi_i}} \qquad (3.41)$$

The Greek symbols, y, g and c are called shift, share, and elasticity parameters of this transformation function. The number one trader's revenue is as following (an Euler function of dual prices for linearly homogenous functions: see Devarajan *et al.* 1994: 26).

$$PD_{i,t}Y_{i,t} = PE_{i,t}E_{i,t} + PXE_{i,t}XE_{i,t} \qquad (3.42)$$

where $PD_{i,t}$ is prices of gross domestic output ($Y_{i,t}$), $PE_{i,t}$ represents export prices to other economies ($E_{i,t}$), and $PXE_{i,t}$ is prices of commodities sold to Nepal-India market ($XE_{i,t}$). Here, the total revenue is decomposed between the revenue from exports and a revenue from sales to the Nepal-India market. The trader chooses an optimum quantity to export to other economies and optimum quantity of sales to trader number two based on the maximization of export revenue subject to the export-transformation function as following.

$$\Re_{i,,w,,t} = PE_{i,t}E_{i,t} + PXE_{i,t}XE - P_{i,t}Y_{i,t} + \Phi_{e,w,t}\left[Y_{i,t} - \Psi(\gamma_i E_{i,t}^{\chi_i} + (1-\gamma_{i_i})XE_{i,t}^{\chi_i})^{\frac{1}{\chi_i}}\right] \qquad (3.43)$$

Maximizing w.r.t $E_{i,t}$, $XE_{i,t}$, $Y_{i,t}$ we get that the ratio of exports to other economies to the sales in Nepal-India market is directly related to the price of exported commodities in the world market and inversely related with the prices of the commodities in the domestic market. This implies that higher the domestic prices more is sold in the domestic market. If the external prices are higher relative to the domestic prices, producers will export more to the other economies.

$$\frac{E_{i,t}}{XE_{i,t}} = \frac{PE_{i,t}}{PD_{i,t}}\left(\frac{1-\gamma_i}{\gamma_i}\right)^{\frac{1}{\chi i}} \qquad (3.44)$$

The parameters of function γ_i and χ_i will influence the magnitude of the ratio.

Commodities produced by such as the transportation sector, public sector, hotel and restaurants, and the electricity, gas and water are non-tradable. There is no revenue maximization decision with respect to exports for traders involved in trading such commodities.

$$XE_{i,t} = Y_{i,t} \tag{3.45}$$

Domestic Sales and Exports to India

The trader number two operates the Nepal-India export business, who purchases all $XE_{i,t}$ goods from the trader number one and decides how much to sell in Nepal market (*NE*) and how much to sell in India (*IE*). The technology of transformation between the Nepalese sales and Indian sales is given by following.

$$XE_{i,t} = \Phi(\xi_i IE_{i,t}^{\iota_i} + (1-\xi_i) NE_{i,t}^{\iota_i})^{\frac{1}{\iota_i}} \tag{3.46}$$

The symbols Φ, ξ, ι are again called shift, share and elasticity parameters of the Nepal India export business. The total revenue from goods sold is the total of revenue from Nepal's sales and the revenue from the exports to India.

$$PXE_{i,t} XE_{i,t} = PD_{i,t} NE_{i,t} + PIE_{i,t} IE_{i,t} \tag{3.47}$$

For a given commodity, PD represents domestic price, PIE represents export price to India and PXE is the aggregate price of the commodities that trader two purchases from trader 1.

The maximization of revenue subject to the constant elasticity of export transformation function can be explained in terms of the following equation.

$$\Re_{i,I,t} = PD_{i,t} NE_{i,t} + PIE_{i,t} IE_{i,t} - PXE_{i,t} XE_{i,t} + \Phi_{i,t}\left[XE_{i,t} - \Phi(\xi_i IE_{i,t}^{\iota_i} + (1-\xi_i) NE_{i,t}^{\iota_i})^{\frac{1}{\iota_i}} \right] \tag{3.48}$$

From the first order necessary condition we get the following result.

$$\frac{IE_{i,t}}{NE_{i,t}} = \left(\frac{PIE_{i,t}}{PD_{i,t}} \frac{(1-\xi_i)}{\xi_i} \right)^{\frac{1}{\iota_i - 1}} \tag{3.49}$$

As before, we find that the ratio of India sale to the domestic sale depends on the terms of trade or the ratio of prices of those commodities in India relative to the price in Nepal and $\Phi_{i,t}$ ξ_i and ι_i the share, shift and substitution parameters.

Again such trading is not necessary in case of transportation, public sector, and hotel and restaurants sectors that are completely non-tradable sectors in the model; for trader number three total domestic sales of goods produced in these sectors is equal to total domestic supply, nothing more and nothing less.

$$NE_{i,t} = XE_{i,t} \tag{3.50}$$

The constant elasticity of trade function can be written in terms of domestic and foreign prices. The exports in the model economy are divided between the exports to India and exports to the other economies. The exports between India and rest of the world in dual formulation, can be expressed by the following transformation function.

$$\Pi^{x}_{j,t} = PX_{j,t} - [(\theta^{I}_{j} PX^{India^{1+\eta_x}}_{j,t} + (1-\theta^{I}_{j}) PX^{RW1+\eta_x}_{j,t})] \leq 0 \tag{3.51}$$

$\Pi^{x}_{j,t}$ = unit profit from exporting one unit of good of tradable sector j,

$PX_{j,t}$ = composite export price of sector j commodity

$PX^{India^{1+\eta_x}}_{j,t}$ = price component due to exports to India

$PX^{RW1+\eta_x}_{j,t}$ = price component due to export to other economies

θ^{I}_{j} = weight of export price to India to total export price

Export to India depends upon the gradient of the profit function:

$$X^{India}_{j,t} = Y_{j,t} \frac{\partial \prod Y_j}{\partial PX_{j,t}} \frac{\partial PX_{j,t}}{\partial PX^{India}_{j,t}} \tag{3.52}$$

similarly the exports to the rest of the world :

$$X^{RW}_{j,t} = Y_{j,t} \frac{\partial \prod Y_j}{\partial PX_{j,t}} \frac{\partial PX_{j,t}}{\partial PX^{RW}_{j,t}} \tag{3.53}$$

Imports

The profits from imports from India and the third countries (RW) depends upon the values of imports that maximize the CES profit function.

The technology of import from other economies and from the domestic producer, called the CES aggregation of M and XM is given by the following function.

$$X_{i,t} = \Omega(\phi_i M_{i,t}^{-\varphi_i} + (1-\phi_i) XM_{i,t}^{-\varphi_i})^{-\frac{1}{\varphi_i}} \tag{3.54}$$

The traders again intend to minimize the cost of total supply that can be broken down into cost of imports from the other economies and cost of supply from the Nepalese and Indian producers. This takes the following form.

$$P_{i,t} X_{i,t} = PM_{i,t} M_{i,t} + PXM_{i,t} XM_{i,t} \tag{3.55}$$

Where P is supply price of composite commodity, M represents the import prices, and PXM is the prices in Nepal-India market.

$$\wp_{i,R,t} = PM_{i,t}M_{i,t} + PXM_{i,t}XM_{i,t} + \Phi^{m}_{i,R,t}\left[P_{i,t}X_{i,t} - \Omega(\phi_i M_{i,t}^{-\varphi_i} + (1-\phi_i)XM_{i,t}^{-\varphi_i})^{-\frac{1}{\varphi_i}}\right] \quad (3.56)$$

The result of optimization can be expressed in terms of ratios of imports depending in the ratios of prices. the lower will be the amount of imports from other economies the lower the prices in Nepal-India market, or higher the prices in the other economies.

$$\frac{M_{i,t}}{XM_{i,t}} = \left(\frac{PXM_{i,t}}{PM_{i,t}}\frac{\phi_i}{(1-\phi_i)}\right)^{\frac{1}{1+\varphi_i}} \quad (3.57)$$

For sector not importing from the other economies, total supply is equals total sales of domestic or Indian producers as following.

$$X_{i,t} = XM_{i,t} \quad (3.58)$$

Thus the total absorption in the economy, A, constitutes of value of final goods and services supplied by domestic producers and imported from India and other economies. The amount each of them depend on relative prices of commodities in these markets.

Imports from India

The trader number three operates on Nepal-India market and supplies goods purchased from trader number two, the operator of Nepal-India trade business, and by importing goods from India that are not sufficiently available in the economy. He decides the composition of domestic supply (NE) and imports from India (IM) looking at the terms of trade with respect to India, or the ratio of prices of goods in the domestic markets and the prices in Indian markets (PIM/PXD). The CES composite of goods (XM) imported from India (MI) and domestic sales of Nepalese firms (NE) is given by the following function.

$$XM_{i,t} = \Gamma(\omega_i MI_{i,t}^{-\varepsilon_i} + (1-\omega_i)NE_{i,t}^{-\varepsilon_i})^{\frac{1}{\varepsilon_i}} \quad (3.59)$$

The traders want to minimize the cost of supply in the domestic market. The cost of supply for Nepal-India sector of the market is given by:

$$PXM_{i,t}XM_{i,t} = PIM_{i,t}MI_{i,t} + PD_{i,t}NE_{i,t} \quad (3.60)$$

For a given commodity, PD is prices of domestic markets, PIM prices of import, and PXM is the aggregate price in the domestic markets. The import cost minimization is subject to possibility of substitution explained in terms of CES is given by the following equation.

$$\wp_{i,I,t} = PXM_{i,t}XM_{i,t} - PIM_{i,t}MI_{i,t} - PD_{i,t}NE_{i,t} + \Phi^{m}_{i,I,t}\left[\Gamma(\omega_i MI_{i,t}^{-\varepsilon_i} + (1-\omega_i)NE_{i,t}^{-\varepsilon_i})^{\frac{1}{\varepsilon_i}}\right] \quad (3.61)$$

The ratio of trade from India to the domestic purchases is derived from the first order necessary condition as following:

$$\frac{MI_{i,t}}{NE_{i,t}} = \left(\frac{PD_{i,t}}{PIM_{i,t}} \frac{\omega_i}{(1-\omega_i)} \right)^{\frac{1}{1+\varepsilon_i}} . \tag{3.62}$$

For sectors not importing from India, such as construction, transportation , tourism and public services, the domestic supply equals domestic production (XD).

$$XM_{i,t} = Y_{i,t} \tag{3.63}$$

Constant elasticity of substitution import function and be written in terms of domestic and foreign prices of importable commodities as following:

$$\Pi^M_{j,t} = P^M_{j,t} - [(\theta^{MM}_{j,India} P_{j,t}^{2-\sigma_{India}} + (1-\theta^{MM}_{j,India}) P_{j,t}^{M^{2-\sigma_{RW}}})]^{\frac{1}{1-\sigma_{MM}}} \leq 0 \tag{3.64}$$

Imports from India are given by

$$M^{India}_{j,t} = A_{j,t} \frac{\partial \prod^A_j}{\partial P^M_{j,t}} \frac{\partial P^M_{j,t}}{\partial P^{India}_{j,t}} \tag{3.65}$$

$A_{j,t}$ is the total supply of commodity in the economy.

similarly the imports from the rest of the world :

$$M^{RW}_{j,t} = A_{j,t} \frac{\partial \prod^A_j}{\partial P^M_{j,t}} \frac{\partial P^M_{j,t}}{\partial P^{RW}_{j,t}} \tag{3.66}$$

Within period market clearance in characterized by the following two conditions.

One, there is no gain from arbitrage between the domestic sales and imports:

$$Y_{j,t} \frac{\partial \prod^Y_{j,t}}{\partial PD_{j,t}} = \frac{\partial P \prod^A_{j,t}}{\partial PD_{j,t}} A_{j,t} \tag{3.67}$$

Two, the Armington supply should equal the total demand in the economy:

$$\Pi^A_{j,t} = P^A_{j,t} - [(\theta^M_j P_{j,t}^{M^{1-\sigma Dm}} + (1-\theta^M_j) P_{j,t}^{1-\sigma Dm})]^{\frac{1}{1-\sigma Dm}} \leq 0 \tag{3.68}$$

The total absorption in the model economy depends upon the domestic supply and imports. The unit Armington (1969) aggregation of domestic sales and imports can be explained by the following function.

INTERTEMPORAL EQUILIBRIUM

The intertemporal equilibrium conditions are derived from the utility maximization problem of households and profit maximization problem of investors.

The Lagrangian of consumers' the inter-temporal problem is

$$\Im^h = \sum_{t=0}^{\infty}(\frac{1}{1+\rho})^t(\frac{C_t^{h1-\sigma}-1}{1-\sigma})+\lambda.[\sum_{t=0}^{\infty} R_t^{-1} * P_t C_t^{h} - WH_t^h] \qquad (3.69)$$

The demand function generated from the constrained intertemporal maximization associated with such type of utility function is of the following form.

$$C_{t+1}^h = [\left(\frac{1+\rho}{1+r_t}\right)\frac{P_{t+1}}{P_t}]^{\frac{1}{\alpha_h-1}} C_t^h \qquad (3.70)$$

Solving the first order difference equation[4] to get the value of C_t , as following:

$$\left(\frac{1}{1+\rho}\right)^t \left(\frac{\left(C_{i,t}^h\right)^{\alpha_h-1}}{\left(C_{i,0}^h\right)^{\alpha_h-1}}\right) = \left(\Pi\frac{1}{1+r_s}\right)\frac{P_t^i}{P_0^i} \qquad (3.71)$$

or, $$C_{i,t}^h = \left[\mu^t R_t^{-1}\frac{P_t^i}{P_0^i}\right]^{\frac{1}{\alpha_h-1}} C_{i,0}^h \qquad (3.72)$$

where $$m^t = \left(\frac{1}{1+\rho}\right)^t .$$

Consistency of the intertemporal budget constraint implies that:

$$\sum_t R_t^{-1}[C_0 + \Omega_1 C_0 + \Omega_2 C_0 + \ldots\ldots] = W \qquad (3.73)$$

where $$\Omega_t = [\mu^t R_t^{-1}\frac{P_t}{P_0}]^{\frac{1}{\alpha_h-1}}$$

$$R_t^{-1}\Omega_t = [\mu^t \frac{P_t}{P_0}]^{\frac{1}{\alpha_h-1}} R_t^{\frac{1}{\alpha_h-1}} R_t^{-1} = [\mu^t \frac{P_t}{P_0}]^{\frac{1}{\alpha_h-1}} R_t^{\frac{\alpha_h}{\alpha_h-1}} \qquad (3.74)$$

As discussed in Rutherford (1995) and Merciner and Mitchel(1994), we use finite descrete-time approximations to approximate the infinite horizon problem faced by consumers in the model economy.

The solution of this maximization problem gives us the following relationship between the consumption at period t and consumption at steady state, $\bar{C}_t$ as following:

$$\frac{C_{t+1}}{C_t} = \frac{\bar{C}_{t+1}}{\bar{C}_t}\left(\frac{P_t}{P_{t+1}}\right)^{\sigma}\left(\frac{\bar{P}_{t+1}}{\bar{P}_t}\right)^{\sigma} = (1+g)(1-r)^{-\sigma}\left(\frac{P_t}{P_{t+1}}\right)^{\frac{1}{\sigma}} \qquad (3.75)$$

Thus the consumption level at steady state can be expressed in terms of growth rate, the rate of interest and intertemporal prices commodities. These are ultimately function of wealth and expenditure of consumers.

In steady state consumption grows as following:

$$\overline{C_t} = (1+g)^t C_0 \tag{3.76}$$

The cost of capital can be decomposed into the true cost of capital, $\overline{r}_j^k$, and the distortion rate, t_j. This can be expressed as:

$$r_1^k = \frac{\overline{r}_j^k}{1-\tau_j} \tag{3.77}$$

In steady state composite present value price move along the following path:

$$\overline{P_t} = (1-r)^t P_0 \tag{3.78}$$

where (1-r) approximates the gross rate of return, i.e. 1/(1+r). The price of composite commodity at the initial period is the numeraire in the model. Two things are noteworthy: first, the general equilibrium implies a set of relative prices consistent with the equilibrium. The absolute prices do not matter. If all prices are multiplied by a constant it will still be the same equilibrium.

It is assumed that at the steady state all sectors grow at the same rate:

$$Y_{i,t+1} = (1+g) Y_{i,t} \tag{3.79}$$

Similarly, the initial labor endowment, in terms of efficiency units, is equals $L_{0,}$ and is assumed to grow exogenously at the g.

$$L_t = L_0(1+g)^t \tag{3.80}$$

One may question the validity of steady state growth rate for each section of the economy. For instance land may not grow at the rate of population growth rate. Urban labor supply may grow faster than the rural labor supply given the trends of migration in these economies. NONSS version of the model considers a case when certain section of the economy grow differently than the steady state growth rate.

Calibration to a Steady State

In the steady state all sectors of the economy grow at the same rate. The bench mark rate of return is calibrated assuming the non-distorted economy being in the steady state in the base year. Calibration of dynamic component of the model is described by the following procedure. I suggest readers to see chapter four for discussion of other parameters of the model.

Investment produces one unit of capital stock in period 2 (P_2^k) from one unit of output in the period one, P_1^k . The present value of one unit of capital in period two is equal to $(1-r)P_1^k$.

$$P_1^l = 1 = P_2^k = (1-r)P_1^k \Rightarrow P_1^k = \frac{1}{1-r}P_2^k \quad (3.81)$$

Here 1-r is the discount rate between two periods, and is approximation to 1/(1+r).

$$\frac{P_{t+1}^k}{P_t^k} = (1-r)$$

One unit of capital at the beginning of period one earns a rate of return today, r_1^k and delivers 1-δ unit of capital for the start of the next period.

$$P_1^k = r_1^k + (1-\delta)(1-r)P_2^k \quad (3.82)$$

This relationship applies to all other periods included in the model.

Using relation between P_2^k and P_1^k, i.e. by substituting out P_1^k from 3.35 using 3.34 this equation becomes:

$$\frac{1}{1-r} = r_1^k + (1-\delta) \quad (3.83)$$

The cost of capital is interest plus the rate of depreciation: $r_1^k = \frac{r}{1-r} + \delta$.

From the base-year SAM we can read the earning of capital

$V_1 = r_1 K_1$ (3.84), and

Now substituting for r_1^k we get the relation between the steady state interest rate r and the parameters of the model as following:

$$K_1 = \frac{V_1}{\frac{r}{1-r} + \delta} \quad (3.85)$$

Then substituting this value of K_1 in I_1 function the relationship between the investment and capital earning component of value added may be expressed as:

$$\frac{I_1}{V_1} = \frac{\delta + g}{\frac{r}{1-r} + \delta} \quad (3.86)$$

If the ratio of investment and capital earning $\left(\frac{I_1}{V_1} = 1\right)$ is equal to one then $g = \frac{r}{1-r}$ or $r = \frac{g}{1+g}$.

When $\frac{I_1}{V_1} \neq 1$, then the key parameter to calibrate is the rate of depreciation, which can be calculated using the relationship between the interest rate, growth rate, depreciation and earning of capital as following :

$$\delta_j = g\frac{V_j}{I_j - V_j} - \frac{r}{1-r}\frac{I_j}{I_j - V_j} \tag{3.87}$$

In a repressionary regime the cost of capital is distorted by a repressionary component of intermediation, t_j , so that price of capital becomes

$$P_1^k = r_1^k(1-\tau_i) + (1-\delta)(1-r)P_2^k \tag{3.88}$$

or the cost of capital

$$r_1^k = \frac{1}{1-\tau_j}\left[\frac{r}{1-r} + \delta\right] \tag{3.89}$$

Decomposing the cost of capital into true cost of capital, $\bar{r}_j^k$, and the distortion rate, τ_j the total cost of capital can be expressed as: $r_1^k = \frac{\bar{r}_j^k}{1-\tau_j}$ Now adjusting (3.39) to take account of distortions in the capital market:

$$\frac{I_1}{V_1} = \frac{\delta + g}{\frac{r}{1-r} + \delta}(1-\tau_j) \tag{3.90}$$

$$\tau_j = 1 - \frac{\bar{r}_j^k}{\delta + g}\frac{I_j}{V_j}$$

Thus the spread between the true cost of capital $\bar{r}_j^k$ and the actual cost of capital r_1^k depends upon the ratio of investment to capital and ratio of natural rate of interest to depreciation plus the growth rate of the economy.

GOVERNMENT SECTOR

Success of the financial sector in mobilizing resources depends to a great extent on the fiscal and balance of payment policy of the government. While a strict discipline on both of these accounts is consistent with the development of the financial system, the whole edifice of the financial structure may crumble when budgetary and trade policy are derailed. This section describes the structure of fiscal and BOP account included in the model.

In the core part of the model the government's budget is balanced in every period, and, therefore government is not involved in intertemporal savings. This essentially implies all government expenditure is basically the government consumption. This assumption can be defended on the ground that policy reforms started during early 1990s have increasingly emphasized on privatization. Government receives revenues from taxes and foreign aids, and spends this amount to provide basic public services. Private sector does the business in this model while by enforcement of property right and contracts the government creates an environment suitable for investment and production activities to be carried by the private sector.

Sources of Revenue

The sources of revenue for the government are taxes on value added, tariffs on imports, sales taxes, income taxes and capital taxes.

$$GR_t = \sum_{R=1}^{2} TARIFF_R + INDTAX_t + INCOM_t + \tau_k RK_t + RENT_t + EXTAX_t + \sum_{R=1}^{2} TTR.TY_R + ITAXREF_t IER_t + AID_t \quad (3.91)$$

where TARRIF is revenues from tariffs on international trade, INDTAX is from indirect taxes, INCOM is from income taxes, RENT is from premium on import quotas, EXTAX is from export taxes, and ITAXREF is from refund from Indian excise taxes; government revenue also includes taxes on capital income $\tau_k RK_t$, tourist's income and international aid. These revenue terms are defined as following

$$TARIFF_{R,t} = \sum_{I} M_{i,R,t}(TM_{i,R,t} + ST_{i,R,t})PWM_{i,R,t}ER_{R,t} \quad (3.92)$$

$$INDTAX_t = \sum_{i} ITAX_{i,t} PX_{i,t} Y_{i,t} \quad (3.93)$$

Lumpsum income taxes are collected from total household income, and such income taxes are assumed to growth at the rate of population growth rate.

$$INCOM_t = (1+g)TAXREV_{h,t-1} \quad (3.94)$$

The amount of rent is equal to the value of imports times the rate of rents on import quotas. In other words it is the ratio of total premium paid by business in order to obtain import licenses.

$$RENT_t = \sum_{I} M_{i,t} R_{i,t} PWM_{i,t} ER_t \quad (3.95)$$

Revenue from the export taxes (*ETAX*) depend upon the amount of exports to the other economies (*E*), world price of those commodities (*PWE*), exchange rate of Nepali Rupee with convertible currencies (*ER*), export tax rates (*ETAX*), the amount of exports to (*IE*), border price of commodities exported to India (*BPIE*), exchange rate of Nepali Rupee with the India Rupee (*IER*), and tax rates on export to India (*EITAX*). The taxes are often imposed to discourage exports of goods that are in shortage in the economy.

$$EXTAX_t = \sum_{i}(ETAX_t E_{i,t} PWE_{i,t} ER_t + EITAX_t IE_i BPIE_i IER_t) \quad (3.96)$$

Tariffs and sales taxes on international trade are imposed upon goods imported from each of the foreign regions. While tariff revenue has been a major source of revenue for the government, they represent extra costs to consumers and producers in the economy. Though an argument for imposing higher tariffs to protect the domestic producers from the international competition has lost its appeal, it may be hard to eliminate them unless other sources of revenue[5] are developed.

In the model, lumpsum income taxes are collected from total household income and such income tax collection is assumed to grow at the rate of population growth rate. In addition there are other sources of government revenue such as export taxes, taxes on tourism, revenue generated from import-licensing and refund of excise taxes from India.

Government Expenditure

Government provides public goods, transfers resources to households and firms in the form of consumption and production subsidies, and needs to serve domestic and foreign debt. The government expenditure is a linear expenditure system of government consumption over the commodities included in the model. In the core part of the model we assume all sorts of non-transfer spending of government goes to public consumption. The export subsidy given to producers of commodities that contribute in enhancing the foreign trade situation of the economy. However, the sustainability of such patronage is questionable. It will be a cause of distortion in relative prices and thus inefficient. Government expenditure can be given by:

$$GD_t = \left(\sum_{i=1}^{12} GLES_{i,t} C_{i,g,t} \right) + \sum_i IG_t + TRN_t + r_{t-1} B_{t-1} + r_f FLG_{t-1} + SUB_t \quad (3.97)$$

Where $C_{g,t} = \left(\sum_{i=1}^{12} GLES_i C_{i,g,t} \right)$, is linear expenditure system of government consumption over the commodities included in the model. In the core part of the model we assume all of government spending takes the form of public consumption, meaning that $\sum_i IG_t = 0$ in the model. TRN is the transfer from government to the households, B the government borrowing, FLG foreign loan to the government, and SUB is the subsidy to the private sector.

The amount of export subsidies depends on exports, export prices and rates of subsidies, $SUBR_{i,t}$ as following:

$$SUB_t = \sum_i (SUBR_{i,t} E_{i,t} PWE_{i,t} ER_t) \quad (3.98)$$

In each period the government must obey the following budget constraint.

$$C_{g,t} + I_{g,t} + SUB_t + TRN_t + r_{t-1} DB_{t-1} + r_f FDB_{t-1} = GR_t + B_t + FLG_t \quad (3.99)$$

Here GR_t is total of taxes, tariffs and aid, B and FLG represent net domestic and foreign borrowing and DB_{t-1} and FDB_{t-1} represent the stocks of domestic and foreign debts respectively. Government retires k fraction of foreign loan, and m fraction of domestic loan each year. The evolution of domestic and foreign debt is as follows.

$$DB_t = (1 - k)DB_{t-1} + B_t \tag{3.100}$$

$$\text{DFBt} = (1 - \text{m})\ \text{DFBt}-1 + \text{FLGt} \tag{3.101}$$

Since we assume that the government expenditure equals the government revenue each period in keeping with the notion of balance budget, the core part of the model, assumes $B_t = 0^6$, though it might be somewhat unrealistic.

In keeping with the notion of budget balance, the core part of the model assumes

$B_t = 0$. If the debt stock is very large in comparison to mobilization of resources, there are two methods of adjustment in the government budget. Government can either borrow more in domestic or foreign capital market or reduce the spending in consumption, investment or subsidies. By ruling out public borrowing, government is bound to retire debts by using its tax revenues. Given the emphasis on privatization, liberalization and financial development of the economy, governments' role is to maintain law and order and to provide basic services such as health, education, and infrastructure. All types of business activities ares left to the private sector. Debt stock accumulated in the past is rolled-over for infinite periods.

Tourism Sector

The tourism sector produces tourism service by using commodities available in the economy as inputs. They spend foreign exchange to buy tourism services. Production of tourism services is equal to total demand for consumption of tourists. The value of tourism services is given by:

$$T_t^s = \sum_{i}^{12} PT_T C_{i,T,t} + TAXREV_{T,t} \tag{3.102}$$

As the preferences and demand structure of tourists are substantially different, this model uses a linear expenditure demand function, described by the coefficient of sectoral expenditure represented by symbol, $\Xi_{i,t}$. These coefficients for tourists consumption are important in studying the link between tourism and the rest of the economy. An effort to expand tourism will create more employment and output in sectors having strong backward and forward linkages with tourism sector. The demand for the tourist services by India and foreign tourists is given respectively by their income:

$$P_{i,t} TD_{i,t} = \Xi_{i,t}(1 - \tau)(TY_t ER_t + TYI_t IER_t) \tag{3.102'}$$

where TD is demand for goods and services by tourists, TY is income of foreign tourists and TYI is income of Indian tourists, ER and EIR are exchange rate Nepalese rupees with foreign and Indian currencies.

For the base year TY and TYI are exogenous. For simplicity I assume their income grows at the rate of growth of the economy. One may take the growth rate of Indian or the rest of the world economy for this purpose.

$$PT_tT_t^d = PVPFX_t(1+g)\sum_{R=1}^{2} TY_R \quad (3.103)$$

Before presenting the market clearing conditions in the goods market I discuss the relation between the domestic and foreign prices and rules for closing the balance of payment accounts. Ultimately these prices are the adjustment factors that make sure the market clearing conditions hold in the model economy.

BALANCE OF PAYMENT AND PRICES OF TRADED COMMODITIES

Prices of capital goods are determined in the competitive market for capital goods. Wages for skilled and unskilled labor are as determined in the labor market . Rates of foreign exchange are assumed to be exogenous in the model, leaving trade balances to be determined endogenously in the model. Prices of commodities are determined at the competitive markets as to be discussed in the last section of this chapter.

The present value price of a commodity in period t+1 (P_{t+1}) is equal to present value (P_t) of period t discounted by the utility discount rate (β) in equation 3.1 taking account of the number of years (*t*) included in the model as following.

$$P_{t+1} = P_t \beta^t \quad (3.104)$$

The value of β here is the same as used in the consumers' intertemporal utility function. Thus the basic notion that consumers care more for present than for the future is built in the model through channels of the price system.

The pre-tax price of gross output supplied by producers to the traders is defined by the following equation. Such prices represents the compensation for factors of production in the form of wages to labors and rental rate of capital ($PV_{i,t}$) and the prices of intermediate goods used in producing an unit of gross output of that sector ($P_{j,t}$ $Z_{i,j,t}$).

$$PD_{i,t}(1 - IT_{i,t}) = PV_{i,t} + \sum_{j,t} P_{j,t}Z_{i,j} \quad (3.105)$$

The price of capital in a given sector, the sector of destination, is weighted average of prices of investment goods of the sector origin. The weights are given by the coefficients in the investment matrix and is given by the equation 3.34 as:

$$PI_{i,t} = \sum_{j,t} P_{j,t} a^I_{i,j,t} \quad (3.34)$$

where PI is price of the investment goods invested in sector i, $a^I_{i,j,t}$ is the investment coefficient matrix that gives the use of sector j good as input in sector i investment.

Domestic Prices of Imported and Exported Commodities

The domestic prices of imported and exported commodities were used in describing the CES and CET functions of international trade in the previous section. Here we give the exact definition of prices of traded commodities.

Assuming a smáll economy all prices are tied down to the world prices through means of tariffs and taxes. It means the difference between the world prices and domestic prices of commodities is due to tariffs and indirect taxes plus the margin charged by traders. In this section we only discuss the relation between the prices in the foreign sector and prices of imported goods in the domestic markets. The reader is requested to look back to equations 3.39 to 3.66 to follow the discussion of prices of trades goods in the model.

Domestic prices of commodities imported (*PM*) from the other economies, faced by trader number four, depend upon the world prices of those commodities (*PWM*) plus tariffs (*TM*), sales taxes (*ST*) and tariff equivalent quota-premium (*R*) and the exchange rate between the Nepalese Rupee and the currency of the country from where these goods are imported. This is given by the following equation.

$$PM_{i,t} = PWM_{i,t}(1 + TM_{i,t} + R_{i,t} + ST_{i,t})ER_{i,t} \tag{3.106}$$

The domestic price commodities exported to the other economies (*PE*) faced by the trader number one in the model is given by following.

$$PE_{i,t} = PWE_{i,t}(1 + SUB_{i,t} + ETAX_{i,t})ER_{i,t} \tag{3.107}$$

where, *PWE* is the prices of commodities in the world market, *ETAX* represents export tax levied by the government , and *SUB* represents subsidies that trader number one can receive from the government for exporting to the other economies that earns valuable foreign exchange which may permit imports of various goods and services from these economies.

The import prices faced by the trader number three are determined by the border prices of commodities imported from India (*BIPM*) adjusted for tariffs in imports from India (*TIM*) and sales taxes on imports from India (*STI*) and the exchange rate between the Nepalese and Indian Rupees (*IER*). For sectors with imports from India, domestic prices of imported goods equal:

$$PIM_{i,t} = BPIM_{i,t}(1 + TIM_{i,t} + STI_{i,t})IER_{i,t} \tag{3.108}$$

Border prices are exogenous in the model. In a sense this is the link between Nepalese and Indian markets. For tradable sectors prices of commodities in Nepalese markets differ by those in the Indian markets by margin of tariffs and taxes. This has far-reaching consequences for Nepalese economic policies in relation to Indian economic policies. If these prices deviate too much from each other goods and factors tend to move to the market with favorable prices through irregular channels, i.e. the parallel markets.

The trader number two who is involved in exporting Nepal goods to India can export any amount to India at the following prices. Domestic prices of export goods to India (*PIE*) are equal to the border prices of commodities net of indirect taxes in India (*BPIE*) plus the export taxes to be paid to the Nepalese government (*EITAX*) on those exports.

$$PIE_{i,t} = BPIE_{i,t}(1 + EITAX_{i,t})IER_{i,t} \tag{3.109}$$

Border prices of exports to India (BPIE) are given by:

$$BPIE_{i,t} = \frac{IPE_{i,t}}{(1 + ITN_{i,t})} \tag{3.110}$$

where ITN is the Indian tariff rates and IPE is the Indian market price of commodities exported from Nepal.

Balance of Payments

The international prices are very important in determining the ratio of domestic sales vs. exports, and ratios of domestic supply vs. imports as we have discussed in the earlier section.

In a small open economy open to international trade, either the foreign exchange rate or the volume of trade is determined endogenously. When capital flows are negligible, clearance of one market implies clearance of the other. In the Nepalese case, exchange rate of Nepalese Rupee with the Indian Rupee and exchange rate between Nepalese Rupees with a basket of other currencies including the U.S. dollar, is essentially fixed (though there is a minor variation daily in the latter). If the foreign exchange rate is exogenously fixed, the trade balance is determined endogenously in the model. Given a large amount of volatility in trade-balances, it is desirable to make trade-balance as the major endogenous variable leaving nominal foreign exchange rate fixed exogenously.

This important fact of foreign trade is captured in the model by developing two sub-models within the Nepal model. In BOPCON model balance of payment constraint applies in each period while in CAPFLOW model agents are free borrow and lend in international market over the model horizon.

Considering the structure of the economy, the balance of payment (BOP) is decomposed into two parts: BOP account with India and the BOP account with other economies. Such a separation is essential because the nature of trade and payment with India is quite different from the nature of trade and payment with other economies.

One may consider three different options to close the balance of payment account. The first rule is a strict rule of balance of payment, i.e., when capital flows are negligible. This implies that imports should be paid by exports plus remittances. We can think of two sorts of foreign exchange regime to implement the model. In one foreign exchange rate is pre-determined leaving trade balances to adjust endogenously. In another, foreign exchange rate may be determined by the market, leaving exogenous determination of trade balance. When foreign exchange rate is determined by the market, we need to introduce the market for foreign exchange, where the supply of foreign exchange comes from exports, remittances and unrequited transfers and demand for foreign exchange originated by imports of goods and services, transfer payment abroad, debt servicing in foreign loans.

In this model we consider the exchange rate to be fixed leaving the trade balance to be determined endogenously. In the second rule, borrowing may be allowed to the tune of the trade gap for some periods, so that the present value of the imports and exports are equal to zero for the time horizon under consideration. Finally in the third rule one might be tempted to the possibility of leaving the balance of payment unbalanced up to a certain percent of GDP particularly counting on conversions of debt stocks in grants eventually.

In the current model the first case is represented by BOPCON sub-model. In this case no foreign borrowing is allowed. Therefore imports need to be paid by exports[7].

$$\sum_{t=0}^{\infty} P_t \left(\sum_{i=1}^{7} (PM_{i,t} M_{i,t} - PE_{i,t} E_{i,t}) \right) ER_t + \sum_{i=1}^{8} (PMI_{i,t} MI_{i,t} - PIE_{i,t} IE_{i,t}) = 0 \quad (3.111)$$

The case where intertemporal borrowing and lending is permitted is explained by the CAPFLOW model. Foreign saving (FS_t) is allowed in this model as given by the following equations.

$$\sum_{t=0}^{\infty} P_t \left(\sum_{i=1}^{7} (PM_{i,t} M_{i,t} - PE_{i,t} E_{i,t}) \right) ER_t + \sum_{i=1}^{8} (PMI_{i,t} MI_{i,t} - PIE_{i,t} IE_{i,t}) = FS_t \quad (3.112)$$

Finally when the borrowing is permitted to a certain fraction of GDP, the CAPFLOW model is modified to the following form:

$$\sum_{t=0}^{\infty} P_t \left(\sum_{i=1}^{7} (PM_{i,t} M_{i,t} - PE_{i,t} E_{i,t}) \right) ER_t + \sum_{i=1}^{8} (PMI_{i,t} MI_{i,t} - PIE_{i,t} IE_{i,t}) = z.Y_t \quad (3.113)$$

The elasticity of substitution between domestic and imported products and the elasticity of transformation between domestic sales and foreign sales become the most crucial parameters in relating the volume of Nepal's imports and exports with the commodity prices in India and other economies. A higher degree of elasticity implies a large trade effect, while a small elasticity implies a small consequences in the trade balances when prices of exported and imported commodities change. The elasticity parameter depends upon the behavior of consumers and technical factors that hinder or promote trade in general.

Similarly, the domestic and foreign interest rates, besides the domestic and foreign price indices play a very important role in resource allocation process in a liberalized economy. In the current situation, the Nepalese exchange rates being essentially fixed with Indian and basket of foreign currencies, any deviation in the purchasing power parity between the convertible currencies and the Indian rupees leaves some ground for artificial economy in the foreign trade sector.

After a complete discussion of supply and demand structure for goods and services in the economy I am in position to define the market clearing condition for goods market as following.

$$A_{j,t} = C_{j,t} + \sum_{j=1}^{12} a_{i,j} Y_{j,t} + G_{j,t} + \sum_{j} a^{I}_{i,j} I_{j,t} + DST_{j,t} + TD_{j,t} \quad (3.111)$$

Here $A_{j,t}$ is total supply in the economy in a sector j should be equal to sum of various components of demand as given on the right hand side, i.e. the consumption of households: $C_{j,t} = \sum_h C_{j,h,t}$, intermediate demands: $\sum_j a_{i,j} Y_{j,t}$, government demand: $G_{j,t}$, investment demand: $I_{j,t} = \sum_j a_{i,j} I_{j,t}$, inventory demand: $DST_{j,t} = DSTR_{j,t} \cdot Y_{j,t}$, and demand by tourists: TD_t^s.

After discussing the factor markets and goods markets in detail, now I turn to discussion of financial structure in the model economy.

ROLE OF THE FINANCIAL SECTOR

How much of the savings in each period is turned into investment depends on return on savings, finance in advance (FIA) constraints, and the cost of financial intermediation.

In period of repression the return on savings are very low, often negative. Therefore financial assets in such period is subject to FIA constraint. This constraint means that households are required to keep a minimum balance of financial assets for transaction purposes even if returns on financial assets are negative. In normal periods this constraint can be explained as following:

$$FA_t \geq aP_tC_t$$

where, a, represents inverse of the velocity of financial assets in a given period. In the repressed regime the FIA constraint assumes it lower bound, $FA_{min} = aP_tC_t$. People cannot avoid this minimum balance condition even if they would like to do so. However, in the framework of present model consumers do not have borrowing constraint over their life time. Therefore they are not subject to any FIA constraint.

For simplicity, we assume that a certain portion of saving dissipates in the process of financial intermediation. Therefore the total investment in the economy is constrained by the savings net of intermediation costs. Moreover, additional resources may be available by liquidating the real unproductive assets (DRA)of the households and firms.

$$c(S_t - \Delta RA_t) = I_t \quad (3.114)$$

Here c is the proportion of saving available for investment purpose, or, 1-c being the cost of financial intermediation. In this model cost of financial intermediation is represented by the distortionary cost of repression, as given by equation 3.30.

Change in real assets, ΔRA, depends on perception of households on the return of financial assets. If it is negative, some of the funds saved during the current period may in fact turn in purchase of real assets. The BLKHOLE sub-model describes leaking of resources in unproductive assets.

Before an economy reaches a steady state, the aggregate growth rate of the economy is related to the cost of financial intermediation and allocations of savings in the financial and unproductive real assets as follows[8].

$$g = (\frac{Y_{t+1}}{Y_t} - 1) = (\frac{K_{t+1}}{K_t} - 1) = \frac{I_t}{K_t} - \delta = A_t^{\frac{1}{1-\theta}} \frac{c_t(S_t - \Delta RA_t) L^{\frac{\theta}{1-\theta}}}{Y_t^{\frac{1}{1-\theta}}} - \delta \qquad (3.115)$$

where A_t, the technology parameter, is normalized to one.

This equation is very powerful in explaining the effect of financial liberalization on the growth rate of the economy. These effects can be grouped in four categories.

(i) If the current inflow of saving is less than the changes in real assets ($S_t < \Delta RA_t$) economic growth will be negative. The magnitude of this negative growth rate will be bigger than the rate of depreciation of capital stocks in the economy.

(ii) If changes in savings and changes in real assets are equal ($S_t = \Delta RA_t$) even then economy will retard at the rate of depreciation.

(iii) Moreover economic growth will be negative even if the change in output brought about by net investment is less than the rate of depreciation in the model economy. $\left(A_t^{\frac{1}{1-\theta}} \frac{c_t(S_t - \Delta RA_t) L^{\frac{\theta}{1-\theta}}}{Y_{i,t}^{\frac{1}{1-\theta}}} < \delta_i \right)$.

(iv) The only condition for positive economic growth is $A_t^{\frac{1}{1-\theta}} \frac{c_t(S_t - \Delta RA_t) L^{\frac{\theta}{1-\theta}}}{Y_{i,t}^{\frac{1}{1-\theta}}} > \delta_i$ All measures for economic growth fail if saving leaks out of the system in hoarding of unproductive assets.

It is interesting to investigate how long cases i-iii will continue? These conditions are essentially the cause of an emergence of informal financial sector or parallel market in the economy. When economy starves for lack of capital, the marginal productivity of capital becomes higher, it becomes profitable for petty businesses to start financial transaction in the informal sector. Detailed analysis of this issue is left for further exercise.

Demand for Funds

The demand for capital function and investment equations (equations 3.37, 3.81-3.90) adjusted for taxes on capital earnings, express the crucial link between financial system and the rest of the economy. Each period amounts investors can invest up to the amount of financial savings not spent in purchasing government bonds and foreign bills. Thus government sector crowds out for funds in the model economy. Similarly, storing wealth by the purchases of foreign exchange or securities essentially have the same effect equal to a spending in unproductive assets. Thus the government deficit and accumulation of foreign currency reserves, both will cause a crowding out in the financial markets for investment funds available to production firms. When the capital stock generated from the self-finance is excluded, change in the capital stock of economy is, i.e., investment, is given by the amount of changes in the financial assets net of government deficit and purchase of foreign assets.

$$\Delta K_t = I_{i,t} = \Delta FA_t - B_t - \Delta FR_t \tag{3.116}$$

$B_t > 0 \Rightarrow DB_t > DB_{t-1}$

When the government operates on a balanced budget ($B_t = 0$), the capital stock of the economy is equivalent to total financial assets minus the outstanding of government debt and accumulation of foreign reserves ($K_t = FA_t - (\overline{DB} + \overline{FR})$). In such case the change in capital stocks, the net investment, will be equal to a changes in the financial assets. In developing economies self finance also contributes towards a sizable portion of capital accumulation. In order to include the capital stock generated from the self-finance, we have used the rate of return in the base-period to estimate the capital stock of the economy consistent with the base year earnings on capital, as described by equation 3.86.

Supply of Funds

The savings of the households in each period is the portion of income not consumed. It should be noted that the net foreign transfer and rents from banks are already included in the income.

$$S_t = \sum_{h=1}^{2} S_{h,t} = \sum_h J_{h,t} - \sum_h C_{h,t} + \sum ER_R \cdot FLP_{R,h,t} \tag{3.117}$$

Saving decisions, as discussed in explanation of equation (3.3) are influenced by the rate of interest prevailing in the economy and the time preference of individuals. Efficiency in the financial system will enhance the amount of saving available in the economy by reducing the wedge between the cost of capital to investors and gains received by the savers. Households buy financial assets to keep their savings which can be used later to satisfy their transaction needs or to meet precautionary demand for funds or to store wealth in more liquid form. If the financial system is very efficient, not only the domestic savers but also the foreign savers will store their unspent current income in the domestic banks.

The amount of depreciation in each period is given by:

$$D_t = \sum_i (d_{i,t} \cdot PK_{i,t} \cdot K_{i,t}) \tag{3.118}$$

Government saving:

$$S_{g,t} = B_t + \sum_R FB_t \cdot ER_{R,t} = GR_t - C_{g,t} - I_{g,t} - TRN_t - SUB_t - r_{t-1} DB_{t-1} - \sum r_R FDB_{R,t-1} \tag{3.119}$$

In case of balanced budget the term $S_{g,t}$ equals zero.

Foreign savings come from India and the rest of the world:

$$FS_t = FSW_t \cdot ER_t + FSI_t \cdot IER_t = \sum_R FLG_{R,t} \cdot ER_{R,t} + \sum_R FLP_t \cdot ER_{R,t} \quad (3.120)$$

Foreign saving (FSWt) is outcome of the current account balance with the other economies and FSI is the current account balance with the Indian economy.

$$FSI_t = \sum_i (MI_{i,t} \cdot BPIM_{i,t} - IE_{i,t} \cdot BPIE_{i,t}) - IREMIT_t - TYI_t - ITAXREF_t \quad (3.121)$$

IREMIT represents remittance income from India, TYI is tourist income from India, ITAXREF is refund of excise taxes levied in India on commodities imported from India.

$$FSW_t = \sum_i (M_{i,t} \cdot PWM_{i,t} - E_{i,t} \cdot PWE_{i,t}) - REMIT_t - TY_t - AID_t \quad (3.122)$$

REMIT represents remittance income from the other economies, TY is tourist income from rest of the world, and AID is net inflow of capital from other economies.

The total of household savings, and government savings constitute the total savings of the economy, which ultimately depends on vector of relative prices, including the exchange rates, the interest rates, indirect taxes, and tariffs.

$$S_t = \sum_{h=1}^{2} S_{h,t} + S_{g,t} \quad (3.123)$$

Balance Sheet of the Consolidated Banking Sector

Assets	*Liabilities*
Capital Stock (K_t)	Financial Assets of Households (FA_t - RA_t)
Outstanding of Government Bonds (DB_t)	
Total Foreign Reserves (FR_t)	

Putting the supply and demand side of financial sector together, we can compute the balance sheet of the banking system as following. Saving-investment, borrowing and lending activities could be represented in terms of changes in the element of this balance sheet.

An increase in the financial assets of the households represents an increase in the capital stock of the economy net of debt outstanding and foreign exchange reserves. I will emphasize on this relation further while studying impacts of financial sector reforms in chapter 5.

DEFINITION OF A COMPETITIVE EQUILIBRIUM

A competitive equilibrium is a set of sequence of prices of composite commodities, $P_{i,t}$; domestic goods sold in domestic markets, $PD_{i,t}$; prices of exported commodities, $PX_{i,t}$; prices of capital goods, $P^k_{j,t}$; prices of terminal capital, $PTK_{j,t}$; wage rates for each categories of labor, $w_{h,t}$; prices of government services, PG_t ; prices of provisions for tourism, PT_t ; prices of transfer, PR_t ; prices of consumption, PU_t ; price of aggregate welfare, PW_t ; price of foreign exchange, PFX_t, present value of foreign exchange, $PVPFX_t$; rental rate of capital for each sector, r_1^k : R+ →R, and sequence of gross output, $Y_{i,t}$; total supply of commodities, $A_{i,t}$; sectoral capital stock, $K_{i,t}$; sectoral investment, $I_{i,t}$; exports, $X_{i,t}$; government services, GOV_t ; level of household utility from consumption, U_t ; and total welfare, W such that given these prices and commodities

(i) households solve intertemporal utility maximization problems subject to life time income constraints (equations 3.4-3.7, 3.67-3.73),
(ii) investors solve intertemporal profit maximization problem (equations 3.8, 3.90) subject to arbitrage conditions in capital markets
(iii) producers solve their profit maximization problem subject to technology and resource constraints (equations 3.12-3.18)
(iv) markets for goods and services, labor , capital clear (equations 3.111)
(v) government account constraints are satisfied (equations 3.90-3.100),
(vi) balance of payments condition is fulfilled (3.111-3.113)
(vii) financial markets are in equilibrium (equations 3.81-3.90,3.24-3.29, 3.116-3.123).

The closure rule of our model is income-expenditure balance over the life period based on perfect foresight of consumers. Capital accumulation is consistent with households optimization problems and growth rate of the economy. Higher income induces more saving as well as more demand for consumption goods.

Equilibrium in this model is a state of rest in a sense that it is intertemporally consistent. It is not at the rest in the sense that from one period to the next given the circumstances, behaviors of economic agents cause changes in variables continuously until the agent has achieved the most advantageous uses of resources available to him. An agent is doing the best he can in light of actions taken by others and actions taken together are technically feasible. This ensures the compatibility of plans of individuals or correspondence between consumers' preferences and firms' technology.

There are mainly two limitations of this model. First, the general equilibrium implies a set of relative prices consistent with the equilibrium. The absolute prices do not matter. If all prices are multiplied by a constant it will still be the same equilibrium. So to compare two prices one needs the ratio, not the absolute difference. Most of the ratios presented in chapter 5 are with reference to the benchmark equilibrium. This applies to quantities as well. Since the quantities are calibrated to arbitrary units one need to provide the percentage changes, or absolute values with appropriate units. All reporting on quantities need to be based on indices compared to the benchmark equilibrium. i.e., in terms of percentage changes in prices and quantities. Second, the model presented here does not contain any adjustment costs or penalties. The role of dynamics in such a model is not to show the pattern of adjustment, but to track the prices of commodities with a multiperiod character, e.g. the capital stock. So any adjustment in the model occurs in the same period the shock has been introduced. Model is suitable to study the impact of a certain policy that change the steady state of the model and thus the growth and welfare of the households over a model horizon. As the economy starts from a steady-state in the base year I am not able to study the costs of dynamic adjustment in the model economy. This requires some refinement in the model.

In spite of this limitation model is capable of generating results that are interesting from a point of view of a policy maker. I use welfare index as the key figure that helps me to make a choice among the different policy alternatives.

MEASURE OF WELFARE

General equilibrium solutions are used to compute equivalent or compensting variations in consumers welfare for given changes in policy regimes. In this model the measure of welfare is defined as:

$$UW^h = \sum_t^{\infty} PU_t^h U_t^h \tag{3.124}$$

where UW^h is a measure of welfare to household h for the period of model horizon, PU_t^h n is the price of utility in each period, and U_t^h is the utility to a household from consumption of goods and services in the economy. These welfare measures indexed to prices PU_t^h in the above equation.

We use welfare measures in order to quantify the impacts of various policy measures. A policy experiment that has greater value of UW^h is desirable than the one with lower one.

Why this Structure of the Model?

One may question why we need such a complex system of production and trade in model economy in order to study the impact of financial sector reforms. Most of the dynamic macro-economic models based analysis on aggregate output and often takes a closed economy (see Grossman and Helpman 1992 for a detailed review). There are three different answers to this question. The first relates to the applicability of such models for policy making. I believe that analysis of results of an one sector closed or open economy models is the beginning, not the end, of policy analysis, that is mostly concerned with inter-sectoral and inter-temporal allocation of resources. Micro-foundation truly does not come unless on levels down to the sectoral details. Different sectors grow differently, and have different impacts on the levels of output, employment and their growth rates and prices of commodities in the economy. Some important political economy questions that are hidden at the aggregate level, surface at the sectoral level. Similarly, major macro and micro economic variables of a small economy are very much influenced by the foreign sector. A thorough analyses of policies on financial development, fiscal policies and international trade requires a multi-secotoral framework. Simultaneous operation of domestic production and imports of same commodity make Armington (1969) specification of product differential by the country of origin more relevant than application of the pure neoclassical trade model that predicts complete specialization in production by these economies. We adopt Armington's trade specification as it is a common practice found in CGE tradition (See Armington 1969, Shoven and Whalley, 1992: Chapter 10, Devarajan et. al 1994).

Secondly, more important from the point of view of implementation of model, the current structure fits on tradition set by the ADB model for the Nepalese economy. The baseyear data-base were readily available from the ADB model (See Maxwell Stamp's report to ADB 1992), so that we could focus on improving dynamic aspect and analysis of financial sector in the model.

Finally, with the development of algorithms to solve the mixed-complementary problem with nested functions in MPSGE/GAMS software, more elaborate specification can be handled easily while implementing the model (See Rutherford, 1995). The complexity of the computation is not a deterrent factor in the model implementation now as it was until very recently.

NOTES

1. The economic intuition of Shephard's lemma can be explained in terms of direct and indirect effect of changes in prices of given input. Suppose an activity requires 1,2,....,n factors of production with input prices given by w_1, w_2, ...w_n. If a firm is operating at the cost minimization point and price w1 increases then the direct effect will result in the increase in the expenditure in the input number one, Besides there will be an indirect effect resulting in the factor mix. Since a firm is operating at a minimum cost point no such changes are profitable for an infinitesimal change in w1 (see Varian p. 54).

   Formally, this is proved as following:

   let x(w, y) be conditional demand function for factor xi as given by: i = 1...n;

   Let x* be the cost minimizing bundle of producing y at price w*, then g(w) = c(w,y) -w.x*

   Since c(w,y) is always cheapest way to produce y, this function is always non-positive. At w = w*

   g(w*) = 0. Since this is the maximum value of g(w) its derivative must vanish.

$$\frac{\partial c(w^*)}{\partial w_i} = \frac{\partial c(w^*,y)}{\partial w_i} - x^* \quad i = 1....n$$

Another way of proving the Shephard's lemma is geometric representation concave cost function c(w,y) with $c = w_1 x_1^* + \sum_{i=2}^{n} w_i x_1^*$ against input price of a single input, say w_1. Then finding a tangency at w* such that the later is tangent to the former.

2. $U(C_t) = \dfrac{C_t^{1-\sigma} - 1}{1-\sigma} \Rightarrow \sigma \neq 1$ and $U(C_t) = \log C_t \Rightarrow \sigma = 1$.

3. By Shephard's Lemma it can be shown that:
Demand for capital is

$$K_{j,t}(P_{j,t}, P_{j,t+1}, Y_{j,t}) = \overline{K}\frac{Y_{j,t}}{\overline{Y_j}}\left(\frac{\overline{P_j^k C_{j,t}}}{P_j^k C_{j,t}}\right)^{\sigma}$$

, where the bar above the variable names used to denote base-year values of those variables.

Demand for labor is

$$L_{j,t}(P_{j,t}, P_{j,t+1}, Y_{j,t}) = \overline{L}\frac{Y_{j,t}}{\overline{Y_j}}\left(\frac{\overline{P_j^L C_{j,t}}}{P_j^L C_{j,t}}\right)^{\sigma}$$

4. Solution for $y_t = by_{t-1} + a$ – is equal to $y_t = [y_0 - (a / 1\text{-}b)]b^t + a / (1 - b)$.
5. From the fiscal year 1996/97 the government is adopting a value-added tax (VAT) system to replace sales and excise taxes imposed on consumers and producers. Given the self-enforcing mechanism of VAT against other indirect taxes are believed to reduce leakage of tax-revenues, though its implementation seem challenging if one considers illiteracy of 67 percent of population in the country. In ideal conditions revenue generated from VAT and taxes on the final product would be the same.
6. Theoretically, there are three major sources to meet this deficit, by selling bonds to the households and banking system, by selling bonds to foreigners, and monetizing. $GR_t - GD_t = B_t + FLG_t + DMB_t$ (56) Which of these three sources is used in a period depends very much upon the objectives of the government in power. A populist policy focused on short-run political gains puts low weight on the inflationary consequences and is detrimental to the development of financial system whereas a small and efficient government fits to an agenda of developing a sound financial system in the long run.
7. In the model number of sectors trading with India and rest of the world are seven and eight respectively.
8. Substitute $K_{i,t+1} = I_{i,t} + (1 - \delta)K_{i,t}$ and use $K_t = f(A_t, L_t, Y_t)$ from the production function and $I_{i,t} = c_t(S_t - RA_t)$ to derive the result (see Pagano, 1993).

8

BASE YEAR DATA AND MODEL SPECIFICATION

A general equilibrium model is valid when a given set of parameters can replicate the base year quantities and prices of a model economy. In dynamic models the benchmark equilibrium is computed along the steady state reference path of the economy. In applied general equilibrium models parameters are calibrated using initial values of variables obtained from a social accounting matrix of the model economy.

In this chapter first I discuss some controversy among the economists regarding the validity of calibration in comparison to econometric estimates in deriving model parameters (Lucas 1976; Jorgenson 1984; Mansur and Whalley 1984). Then I present the he social accounting matrix and financial accounting matrix of the Nepalese economy which is used to calibrate the model parameters. Finally, I refer to the MPSGE/GAMS modeling language and the PATH algorithm which is used to solve my model followed by a brief comment on the effect of quality of data in model outputs.

CALIBRATION VS. ECONOMETRIC ESTIMATION OF PARAMETERS

There is a debate among economic policy analysts about the appropriate method of deriving model parameters. Some prefer econometric estimates; others can live with "point estimate" or calibration of the model parameters. Since Lucas' critique on policy evaluation (Lucas 1976) economists prefer forecasting technique based on rational expectation: the method that predicts the value of target variables at *t+1* period conditional on the information set available at period *t*. In Lucas' world, a change in parameter set (l) affects the behavior of the system [$y_{t+1} = F(y_t, x_t, \theta(\lambda), \varepsilon_t)$] either by changing the behavior of a policy variable, x_t, or by changing the policy response function, $\theta(\lambda)$. Earlier econometricians treated l as fixed once it is estimated by a linear or non-linear technique. Lucas opposed the idea of treating x_t as exogenous, l as fixed and e_t representing the all stochastic elements in a model arguing that once people know relations between x_t, and l, they change behavior according to $\theta(\lambda)$. Over time x_t, l, and e_t become interdependent and this affects the system represented by y_{t+1}. Econometric techniques for estimating parameters of a multi-sectoral forward looking general equilibrium model taking account of rational expectation remains still a challenge among the econometricians.

The calibration technique assumes equilibrium in the base year and derives parameters from equilibrium conditions in goods and factor markets. Properly calibrated parameters in light of the intuition from economic theories produce sensible results over an intermediate or long-term period, they can stand out even if judged according to the mean absolute deviation (MAD) and mean square error (MSE) criteria. Therefore the calibration technique is widely used in applied general equilibrium models.

It should be noted, however, that there are several criticisms against the calibration approach. Some argue that calibrated parameters are simply "drawn out of hat" or based on subjective prior beliefs of the modeler or copied from the results of other empirical studies (Lau 1984 commenting on Mansur and Whalley 1984). In the calibration approach, parameters are estimated with a functions $F(y, x, \lambda, \varepsilon) = 0$, where the stochastic random term, e, is simply set equal to zero and the parameter λ, is found from the resulting system of equations using a single observation of endogenous variables, y, and exogenous variables, x. This means that no factors other than those already included in the model affects the values of the endogenous variable in the benchmark period and none are expected to affect them in any future period. Lau (1984) outlines three problems with such approach. First, the calibration approach is prone to underidentification - "that is, the inability to determine all parameters of the model given the data (ibid)". In econometrics, if one has a problem in determining whether a parameter obtained by observations on prices and quantities belongs to a demand or supply curve, a standard procedure is to introduce another exogenous variables that shifts one curve without sifting the other in order to identify the function corresponding to the parameter. In contrast, in calibration techniques used in general equilibrium analysis, the number of independent unknown components of λ, cannot exceed the number of equations. "Adding exogenous variables whose effects are not known a priori increases the number of independent unknown components of l that must be estimated and thus worsens the underidentification problems (*ibid*)". The second problem with calibration techniques is that in a two commodity general equilibrium model "it is easy to see that given only one observation, an unaccountably infinite number of pairs of curves can serve as the calibration candidate of indifference and production possibility frontier. Thus it is not possible to identify either the indifference curve or the production possibility frontier without additional a priori non-data-based restrictions on these curves". The applied CGE model some how need to be calibrated to estimates of elasticity parameters existing in the literature. The third problem of calibration approach is the "lack of measure of the degree of reliability of the model and its parameters. If the parameters are determined completely by the solution of equations for the benchmark period, they might be quite sensitive to the choice of the benchmark period (*ibid*)". While the econometric method provides measures of the reliability of model in terms of variance-covariance matrix of estimator parameters and other within-sample goodness of fit statistics to judge the stationarity and stability of the model, these are not available in the calibration approach.

In spite of shortcomings outlined above calibration of parameters is almost universal in empirical general equilibrium models. I will rely on calibration as the virtues of this approach-such as parsimony of data requirement, the ease with which the values of the independent unknown parameters can be determined, and possibility of sensitivity analysis to investigate appropriateness of alternative key parameters of the model-outweigh the problems of econometric methods as mentioned above. After all, there is very little difference using calibrated parameters against econometrically estimated parameters. In theory any model that can be calibrated can be econometrically estimated but not vice versa (Lau 1984, see Jorgenson 1984 for econometric estimation for Applied General Equilibrium models). Some authors have suggested a routine for conditional or unconditional systematic sensitivity analysis (Harrison, Jones, Kimbell and Wigle 1993), CSSA or USSA, to improve the robustness of model outcomes. Given the fact that the performance of well specified CGE models in tracking the evolution of model economies, as measured by the mean absolute deviation (MAD) or mean square error (MSE) of model predictions, AGE or CGE models are widely used for policy analysis.

Another important point to be noted is the construction of a reference path of the model. Generally static models are solved for a base year and when the model reproduces the base year data, then model is considered to be a valid representation of the economy. Model validation is more challenging in dynamic models, as we do not yet have any realized information about the future of the economy. Modelers solve this problem by choosing a model horizon, a balanced growth rate and investment rate in the terminal year along with the intertemporal maximization problem to compute a benchmark equilibrium that serves as a reference path of the model (Rutherford 1995; Mercenier and Michel 1994). This essentially means looking at the time path of model variable over the model horizon assuming all sorts of policies and structure of economy be continued in the future. Then a modeler studies the evolution of the economy associated with one or more policy instruments. Following this procedure we have solved the forward-looking CGE model of Nepal explained in detail in chapter five with initial values for the base year 1990 and various terminal conditions relating to the growth rate of the economy, labor force, and investment (Appendix IV). The bench mark equilibrium path of variables in this model are computed assuming that the economic policy structure of the base year will be continued in the following years. Then some other counter-factual simulations are made to study the general equilibrium effect of changes in financial sector policies.

I have calibrated parameters such as share of labor and capital income in total value added, rate of return to capital by sector, the distortion coefficient due to repression of financial system, wage rates, the share of spending on commodities in the consumer's budget, supply index of labor force in the economy from the base year data. Alternative estimates of parameters that drive the dynamics of the model such as utility discount factor, rate of depreciation, bench mark rate of return were set after studying the sensitivity of model outcomes to these parameters.

MODEL DIMENSIONS AND DATA STRUCTURE

Since the primary focus of this modeling exercise was in introducing a forward looking behavior in a multisectoral setting, my effort on updating the data structure of the Nepalese economy has remained minimal. In fact improving data structure suitable for this model deserves a separate research. For the time being, I have adopted the sectoral and institutional structure of the ADB model (Maxwell Stamp, ADB, 1992).

Table 4.1
Dimensions of Nepal Model

Production Sectors	*Primary Factors*	*Labor Type*	*Institutions*	*Foreign Sector*	*Time period*
1. Food Crop 2. Cash Crop 3. Food-Processing 4. Textile 5. Chemical 6. Capital 7. Transport 8. Electricity 9. Construction 10. Tourism 11. Services 12. Public Services	1. Labor 2. Capital	1. Urban 2. Rural	1.Urban Households 2. Rural Households 3. Firms 4. Government 5. Banks	1. India 2. Other economies	It actually depends on choice of policy horizon. For a long run growth model it is desirable to choose a time period long enough so that model results for the chosen horizon are insensitive to terminal conditions imposed on the model. It is desirable to compare turn-pike properties of the model in order to determine the most appropriate horizon for the model

The dimension of data in this model is defined in terms of 12 production sectors, 2 types of labor, five types of institutions as presented in Table 4.1. The listing of data sources is provided in appendix IV.

A big model, such as the one discussed here, demands a lot information about the economy. Several sources have been pulled together to find data required by the model. The base year data are drawn from the social accounting matrix of Nepal that was prepared by Asian Development Bank (Appendix IV). Maxwell Stamp and Buehrer-Mauro have used this SAM for the static CGE model of Nepal (Maxwell Stamp 1991, Buehrer-Mauro 1993). This SAM presents detailed disaggregation of Nepalese economy, material balances between demand and supply of various commodities and factors of production, income and expenditure of households, firms, government and international sector for the base year. The capital account in the SAM links the social accounting matrix to financial accounting matrix trough flows of savings and investment.

Social Accounting Matrix (SAM)

A social accounting matrix (SAM) is designed to present an overall picture of the circular flow of resources in a market economy. It brings consistently the transactions of the various actors whose behavior is being modeled. Generally SAM follows the conventions for national accounts established by the United Nations Statistical Office.

A careful study of a SAM reveals salient features of an economy: saving - investment gap, trade gap, public deficit, household income and savings, domestic production and absorption. The rows of a SAM are interpreted as receipts or revenue accounts. The columns on the other hand represent, the expenditure accounts. In an economy expenditure of one sector is income of the other sector. The accounting principle that revenue should equal expenditure implies that the sum of corresponding rows and columns should be equal to each other in a SAM table. A brief discussion of the structure of Nepal SAM is in order (Maxwell Stamp 1991).

The first two accounts in the SAM, the activities and commodities, represents the production and supply system of the economy. The activities account represent the domestic production by producers and its disposition between domestic markets and exports. The value of intermediate inputs is the value of inter-industry flows; these intermediate inputs are received from the commodity accounts. When combined with value added, wages and rental payments, and excise taxes, it gives the value of output at market price. This value of output, in turn, should equal the revenue received from the domestic sales and exports.

The commodities account gives the total demand and supply of goods and services in the economy. Supply includes outputs sold by domestic industries and goods imported from foreign market plus tariffs paid on those goods. This total value of imports should equal the total absorption in the economy; the intermediate demand, consumption of households, government, tourists, investment.

The income in the factors account is payment made by domestic producers to labor and capital employed in production. These incomes are then flow to households after deducting taxes to the government, retained earnings of the corporations, and repatriation of profits to foreigners for their contribution in the production process.

Households receive income from supplying the factors of production to the domestic producers, or transfer payment from the government or remittances from the foreign account. The households spend their income in consumption, paying income and property taxes to the government, and transferring a part to citizens abroad. Then a part of their income is left for consumption.

The government account records the revenue and expenditure of the government. Government's revenue consists of indirect taxes paid by the domestic producers, tariffs, income taxes, taxes on labor and capital income. In addition

Table 4.2
Structure of Social Accounting Matrix-1

Receipt	Expenditure *Activities*	*Commodities*	*Factors*	*Households*	*Tourists*	*Government*	*Capital Acct.*	*Row*	*Total*
Activities		*Domestic Sales*				*Export Tax or Subsidy*		*Exports*	*Total Domestic Output*
Commodities	Intermediate inputs			HH consumption	Tourist Consumption	Government Consumption	Public and Private Investment		Absorption
Factors	Value Added								Value Added
Households			HH Allocation			Transfer		Remittances and Factor Income	Household Income
Tourists								Tourist Expense	Tourist Income
Government	Indirect Taxes	Tariffs	Income Tax	Household Tax	Tourist Taxes		Public Borrowing from Private HH	Foreign Aid and Loans	Public Revenue
Capital Acct.			Retained Profit	Household Saving		Government Saving			National Saving
Row		Imports	Repatria- tion	Transfer Abroad		Payment of foreign debt			Import Expenses
Total	Domestic Output	Absorption	Uses of Factor Income	Household Expenditure	Tourist Expenditure	Government Expenditure	National Investment	Export Income	634773

government receives aid from the foreigners and borrows from the domestic capital market.

The capital account is equivalent to the bank's account in the model. There are three sources of funds to the banks; household savings, government savings, and corporate savings. I modify the capital account of the government in the ADB SAM re-categorizing all government expenditure as public consumption. Rs. 11977.3 million were moved from governments capital account to public consumption account. This modification was to address balanced budget assumption that I made in the current model.

In the model the corporate savings are lumped together with the household saving. Banks use their deposits to purchase investment goods, or to lend the government or to buy foreign reserves in order to pay for the deposits made by the foreigners.

Finally the foreign account records the inflows and outflows of foreign exchange in the economy. The foreign sector pays for the exports made by the domestic producers, for remittances paid to households by their relatives and friends abroad, foreign aid received by the government and foreign savings (or withdrawal from) in the banking sector. In return foreigner are paid for imports of goods and services, repatriation of profits by foreigners, payment by households to their relatives and friends abroad, debt servicing by the government and repayment of private foreign debt. I draw on information contained on a social accounting matrix (SAM) for 1991 and a financial accounting matrix (FAM) of the economy 1991, to present a snapshot of the Nepalese economy and the financial sector. The SAM and FAM would provide an overview of economy, and are useful in calibrating parameters on production, consumption, trade, and financial blocks of the model.

I use the social accounting matrix of 1991 prepared by a research team of the Asian Development Bank in Manila, and develop a financial accounting matrix for the economy based on data published in the economic survey 1994 (MOF), economic bulletin 1994 (NRB), and Nepal in Figures 1994 (CBS). Combining both SAM and FAM is major undertaking in this section.

Table 4.3
Aggregated NEPAL SAM 1990/91(Millions of Rs.)

	Activities	*Commodities*	*Factors*	*Households*	*Tourism*	*Government*	*Capital Account*	*Row*	*Total*
Activities		156536				-78.499		9366.94	165824
Commodities	64904.1			87950	3298.5	22463.3	8397.6		187014
Factors	98296								98296
Households			92273.8					2984.8	95258.6
Tourism								3587.6	3587.6
Government	2624.3	4354.2	1194.5	1977.7	289.1		4398.5	8633.04	23471.3
Capital Account			4827.67	3365.13		0		5875.6	14068.8
Row		26123.4		1965.8		1086.5	1272.3		30448
Total	165824	187014	98296	95258.6	3587.6	23471.3	14068.8	30448	

Source: Maxwell Stamp, ADB model 1992; See appendix for a disaggregated SAM.

Activities and commodities sectors are further disaggregated in order to capture the major sectors of the economy. The ADB SAM incorporates twelve different sectors (Appendix V). Intersectoral linkages among these sectors in the base year is explained by the input-output table contained in the social accounting matrix.

Production sectors included in the model use investment goods from various sectors. The composition of inter-sectoral investment-flows is given in terms of capital coefficient matrix for the base year Table 4.9. In the dynamic version of the model, the amount of intersectoral investment flow changes as there will be a change in the total sectoral investment depending on the rate of return on such investment.

Sectoral investment cost index is assumed to be unity in the benchmark scenario. Financial policies favoring one sector against the another would bring a change in this index. Terminal conditions of the model are assigned such that level of investment beyond the model horizon is enough to cover the growth rate and the depreciation rate of the capital.

Financial Accounting Matrix (FAM)

A financial accounting matrix is a simplified representation of the major financial linkages in the model economy. Like SAM, FAM is a square, in which columns represent liabilities and rows represent assets. Accounting identity is maintained when sum of a column equals sum of the corresponding row. A simple financial accounting matrix of the formal financial system of Nepal is constructed from data available in the economic survey. It shows that in 1990/91, financial assets of household are given by their deposits in the banks (FA_t), saving for a years is ($S_{h,t}$-$\Delta RA_{h,t}$) which represents a change in the financial asset of households. Households accumulate financial assets by making deposits over the years, $\sum_{s=0}^{t}(S_{h,s} - \Delta RA_t)$. The effects of leakage of savings, ΔRA_t, is approximated by flow of income going to unproductive assets which does not return to the economic system. In essence such a flow increases under financial repression and decreases as the financial sector become more competitive.

The government borrows from the foreign sector and banks (B_t) and owes a debt stock $\sum_{s=0}^{t} FLG_s$ to foreigners and debt stock DB_t to domestic banks and D_t is the total debt stock of the government at the end of the year. While the government borrowing represents assets of the foreign sector, the foreign exchange reserve with the banking system represents the liabilities to the foreign sector. Finally the banking sector reconciles the financial account of the economy. Its assets are represented by the funds received from the households, the government bonds and the foreign exchange reserves, while its liabilities are made of their deposits. In turn financial assets of households are bank's liabilities.

The savings entries in the first column represent flows from current accounts to capital accounts. This essentially is injections of savings to loanable funds market. These saving entries are sensitive to interest rates and time preference of

Table 4.4
The Structure of a Simple Financial Accounting Matrix

	Δ in Assets From SAM	*Assets of Institutions Households*	*Government*	*Foreign Sector*	*Banks*	*Total Asset in Period t*
Households	$S_{h,t}-\Delta Ra_{h,t}$				FA_{t-1}	FA_t
Government	$B_t = S_{g,t}$			$\sum_{S=0}^{t} FLG_S$	DB_{t-1}	D_t
Foreign Sector	ΔFR_t		$\sum_{S=0}^{t} FLG_S$		FR_{t-1}	FR_t
Banks	$(S_{h,t}-\Delta RA_{h,t})$ + $(B_t + \Delta FR_t)$	$\sum_{S=0}^{t}(S_{h,s}-\Delta RA_s)$	$\sum_{S=0}^{t} B_S$	$\sum_{S=0}^{t} \Delta FR_S$		Total Loans
Total	Savings	Household Savings	Public Debt	Foreign Reserves	Deposits	

Table 4.5
A Simple Financial Accounting Matrix of Nepal 1990/91
(Millions of Rs.)

	From SAM			*Financial Accounts*		
	Δ in Assets	*Households*	*Government*	*Foreign*	*Banks*	*Total Liabilities*
Households	3365				36134	39499
Government	0			59398	13907	73305
Foreign	5876		59398		12014	77288
Banks	-9241	39499	13907	17890		62055
Total Assets		39499	73305	77288	62055	

Source: ADB SAM for Savings and Economic Survey Tables 6.6, 7.3, 7.1, 8.10 and 8.11; Table 4.6: Foreign exchange reserve of banks; Table 7.1: Currency holding ; Table 7.3: Total deposit; Table 8.10: Foreign Debt; Table 8.11: Internal Borrowing of Government.

consumers. The economy wide equilibrium requires that total savings in the formal sector be equal to total investment. The rest of FAM describes the transformation of these loanable funds accumulated over years to different types of financial assets.

The balance sheets of the financial institutions is an outcome of the portfolio allocation decision of households, firms, government and the foreign sector. Financial assets net of government bonds and foreign reserves are used to make loans firms. The capital stock resulting from such loans is given in the last column of the table. Changes in the foreign exchange account affect the capital account and the current account simultaneously. Balance of international payment requires that a deficit in the current account be financed by a net inflow foreign capital. The government can crowd out in the loanable funds market through domestic borrowing.

The data structure obtained from SAM and FAM can be used to calibrate the parameters of the model. Information on share parameters on demand functions and production functions and associated wage rates, direct and indirect tax rates, foreign exchange rates, remittances, is based on base year SAM. Some basic parameters of the model such as utility discount factors of the households, growth rate of the labor force, elasticity of substitutions and transformation in tradable-goods-producing sectors are set after a sensitivity analysis. The rate of return on capital are obtained by imposing equilibrium steady state condition on the base year.

MODEL PARAMETERS

This section presents the crucial parameters of the model calibrated from the quantities obtained from the base year social account matrix of Nepal. These parameters are important in interpreting model results in the next chapter.

Financial Sector Parameters

Nepal is poor in physical capital: machinery, land and construction used in the production process. Maxwell-Stamp (1992: 95) estimated total capital stock of the Nepalese economy for 1990/91 equal to Rs. 131 billion, compared to total domestic output of 166 billions (see Table 5.1) for that year. The stock of capital in agriculture, livestock and land far outweighs the capital stock in other industries. This is mainly because of the size of the agriculture in the economy rather than to the intensity of capital in the production process (Fig. 4.1 and Table 4.9 for capital-output ratios by sector). There is plenty scope for expanding the growth rate of the economy by increasing the stock of capital in the production process. Increase in the capital stock requires investment which may come through the development of an efficient financial system.

Fig. 4.1
Capital Stock by Sector, 1990/91
(Billions of Rs. in 1990 prices)

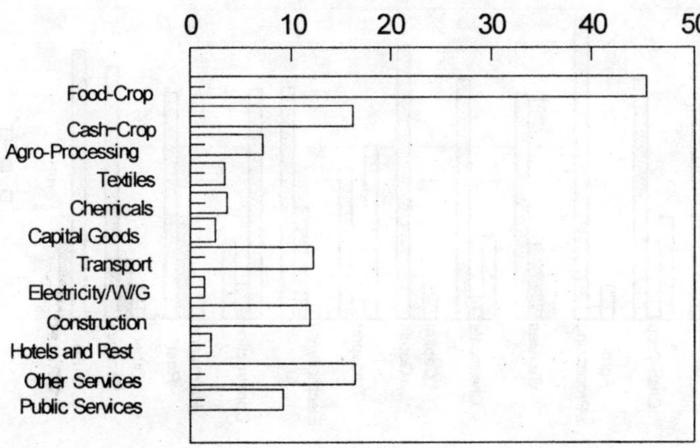

Source: Maxwell Stamp (1992).

Capital's Share in Income

The share of labor and capital in sectoral output in the base year is given in Table 4.6 and 6.2. These figures are derived by dividing the payments made to the labor and capital by total product of the sector at factor prices (payments made by activities accounts in the SAM).

Table 4.6
Factor Share's in Income

	Labor's Shares		*Capital's*	*Total*
	Rural	*Urban*	*Share*	
FOOD-CROP	0.191	0.013	0.796	1.000
CASH-CROP	0.265	0.006	0.729	1.000
FOOD-PROC	0.047	0.017	0.936	1.000
TEXTILES	0.049	0.083	0.868	1.000
CHEMICAL	0.103	0.027	0.870	1.000
CAPITAL	0.022	0.038	0.940	1.000
TRANSPORT	0.194	0.022	0.784	1.000
ELECTRIC 1	0.000	0.265	0.735	1.000
CONSTRUCT	0.359	0.055	0.586	1.000
TOURISM	0.027	0.112	0.861	1.000
SERVICES	0.036	0.067	0.897	1.000
PUBLIC	0.449	0.128	0.423	1.000

Source: Nepal SAM, 1991: Appendix V.

Fig. 4.2

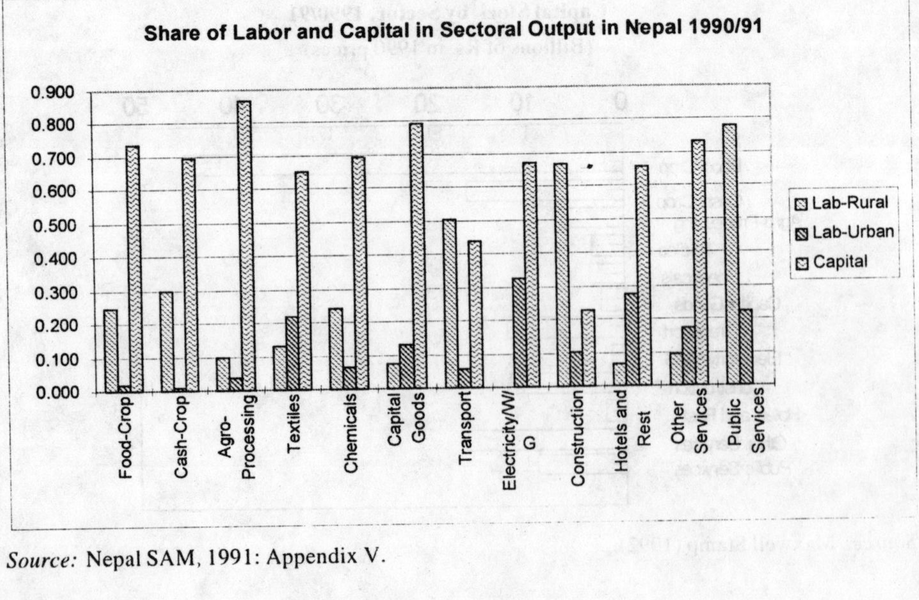

Source: Nepal SAM, 1991: Appendix V.

Share of capital is on average 75 percent of the total output which leaves remaining 25 percent to the laborers. The division of income between labor and capital in the Nepalese economy is just about the reverse of one usually found in a more advanced economy. For instance in the US economy labor receives about 75 percent of the total income remaining 25 percent leaving to the owners of capital (Barro and Sala-i-Martin 1995). Low share of wage-bills in income can be explained by a very low wage rates due to the abundant supply of labor resource in the economy. The marginal productivity of capital is very high because of very low capital stock per capita. This results in a very high share of capital in total income. Share of capital income in total income shown in Table 4.6 point to the significance of capital formation in the process of economic development . Unless capital stock per-capita is increased, the productivity of workers will remain low making the share of labor income lower than that of the capital income.

A few important macro-economic ratios are given in table 4.7. Saving rate of urban households is 15 percent in comparison to a 1 percent of rural households. Urban households receive 13 percent of their income in form of transfers, i.e. pensions. Share of capital income higher in rural areas mainly because of predominance of land-assets on earning in rural areas.

Table 4.7
Selected Economic Ratios in the Base Year

Base year Ratios	*Urban*	*Rural*
Saving to income	0.1515	0.0132
Income tax rate (% of GDP)	0.0206	0.0208
Net transfer abroad to income (includes net transfer from abroad)	0.1298	0.0
Remittance to income	0.0565	0.0266
Capital income to total income	0.5250	0.6053
Depreciation Rate of Capital (annual)	0.05	
UDR (% per year)	0.1	0.1
Growth Rate of Labor	0.03	0.03

Source: Nepal SAM 1990/91, appendix 5.1

User Cost of Capital and Spread Between Lending and Borrowing Rates

The user cost of capital consists of two parts; the net rate of return and the rate of depreciation. Both of these vary from one sector to another. The bench-mark rate of return is obtained by dividing capital income by the total stock of sectoral capital for the base year. The rate of return on capital also is different from one sector to another as shown in Table 4.8. For simplicity the annual depreciation rate of capital is assumed to be 5 percent in each sector.

It should be mentioned that derivation of rate of interest across sectors in this manner and applying that to study the growth path of the economy has serious limitations. Therefore the model results based on these data should be judged carefully while applying for policy analysis.

In the financial sector, the base year is characterized by a repression of the banking system. It is reflected in the spread between the lending and borrowing rates in the economy. The spread between the lending and borrowing rates is calculated assuming a steady state equilibrium rate of interest equal to five percent. The spread is a percent deviation from the equilibrium rate of interest and is measured by t as given in the last column of Table 4.8.

Table 4.8
Net Rate of Return to Capital and Distortion in the Cost of Capital

	RKO	*TAU (t)*
FOOD-CROP	0.3	0.591
CASH-CROP	0.3	0.591
FOOD-PROC	0.3	0.591
TEXTILES	0.291	0.578
CHEMICAL	0.264	0.536
CAPITAL	0.213	0.424
TRANSPORT	0.117	-0.047
ELECTRIC	0.106	-0.157
CONSTRUCT	0.092	-0.336
TOURISM	0.146	0.161
SERVICES	0.124	0.011
PUBLIC	0.058	-1.118

Source: Nepal Model.

It is clear that a few sectors, i.e. the food and cash crops, textiles, chemicals and capital sectors are repressed. These sectors paid up to 60 percent higher than the normal rate of interest. Some other sectors such as electricity, construction, transport and public services are subsidized sectors. The subsidy content of the loans in the public sector is very high which covers more than the cost of funds.

Financial liberalization reduces the wedge between lending and borrowing rates. We start from an investment cost index equal to unity in the base year and allow a reduction in this wedge among different sectors differently in order to study the multi-sectoral impacts of financial policies designed to reduce the cost of capital in specific sectors of the economy.

Intersectoral Linkage Coefficients

Intersectoral linkage is a key concept in a multi-sectoral model and is explained by investment coefficient matrix ($a^I_{i,j,t}$: equation 3.25) and input-output matrix ($a_{i,j}$: equation 3.39), updated for the base year in Table 4.9 (see end of this chapter). An increase in investment demand in a particular sector affects the sales of investment goods in other sectors as described by the capital coefficient matrix of the economy. Thus individual firms making total investment plans simultaneously increase the demand for investment goods from other firms as well. The sum of coefficients in a row of the investment matrix maps investment from origin into the investment by destination. Gross output in each sector, Yj,t was explained by the nested production function between the value added, Vj,t and the intermediate inputs, $a_{i,j}Y_{j,t}$ in equation 3.39.

Present Value Factor

The basic notion that consumers care more for present than for the future is built in the model through channels of the price system. The present value price of a commodity in period t+1 (P_{t+1}) is equal to present value (P_t) of period t discounted by the utility discount rate (β). Given a time preference factor for consumers ρ, β is approximated by $(1-\rho)^t$. Hence the *P* is different for a different value of ρ and *t*. For instance P value for ρ = 0.1, when *t* assumes 1,2,3 is as following.

Table 4.10
Present value factor by Periods (*P*)

Number of Years in a period (t)	*1*	*2*	*3*	*4*	*5*	*6*	*7*	*8*	*9*	*10*	*11*	*12*
1	1.000	0.900	0.810	0.729	0.656	0.590	0.531	0.478	0.430	0.387	0.349	0.314
2	1.000	0.810	0.656	0.531	0.430	0.349	0.282	0.229	0.185	0.150	0.122	0.098
5	1.000	0.590	0.349	0.206	0.122	0.072	0.042	0.025	0.015	0.009	0.005	0.003

In other words, one unit of a certain commodity after 12 periods will be worth 0.003 unit now if each period consists of five years, worth 0.098 units if each periods are made of two years, or worth 0.314 units if each period consists of one year.

All prices in dynamic equilibria should satisfy this time preference factor specified in the model. The present value factor is the crucial link between the current prices and future prices of commodities in the model.

Other Parameters

Share of Consumers' Spending on Composite Commodities

Share of spending on a commodity by a household α_i^h comes from income-expenditure surveys of households. These shares of spending of rural households differ from shares of the urban households according to tastes and preferences of consumers. Weight of a particular commodity in consumers' budget also vary according to the income of consumers. Engel's law explains such behavior in consumption. If the domestic suppliers are not able to satisfy consumer demands international trade allows consumers to receive commodities at competitive prices. The demand structure generated from preference parameters α_i^h significantly influences the production structure of an economy.

The utility function requires the shares of income spent on different commodities by two different categories of households. Values of these parameters in the base year are given on Table 4.11.

Notice that the consumers do not spend anything on products of construction and public service sectors. The output of the construction sector is used completely for investment purposes (Table 4.9). The output of the public service sector is a public good provided by the government. My model does not include public goods

Table 4.11
Share of Consumers' Spending by Sector

	Consumption Shares		
	RURAL	*URBAN*	*Tourists*
FOOD-CROP	0.497	0.203	
CASH-CROP	0.039	0.029	
FOOD-PROC	0.116	0.078	
TEXTILES	0.061	0.031	0.07060
CHEMICAL	0.073	0.046	
CAPITAL	0.072	0.038	0.07170
TRANSPORT	0.016	0.019	0.04220
ELECTRIC	0.005	0.003	
TOURISM	0.008	0.01	0.55850
SERVICES	0.104	0.284	0.2570
TOTAL	0.992	0.74	
SAVING	0.008	0.26	

Source: Nepal SAM 1990/91

in the household utility function. Capital sector includes metals and consumer durables, and chemical sector includes pharmaceuticals. Each type of households pay certain portion of their income in these two goods.

Wage Rates

The next information required in the model is sources of income for the consumer. In this model households earn labor income, capital income, income from the banks, remittances from abroad and transfers from the government. Among them, labor and capital income are the major sources of income to the households. During the base year, such income flow are given in Table 4.12.

There is a wide variation in wage rate by sectors. The base-year data on the wage bill of urban and rural labor force is updated using information contained in the 1991 Census.

Table 4.12
Annual Wage Rate in the Base Year (000' Rs.)

	Rural	*Urban*
FOOD-CROP	1.76	4.638
CASH-CROP	5.323	8.967
FOOD-PROC	8.703	16.495
TEXTILES	3.899	30.58
CHEMICAL	13.282	14.068
CAPITAL	1.965	17.679
TRANSPORT	9.297	12.645
ELECTRIC	10.133	15.231
CONSTRUCT	13.637	14.954
TOURISM	3.53	26.698
SERVICES	3.037	19.089
PUBLIC	23.562	27.263

Source: SAM 1990/91 for wages and CBS 1995 for rural -urban labor force.

We have used CES production functions to analyze production activities of sectors contained in the model. The basic parameters of the model are elasticity of output with respect to capital and labor. The elasticity of substitution between skilled (urban) and non-skilled (rural) labor is assumed to be 3 and the between the labor and capital is equal to one. In case of agricultural sector land is an additional factor of production and the elasticity between the land, labor and capital is assumed to be one. All production functions in the model are of constant return to scale type. According to Euler theorem income shares of factor should add up to one implying that economic rent to be zero in equilibrium.

Elasticity of Import Substitution and Export Transformation

The elasticity of substitution of production and trade are important components in CGE modeling. These elasticities define the nested production, Armington trade function, and the CET export supply functions. It is assumed that Nepalese goods are closer substitutes to the Indian goods than to the goods imported from the other economies. Table 4.13 reports on the elasticity of substitution between domestic and imported products. Ideally these elasticities need to be estimated, but for the present study these are taken from the ADB model.

The elasticity values less than one indicate that the demand response to a change in relative prices would be less than proportional, indicating not close substitutes. Values equal to unity imply a unitary elasticity, with a one to one change in demand and relative prices. The closely substitutable goods have an elasticity greater than one. This means a small change in price will have a great switch-over effects.

Table 4.13
Elasticities of Import Substitution and Export Transformation

	Between Nepalese goods and third country imported goods (SIGC)	*Between Napalese goods and imports from India (SIGCM)*	*Between Nepalese goods and third country exported goods (SIGT)*	*Between Nepalese goods and exports from India (SIGTE)*
FOOD-CROP	0.75	1.5	0.75	1.5
CASH-CROP	0.75	2.5	0.75	2.5
FOOD-PROC	1.5	2.5	1.5	2.5
TEXTILES	1.5	2	1.5	2
CHEMICAL	1.5	1.5	1.5	1.5
CAPITAL	1.5	1.5	1.5	1.5
TRANSPORT	0.75	0.75	0.75	0.75
ELECTRIC	0.75	2.5	0.75	2.5
CONSTRUCT	0.75	0.75	0.75	0.75
TOURISM	0.75	0.75	0.75	0.75
SERVICES	1.5	2.5	1.5	2.5
PUBLIC	0.75	0.75	0.75	0.75

Source: CGE Model of Nepal, ADB, Manila, 1992.

Import and Export Prices and tax and Tariff Rates

Government revenue and expenditure was discussed in section 3.6. Basic parameters of government sector in the base year. Indirect taxes rate on exports and imports during the base year are presented in table 4.14.

Table 4.14

Prices of Traded and Non-traded Goods with Tax Rates and Tariffs in the Base Year

	Export Prices		*Import Prices*		*Tariff Rates*		*Sales and Excise*	*Uniform Export tax tax*
	India	*ROW*	*India*	*ROW*	*India*	*ROW*		
FOOD-CROP	0.99	0.99	1	1			0.004	0.01
CASH-CROP	0.99	0.99	1.119	1.185	0.119	0.185	0.011	0.01
FOOD-PROC	0.99	0.99	1.132	1.279	0.113	0.279	0.047	0.01
TEXTILES	0.99	0.99	1.17	1.337	0.17	0.337	0.06	0.01
CHEMICAL	0.989	0.99	1.133	1.073	0.133	0.073	0.045	0.01
CAPITAL	0.99	0.99	1.191	1.372	0	0	0.08	0.01
TRANSPORT	1	1	1	1	0	0	0.005	0.01
ELECTRIC	1	1	1	1	0	0	-0.014	0.01
CONSTRUCT	1	1	1	1	0	0	0	0.01
TOURISM	1	1	1	1	0	0	0.001	0.01
SERVICES	1	1	1	1	0	0	0.025	0.01
PUBLIC	1	1	1	1	0	0	-0.175	0.01

Source: Nepal SAM 1990/91.

Import tax rates include tariffs, quota premiums, and sales taxes on imported commodities. Prices of all sectors are unity in the base year except prices of imported and exported goods and services, which includes taxes and are modified as following in the base year.

Reference Quantities and Prices in the Steady State

Reference prices vary according to the utility discount factors of consumers. These utility discount factors convert future utility at par with the utility at the present period. Reference quantities in the steady state growth path depend upon the growth rate of the labor force as explained in section 3.5. For the current model labor supply growth rate is assumed to be 2 percent per year which is very close figures obtained from the population census 1991.

Consumers' intertemporal optimization decisions are affected by the utility discount factors. Utility discount factor converts future utility at par with the utility at the present period.

MODELING LANGUAGE AND ALGORITHM

The data structure and calibration techniques adopted by model builders depend upon the solution algorithm available to solve the general equilibrium model. In fact in the past, solution techniques have been limiting factors to implement more complete models numerically. The models of Harberger (1962, 1966), Scarf (1967,

Table 4.15
Reference Quantities and Prices in the Steady State

	QREF	*PREF*		*QREF*	*PREF*
1991	1.02	0.95	2009	1.457	0.377
1992	1.040	0.903	2010	1.486	0.358
1993	1.061	0.857	2011	1.516	0.341
1994	1.082	0.815	2012	1.546	0.324
1995	1.104	0.774	2013	1.577	0.307
1996	1.126	0.735	2014	1.608	0.292
1997	1.149	0.698	2015	1.641	0.277
1998	1.172	0.663	2016	1.673	0.264
1999	1.195	0.630	2017	1.707	0.250
2000	1.219	0.599	2018	1.741	0.238
2001	1.243	0.569	2019	1.776	0.226
2002	1.268	0.540	2020	1.811	0.215
2003	1.294	0.513	2021	1.848	0.204
2004	1.319	0.488	2022	1.885	0.194
2005	1.346	0.463	2023	1.922	0.184
2006	1.373	0.440	2024	1.961	0.175
2007	1.400	0.418	2025	2.000	0.166
2008	1.428	0.397	2026	2.040	0.158

1973), Shoven and Whalley (1976) were modest and essentially for pedagogical purposes. The applied equilibrium models had some shortcoming regarding the treatment of time. Using static expectations to determine the investment rates some models built a recursive dynamic structure using a sequence of static equilibria (Robinson (1978), Bourguignon et. al (1991) and the ADB model of Nepal). The approach is basically inconsistent with the dynamic equilibrium concept; such type of dynamic equilibrium do not maximize agents' inter-temporal welfare. The major reason for updating of static equilibrium was the difficulty of implementation of models with infinitely lived consumers (Ballard 1983). The situation has significantly improved after the development of more efficient languages in recent years, after the development of more efficient solution algorithms.

MPSGE/GAMS

The forward looking CGE model of Nepal discussed in chapter 5 is formulated in Mathematical Programming System for General Equilibrium (MPSGE: Rutherford 1993) and uses PATH (Ferris and Dirkse 1994) as the solution algorithm. The computer program of this model is presented in appendix I to III .Both MPSGE and PATH are active research areas at the moment. MPSGE is the most useful, transparent and relatively painless way to write down and analyze the complicated system of nonlinear inequalities contained in a multi-sectoral model. Originally it was designed for solving Arrow-Debreu economic equilibrium models, allowing very concise specification of complicated non-linear models in four classes of variables namely, sectors, commodities, consumers and auxiliary, and nested CES or CET functions for preferences and technologies. MPSGE uses the General

Algebraic Modeling System (GAMS: Meeraus *et al.* 1988) at the front end and back end to facilitate data handling and report writing (Rutherford 1993). The essential steps in MPSGE/GAMS include declaration and definition of sets, parameters, scalars, input data, variables, equations and model, and solving them with linear, non-linear or mixed integer programming algorithms such as MINOS 5, PATH, MILES and others (Meeraus *et al.* 1988, and Deverajan. Lewis and Robinson 1991). One advantage of using MPSGE over algebraic GAMS is that given the values of elasticity and functional forms of production or utility functions, MPSGE automatically generates model equations for variables to the base year data in terms of unit functions. In other words, using benchmark quantities and prices, MPSGE automatically calibrates function coefficients and generates non-linear equations and Jacobeans. This simplicity inherent in MPSGE is a virtue if one intends to incorporate a forward looking behavior of the households in the economy.

PATH Algorithm

The PATH algorithm designed by Dirkse and Ferris (1994) is a damped Newton method for solving mixed complemetarity and variational inequality problems. It is robust and efficient in computing general equilibria. It consists of two parts; the front end and the solver. The front end basically is an interface to the routines which evaluate the function F and its Jacobean J, the initial values and lower and upper bounds for the problems variables z, and other data-specific problem. The solver is called by the front end to solve the mixed complementary problem (MCP) defined on F and bounds B. The process of solution is carried out in two steps: the construction of path and stabilization technique to determine a pathsearch. In the path construction phase the basis updating scheme is used in order to find the sequence of directions. The path construction phase of the algorithm terminates at a Newton point, at the base of a ray or as the result of an iteration interrupt.

The PATH algorithm (Dirkse and Ferris 1994) uses pivotal techniques to construct a path $p^k(.)$ parameterized by t, from the current point x^k to the Newton point x_N^k of the nonsmooth equation $F_b(x) = 0; F_b(x^*) = 0$. A Newton point x_N^k is given by $x_N^k = x^k + d^k$, where d^k is Newton direction. The next iteration in the Newton process is determined by a linear search along this direction such that the new point [$x^{k+1} = x^k + \lambda d^k$] is chosen to satisfy some descent criteria in $\|F\|$ with the ultimate goal finding a point x^* such that $\|F(x^*)\| = 0$. At this point also $F(x^*) = 0$. The watchdog stabilization technique is used to determine whether the path should be searched for a point $p^k(t)$ satisfying monotone descent condition, if the Newton point should be accepted without searching the path. The PATH solver, written primarily in C language (also in FORTRAN) is an implementation of the PATH algorithm. The process of the algorithm can explained in terms of the above figure. The contour lines shown represent the Euclidean norm of the piecewise-linear functions F_b while the paths to the Newton point for each mapping

Fig. 4.3

Path Algorithm: Piecewise-Linear Function to Newton Point (np)

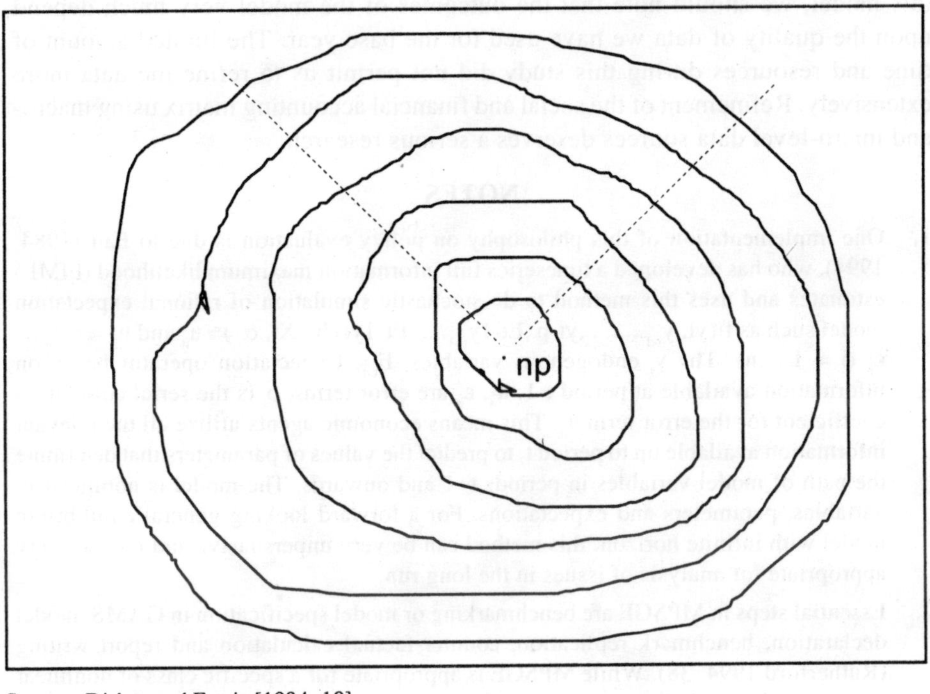

Source: Dirkse and Ferris [1994: 10].

are given by dashed lines.

Dirkse and Ferris(1994) warn of some possible problems in constructing the path, e.g., the initial basis may not be invertible, the value of t may not increase monotonically on the path (0 £ t £ 1; at Newton point t =1) due either to a cycling of bases or ray termination. The stabilization technique determines whether a path search is necessary using information stored on the stack. If necessary a backtrace of the path is performed in which the path is reconstructed in reverse order from its computation (see Dirkse and Ferris ibid:13).

MODEL OUTCOMES AND QUALITY OF DATA

My model outcomes are based on forward looking general equilibrium solutions of a decentralized market economy. Conditions on the market of goods and services, of factors of production and of financial assets determine sectoral outputs and sectoral price indices which helps in evaluating the dynamic effects of alternative economic policies. Policy makers are mainly interested in the allocation of economic resources across various sectors and the distribution of income. It generates an optimal level of consumption and savings and associated utility and welfare indices for consumers living in urban and rural areas. Given the rate of depreciation model solves for the stock of capital for each sector as a function of equilibrium rental rate of capital.

In spite of the comprehensive pictures of the economy which emerge from this model, we should note that the outcomes of the model very much depend upon the quality of data we have used for the base year. The limited amount of time and resources during this study did not permit us to refine the data more extensively. Refinement of the social and financial accounting matrix using macro- and micro-level data sources deserves a serious research.

NOTES

1. One implementation of this philosophy on policy evaluation is due to Fair (1984, 1994), who has developed a timeseries full information maximum likelihood (FIML) estimates and uses this method to do stochastic simulation of rational expectation model such as fi(yt, y_{t-1}........,yt-p ,Et-1y_{t+1}......Et-1yt+h , Xt, α_1)= u_{lt} and $u_{lt} = \rho_l u_{lt-1} + \varepsilon_{it}$ (i = 1.....n). The y_t endogenous variables, E_{t-1}. Expectation operator based on information available at period t-1, u_{it}, ε_{it} are error terms, ρ_i is the serial correlation coefficient for the error term u_{it}. This means economic agents utilize all the relevant information available up to period t, to predict the values of parameters that determine the path of model variables in periods t+1 and onwards. The model is nonlinear in variables, parameters and expectations. For a forward looking general equilibrium model with infinite horizon, this method can be very unpersuasive and it is not very appropriate for analysis of issues in the long run.
2. Essential steps in MPSGE are benchmarking or model specification in GAMS, model declaration, benchmark replication, counter-factual calculation and report writing (Rutherford 1994, 38). While MPSGE is appropriate for a specific class of nonlinear equations, the GAMS is capable of representing any system of equations.

Table 4.9
Investment Coefficient Matrix

	Food-Crop	Cash-Crop	Agro-Processing	Textiles	Chemicals	Capital Goods	Transport	Electricity/ W/G	Construction	Hotels and Rest	Other Services	Public Services
Food-Crop	0.157	0.142	0.000	0.000	0.000	0.000	0.000	0.000	0.000	0.000	0.000	0.000
Cash-Crop	0.000	0.211	0.152	0.000	0.003	0.010	0.000	0.000	0.000	0.000	0.000	0.000
Capital Goods	0.178	0.052	0.324	0.407	0.349	0.285	0.810	0.697	0.644	0.307	0.026	0.083
Construction	0.666	0.595	0.524	0.593	0.648	0.706	0.190	0.303	0.356	0.693	0.974	0.917
Total	1.000	1.000	1.000	1.000	1.000	1.000	1.000	1.000	1.000	1.000	1.000	1.000

Source: Unpublished manuscript of CGE Model of Nepal, Buehrer and Mauro, 1993.

Capital Output Ratio by sector, 1990/91

Food-Crop	Cash-Crop	Agro-Processing	Textiles	Chemicals	Capital Goods	Transport	Electricity/W/G	Construction	Hotels and Rest	Other Services	Public Services
1.500	1.970	1.620	1.370	1.620	1.620	1.750	2.500	1.500	1.250	1.000	1.500

Source: Maxwell-Stamp 1991:p95.

Input-Output Coefficient Matrix, 1990/91

	Food-Crop	Cash-Crop	Agro-Processing	Textiles	Chemicals	Capital Goods	Transport	Electricity/ W/G	Construction	Hotels and Rest	Other Services	Public Services
Food-Crop	0.0997	0.0609	0.4225	0.0000	0.0000	0.0000	0.0000	0.0000	0.0000	0.3758	0.0002	0.0000
Cash-Crop	0.1059	0.0189	0.0390	0.4880	0.4336	0.3979	0.0001	0.0000	0.0197	0.0000	0.0110	0.0000
Agro-Processing	0.0000	0.0003	0.0003	0.0002	0.0097	0.0015	0.0029	0.0002	0.0000	0.0157	0.0010	0.0689
Textiles	0.0000	0.0001	0.0001	0.0130	0.0019	0.0015	0.0041	0.0004	0.0000	0.0000	0.0042	0.0114
Chemicals	0.0005	0.0008	0.0007	0.0036	0.0278	0.0103	0.0130	0.0090	0.1773	0.0182	0.0243	0.0261
Capital Goods	0.0004	0.0002	0.0002	0.0011	0.0017	0.0787	0.0128	0.0109	0.1752	0.0000	0.1140	0.0453
Transport	0.0103	0.0086	0.0030	0.0162	0.0161	0.0196	0.2030	0.0089	0.0176	0.0860	0.1722	0.1798
Electricity/W/G	0.0000	0.0002	0.0006	0.0062	0.0110	0.0059	0.0127	0.0083	0.0000	0.0333	0.0064	0.0023
Construction	0.0000	0.0000	0.0000	0.0000	0.0000	0.0000	0.0000	0.0000	0.0000	0.0000	0.0000	0.0000
Hotels and Rest	0.0000	0.0000	0.0000	0.0001	0.0002	0.0003	0.0196	0.0002	0.0000	0.0099	0.0043	0.0073
Other Services	0.0112	0.0060	0.0008	0.0120	0.0158	0.0115	0.3424	0.1639	0.0552	0.0515	0.2502	0.0814
Public Services	0.0000	0.0000	0.0004	0.0175	0.0088	0.1040	0.0000	0.0000	0.0171	0.0000	0.0000	0.0000

Source: Derived from the Nepal SAM 1990/91 given in the appendix.

9

ANALYSIS OF MODEL RESULTS

This chapter reports on the impact of financial sector liberalization in Nepal applying the forward-looking general equilibrium model developed in chapter three and using parameters and elasticities discussed in the previous chapter. My focus is on the efficiency of allocation of resources and distribution of income between rural and urban households under liberalized financial arrangements.

Financial liberalization impacts the model economy through its effect on the volume of savings and investment. The volume of savings increases after liberalization, if the substitution effect from an increase in the real interest rate after the liberalization dominates the income effect. A priori it is not clear which one of these two effects is stronger and most influences the volume of savings. The volume of investment will increase if the impact of an increase in the cost of capital after liberalization is over-compensated by the positive impact of improvement in efficiency of allocation.

It is not obvious, in theory, whether the reallocation effect dominates the interest rate effect after liberalization. In addition to pure interest rate effects under the inter-temporal optimization framework, there are other aspects of mobilization of productive resources when an economy is moving from a condition of repression to a free economy. Unproductive assets are converted into productive assets once households are convinced that the financial system pays positive interest rates on savings. Most of the funds flowing through informal channels under repression take formal routes after liberalization. Ultimately the effect of changes in savings and investment are reflected in the indices of welfare, accumulation of capital and output over the period derived from the model solutions. Increase in each of these means that the substitution effect dominates income effect on savings side and the reallocation effect dominates the interest effect on the investment side. Therefore I consider the assessment of model solutions on welfare, capital stock and output sufficient enough to study the efficiency and redistribution impacts of liberalization in the economy.

From model results I find that, by eliminating the distortionary costs of capital, financial liberalization, improves efficiency on allocation of resources in the economy. Reallocation of capital after the liberalization increases total output, employment and capital accumulation over the model horizon. Overall welfare of consumers increases. Welfare gains of rural households are higher than the welfare gains of urban households. This indicates a significant effect of liberalization on redistribution of income. The degree of liberalization matters. Impact of complete liberalization is greater than the impact of a partial or a piecemeal liberalization for both efficiency and redistribution.

The impact of financial liberalization policy vary according to conditions and structure of the entire economy upon which these policies are undertaken. Financial sector policies are closely linked with fiscal, trade and labor market policies and therefore cannot be analyzed in vacuum. These other policies create certain subtle conditions under which a financial liberalization policy operates.

The baseline model takes current policy environment to be continued over the model horizon. Solutions of this version of the model serve as the benchmark for studying the differences in impact due to structural and institutional variations. I consider other four variations in the structure of the model. Three of these relate to structural differences in the capital market of the model economy. The fourth one analyzes the impact of liberalization when the growth rates of urban labor and productivity of agricultural land differ from steady state growth rates assumed in the baseline model.

I modify the structure of the baseline model to assess the closed versus open economy approach to the capital markets in Nepal. Liberal economists commonly think that Nepal can benefit by opening up and integrating Nepal's capital market to the international capital markets. The rate of return to capital are higher in Nepal because of an overall scarcity of capital goods. Free capital market policies promote direct foreign investment and inflows of financial resources in response to these higher returns. Optimists even believe that by strengthening the financial sector Nepal can act as a financial hub for the South Asia region. Unrestricted international borrowing and lending opportunities increase supply of capital required for a higher growth rate of the economy. Higher growth means higher wages and allows for redistribution by means of greater economic growth.

Radical economic thinkers prefer self-reliance approach in contrary to free capital market policies of liberal economist. They view that free capital market policies can only contribute to a further depletion of meager capital resources existing in the economy. They argue that Nepalese economy is a high cost economy constrained by geographical, institutional, and skill barriers. Rate of return to capital cannot be higher in Nepal than elsewhere. As there is a growing tendency of migration of skilled workers out of the economy and so will capital fly to the international capital markets if permitted. Nepal becomes a debt-trapped economy and the growth process stops for perceivable future. Therefore Nepal should limit imports according to size of the export earnings. Clear restrictions on international lending and borrowing are necessary to generate the growth process inside the economy.

Another modification in the baseline model relates to model treatment of portfolio allocation decisions of rural and urban households. Financial community in Nepal widely shares a view that a significant proportion of savings takes the form of possession of precious metals, gold and jewelry, purchase of urban lands, and possession of foreign currencies. In spite of the development of financial institutions during the last three decades, a significant amount of savings leak out in unproductive uses in this manner. The main reason for such leakage is the negative rate of return on financial assets under the conditions of financial repression. The liberalized regime guarantees true cost of capital to the savers and helps saving flow in the form of productive investment through financial institutions and reconvert the unproductive assets in productive investment once returns in these assets can serve as the precautionary and inflationary hedge as well as guarantee reasonable rates of returns.

In addition to the affect of above mentioned capital market conditions, impacts of financial liberalization are also influenced by the growth conditions in labor markets and productivity of agricultural lands. Growth rates of urban labor force are largely determined by the rural urban migration, the productive of agricultural lands are affected by the rate of adoption of an improved production technology. Differences from the steady state growth rates of urban labor and productivity of agricultural land , may change the conclusions on impacts of financial liberalization policy in the economy.

Five different versions of the model are used in order to incorporate these various aspects in studying the impacts of financial liberalization policy under different circumstances in the model economy. Names and underlying assumptions of these models are listed in the table 5.1 (see Appendix I ,II and III for program formulation in the MPSGE).

Table 5.1
Models and Assumptions Used in the Analysis of Financial Liberalization in Nepal

Name of the Model	*Assumptions*
Base-line Model	Calibrated assuming a steady state equilibrium in the base-year
Complete Market Model (CAPFLOW)	Steady state growth rate across all sectors; Unrestricted capital flows to close the BOP gap;Exogenous interest rates;
Incomplete Market Model (BOPCON)	Steady state growth rates across all sectors Period by period BOP constraint
Black-hole intermediation cost model (BKLHOLE)	Period by period BOP constraint; Steady state growth path;Real cost of financial intermediation, i.e., part of savings are converted into the unproductive assets e.g. accumulation of foreign exchange.
Non-steady state model (NONSS)	Free flows of capital and exogenous interest rates; Land grows at 1/3 of the steady state growth rate; Urban labor grows 2 times the rate of steady state growth rate

Results of these models are quite different. The financial liberalization impacts model economy more when international capital market conditions guarantee unlimited freedom of lending and borrowing compared to restricted access to international capital markets. Black-hole seem to be important and differences in growth rates between the urban and rural labor produce different results. These differences represent the importance of the underlying structure of liberalization policy in the model economy.

The base-line model traces the path of the economy assuming a steady-state in the base-year. As mentioned in section 3.5, in a steady state all sectors grow at the same rate and that is mainly determined by the growth rate of the population. The model assumes that the growth in capital stock is sufficient to maintain the per capita capital stock at the steady state level. Consumers maximize utility subject to their life-time budget constraint and investors allocate capital among various sectors in order to maximize inter-temporal profits. The government budget is balanced and there is a limited inflow of capital to close trade imbalances. Competitive equilibrium conditions on commodity markets and factor markets guarantee that prices are market clearing.

As explained in section 3.9, a general equilibria in all models discussed here imply a set of relative prices consistent with the equilibrium. Absolute prices do not matter. If all prices are multiplied by a constant it will still be the same equilibrium. So to compare two prices one should use ratios of prices and quantities but not the absolute differences between model solutions. Any change to the steady state in the model will give some changes in prices and quantities. Since the quantities are calibrated to arbitrary units one need to provide the percentage changes, or absolute values with appropriate units. All reporting on quantities and prices in this chapter is based on indices, percentage changes, compared to the benchmark equilibrium. Within the structure of the baseline model, financial liberalization is represented by a complete or partial elimination of repression elements in the cost of capital.

The base-line model is a kind of all purpose model. It can be modified easily to look at various other policy issues permitted by the structure of the model. However, this model does not contain any adjustment costs or penalties. The role of dynamics in the current model is not to show the pattern of adjustment, but to track the prices of commodities with a multi-period character, e.g. the capital stock. A study on dynamic adjustment to a steady state requires further modification in the current model.

The CAPFLOW model builds on the assumption of a complete mobility of capital resources in and out of Nepalese economy. Households and investors are free to borrow from domestic and international capital markets. This is the basic difference of the CAPFLOW model from the base-line model. The rate of interest rate in this model is given by the rate of interest in the world market, which for the present exercise is taken exogenously to be at five percent. Linking domestic interest rates to a foreign interest rate is not irrelevant given the size of the Nepalese economy. A proper analysis of effects of foreign capital inflows are very important in case of the Nepalese economy where more than 60 percent of development expenditure in the public sector are financed by international borrowing and foreign aid and the role of direct foreign investment in modern sectors, i.e. the hydro-electric and tourism sectors, are perceived to be a key for generating a momentum of development in the economy.

The structure of CAPFLOW model is relevant to consider a number of external trade issues in the Nepalese economy. The volume of exports are small because of the small scale of production. The level of production is low because of lack of sufficient funds required to import primary inputs. Does a freedom to borrow at the international markets accompanied by an efficient financial system guarantee an expansion in the economy? The CAPFLOW model allows us look at this issue further in depth than the base-line model.

The BOPCON model assumes a complete self-reliance on capital approach in the model economy. This means a strict adherence to balance of payment conditions; strictly limiting imports to be equal to exports. This is an economy with non-existence of the foreign capital market, and hence, economy is subject to a period by period balance of payment constraint. Though this may not be a very realistic scenario but it serves the purpose of comparison. A contrast between the CAPFLOW and BOPCON model illustrates the importance of foreign capital inflows in the model economy.

The black-hole model is different from other models discussed here. It presents a typical case of a developing economy under financial repression where a significant amount of financial resources can be recovered by liberalization. It captures the essential features described in section 3.8. The rate of interest in a repression is often negative. Households prefer to keep their savings in unproductive real assets such as gold, jewelry, urban lands and foreign currencies. The leakage of savings in unproductive assets reduces the volume of productive investment. A reduction in productive investment lowers the income and output in the economy. Financial liberalization reduces leakage in unproductive assets by raising the rate return on productive assets.

In this process, investment can be more than the total amount of savings as the additional resources may be available for investment by liquidating the real unproductive assets of the households and firms. I use the results of black-hole model to see how the black-hole phenomena affects efficiency in allocation and distribution of income over the model horizon?

All versions of the model discussed so far assume steady state growth rates in all sectors of the model economy. What will happen if all sectors do not grow at the same rate ? How would efficiency and distribution effects of financial liberalization be if some sectors grow at higher or lower rates than other sectors? This question is studied using non-steady state model, NONSS.

I consider two types of liberalization: Economy-wide liberalization and piecemeal liberalization. Economy-wide liberalization is further classified into a partial and a complete liberalization depending upon the amount of reduction in the spread under two model horizons. In case of economy-wide liberalization the distortionary cost of financial intermediation (t), the spread between the lending and borrowing rates, is changed across all sectors at the same rate. In this chapter, it is called partial economy-wide liberalization if t is reduced by a fifty percent, and a complete liberalization if t equals zero. In the case of piecemeal liberalization, the distortionary cost of financial intermediation is reduced only for one or a few selected sectors. For instance, would a cut in the subsidy on the cost of capital to the public sector increase the volume of investment in other sectors or does a reduction in the premium on cost of capital in food sector or a cash crop sector matter? Will there be some improvement in the efficiency of allocation and a significant redistribution? I search answers to these questions solving the model for piecemeal liberalization of 9 different sectors.

To sum up, the reporting framework is organized in terms of five models, i.e. (1) Base-line model; (2) CAPFLOW model; (3) BOPCON model; (4) BLKHOLE model; (5) NON-SS model and two different major scenarios, i.e., (1) economy-wide liberalization, and (2) piecemeal liberalization. I believe that assessment of growth under these various scenarios are enough to highlight the role of financial sector reforms in the economy.

The numerical output generated from these models is enormous because of sectoral and time dimensions and five sum-models for three different scenarios (see chapter 4 for details on dimensions of the model). One variable has thus 30 . 5 . 3 = 450 different solutions. Variables and scenarios I choose to study the efficiency and redistribution are only illustrative and I leave much details for further study. Important variables I report in this chapter are the welfare indices of urban and rural households and wage rate indices for urban and rural labor, the rates of returns to the capital across the sectors and indices of the stock of capital and output in the model economy. An analysis of path of these variables is enough to conclude on what are the efficiency and redistribution impacts of financial liberalization.

As mentioned in chapter one the distribution of income after the liberalization, has been a key issue of debate among the policy makers. The major indicator for judging the distribution impact after the liberalization is welfare of households. Does financial liberalization lead to an overall increase in the welfare of households? If it does, are urban households better off than the rural households or vice-versa or does the liberalization benefit each type of households equally? If these benefits are not equal, to what extent do they differ from each other? How do these differences occur? Are changes in wage rates important for analysis of welfare? I compare wage rate indices of rural and urban households to answer these questions. The rates of returns to capital across sectors are important for consideration of efficiency effect of reallocation. These rates affect the level of investment across sectors. Do these rates of return to capital increase or decrease after liberalization? How do they affect the level of investment in one sector to that of another? In a competitive economy, one would expect the reallocation process to continue until rate of return become the same across all sectors. Does it happen after liberalization? When the investment in one sector increases, does it lead to an expansion in production and productivity? I use the index of capital and output to study these questions in the model economy.

Each of five models listed above can be solved for any time horizons one is interested to design a policy framework. For this study, each of these models was solved for a 30 years horizon form 1990 to 2020. Each of them was also solved for 35 years' horizon 1990-1925 and a 100 years' horizon which ensured the turn-pike properties of the model. With the parameters calibrated for this model, a 30 years' horizon is enough for output and prices to converge to the steady state conditions of the economy.

WELFARE IMPACTS OF LIBERALIZATION

In each of the above models, rural and urban households maximize utility over the model horizon subject to life-time wealth constraints. Welfare is the sum of discounted utilities and these discount rates are given by the time preference of individuals. Overall and household specific welfare indices equal to one in the baseline model. The welfare in various other sub-models are indexed to the welfare of the base-line model in table 5.2. The numbers in the cells of the table represent overall welfare and its break down by rural and urban houscholds in the various scenarios of the model. Because of the overwhelming dimension of the model, I report only the solutions of the CAPFLOW model in case of piecemeal liberalization.

The overall gains in welfare from financial sector liberalization are significant. The greatest welfare gain is up to 14.4 percent more than the base line model in NONSS version of the model under complete liberalization, compared with 9.3 percent gain in CAPFLOW and BLKHOLE model. These results indicate the importance of growth conditions in the labor market and the growth in productivity of agricultural land in analyzing the impacts of financial liberalization. They also highlight the importance of international capital flows and re-conversion of savings from unproductive to productive assets. Welfare gains under partial liberalization are smaller than in the case of complete liberalization but still they are sizable. Overall welfare under partial liberalization is up 6 percent in CAPFLOW and BLKHOLE model compared to 2 percent in NONSS model. Overall welfare gains of sector wise piecemeal liberalization are positive except in case of construction and tourism sectors. This is mainly because of less dependency of these sectors as reflected by the input-output coefficients and investment coefficient matrix discussed in chapter four. The overall welfare results show that distortions in capital markets results in welfare losses over the model horizon and removal of these distortions increase the level of welfare under different model scenarios.

These overall welfare effects are comparable to findings of many other studies in the tax reforms and trade liberalization (Shoven and Whalley (1984) Robinson (1989) and Deverajan et. al (1996)).

The redistribution impacts of liberalization are noticeable. The model solutions generally show that the process of financial liberalization favors rural households in comparison to the urban households. This result might seem counter-intuitive as one would expect urban households to benefit more from the financial liberalization. But under liberalization, firms in urban areas have more access to financial institutions compared to those in rural areas as I mentioned in sections

2.3-2.4. Various channels of capital and labor markets make rural households better off compared to urban households after liberalization. In repression, credit rates are kept artificially low by means of interest rate subsidies in the name of promoting small scale enterprises, promoting one or another industry located in urban areas.

The financial liberalization eliminates cheap credit facilities for privileged firms located in urban areas, forcing all firms to compete for the capital on the basis of productivity. Firms operating with a heavy subsidy under repression, i.e. the public sector, can attract less capital and tend to substitute labor to capital after liberalization. Firms employing unskilled (rural) labor intensively, such as textiles, food-crops and cash-crop sectors expand their investment and production in response to increased access to funds in liberalized regime. They demand more unskilled labor than skilled labor to complement the additional capital. The endowment of unskilled labor is larger than the endowment of skilled labor in the Nepalese economy. Easy access to credit markets for labor intensive firms have positive consequences in market for rural labor. Demand for labor increases leading to an increases in the wage rates of the rural labor. Liberalization of formal financial sector also has an widespread effect on informal credit markets in the rural sector.

As mentioned in section 2.3, Nepal's rural credit market is dominated by the informal sector. In repression, access of rural firms or households to financial institutions is limited and the local money lenders exercise their market power charging very high rate of interest. After liberalization more savings and lending flow through formal channels. Therefore local money lenders have to provide attractive lending and borrowing rates if they want to continue their business. This implies liberalization opens competition even in the rural areas where the formal financial institutions are not accessible. Cheap credit facilities increase rural investment and the productivity of the rural labor.

Table 5.2
Welfare Indices under Complete Liberalization

	CAPFLOW			*NONSS*			*BLKHOLE*		
	Rural	*Urban*	*Overall*	*Rural*	*Urban*	*Overall*	*Rural*	*Urban*	*Overall*
Partial	1.103	0.747	1.0674	1.045	0.822	1.0227	1.103	0.718	1.0645
Complete	1.166	0.441	1.0935	1.166	0.947	1.1441	1.166	0.441	1.0935
Public	0.986	1.158	1.0032	1.104	0.529	1.0465	0.986	1.163	1.0037

Welfare Indices in Piecemeal Liberalization under CAPFLOW model

	Rural	*Urban*	*Overall*
Food-Crop	1.063	0.669	1.0236
Cash-crop	1.035	0.874	1.0189
Food-Proc.	1.015	0.919	1.0054
Textiles	1.051	0.917	1.0376
Chemical	1.015	0.917	1.0052
Capital	1.006	0.948	1.0002
Construct	0.994	1.029	0.9975
Tourism	1.001	0.988	0.9997

From a comparison of the figures in table 5.2 it becomes clear that the benefits of financial liberalization flow to the rural households. The only exception is the piecemeal liberalization of the public sector under the CAPFLOW and BLKHOLE models. Providers of public services are mainly the urban households. A cut in subsidies going to the public sector in the process of liberalization means increase in prices of public services. This would increase the income of urban households from providing public services. Meanwhile, it raises the cost of living of the rural households who are the major consumers of public services. Therefore, in contrast to a complete liberalization piecemeal liberalization of public sector favors the urban households, mainly by continuing some of the repressionary conditions.

The welfare indices in case of the non-steady state (NON-SS) model also follow the pattern seen in CAPFLOW and BLKHOLE model. The rural households gain more than urban households both in partial as well as the complete liberalization. This is mainly because of two times higher than a steady state growth rate of the urban labor force in the model economy. Even in NON-SS model urban wages rates grow less than rural wage rates because of supply and demand conditions in the rural and urban labor markets. Even a partial liberalization is enough to generate investment effects sufficient enough to affect the redistribution of income in favor of rural households. The rural households mainly in the agricultural sector get their credit needs fulfilled even by the partial liberalization. Even a fifty percent liberalization allows them to produce at a lower cost of investment and an increase their income and consumption.

The overall and household specific welfare indices in the case of BLKHOLE model are comparable to those in CAPFLOW model. Households' overall gain is 6 percent in partial liberalization and 9 percent in complete liberalization. Rural households do better than urban households in both of these scenarios. This means liberalization releases extra resources by redirecting the flows of savings from unproductive assets to productive assets. In the liberalized environment households even reconvert unproductive assets into productive assets. As in other models rural households gain more than urban households both in partial and complete liberalization scenarios.

In the limited market model (BOPCON), a period by period BOP constraint, the financial liberalization in not effective; the effect of liberalization on welfare is minimal. It implies that when the economy cannot borrow or lend intertemporally, several instruments of the financial system become inapplicable. The rental cost of capital is higher in solutions of BOPCON model than in the solutions of any other model. The wage rates of rural and urban labor remain same as compared to the benchmark equilibrium. If the economy cannot participate internationally, markets are not free, so the liberalization has no reallocation effect.

From analysis of welfare figures I can conclude that in general the financial liberalization leads to an overall increase in welfare, and welfare gains of rural households are larger than the welfare gains of urban households.

WAGE RATE IMPACTS OF LIBERALIZATION

Wages are key components in intertemporal budget constraints of households. Increase in wage rates increase their income, consumption and utilities and hence in the overall welfare over the model horizon. Redistribution takes place over the period if the wage rates of rural households increase faster than the wage rates of the urban households or vice-versa. As can be seen from table 5.3, the increase in wage rates of rural labor in comparison to the urban labor is the major source of redistribution of income following from the financial liberalization. Reforms in the financial sector provide an easy access to credit to rural labor intensive firms in urban areas. These firms increase the demand for rural labor to complement addition in capital stock acquired from cheap credits. The competition on credit market reduces interest rates in the informal markets in rural areas. Rural firms are able to purchase more capital stock which make rural labor more productive. Households convert their savings from unproductive assets to formal channels in order to earn interests. This re-conversion of capital takes places in rural sectors favoring rural households more than urban households.

Lower rates of credit lead to more investment and greater demand for labor. Gradually segmentation of the labor markets characteristic to a repressed economy fades away towards the emergence of an integrated labor market where the rural labor is paid according to its productivity.

I present the complete path of indices of wage rates of rural labor relative to the wage rates of urban labor under partial and full liberalization scenarios of CAPFLOW, NONSS and BLKHOLE models in table 5.3. In all scenarios the wage rate increase is higher for the rural labor relative to wage rates of the urban labor. Greater demand for rural labor drives up the rural wage rate after liberalization. Significantly higher rural wage rate in NONSS model is indicative of cuts in urban wages due to a higher growth rate of urban labor force.

Model results in table 5.3 show that increase in wage rates depend upon the degree of liberalization. Wage rate effects are higher in case of complete liberalization than in the case of partial liberalization. Wage effects are greater in a non-steady state model because of the assumption that the urban labor force grows twice the rate of steady state growth rate of the economy. Increase in urban labor supply causes a slower growth rate in the urban wages rates in comparison to rural wage rates.

From analysis of wage rate indices in liberalized regime in comparison to base-line model I can conclude that financial liberalization leads to a significant redistribution of income in favor of rural households.

IMPACT OF LIBERALIZATION ON THE RATE OF RETURNS TO CAPITAL ACROSS SECTORS

Next I consider how much the financial liberalization improves the efficiency of allocation of capital resources in the economy. I have taken the sectoral rates of returns to capital as the indicator of efficiency in allocation of capital across various sectors. In repression an artificial rule of allocation makes rate of returns vary

Table 5.3
Rural/Urban Wage Ratios Under Different Model Assumptions

	CAPFLOW		*NONSS*		*BLKHOLE*	
	Partial	*Complete*	*Partial*	*Complete*	*Partial*	*Complete*
1990	1.028	1.049	0.995	1.024	1.029	1.049
1991	1.025	1.047	0.999	1.026	1.025	1.047
1992	1.016	1.034	1.008	1.024	1.016	1.034
1993	1.013	1.025	1.017	1.031	1.013	1.025
1994	1.01	1.019	1.026	1.036	1.010	1.019
1995	1.010	1.016	1.036	1.043	1.010	1.016
1996	1.008	1.014	1.043	1.051	1.008	1.014
1997	1.007	1.014	1.052	1.059	1.007	1.014
1998	1.006	1.012	1.063	1.068	1.004	1.012
1999	1.004	1.011	1.071	1.074	1.004	1.011
2000	1.003	1.010	1.081	1.083	1.003	1.010
2001	1.005	1.011	1.089	1.092	1.005	1.011
2002	1.003	1.010	1.099	1.103	1.003	1.010
2003	1.004	1.010	1.108	1.112	1.002	1.010
2004	1.004	1.009	1.118	1.119	1.004	1.009
2005	1.004	1.009	1.125	1.132	1.002	1.009
2006	1.004	1.010	1.137	1.138	1.002	1.010
2007	1.002	1.008	1.146	1.147	1.002	1.008
2008	1.002	1.009	1.155	1.160	1.002	1.009
2009	1.002	1.009	1.169	1.168	1.002	1.009
2010	1.003	1.010	1.176	1.179	1.003	1.010
2011	1.003	1.010	1.188	1.187	1.003	1.010
2012	1.003	1.008	1.196	1.196	1.003	1.008
2013	1.003	1.006	1.209	1.209	1.003	1.006
2014	1.003	1.009	1.213	1.219	1.003	1.009
2015	1.000	1.006	1.227	1.224	1.000	1.006
2016	1.000	1.003	1.236	1.241	1.000	1.003
2017	0.996	1.004	1.246	1.247	0.996	1.004
2018	0.996	1.000	1.256	1.253	0.996	1.000

from one sector to another. Rental rates are not necessarily tied down to the rate of returns or productivity of capital. Subsidies on interest rates reduce the rental rates in selected sectors against the burden of higher rental rates for other sectors. In liberalized regime capital is allocated according to its marginal productivity. It means that more productive sectors receive more capital. Reallocation of capital continues until the rate of returns across the sectors are equal and all of these returns are equal to the cost of capital net of depreciation. I will report on how these improved rental rates affect the accumulation of capital and output in various sectors by using indices of capital stock and output over the model horizon.

Table 5.4 reports on the rates of returns to capital in different sectors and under different models. Under financial liberalization, one would expect rental rates and the rate of returns to capital to be equal across sectors over a period. The distortions occurring in a repression regime are removed as rental rates become equal across the sectors. Among the four models, CAPFLOW, NONSS and BLKHOLE models produce this outcome except the BOPCON model, which truly reflects the phenomena of an incomplete market assumed in that model.

Table 5.4
Real Rate of Return across the Sectors Under Complete Liberalization Across Models

	Rental Rate of Capital in Year 2020 (Base year 1990)				
	BASELINE	*CAPFLOW*	*BOPCON*	*NONSS*	*BLKHOLE*
FOOD-CROP	0.037	0.026	0.064	0.024	0.026
CASH-CROP	0.037	0.027	0.064	0.025	0.027
FOOD-PROC	0.036	0.025	0.064	0.023	0.025
TEXTILES	0.035	0.025	0.062	0 023	0.025
CHEMICAL	0.035	0.025	0.057	0.023	0.025
CAPITAL	0.032	0.026	0.046	0.024	0.026
TRANSPORT	0.023	0.022	0.025	0.021	0.022
ELECTRIC	0.022	0.023	0.023	0.022	0.023
CONSTRUCT	0.021	0.023	0.02	0.021	0.023
TOURISM	0.028	0.026	0.031	0.023	0.026
SERVICES	0.027	0.028	0.027	0.025	0.028
PUBLIC	0.017	0.027	0.012	0.025	0.027

The cost of capital is different in different sectors in the base-year 1990 as presented in table 4.8, because of the repression in the financial system. When the economy is subject to period by period constraints in balancing international accounts, as in BOPCON model, the rental rates of capital can become even more unequal with financial liberalization. Capital cannot be allocated across sectors according to the marginal productivity rules because of the constraints in the external account. In the base year many capital goods are supplied by imports and such imports are financed by the inflow of foreign capital. It is obvious that when such inflows need to match by the value of exports, many investment projects remain constrained by the position of international account.

I use figures 5.1 and 5.2 to compare the rental rates of returns to capital across different sectors in the CAPFLOW model. The repressionary situation is represented by the marked square boxes that connect the rental rate of capital across sectors during the base year of the model, 1990. In repression, the cost of capital to the private or non-subsidized sectors is significantly higher than the cost of capital in the public or subsidized sectors.

The process of liberalization removes all distortionary elements in the cost of capital. The reduction in the cost of capital is represented by two lines at the bottom of the figure. It should be noted that the rental rates represented by these lower lines are for the year 2020, after the liberalization process has fully worked out for three decades.

Rental rates of capital falls to around 2.5 percent , which reflects the true cost of capital in the steady state.

Thus under the perfect market model rental rate of capital among the sectors are equalized by the financial liberalization. Capital is allocated across sectors according to marginal productivity.

The statement on the rate of returns on capital across the sectors made in the previous paragraph is based on the solutions of the CAPFLOW model. It is

Fig. 5.1
Cost of Capital Across Sectors in CAPFLOW Model

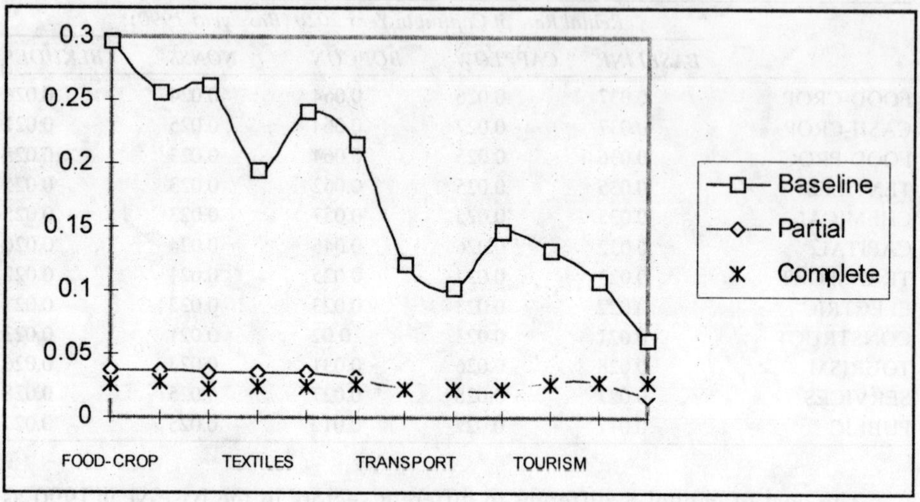

interesting to see that is valid even in other modeling environment. Figure 5.2 presents rental rates across various sectors under different model assumptions.

As one would expect, when markets are free to set the interest rates, the cost of capital to various sectors are lower in the CAPFLOW model. When markets cannot function properly, as in the case of BLKHOLE and NONSS models, the rental rate is generally higher for all sectors. When the economy cannot borrow or lend the differences between the lending and borrowing across sectors persist for a long time. The solutions of different models are compared in the following figure.

The rental rates in the least favored sectors such as food and cash crop sectors are expected to decline after liberalization. Still, some other sectors that are very close to market rates in the base-year would be affected minimally by the process

Fig. 5.2
Rental Rate of Capital in Capital Goods Sector

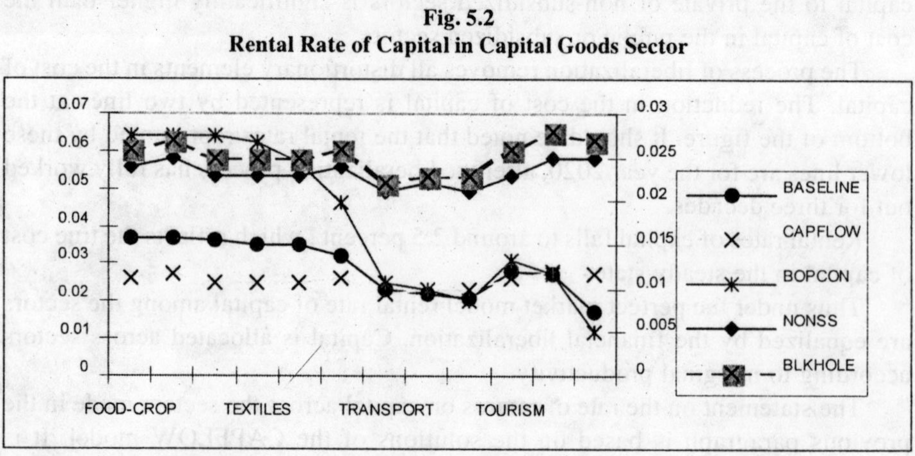

of liberalization. Two cases are presented below in order to illustrate how the rental rates converge over period after the liberalization. In figures 5.3 the capital goods sector faces a rental cost of capital well above the steady state rate, while in the figure 5.4 the rental rate in the construction goods sector is very close to the steady rate in the model. These figures also show the time path of convergence towards the steady state rate under the partial or complete liberalization.

In case of capital goods sector, there is a noticeable deviation of rental rates under partial and complete liberalization from the steady state cost of capital. Some explanation is required why the rental rate is higher with complete liberalization compared to the rate in partial liberalization and the bench-mark equilibrium rate of interest.

Fig. 5.3
Rental Rate of Capital in Capital Goods Sector

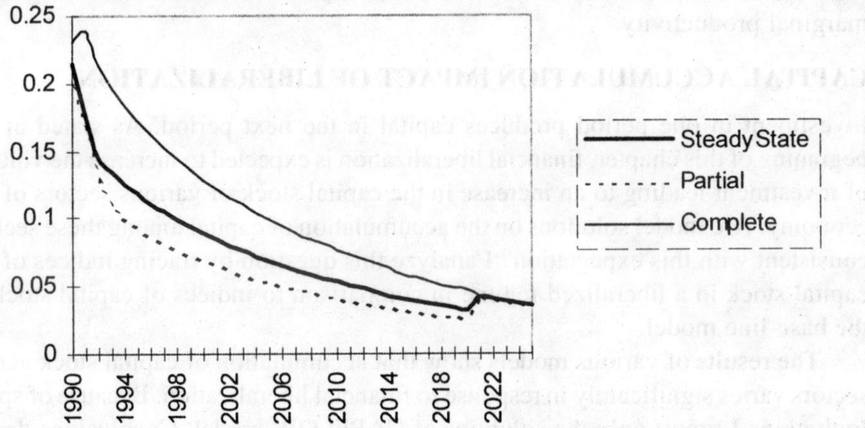

With complete liberalization, there is more demand for capital as the demand for investment increases across all sectors. This causes an increase in the demand for investment goods in the economy which are supplied mainly by the capital goods sector. This in turn leads to a greater accumulation of capital in the capital goods sector, which causes a reduction in the marginal productivity of capital in this sector. Therefore, the rental rate of capital increases in the capital goods sector.

In contrast to the cost of capital in capital goods sector, the rental rate is least affected in the construction goods sector. There are two reasons. First, the bench-mark rental rate in the construction goods sector is very close to the true market rate, therefore, there is little reason for the rental rate in the construction goods sector to vary with the process of liberalization. Another reason is that the construction sector is non-tradable sector, therefore the freeing of the capital market does not affect this sector as much as the capital goods sector.

From analysis of rental rates I conclude that financial liberalization improves efficiency in allocation by equalizing the rental rate of capital across the sectors.

Fig. 5.4
Rental Rate of Capital on Construction Goods Sector

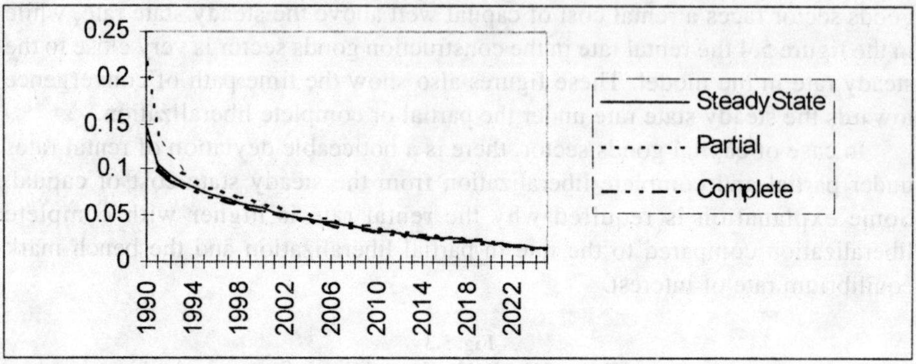

Model results assure that after liberalization capital is allocated according to its marginal productivity.

CAPITAL ACCUMULATION IMPACT OF LIBERALIZATION

Investment in one period produces capital in the next period. As stated at the beginning of this chapter, financial liberalization is expected to increase the volume of investment leading to an increase in the capital stock of various sectors of the economy. Are model solutions on the accumulation of capital among these sectors consistent with this expectation? I analyze this question by tracing indices of the capital stock in a liberalized regime in comparison to indices of capital stock in the base-line model.

The results of various models show that accumulation of capital stock across sectors varies significantly in response to financial liberalization. Because of space limitations I report only the solutions of CAPFLOW model. Conclusions drawn from the analysis of these results also apply to NONSS and BLKHOLE models as the output and capitals stock indices of those models are similar to that of CAPFLOW model.

I present capital stock indices from the solutions of CAPFLOW model in table 5.5. This shows different indices of capital stock for different sectors. The growth path of capital stocks in textiles, food crops, cash crops and chemical sectors are higher than its growth path in electricity, construction, and services sectors. One need to reflects on the structure of demands for factors and goods and the elasticity of substitution in consumption, production and trade of the model economy to answer these questions. Liberalization reduces the costs of capital to producers of textiles, food crops and cash-crops more than to other sectors. Increase in income of households result in increased demand for these products according to weight of these commodities in consumers' total expenditure. These accumulation rates are directly related to removal of distortions in the capital markets. In fact the accumulation rate closely corresponds to the distortionary element of capital in a repressionary regime as presented in table 4.8. Accumulation

Table 5.5
Indices of Capital Stock Compared to Benchmark Equilibrium: CAPFLOW Model with Partial Liberalization

	Food-Crop	*Cash-Crop*	*Food-Proc*	*Textiles*	*Che-mical*	*Capital*	*Trans-port*	*Electric*	*Cons-truct*	*Tourism*	*Services*	*Public*
1990	1.00	1.00	1.00	1.00	1.00	1.00	1.00	1.00	1.00	1.00	1.00	1.00
1991	1.38	1.21	1.33	1.02	1.25	1.10	0.98	0.91	1.37	0.91	0.91	0.91
1992	1.61	1.60	1.50	1.68	1.40	1.15	1.00	0.96	1.38	0.97	0.85	0.83
1993	1.65	1.69	1.55	1.92	1.44	1.13	1.04	1.00	1.39	0.99	0.87	0.83
1994	1.68	1.78	1.57	2.11	1.45	1.15	1.05	1.02	1.35	1.00	0.89	0.85
1995	1.70	1.84	1.59	2.27	1.46	1.16	1.06	1.03	1.32	1.01	0.90	0.85
1996	1.71	1.89	1.60	2.39	1.46	1.17	1.07	1.04	1.30	1.01	0.91	0.86
1997	1.72	1.92	1.61	2.48	1.47	1.17	1.07	1.05	1.28	1.02	0.91	0.87
1998	1.73	1.95	1.61	2.54	1.47	1.17	1.08	1.06	1.27	1.02	0.92	0.87
1999	1.74	1.97	1.62	2.59	1.47	1.18	1.08	1.06	1.26	1.03	0.92	0.87
2000	1.74	1.99	1.62	2.63	1.47	1.18	1.08	1.06	1.25	1.03	0.92	0.87
2001	1.75	2.00	1.62	2.66	1.47	1.18	1.08	1.07	1.25	1.03	0.93	0.87
2002	1.75	2.00	1.62	2.68	1.47	1.18	1.08	1.07	1.24	1.03	0.93	0.88
2003	1.75	2.01	1.62	2.69	1.47	1.18	1.08	1.07	1.24	1.03	0.93	0.88
2004	1.75	2.01	1.63	2.71	1.47	1.18	1.08	1.07	1.24	1.03	0.93	0.88
2005	1.75	2.02	1.63	2.71	1.47	1.18	1.08	1.07	1.24	1.03	0.93	0.88
2006	1.75	2.02	1.63	2.72	1.47	1.18	1.08	1.07	1.23	1.03	0.93	0.88
2007	1.75	2.02	1.63	2.73	1.47	1.18	1.08	1.07	1.23	1.03	0.93	0.88
2008	1.75	2.02	1.63	2.73	1.47	1.18	1.08	1.07	1.23	1.03	0.93	0.88
2009	1.75	2.02	1.63	2.73	1.47	1.18	1.08	1.07	1.23	1.03	0.93	0.88
2010	1.75	2.02	1.63	2.74	1.47	1.18	1.08	1.07	1.22	1.03	0.93	0.87
2011	1.75	2.02	1.63	2.74	1.47	1.17	1.08	1.07	1.22	1.03	0.93	0.87
2012	1.75	2.02	1.63	2.75	1.47	1.17	1.08	1.07	1.21	1.03	0.93	0.87
2013	1.75	2.02	1.63	2.76	1.46	1.16	1.08	1.07	1.20	1.03	0.93	0.87
2014	1.75	2.02	1.62	2.77	1.46	1.16	1.08	1.07	1.18	1.03	0.92	0.87
2015	1.74	2.02	1.62	2.78	1.45	1.14	1.07	1.07	1.16	1.03	0.92	0.86
2016	1.74	2.02	1.62	2.81	1.44	1.13	1.07	1.07	1.14	1.02	0.92	0.86
2017	1.74	2.02	1.62	2.83	1.43	1.11	1.07	1.06	1.10	1.02	0.92	0.85
2018	1.73	2.02	1.61	2.88	1.42	1.08	1.06	1.06	1.05	1.02	0.91	0.84

rate is higher for sectors seriously repressed before the liberalization, medium for less seriously repressed sectors. Possibility of trade also affects the model outcome. Capital accumulation rate is higher in tradable goods producing sectors and lower in non-tradable goods producing sectors. Capital accumulation is lower than the baseline model for services and public sectors, which were receiving sizable subsidies before the liberalization.

Table 5.6
Indices of Capital Stock Compared to Benchmark Equilibrium: CAPFLOW Model with Complete Liberalization

	Food-Crop	*Cash-Crop*	*Food-Proc*	*Textiles*	*Che-mical*	*Capital*	*Trans-port*	*Electric*	*Cons-truct*	*Tourism*	*Services*	*Public*
1990	1.00	1.00	1.00	1.00	1.00	1.00	1.00	1.00	1.00	1.00	1.00	1.00
1991	1.55	1.20	1.47	0.91	1.38	1.00	0.99	0.91	1.57	0.91	0.91	0.91
1992	1.93	1.80	1.77	1.72	1.63	1.29	1.00	0.88	1.53	0.92	0.83	0.83
1993	2.18	2.28	1.97	2.66	1.77	1.27	1.02	0.95	1.54	0.97	0.76	0.76
1994	2.28	2.52	2.04	3.22	1.80	1.26	1.06	1.00	1.49	1.00	0.78	0.69
1995	2.34	2.68	2.09	3.61	1.82	1.24	1.08	1.02	1.44	1.01	0.80	0.64
1996	2.36	2.77	2.10	3.80	1.82	1.25	1.09	1.04	1.41	1.02	0.81	0.64
1997	2.38	2.83	2.11	3.96	1.83	1.25	1.09	1.04	1.39	1.03	0.81	0.65
1998	2.39	2.88	2.12	4.07	1.83	1.25	1.09	1.05	1.37	1.03	0.82	0.65
1999	2.40	2.91	2.13	4.16	1.83	1.25	1.10	1.06	1.36	1.03	0.82	0.65
2000	2.41	2.94	2.13	4.23	1.83	1.25	1.10	1.06	1.35	1.03	0.83	0.65
2001	2.41	2.96	2.14	4.28	1.83	1.25	1.10	1.06	1.35	1.04	0.83	0.66
2002	2.42	2.98	2.14	4.32	1.83	1.25	1.10	1.07	1.34	1.04	0.83	0.66
2003	2.42	2.99	2.14	4.35	1.83	1.25	1.10	1.07	1.33	1.04	0.83	0.66
2004	2.42	3.00	2.14	4.37	1.83	1.25	1.11	1.07	1.33	1.04	0.83	0.66
2005	2.42	3.00	2.14	4:39	1.83	1.25	1.10	1.07	1.33	1.04	0.83	0.66
2006	2.42	3.01	2.14	4.40	1.83	1.25	1.10	1.07	1.32	1.04	0.83	0.66
2007	2.42	3.01	2.14	4.41	1.83	1.25	1.11	1.07	1.32	1.04	0.83	0.66
2008	2.42	3.01	2.14	4.42	1.83	1.25	1.11	1.07	1.32	1.04	0.83	0.66
2009	2.42	3.02	2.14	4.43	1.83	1.25	1.10	1.07	1.31	1.04	0.83	0.66
2010	2.42	3.02	2.14	4.44	1.82	1.25	1.10	1.07	1.31	1.04	0.83	0.66
2011	2.42	3.02	2.14	4.45	1.82	1.24	1.10	1.07	1.30	1.04	0.83	0.66
2012	2.42	3.02	2.14	4.46	1.82	1.24	1.10	1.07	1.29	1.04	0.83	0.65
2013	2.42	3.02	2.14	4.47	1.81	1.23	1.10	1.07	1.28	1.04	0.83	0.65
2014	2.41	3.02	2.14	4.49	1.81	1.22	1.10	1.07	1.26	1.04	0.83	0.65
2015	2.41	3.02	2.13	4.52	1.80	1.21	1.09	1.07	1.24	1.03	0.82	0.65
2016	2.40	3.02	2.13	4.56	1.78	1.19	1.09	1.07	1.20	1.03	0.82	0.64
2017	2.39	3.01	2.12	4.62	1.76	1.15	1.08	1.06	1.16	1.03	0.82	0.63
2018	2.37	3.02	2.11	4.72	1.73	1.12	1.07	1.06	1.07	1.02	0.81	0.62

Thus overall conclusion emerging from analysis of table 5.5 is that the liberalization impacts for accumulation of capital are different across sectors as these sectors were subject to various capital market conditions before the liberalization and parameters in consumption, production and trade functions are different for different sectors. Though all of these sector come under same rule (i.e. the rate of marginal productivity of capital) after the liberalization, differences in parameters defining the model structure result in differences in model outcomes. The readjustment process continues for a long period after reforms as seen by tracing the path of capital stock of expanding and contracting sectors.

The reallocation of capital after the financial liberalization to more productive from less productive sectors can be seen from table 5.5 and 5.6. The capital stock expands faster in the textile, food crops and cash crop sectors compared to the benchmark equilibrium implying more access to finance after liberalization. The capital stock decreases in the services and public service sector because of a reduction in interest rate subsidies under partial liberalization.

The growth path of capital stock in complete liberalization closely corresponds to the growth path in the partial liberalization except that the rate of readjustment is greater in case of complete liberalization. This can be seen if we compare the figures in corresponding cells in tables 5.5 and 5.6. For instance, the index of capital stock in the textile sector in 1918 is 2.88 in the case of partial liberalization, and 4.72 in case of complete liberalization. The impact of complete liberalization is 61 percent higher than that in the partial liberalization. Similarly, capital stock index in public service sector in complete liberalization is 73 percent of partial liberalization. The impact in other sectors vary between these two extremes. Thus the extent of adjustment is slowed down by the degree of liberalization.

From an analysis of model solution in Table 5.5 and 5.6, I conclude that an improvement in the efficiency of allocation of capital stock leads to an increase in the overall stock of capital in the economy. The capital stock shrinks in public services and service sectors implying substitution of labor for capital in these sectors following the removal of interest rate subsidies after the liberalization. The stronger capital re-allocation effect under a complete liberalization compared to a partial liberalization implies that conventional practice of creating special rules for the promotion of selected sectors is not effective in the long run. The best rule for a greater accumulation of capital is to remove these special rules and let the capital market operate according to demand and supply forces of the liberalized market economy.

From the model results it is safe to conclude the substitution effect dominates the income effect of the increase in rate interest on savings side and the capital reallocation effect dominates the increase cost of capital effect on investment side. Thus both supply and demand side of the capital market respond positively to liberalization policies. Overall effect of liberalization is increase in both savings and investment that ultimately lead to a higher rate of capital accumulation and growth after liberalization.

OUTPUT IMPACTS OF LIBERALIZATION

The model solutions for output indices compared to the base-line model are presented in table 5.7 and 5.8. It can be seen that output increases in all sectors after liberalization. Output expansion in primary rural-labor intensive sectors, such as textiles, food-crops, cash-crops and chemical (mining and querying) sectors, are greater than in secondary sectors, i.e. transportation, electricity, tourism and construction. Output increases even in public and services sectors in spite of some reductions in capital stocks in these sectors compared to baseline model. This suggests that in response to elimination of subsidies on interest rates, these sectors substitute of labor for capital in the liberalized regime, keeping the production technology defined by the production functions of the model constant.

One very important difference between the growth paths of capital stock and output is that output growth indices are greater than one for every sector. None of the production sectors are experiencing any reduction in the level of output compared to baseline model. This reflects the fact that producers maximize profits by substituting capital and labor until the wage rental ratios are equal to marginal productivity ratios of capital and labor. Even if the capital stock de-accumulates in public and service sectors because of factor substitution, production index is still greater than one. A careful comparison of capital accumulation path and output path indicates this underlying process of substitutions between capital and labor by producers intending to maximize intertemporal profits. Increase in the capital stock complements to urban and rural labor in the production of goods and services in the economy. However it should be recognized that increase in the capital stock is a sufficient but not a necessary condition for increase in the output. The level of output can expand even by an increase in the employment of labor for a given stock of capital. Changes in wage rental ratios implies changes in capital labor ratios in order to fulfill the requirements for profit maximization. Thus, increases in the capital stock leads to an increase in output but the output can

Table 5.7
Production Indices Compared to Benchmark Equilibrium :
CAPFLOW model with Partial Financial Liberalization

	Food-Crop	*Cash-Crop*	*Food-Proc*	*Textiles*	*Che-mical*	*Capital*	*Trans-port*	*Electric*	*Cons-truct*	*Tourism*	*Services*	*Public*
1990	1.002	0.887	0.935	0.858	0.954	0.992	0.98	0.978	1.377	0.95	0.954	1.005
1991	1.059	0.968	1.067	0.886	1.14	1.075	0.971	0.942	1.525	0.929	0.907	1.031
1992	1.09	1.127	1.125	1.424	1.247	1.115	0.977	0.992	1.458	0.96	0.88	1.058
1993	1.111	1.189	1.153	1.643	1.29	1.105	1.008	1.037	1.461	0.988	0.913	1.08
1994	1.133	1.25	1.179	1.837	1.322	1.144	1.038	1.073	1.441	1.015	0.944	1.103
1995	1.155	1.304	1.204	2.003	1.353	1.175	1.066	1.107	1.432	1.041	0.973	1.126
1996	1.178	1.352	1.23	2.145	1.382	1.205	1.093	1.138	1.43	1.066	1	1.15
1997	1.202	1.397	1.255	2.267	1.411	1.233	1.118	1.168	1.436	1.09	1.025	1.173
1998	1.226	1.438	1.28	2.373	1.44	1.26	1.144	1.197	1.447	1.114	1.049	1.197
1999	1.25	1.476	1.306	2.466	1.469	1.287	1.169	1.225	1.463	1.138	1.073	1.222
2000	1.275	1.513	1.332	2.549	1.499	1.314	1.194	1.252	1.482	1.162	1.097	1.246
2001	1.3	1.549	1.359	2.626	1.529	1.341	1.219	1.279	1.504	1.186	1.12	1.271
2002	1.326	1.584	1.386	2.698	1.56	1.368	1.244	1.306	1.528	1.21	1.144	1.297
2003	1.353	1.618	1.414	2.766	1.591	1.396	1.27	1.334	1.554	1.235	1.168	1.323
2004	1.38	1.653	1.443	2.832	1.622	1.424	1.295	1.361	1.582	1.26	1.192	1.35
2005	1.407	1.688	1.471	2.898	1.655	1.452	1.322	1.389	1.61	1.285	1.216	1.377
2006	1.435	1.723	1.501	2.962	1.688	1.481	1.348	1.417	1.64	1.311	1.241	1.404
2007	1.464	1.759	1.531	3.027	1.721	1.509	1.375	1.446	1.67	1.338	1.266	1.432
2008	1.493	1.795	1.562	3.093	1.755	1.538	1.403	1.475	1.7	1.364	1.291	1.461
2009	1.523	1.832	1.593	3.161	1.789	1.567	1.431	1.505	1.73	1.392	1.317	1.49
2010	1.554	1.869	1.625	3.23	1.824	1.596	1.459	1.535	1.759	1.42	1.343	1.52
2011	1.585	1.908	1.657	3.302	1.859	1.624	1.488	1.566	1.787	1.448	1.369	1.55
2012	1.617	1.948	1.69	3.378	1.894	1.651	1.518	1.598	1.813	1.477	1.396	1.58
2013	1.65	1.989	1.724	3.459	1.929	1.677	1.548	1.63	1.837	1.507	1.424	1.612
2014	1.683	2.031	1.759	3.546	1.964	1.7	1.578	1.662	1.855	1.537	1.451	1.643
2015	1.717	2.075	1.794	3.642	1.997	1.72	1.608	1.696	1.866	1.568	1.479	1.675
2016	1.752	2.122	1.83	3.75	2.029	1.733	1.639	1.73	1.867	1.599	1.506	1.708
2017	1.788	2.172	1.867	3.875	2.058	1.739	1.67	1.765	1.853	1.631	1.534	1.74
2018	1.826	2.226	1.904	4.026	2.083	1.723	1.7	1.801	1.817	1.664	1.561	1.772
2019	1.864	2.29	1.943	4.222	2.099	1.714	1.73	1.838	1.736	1.698	1.586	1.805
2020	1.904	2.353	1.981	4.418	2.107	1.703	1.757	1.875	1.631	1.731	1.608	1.838

increase even by increase in the labor for a given stock of capital. Firms operating the expanding sectors tend to increase employment of both labor and capital to raise production sufficient enough to meet the increased demand for goods and services in the economy.

Expansion in output are supported by increase in demands. As mentioned in chapter three. growth in demand may take the forms of increased consumption of the households, and tourists, increased level of investment and a increased volume of exports. Even the government demand increases corresponding an increase in revenue due to expansion in income.

By reducing the cost of capital the financial liberalization lowers prices of commodities supplied by domestic producers. A large proportion of demand met by imports before liberalization, particularly in the expanding sectors food crops, cash crops and textiles, are met by internal production after liberalization.The growth prospects of various sectors closely correspond to the consumption shares presented in table 4.11, import and export prices as given in table 4.14. The food crops, processed foods, textiles and chemicals and services constitute the major portion of household consumption in the base year. These consumption share parameters influence the total demand for a particular product and hence their growth path in the model economy.

The expanding tradable sectors, such as food processing, textiles, chemicals and capital goods sectors are subject to tariffs and export subsidies in the base year. These transfers and subsidy rates are taken as exogenous for computing the impacts of financial liberalization in all versions of the model. In spite of liberalization of trades, tariff rates are higher than export taxes in the base year, as given in table 4.14. This implies reducing the cost of production in the economy, some increase in output after liberalization effectively substitutes imports of these commodities. Meanwhile the lower prices of exportable increases demands for these goods in international markets.

The output indices in tables 5.6 and 5.7 show that liberalization favors some sectors more than others. The highest growth rate is realized in the textile goods sector followed by cash-crop and food crop sectors. Regarding the degree of liberalization, the output effect is similar to capital stock effect; the impact of complete liberalization on output is greater than of the partial liberalization. Output index of textile sector in 2018 was 4.4 in partial liberalization compared to 5.7 in complete liberalization. The cost of capital decreases in these sectors after the liberalization. The capital stock decreases in the public service and services sector are in response to the reduction in interest subsidies after the liberalization. This is in response to an increase in the cost of capital compared to the base year.

The output indices presented in table 5.7 and 5.8 are very intuitive in considering the growth strategy for the Nepalese economy. If distortions are removed economy starts growing through expansion of primary sectors, agriculture and its related sectors. Producers in these sectors respond to reduced cost of production by increasing output. The textiles production expands to meet internal and international demands. Expansion rate of ancillary sectors, i.e. transport,

Table 5.8
Production Indices Compared to Benchmark Equilibrium: CAPFLOW model with Complete Financial Liberalization

	Food-Crop	*Cash-Crop*	*Food-Proc*	*Textiles*	*Che-mical*	*Capital*	*Trans-port*	*Electric*	*Cons-truct*	*Tourism*	*Services*	*Public*
1990	0.986	0.798	0.882	0.758	0.91	0.957	0.95	0.944	1.722	0.906	0.903	1.009
1991	1.062	0.877	1.06	0.717	1.174	0.957	0.945	0.909	1.949	0.89	0.861	1.033
1992	1.104	1.089	1.149	1.317	1.336	1.202	0.952	0.927	1.803	0.908	0.827	1.067
1993	1.132	1.258	1.2	1.999	1.426	1.181	0.957	0.989	1.727	0.936	0.792	1.093
1994	1.154	1.361	1.23	2.426	1.467	1.179	0.99	1.042	1.662	0.967	0.823	1.117
1995	1.176	1.443	1.256	2.752	1.498	1.18	1.021	1.084	1.613	0.995	0.856	1.14
1996	1.199	1.501	1.282	2.955	1.528	1.208	1.048	1.117	1.609	1.019	0.88	1.164
1997	1.223	1.555	1.307	3.13	1.559	1.234	1.073	1.149	1.613	1.042	0.903	1.189
1998	1.247	1.604	1.333	3.283	1.59	1.259	1.098	1.178	1.623	1.065	0.926	1.213
1999	1.271	1.649	1.359	3.419	1.621	1.285	1.122	1.207	1.638	1.088	0.947	1.238
2000	1.296	1.693	1.386	3.541	1.653	1.311	1.147	1.235	1.658	1.111	0.968	1.263
2001	1.322	1.735	1.414	3.653	1.686	1.338	1.171	1.263	1.68	1.134	0.99	1.289
2002	1.348	1.776	1.442	3.758	1.719	1.365	1.196	1.29	1.706	1.157	1.011	1.315
2003	1.375	1.816	1.471	3.858	1.753	1.392	1.221	1.318	1.734	1.181	1.032	1.341
2004	1.403	1.856	1.5	3.954	1.788	1.419	1.246	1.346	1.763	1.205	1.053	1.368
2005	1.431	1.896	1.53	4.048	1.824	1.447	1.271	1.374	1.794	1.229	1.075	1.396
2006	1.459	1.936	1.561	4.141	1.86	1.475	1.297	1.402	1.826	1.254	1.097	1.423
2007	1.488	1.977	1.592	4.234	1.896	1.504	1.323	1.43	1.859	1.279	1.119	1.452
2008	1.518	2.018	1.623	4.328	1.933	1.533	1.349	1.46	1.892	1.305	1.141	1.481
2009	1.549	2.06	1.656	4.424	1.971	1.561	1.376	1.489	1.925	1.331	1.164	1.51
2010	1.58	2.103	1.689	4.522	2.009	1.589	1.404	1.519	1.957	1.358	1.187	1.541
2011	1.611	2.147	1.723	4.625	2.047	1.617	1.432	1.55	1.988	1.385	1.211	1.571
2012	1.644	2.192	1.757	4.733	2.086	1.643	1.46	1.581	2.016	1.413	1.234	1.602
2013	1.677	2.239	1.792	4.848	2.124	1.668	1.489	1.613	2.039	1.441	1.258	1.634
2014	1.711	2.289	1.828	4.974	2.161	1.688	1.518	1.646	2.057	1.47	1.282	1.666
2015	1.746	2.341	1.864	5.114	2.196	1.704	1.547	1.68	2.065	1.499	1.306	1.698
2016	1.781	2.396	1.901	5.274	2.228	1.714	1.576	1.714	2.058	1.529	1.33	1.731
2017	1.818	2.457	1.938	5.468	2.257	1.694	1.605	1.749	2.032	1.56	1.353	1.763
2018	1.856	2.533	1.976	5.738	2.273	1.685	1.633	1.788	1.947	1.591	1.375	1.796

electricity, construction and service is lower than the growth rates of the primary sectors.

Thus an analysis of solutions of a forward-looking inter-temporal general equilibrium model bring us to believe that the financial sector liberalization policy actually turns out to be equivalent to an agriculture-led growth strategy for the Nepalese economy.

To sum up, from the model results of output indices I conclude that financial liberalization leads to an expansion in output of all sectors and rural-labor intensive agricultural sectors in particular. The impact of complete liberalization on output are greater than the impact of partial liberalization.

CONCLUSIONS

The main results from the model I perform are:

1. Liberalization favors rural households over urban households, as reflected in a higher welfare index for rural households in comparison to urban

households. In this sense liberalization redistributes income from urban to rural households.

2 The redistribution of welfare occurs through the effect of liberalization on wage increases. The wages of unskilled labor increase faster than the wages of skilled labor.

3 Liberalization equalizes the rates of return across sectors. This insures efficiency in the allocation of resources. Welfare and accumulation effects are greater when domestic capital markets are integrated with international capital markets. Non-steady state growth rates of urban labor force and agricultural productivity can influence these liberalization effects to some extent.

4 The efficiency in allocation causes a larger increase in the capital stock of sectors that were more repressed before liberalization started. It causes a reduction or a slower growth of the capital stock in sectors that used to be subsidized before repression. Ultimately all sectors return to the steady state growth rate of the economy.

5 The expansion in capital stock allows production to expand accordingly. The output expansion is greater in sectors that were more heavily repressed before the liberalization.

6 The modeling exercises reported on this chapter show that it is possible to develop a well disaggregated general equilibrium model by using inter-temporal behavior of households and producers and to study the effects of economy-wide and sector specific policy issues aimed at increasing efficiency and welfare in the economy.

7 Numberical solutions of model imply that the substitution effect of the increase in rate interest dominates the income effect on savings side and the efficiency in capital reallocation effect dominates the increased cost of capital effect on the investment side. Overall effect is increase in both savings and investment after the liberalization leading to a higher rate of capital accumulation and output after liberalization.

10

SUMMARY AND EXTENSIONS

SUMMARY

The major argument advanced in this dissertation is that financial sector reforms in Nepal have released extra resources for investment by improving efficiency in resource allocation, and increased the volume of savings available for productive investment as spending was cut on unproductive assets to meet unseen contingencies in the future. It also argues that the Nepalese reform process has redistributed income from urban to rural households. Financial liberalization has increased the demand for rural labor to complement added capital stocks in rural-labor intensive sectors. Wage rates for rural labor increase more than that of the urban labor, leading to an increase in their welfare.

Financial sector reforms have their main impacts on the volumes of saving and investment. However, economic theory alone cannot determine the magnitudes of changes in the volume of savings and investment concomitant to such reforms. Whether the volume of saving increases with financial liberalization or not, depends upon whether the income effect from a change in the rate of interest dominates the substitution effect. Saving will increase only if the substitution effect is stronger than the income effect. Thus the effect of financial sector reform on saving is ambiguous. Similarly, financial sector reform is often characterized by an increase in the real interest rate. Standard theory states that when the cost of investment funds increases, the amount of investment is likely to fall. The net effect of the reforms on investment, then, depends upon whether the efficiency gains of reallocation of capital can compensate for the increased costs of investment after liberalization.

In Nepal the financial reform process started in mid 1980s and took major shape in 1992 under a new government. Before the 1992 reforms, the Nepalese financial sector was characterized by ceilings on interest rates, credit controls, high reserve requirement, tight regulations on entry and exit of financial institutions, controls on foreign exchange, uncontrolled budgetary deficits and underdeveloped capital markets. The financial repression from all these features resulted in higher transaction costs for borrowers, and often negative rates of interest for savers. High subsidies on credits to selected sectors coexisted with higher interest rates for other sectors. The distortionary effects of repression were wide ranging. Though the reform measures have removed many of the distortionary elements involved debate on efficiency and redistribution effects of further reforms continues.

I consider the economy-wide long-run consequences of financial sector liberalization using a forward-looking multi-sectoral computable general equilibrium (CGE) model of the Nepalese economy with financial intermediation. The model is used to investigate efficiency, redistribution and welfare effects of financial sector reform as the economy evolves. In the model, consumers are located in urban and rural areas. Their decisions between saving and consumption are studied under life-cycle behavior. There are 11 producers of goods and services. Investors' decisions regarding the allocation of the capital stock reflect inter-temporal profit maximization. Traders sell products both in domestic and foreign markets. The government collects revenues from taxes on income, consumption and international trade and spends all of these revenues. The laws of motion of capital and exogenous growth rate of the population determine the growth path of the economy.

The model is applied to study the effects of partial and complete economy wide reforms, as well as piecemeal reforms. A partial reform refers to a 50 percent reduction in the distortionary cost of financial transactions after the reform, while a complete liberalization means the elimination of all distortions across all sectors. Piecemeal liberalization is sector specific.

The major conclusions from the model analyses are following:

1. By equalizing rates of return across sectors, liberalization ensures efficiency in the allocation of resources. Efficiency in resource allocation increases the capital usage in sectors that were more repressed before liberalization. It causes a reduction, or slower growth, of capital use in sectors that used to be subsidized before repression. Ultimately all sectors return to their output and capital use levels on a steady state growth. The expansion in the capital stock allows production to expand accordingly. Output expansion is greater in sectors that were repressed heavily before the liberalization.
2. The benefits of liberalization accrue more to the rural households than to the urban households. Following liberalization rural labor intensive sectors invest more in response to an increased access to financial institutions. More labor is required to complement additional capital. Demand for unskilled labor increases faster than the demand for skilled labor. This means increases in wage rates of rural labor is greater than the increases in the wages rates of the rural labor. Consequently welfare gains of rural households are larger in comparison to the welfare gains of urban households. In this sense, liberalization redistributes income from urban to rural households. The redistribution of welfare occurs by increasing wages of unskilled labor in comparison to the wages of skilled labor.

The rich institutional structure contained in forward-looking CGE models allows one to experiment with many structural assumption characterizing the particular economy under investigation. Therefore this framework is definitely an improvement over the staples of growth models including the fixed coefficient Harrod-Domar growth model, neoclassical growth models, one sector endogenous growth models as well as static and sequential dynamic CGE models available in the literature. Specification of a multi-sectoral wedge in the cost of capital an its impact on the economy over the period is a new approach for analysis of financial repression and liberalization of decentralized market economy. Model contained in this dissertation is an important empirical tool to study long run growth and distribution in an inter-temporal and inter-sectoral framework. However, this model could benefit from further work on specification of dynamic adjustment process in a steady state growth path of the model economy.

The dynamic general equilibrium framework contained in the base-line model can be applied to analyze several other issues of the Nepalese economy particularly related to study the impacts of fiscal reforms, liberalization of international trade, policies on labor market and human resource development policies. It can be an appropriate model for studying migration, regional and sectoral development, and parallel markets, with a very few modifications.

EXTENSIONS

Extension of model is possible by adding new features or by refining the data-structure. Some hints are listed below for some important issues that could not be covered in this paper, as guidelines for further research.

Government Finance

The government's fiscal policy discussed in the section 3.6 assumed a period by period balance in the government budget. This may be relaxed to accommodate government deficit ($GR_t - GD_t$) to a certain percent of GDP. Theoretically, there are three major sources to meet this deficit; selling bonds to the households and banking system (B_t), selling bonds to foreigners (FLG_t), and, monetizing (DMB_t).

$$GR_t - GD_t = B_t + FLG_t + DMB_t \tag{6.1}$$

Which one of these three sources is used in practice depends very much upon the objectives of the government in power. A populist policy focused on short-run political gains may put a low weight on the inflationary consequences and is very different from the point of a sustainable policy that would emphasize on increased mobilization of savings including inflows of foreign capital. Additional revenue requirement may be met by increase in value added taxes or tariffs or income taxes. Each of these have different impacts on behaviors of producers, savers and consumers. These and other issues of budgetary policy can be studied using the current model without much elaboration.

Public sector investment, $I_{g,t}$, in education and health of population, in construction of roads, highways, airports, communication systems, and hydro-energy and so on creates basic infrastructure, based upon which private firms will invest, $I_{i,t}$, and adopt new technologies either in starting a new production process or replacing the old machines in existing production plants. The current model can be used without further changes to study impacts of various components of public expenditure policies in the model economy.

More Elaboration on Financial System

The dynamic model contained in this dissertation does not include portfolio allocation decisions of household in the short run. Allocation between consumption and savings n the long-run models are guided by one price of risk-less capital that applies to all kinds of assets of the households. In the short run, households allocate their savings on a mix of new assets, e.g., in currency, demand deposits, foreign deposits, and equity and these assets are imperfect substitutes in their portfolio. The mix on portfolio really depends upon the rental rate of capital, inflation, the domestic interest rate, and the foreign interest rates. Demand for money depends on prices, interest rates and income of the people. Firms issue new equity to reflect increases in their capital stock. This new equity is owned by households and government. The current model with some modifications on the steady state and terminal conditions can be appropriate to study a short-run portfolio allocation decisions of households responding to capital market conditions in the economy.

Another important phenomena that can be covered in extension is the segmentation of the financial market between formal and informal sector. Total savings of the economy is divided between the formal (*bSt*) and informal sector (*1-b*) *St*. If the rate of return on formal sector activities is not attractive, funds will flow through the informal sector in repression. The return in formal sector activities may not be attractive owing to appreciation of currency that makes the domestic interest rate lower than the international interest rate. If such condition continues for a long period capital tend to fly out resulting in a reduction in the volume of investment in the economy. When saving cannot reach to investors it cannot contribute towards economic growth.

$$S_t = bS_t + (1 - b)S_t \tag{6.2}$$

$$FA_t = bFA_t + (1 - b)\ FA_t \tag{6.3}$$

The share parameter b, $0 < b < 1$, shows segmentation of saving between formal and informal markets. Such segmentation leads to distortions in the capital market. While the preferred borrowers have unlimited access to credit at regulated rates, other borrowers obtain a large proportion of their funds at competitive rates or from an unofficial "curb" market (Wijnbergen).

Another area of extension is foreign exchange markets. In this model I considered a fixed exchange rate regime leaving the trade balance to be determined endogenously. A foreign exchange market need to be included if one wants to study an economy where the foreign exchange rate is determined endogenously by the market model. The supply of foreign exchange comes from exports, remittances and unrequited transfers and demand for foreign exchange is originated by imports of goods and services, transfer payment abroad, debt servicing in foreign loans. The basic rule in this case is to let the exchange rate clear the demand and supply of foreign exchanges which will have further implications on inflows and outflows of capital from the model economy.

Labor Market and Man Power Development

Some refinement in the labor market specification in the current model is worth-taking to study the general equilibrium effects on rural-urban migration and international migration across Nepal-India border, to trace the link between subsistence and mainstream economy and to analyze the impact of human capital formation in the economy.

In the model growth rate of labor force is exogenous. Migration could be made endogenous making labor movement from rural to urban areas respond to wage rates and other employment conditions in these two locations.

In each period *(1-u)* remains unemployed, which may be due to seasonal factors in agriculture, low capacity utilization in the manufacturing sector or shocks on raw materials; job search process in the urban sector. Employed labor force is either employed in the rural sector or in the urban sectors.

$$u_t L_t = \sum_{h,i} L_{h,i,t} = L_{r,t} + L_{u,t} \tag{6.4}$$

The size of urban labor force can be related to non-agricultural value added relative to the agricultural value added adjusted for the capital intensity as following:

$$L_u = \left(\frac{Y_{na,t}}{Y_{a,t}}\right)^j \left(\frac{K_{na,t}}{L_{na,t}}\right)^q \left(\frac{w_{na,t}}{w_{a,t}}\right)^p \tag{6.5}$$

where subscripts u, *a* and *na* represent urban, agricultural and non-agricultural sectors respectively. Variables *L, K, Y* and *W* are labor, capital, output and wage rates. The migration of labor from rural to urban areas, LM_t, can be accounted by a change in the level of employment of urban (skilled) labor between *t* and *t+1* periods.

$$LM_t = L_{u,t-1} - L_{u,t} \tag{6.6}$$

Producers indirectly determine the rate of migration from rural to urban areas while determining the level of output, and employment of labor and capital.

The Nepalese labor market is very closely related with the labor market in India for various reasons. First, Nepal is land-locked and has an open border with India in the East, South and West. Secondly, these two countries have long cultural and social ties. Third, most of the Indian languages are easy to learn to Nepalese people and vice-versa as both Nepali and several Indian languages have a common root in Sanskrit. Owing to these factors there is a long history of international migration of labor between India and Nepal. A lot of the professional labor force in Nepal has received one or another sort of training from India. Because of the size and free mobility across the borders, labor market conditions in India dominates the labor market in Nepal. For these reasons specification of labor market in Nepal is incomplete without relating it to the Indian labor market. The simplest possible specification, though labor market is very different for one category of skills to another, is to subject net migration to India, $LMI_{h,t}$, as a function of the wage rate in Nepalese labor market w_n relative to an average wage rate in India, w_I as following:

$$LMI_{h,t} = v.(w_n/w_I)^h \tag{6.7}$$

The motivation for migration exists until the wage rate between these two economies equalize. There are two sorts of outcome due to such labor market situation. First, wage rates in Nepal are driven by wages in India, if a free mobility of labor is allowed along the border. Any gain in Nepal's labor market cannot remain not shared with the Indian labor market. This sort of analysis would be useful for analyzing implications of common labor market policies as suggested by the South Asian Preferential Trade Arrangements (SAPTA, 1995).

Another areas in labor market relates to treatment of subsistence and self-employment sector. Along with the firms in the formal sector, there are many subsistence sector firms operated by poor households in rural and urban areas. Their self-employment sector production functions can be specified as:

$$Y^r_{I,t} = A^r_{I,t}(L^r_{I,t})^{\theta_r}(K^r_{I,t})^{1-\theta_r} \tag{6.8}$$

$$Y^u_{I,t} = A^u_{I,t}(L^u_{I,t})^{\theta_u}(K^u_{I,t})^{1-\theta_u} \tag{6.9}$$

where subscripts r and u refer to rural and urban locations, *A*,*K*,*L*,and *Y* technology, capital, labor and output as usual. All self-employment sector income goes to the subsistence households. Though on average, such subsistence income is less than what a regular employee in the formal sector would earn, such activities will continue until the growth in the formal sector is sufficient to absorb all people employed in the subsistence sector.

Most of the output of rural subsistence sector do not appear in the market and only a portion of output such as milk, wood, animals, and forest products is sold in the market in exchange of necessary goods such as clothes, medicine, and simple tools. We assume that part of the income not consumed by the rural subsistence households is used in self-financing small scale investment activities in the rural areas. These may include improvement of agricultural farms, increase in size of livestock, purchase and maintenance of tools.

Poor households in urban subsistence sector operate informal firms that provide services in rich urban households. The list of these services is very extensive and includes pulling carts, rickshaw, portering, haircutting, shoe-shining, vending vegetables and fruit, and selling other consumption goods from door to door, and maintaining small corner shops or an unit in an open market. This sector grows with urbanization, as the demand for such services grows with the size of the population living in the urban areas.

A part of the income saved by the household in the urban sector is used in self-financing activities, so that their business continues to provide them with self-sustenance over their life time.

$$P_{i,t}Y^{r}_{l,t} \le P_{i,t}Y^{u}_{l,t} \le w_{i,t}L_{i,t} \tag{6.10}$$

To be consistent with the migration function outlined above one may assume that income in the subsistence sectors in rural areas is less than income in the informal sector, which itself is less than wage income in formal sectors. There is always a queue of people waiting for jobs in the formal sector.

Sometimes, depending on the economic policy regime, it is not uncommon to find bigger size firms involved in financial services, foreign exchange and international trade through informal channels. These bigger firms use small firms in the informal sector to distribute goods and services supplied by the parallel economy.

Incorporation of self-employment and subsistence sectors explicitly would make the current model more realistic to the Nepalese economy.

Informal Sector and International Trade

International trade policies have significant effect on prices of commodities, public revenues, incentive of producers and investors in the economy. Various aspects of international trade policy and their link with economic growth rates, can be studied under the current model without much extension. One area where the current model can benefit is by proper modification of informal market for commodities and factors. In commodity markets, the heavy tariff on international trade promotes an illegal trade mostly along the open Indian border. Such deflection in trade due to the difference in trade regime between India and Nepal in the past has been an issue in trade disputes. As an example of the worst dispute one can take the trade embargo by India against Nepal from March 1989 to June 1990, when only two out of 15 trade points were not closed down from the Indian side. Similarly quota restrictions also have promoted the smuggling of goods through the informal markets, and rampant corruption.

Given the importance of informal sector in the Nepalese economy, it may be desirable to supplement the traditional SAM with an augmented SAM that also incorporates informal sector in commodities, factors, capital and foreign exchange markets. An augmented SAM can help us estimate such underground activities in the economy. Though with the gradual process for liberalization of economies in the South-Asian economies, particularly of the Indian economy, one can expect the issue of deflection in international trade will become a minor issue in coming years, proper understanding of informal sector activities will remain useful for studying the impacts of various policies designed for development of the economy.

Applications outlined here are only indicative. The base-line model contained in dissertation is an all-purpose model. With slight modification it can be applied for analysis of many other issues in the Nepalese economy which are amenable to general equilibrium analysis.

APPENDICES

APPENDIX I

```
$TITLE An Intertemporal CGE Model for Nepal—ref case w/ capital flows
SET    MDL Alternative models /CAPFLOW, BOPCON, NONSS, BLKHOLE/;
SET    TP /1990*2025/, TFIRST(TP) /1990/, TLAST(TP), HORIZON(TP);
SET    SC Two of the scenarios /PARTIAL, COMPLETE/;
SCALAR        CAPFLOW Switch for free capital flows            /1/,
       BLKHOLE Switch for rent-seeking losses           /1/,
       NONSS Switch for non-steadystate growth path     /0/,
       DEBUG  Switch for benchmark replication          /0/;

$INCLUDE scenario
*      Set switches for alternative model structures:
IF (STRUCT("CAPFLOW"),
       BLKHOLE = 0;
       NONSS = 0;
       CAPFLOW = 1;
);
IF (STRUCT("BOPCON"),
       BLKHOLE = 0;
       NONSS = 0;
       CAPFLOW = 0;
);
IF (STRUCT("BLKHOLE"),
       BLKHOLE = 1;
       NONSS = 0;
       CAPFLOW = 1;
);
```

```
IF (STRUCT("NONSS"),
        BLKHOLE = 0;
        NONSS = 1;
        CAPFLOW = 1;
);
SCALAR BOPCON Switch for period by period capital flow constraints;
BOPCON = 1 - CAPFLOW;

$INCLUDE nepaldat.gms
*       Initialize as though we are solving the entire horizon
*       in one shot:
SCALAR          G           POTENTIAL GROWTH RATE /0.02/
        NR      NET INTEREST RATE       /0.05/
        DEPR    DEPRECIATION RATE       /0.07/
        GOVFX               Government foreign exchange balance
        GOVEXP              Government net income;
SET URBAN(HH) /URBAN/;
PARAMETER       QREF(TP)            STEADY STATE QUANTITY INDEX
                PREF(TP)            PRESENT VALUE PRICE
                QLAND(TP)           GROWTH RATE OF ARABLE LAND
                QLABOR(LC,TP)               GROWTH RATE OF LABOR
                YEAR(TP)            YEAR ASSOCIATED WITH PERIOD TP
                INCBAL(*)           CHECK OF INCOME BALANCE
                I0(J)               BASE YEAR INVESTMENT BY SECTOR
                LAND(I)             LAND INPUTS
                VKCHK(I,*)          CAPITAL VALUE CROSS-CHECKS
                TAU(I)              CALIBRATED SPREAD IN CAPITAL RENTS,
                RK0(*)              BASE YEAR USER COST OF CAPITAL
                K0(I)               BASE YEAR CAPITAL STOCK
                FXCHK               CROSS CHECK OF FOREIGN EXCHANGE

                W0(HH)              REFERENCE CONSUMPTION LEVEL
                THETA(HH)           HOUSEHOLD SHARE OF GOVERNMENT
 INCOME&EXPENSE
                KSHR(HH)            HOUSEHOLD SHARE OF INITIAL CAPITAL
                LSHR(HH)            HOUSEHOLD SHARE OF LAND
                EXOGFX(TP,HH)               EXOGENOUS FOREIGN INCOME
                INCADJ(HH)          INTER-HOUSEHOLD TRANSFERS
                BOPDEF              BASE YEAR FOREIGN EXCHANGE DEFICIT
```

```
                    ESUBT(HH)      INTERTEMPORAL ELASTICITY OF
                                   SUBSTITUTION / RURAL 0.25, URBAN 0.5 /;

*       Set up the time horizon:
YEAR(TP) = 1990 + (ORD(TP)-1);
LOOP(TARGET, HORIZON(TP) = YES$(YEAR(TP) LE YEAR(TARGET)) );
TLAST(TP) = YES$(ORD(TP) EQ CARD(HORIZON));
*       Check income balances in the base year data:
INCBAL(HH) = SUM(I,D0(I,HH)) + SAVING(HH) -
        (ENDOW("L",HH)
        + ENDOW("K",HH)
        + SUM(R,ER(R)*(REMIT(R,HH)-FTRN(HH,R)))
        - ER("ROW")*LOANS(HH)
        - TAXREV(HH) );
INCBAL("GOVT") = SUM(I,D0(I,"GOVT")) + SAVING("GOVT") - (
                SUM((I,R), X0(I,R) * TX(I,R))
               + SUM((I,R), M0(I,R) * TM(I,R))
               + SUM(I, D0(I,"TOURIST") * TTR)
               + SUM(J, Y0(J)*TI(J))
               + SUM(HH, TAXREV(HH))
               + SUM(LC,INCTAX(LC))
               + TAXREV("CORP")
               + FSAV
               + ER("ROW")*(LOANS("AID")-LOANS("GOVT"))
               + ER("INDIA")*LOANS("REFUND")
               - SUM(I,D0(I,"STOCK")) );
DISPLAY INCBAL;
*       Move non-capital inputs from the investment demand to the stock
*       change vector:
SET     IK(I)       Capital formation goods /CAPITAL, CONSTRUCT/;
D0(I,"STOCK") = D0(I,"STOCK") + SUM(J,IMA(I,J))$(NOT IK(I));
IMA(I,J)$(NOT IK(I)) = 0;
I0(J) = SUM(I, IMA(I,J));
*       Extract land rents from capital income in the agricultural
*       sectors:
SET IAGR(I) Agricultural goods /FOOD-CROP,CASH-CROP,FOOD-PROC/;
LAND(IAGR) = VK0(IAGR) - I0(IAGR) / 0.3;
VK0(IAGR) = VK0(IAGR) - LAND(IAGR);
```

```
DISPLAY LAND;
*       Report statistics on the rates of return to capital and land, etc:
VKCHK(I,"KVS") = (PROFIT(I)+SUPPLY(I,"DEP")) /
        (LAND(I) + PROFIT(I)+SUPPLY(I,"DEP") + SUM(LC,WAG(I,LC)));
VKCHK(I,"LAND") = LAND(I) /
        (LAND(I) + PROFIT(I)+SUPPLY(I,"DEP") + SUM(LC,WAG(I,LC)));
VKCHK(I,"PROFITSHR") = PROFIT(I)/VK0(I);
VKCHK(I,"IKRATIO") = I0(I) / VK0(I);

*       Calibrate the spread from the base year investment, growth,
*       depreciation, interest rate and capital rents:

TAU(I) = 1 - (DEPR + NR/(1-NR))*I0(I)/((DEPR+G)*VK0(I));
RK0("RISKLESS") = NR/(1-NR) + DEPR;
RK0(I) = ( NR/(1-NR) + DEPR ) / (1-TAU(I));
K0(I) = VK0(I) / RK0(I);

DISPLAY RK0;
*       Reporting capital-output ratio:
VKCHK(I,"KYRATIO") = K0(I) / Y0(I);
VKCHK(I,"TAU") = TAU(I);
DISPLAY VKCHK;
*       Steady state growth path quantity and price indices:
QREF(TP) = (1+G)**(ORD(TP)-1);
PREF(TP) = (1-NR)**(ORD(TP)-1);
QLAND(TP) = QREF(TP);
QLABOR(LC,TP) = QREF(TP);
DISPLAY QREF,PREF;
*       Calibrated foreign exchange flows (the whole economy):
BOPDEF =
        FSAV
        + SUM(R, TY(R))
        + ER("ROW")       * LOANS("GOVT")
        + ER("ROW")       * LOANS("AID")
        + ER("INDIA")     * LOANS("REFUND")
        + ER("ROW")       * SUM(HH, LOANS(HH))
        + SUM((HH,R), ER(R) * REMIT(R,HH))
        - SUM((HH,R), ER(R) * FTRN(HH,R));
```

```
FXCHK = BOPDEF - SUM((I,R), M0(I,R)-X0(I,R));
DISPLAY FXCHK;

$ONTEXT

$MODEL:NEPAL

$SECTORS:
      W(HH)                           ! Welfare index
      Y(I,TP)$HORIZON(TP)             ! PRODUCTION
      K(I,TP)$HORIZON(TP)             ! CAPITAL
      INV(I,TP)$HORIZON(TP)           ! INVESTMENT
      X(I,TP)$(VX0(I)$HORIZON(TP))    ! EXPORT
      A(I,TP)$HORIZON(TP)             ! ARMINGTON AGGREGATION
      GOV(TP)$HORIZON(TP)             ! GOVERNMENT OUTPUT
      U(HH,TP)$HORIZON(TP)            ! UTILITY INDEX
      T(TP)$HORIZON(TP)               ! PROVISION OF TOURISM

$COMMODITIES:
      P(I,TP)$HORIZON(TP)             ! SUPPLY PRICE
      PD(I,TP)$HORIZON(TP)            ! DOMESTIC OUTPUT PRICE
      PX(I,TP)$(VX0(I)$HORIZON(TP))   ! EXPORT PRICE AGGREGATE
      RK(I,TP)$HORIZON(TP)            ! CAPITAL RENTAL RATE
      PK(I,TP)$HORIZON(TP)            ! CAPITAL PRICE
      PL(LC,TP)$HORIZON(TP)           ! WAGE RATE
      PLAND(TP)$HORIZON(TP)           ! RENTAL RATE ON LAND
      PG(TP)$HORIZON(TP)              ! GOVERNMENT OUTPUT
      PT(TP)$HORIZON(TP)              ! TOURSIST PRICE
      PR(TP)$HORIZON(TP)              ! PRICE INDEX FOR GOVERNMENT
TRANSFER
      PU(HH,TP)$HORIZON(TP)           ! CONSUMPTION PRICE
      PW(HH)                          ! Welfare price index
      PTK(I)                          ! TERMINAL INVESMENT PREMIUM
      PVPFX$CAPFLOW                   ! PRESENT VALUE EXCHANGE RATE
      PFX(TP)$(BOPCON$HORIZON(TP)) ! PRESENT VALUE EXCHANGE RATE

$CONSUMERS:
      TOURIST(TP)$HORIZON(TP)         ! TOURISM DEMAND
      GOVT(TP)$HORIZON(TP)            ! GOVERNMENT
      RA(HH)                          ! REPRESENTATIVE AGENT
      FININT(TP)$(BLKHOLE$HORIZON(TP)) ! FINANCIAL INTERMEDIATION
```

```
COST

$AUXILIARY:
        TK(I)                  ! TERMINAL CAPITAL DEMAND

$PROD:Y(I,TP)$HORIZON(TP) s:0 t:ETRNDX(I) VA:1 L(VA):3
        O:PD(I,TP)           Q:(Y0(I)-VX0(I)) A:GOVT(TP) T:TI(I)
        O:PX(I,TP)           Q:VX0(I)         A:GOVT(TP) T:TI(I)
        I:P(J,TP)            Q:IOF(J,I)
        I:PL(LC,TP)          Q:WAG(I,LC)      L:
        I:PLAND(TP)          Q:LAND(I)        VA:
        I:RK(I,TP)           Q:K0(I) P:RK0(I) VA:

$PROD:K(I,TP)$HORIZON(TP+1) s:0
        O:RK(I,TP)           Q:K0(I)
+       A:RA("URBAN")$(NOT BLKHOLE) A:FININT(TP)$BLKHOLE T:TAU(I)
        O:PK(I,TP+1)         Q:(K0(I)*(1-DEPR))
        I:PK(I,TP)           Q:K0(I)

$PROD:K(I,TP)$TLAST(TP) s:0
        O:RK(I,TP)           Q:K0(I)
+       A:RA("URBAN")$(NOT BLKHOLE) A:FININT(TP)$BLKHOLE T:TAU(I)
        O:PTK(I)             Q:(K0(I)*(1-DEPR))
        I:PK(I,TP)           Q:K0(I)

$PROD:INV(I,TP)$HORIZON(TP+1) s:0
        O:PK(I,TP+1)         Q:I0(I)
        I:P(J,TP)            Q:IMA(J,I)

$PROD:INV(I,TP)$TLAST(TP) s:0
        O:PTK(I)             Q:I0(I)
        I:P(J,TP)            Q:IMA(J,I)
*       EXPORT ACTIVITY—THIS IS A CET COMPOSITE OUTPUT OVER
*       FLOWS TO DIFFERENT TRADING PARTNERS.

$PROD:X(I,TP)$(VX0(I)$HORIZON(TP)) t:ETRNXX(I)
 O:PVPFX#(R)$CAPFLOW
+       Q:(X0(I,R)*PREF(TP)) P:(PX0(I,R)/PREF(TP)) A:GOVT(TP) T:TX(I,R)
O:PFX(TP)#(R)$BOPCON Q:X0(I,R) P:PX0(I,R) A:GOVT(TP) T:TX(I,R)
I:PX(I,TP)           Q:VX0(I)
*    ARMINGTON SUPPLY AGGREGATES DOMESTIC AND IMPORTED GOODS.
*    LIKE EXPORTS, HERE WE HAVE ONE IMPORT COEFFICIENT FOR EACH
*    REGION R.
```

```
$PROD:A(I,TP)$HORIZON(TP) s:SIGMADM(I) m:SIGMAMM(I)
O:P(I,TP)           Q:S0(I)
I:PD(I,TP)          Q:(Y0(I)-VX0(I))
I:PVPFX#(R)$CAPFLOW
+    Q:(M0(I,R)*PREF(TP)) P:(PM0(I,R)/PREF(TP)) A:GOVT(TP) T:TM(I,R) m:
I:PFX(TP)#(R)$BOPCON Q:M0(I,R) P:PM0(I,R) A:GOVT(TP) T:TM(I,R) m:

$PROD:GOV(TP)$HORIZON(TP)
    O:PG(TP)            Q:(SUM(I,D0(I,"GOVT")))
    I:P(I,TP)           Q:D0(I,"GOVT")

$PROD:U(HH,TP)$HORIZON(TP) s:1
    O:PU(HH,TP)         Q:(SUM(I,D0(I,HH)))
    I:P(I,TP)           Q:D0(I,HH)

$PROD:W(HH) s:ESUBT(HH)
    O:PW(HH)            Q:W0(HH)
    I:PU(HH,TP)$HORIZON(TP)   Q:(QREF(TP)*SUM(I,D0(I,HH))) P:PREF(TP)

$PROD:T(TP)$HORIZON(TP)
    O:PT(TP)            Q:(SUM(I,D0(I,"TOURIST"))+TAXREV("TOURIST"))
    I:P(I,TP)           Q:D0(I,"TOURIST") A:GOVT(TP) T:TTR

$DEMAND:FININT(TP)$(BLKHOLE$HORIZON(TP))
    D:PFX(TP)$BOPCON
    D:PVPFX$CAPFLOW

$DEMAND:TOURIST(TP)$HORIZON(TP)
    E:PVPFX$CAPFLOW          Q:(PREF(TP)*QREF(TP)*SUM(R, TY(R)))
    E:PFX(TP)$BOPCON Q:(QREF(TP)*SUM(R, TY(R)))
    D:PT(TP)                 Q:(QREF(TP) * SUM(R, TY(R)))

$DEMAND:GOVT(TP)$HORIZON(TP)
    E:PVPFX$CAPFLOW          Q:(QREF(TP)*PREF(TP)*GOVFX)
    E:PFX(TP)$BOPCON Q:(QREF(TP)*GOVFX)
    E:P(I,TP)                Q:(-QREF(TP)*D0(I,"STOCK"))
    E:PL(HH,TP)              Q:(QLABOR(HH,TP)*(TAXREV(HH)+INCTAX(HH)))
    D:PR(TP)                 Q:(QREF(TP)*GOVEXP)

$DEMAND:RA(HH)
    E:PFX(TP)$((BLKHOLE*BOPCON)$HORIZON(TP)$URBAN(HH))
+              Q:(SUM(I,    TAU(I)*K0(I)*RK0(I)*QREF(TP)))
    E:PVPFX$((BLKHOLE*CAPFLOW)$URBAN(HH))
```

```
+     Q:(SUM((I,TP)$HORIZON(TP),TAU(I)*K0(I)*RK0(I)*QREF(TP)*PREF(TP)))
      E:PW("URBAN")             Q:INCADJ(HH)
      E:PVPFX$CAPFLOW       Q:(SUM(TP$HORIZON(TP),
PREF(TP)*EXOGFX(TP,HH)))
      E:PFX(TP)$BOPCON         Q:EXOGFX(TP,HH)
      E:PR(TP)$HORIZON(TP)      Q:(QREF(TP)*GOVEXP*THETA(HH))
      E:PL(HH,TP)$HORIZON(TP)  Q:(QLABOR(HH,TP)*(ENDOW("L",HH)-
TAXREV(HH)))
      E:PLAND(TP)$HORIZON(TP) Q:(QLAND(TP)*SUM(I,LAND(I))*LSHR(HH))
      E:PK(I,TFIRST)                Q:(K0(I)*KSHR(HH))
      E:PG(TP)$HORIZON(TP)        Q:(-
QREF(TP)*SUM(I,D0(I,"GOVT"))*THETA(HH))
      E:PTK(I)                      Q:(-K0(I)*KSHR(HH))      R:TK(I)
      D:PW(HH)                      Q:W0(HH)

$CONSTRAINT:TK(I)
    PTK(I)*I0(I) =E= SUM((J,TLAST), P(J,TLAST)*IMA(J,I));

$OFFTEXT
$SYSINCLUDE mpsgeset NEPAL

P.L(I,TP)              = PREF(TP);
PFX.L(TP)              = PREF(TP);
PD.L(I,TP)             = PREF(TP);
PX.L(I,TP)$VX0(I)      = PREF(TP);
RK.L(I,TP)             = PREF(TP)*RK0(I);
PK.L(I,TP)             = PREF(TP)/(1-NR);
PL.L(LC,TP)            = PREF(TP);
PLAND.L(TP)            = PREF(TP);
PG.L(TP)               = PREF(TP);
PT.L(TP)               = PREF(TP);
PU.L(HH,TP)            = PREF(TP);
PR.L(TP)               = PREF(TP);

Y.L(I,TP)              = QREF(TP);
K.L(I,TP)              = QREF(TP);
INV.L(I,TP)            = QREF(TP);
X.L(I,TP)$VX0(I)       = QREF(TP);
A.L(I,TP)              = QREF(TP);
GOV.L(TP)              = QREF(TP);
U.L(HH,TP)             = QREF(TP);
T.L(TP)                = QREF(TP);
```

```
*     Allocate 20 megabytes of workspace for the solver:

NEPAL.WORKSPACE = 10;
NEPAL.OPTFILE = 1;

*     Set price distortion levels:

TLAST(TP)        = YES$(ORD(TP) EQ CARD(HORIZON));

DISPLAY HORIZON, TLAST, TAU;

PTK.L(I)         = SUM(TLAST, PK.L(I,TLAST)*(1-NR));
TK.L(I)          = (1+G)*SUM(TLAST,QREF(TLAST));

W0(HH) = SUM(TP$HORIZON(TP),PREF(TP)*QREF(TP)*SUM(I,D0(I,HH)));

GOVFX =          FSAV   + ER("ROW")     * LOANS("GOVT")
                        + ER("ROW")     * LOANS("AID")
                        + ER("INDIA")   * LOANS("REFUND");

GOVEXP = GOVFX - SUM((I), D0(I,"STOCK"))
                 + SUM(HH, TAXREV(HH)+INCTAX(HH))
                 + SUM(I, D0(I,"TOURIST")*TTR)
                 + SUM((I,R), M0(I,R)*TM(I,R))
                 + SUM((I,R), X0(I,R)*TX(I,R))
                 + SUM(I, Y0(I) *TI(I));

EXOGFX(TP,HH) = QREF(TP) * (
                        +        ER("ROW") * LOANS(HH)
                        + SUM(R, ER(R) * REMIT(R,HH))
                        - SUM(R, ER(R) * FTRN(HH,R) ) );

THETA(HH) = SAVING(HH) / SUM(H, SAVING(H));

KSHR(HH) = ENDOW("K",HH) / SUM(H, ENDOW("K",H));

LSHR("RURAL") = 1;

INCADJ(HH) =
    PW.L(HH)*W0(HH)
    + SUM(I, PTK.L(I)*(K0(I)*KSHR(HH))*TK.L(I))
    + SUM(TP$HORIZON(TP),
PG.L(TP)*QREF(TP)*SUM(I,D0(I,"GOVT"))*THETA(HH))
    - SUM(TP$HORIZON(TP), PREF(TP)*EXOGFX(TP,HH))
    - SUM(TP$HORIZON(TP), QREF(TP) * (
```

```
                    PR.L(TP)          * GOVEXP*THETA(HH)
                  + PL.L(HH,TP)       * (ENDOW("L",HH)-TAXREV(HH))
                  + PLAND.L(TP)       * SUM(I,LAND(I))*LSHR(HH) ))
    - SUM((I,TFIRST), PK.L(I,TFIRST)*(K0(I)*KSHR(HH)));

INCADJ("URBAN") = INCADJ("URBAN")
    - SUM((I,TP)$HORIZON(TP), K0(I)*K.L(I,TP)*RK.L(I,TP)*TAU(I));
DISPLAY INCADJ;

*   Work with a non-steady state baseline:
*   Assume that arable land grows at 1/3 the growth rate of other
*   factors, and urban labor grows at twice the underlying growth
*   rate:

IF (NONSS,
    QLAND(TP) = (1+G/3)**(ORD(TP)-1);
    QLABOR("URBAN",TP) = (1+2*G)**(ORD(TP)-1);
);

IF (DEBUG,

NEPAL.ITERLIM = 0;
$INCLUDE NEPAL.GEN
SOLVE NEPAL USING MCP;

ELSE
TAU(I)$SCENARIO(I) = 0;
TAU(I)$SCENARIO("PARTIAL") = TAU(I) / 2;
TAU(I)$SCENARIO("COMPLETE") = 0;
$INCLUDE NEPAL.GEN
SOLVE NEPAL USING MCP;
);

PARAMETER
SOLUTION ACTIVITY LEVELS AND FUTURE VALUE PRICES (% CHANGE FROM
BASELINE);
*   Record all the activity levels from this solution:
SOLUTION("L",TLAST,TP,I,"Y",STRUCT,SCENARIO)$HORIZON(TP)
    = ROUND(100 * (Y.L(I,TP)-QREF(TP))/QREF(TP), 1);
SOLUTION("L",TLAST,TP,I,"K",STRUCT,SCENARIO)$HORIZON(TP)
    = ROUND(100 * (K.L(I,TP)-QREF(TP))/QREF(TP), 1);
SOLUTION("L",TLAST,TP,I,"INV",STRUCT,SCENARIO)$HORIZON(TP)
    = ROUND(100 * (INV.L(I,TP)-QREF(TP))/QREF(TP), 1);
```

```
SOLUTION("L",TLAST,TP,I,"X",STRUCT,SCENARIO)$(VX0(I)$HORIZON(TP))
    = ROUND(100 * (X.L(I,TP)-QREF(TP))/QREF(TP), 1);
SOLUTION("L",TLAST,TP,I,"A",STRUCT,SCENARIO)$HORIZON(TP)
    = ROUND(100 * (X.L(I,TP)-QREF(TP))/QREF(TP), 1);
SOLUTION("L",TLAST,TP,HH,"U",STRUCT,SCENARIO)$HORIZON(TP)
    = ROUND(100 * (U.L(HH,TP)-QREF(TP))/QREF(TP), 1);
SOLUTION("L",TLAST,TP,"x","T",STRUCT,SCENARIO)$HORIZON(TP)
    = ROUND(100 * (T.L(TP)-QREF(TP))/QREF(TP), 1);

PARAMETER PNUM(TP) NUMERAIRE PRICE INDEX (RURAL CONSUMPTION
BASKET);
PNUM(TP) = PU.L("RURAL",TP);
*   Record all the prices from this solution:


SOLUTION("P",TLAST,TP,I,"P",STRUCT,SCENARIO)$HORIZON(TP) =
    ROUND(100 * ( P.L(I,TP) / PNUM(TP) - 1), 1);
SOLUTION("P",TLAST,TP,I,"PD",STRUCT,SCENARIO)$HORIZON(TP) =
    ROUND(100 * ( PD.L(I,TP) / PNUM(TP) - 1), 1);
SOLUTION("P",TLAST,TP,I,"PX",STRUCT,SCENARIO)$(VX0(I)$HORIZON(TP))
    = ROUND(100 * ( PX.L(I,TP) / PNUM(TP) - 1), 1);
SOLUTION("P",TLAST,TP,I,"RK",STRUCT,SCENARIO)$HORIZON(TP) =
    ROUND(100 * ( RK.L(I,TP) / PNUM(TP) - 1), 1);
SOLUTION("P",TLAST,TP,I,"PK",STRUCT,SCENARIO)$HORIZON(TP) =
    ROUND(100 * ( PK.L(I,TP) / PNUM(TP) - 1), 1);
SOLUTION("P",TLAST,TP,LC,"PL",STRUCT,SCENARIO)$HORIZON(TP) =
    ROUND(100 * ( PL.L(LC,TP) / PNUM(TP) - 1), 1);
SOLUTION("P",TLAST,TP,HH,"PU",STRUCT,SCENARIO)$HORIZON(TP) =
    ROUND(100 * ( PU.L(HH,TP) / PNUM(TP) - 1), 1);
SOLUTION("P",TLAST,TP,"x","PLAND",STRUCT,SCENARIO)$HORIZON(TP) =
    ROUND(100 * ( PLAND.L(TP) / PNUM(TP) - 1), 1);
SOLUTION("P",TLAST,TP,"x","PT",STRUCT,SCENARIO)$HORIZON(TP) =
    ROUND(100 * ( PT.L(TP) / PNUM(TP) - 1), 1);
SOLUTION("P",TLAST,TP,"x","PG",STRUCT,SCENARIO)$HORIZON(TP) =
    ROUND(100 * ( PG.L(TP) / PNUM(TP) - 1), 1);
SOLUTION("P",TLAST,TP,"x","PFX",STRUCT,SCENARIO)$(BOPCON$HORIZON(TP))
                              = ROUND(100 * ( PFX.L(TP) / PNUM(TP) - 1), 1);
*   Save the activity levels and prices in the solution file so
*   that they may be retrieve to the PC:
PUT KSOL '$offlisting'/;
$BATINCLUDE gams2txt SOLUTION
DISPLAY SOLUTION;
```

APPENDIX II

```
$STITLE 1990/91 Base Year Data for Nepal (nepaldat.gms)

SET

    F   Primary factors /L, K/,
    I   Sectors /

            FOOD-CROP  Agricultural food crops
            CASH-CROP  Agricultural cash crops
            FOOD-PROC  Food processing
            TEXTILES   Textile goods
            CHEMICAL   Chemical and minerals
            CAPITAL    Metal products
            TRANSPORT  Transport
            ELECTRIC   Electricity
            CONSTRUCT  Construction
            TOURISM    Tourism and distribution
            SERVICES   Private services
            PUBLIC     Public services /

HH          Households and labor categories /RURAL, URBAN /,
R           Trading partners /INDIA, ROW/;

ALIAS (I,J), (LC,HH), (H,HH);

PARAMETER
```

ER(R) Base year exchange rates

/ INDIA 1.68

ROW 49.78 /

INCTAX(HH) Income tax payments ('91 million Nepal Rs) /

URBAN 855.1 /

TAXREV(*) Tax revenue ('91 million Nepal Rs) /

URBAN 312.7

RURAL 1664.9

CORP 663.2

TOURIST 289.1 /

TY0(R) Gross tourist income ('91 million Nepal rs) /

INDIA 1593.8

ROW 1993.8 /

LOANS Financial flows associated with various loans /

* Foreign aid income and loans M. US$

AID 295.5

* Govt payments on foreign loans M.US$

GOVT 31.5

* Private payments on foreign loans M.US$

URBAN 44.6

* Indian exise tax refund (million Indian Rs)

REFUND 448.7

* Loans to government from private sector M.RP

LOAN 154.3 /

FTRN(HH,R) Payments by households to foreigners M.US$

/ URBAN.ROW 69.0 /;

TABLE REMIT(R,HH) Ghorka remitances in foreign currency - M. US$ & India Rp

	RURAL	URBAN
ROW	19.3	28.1
INDIA	939.7	33.8;

TABLE ENDOW(F,HH) Factor income M. N Rp

	RURAL	URBAN
L	29498.7	6338.3
K	48485.4	7952.4;

TABLE IOF(I,J) Input-output flows ('91 million Nepal Rs)

FOOD-CROP CASH-CROP FOOD-PROC TEXTILES CHEMICAL CAPITAL

FOOD-CROP 5319.847 1011.540 3762.978

CASH-CROP 5648.229 314.546 348.228 4013.569 2691.578 1738.541

FOOD-PROC 4.879 2.833 1.986 60.261 6.696

TEXTILES 2.195 0.683 108.094 11.928 6.708

CHEMICAL 24.254 12.992 6.127 29.677 172.329 45.050

CAPITAL 21.930 3.406 1.341 8.933 10.325 343.970

TRANSPORT 550.367 143.483 26.304 133.132 100.105 85.416

ELECTRIC 0.360 3.103 4.972 50.936 68.010 25.623

TOURISM 0.425 0.156 0.562 1.419 1.440

SERVICES 598.829 99.996 6.934 98.362 98.081 50.306

PUBLIC 3.135 143.826 54.927 454.141

\+ TRANSPORT ELECTRIC CONSTRUCT TOURISM SERVICES PUBLIC

FOOD-CROP 1170.105 6.384

CASH-CROP 1.194 264.234 294.285

FOOD-PROC 35.898 0.263 48.868 28.940 783.223

TEXTILES 51.078 0.390 0.057 112.593 130.203

CHEMICAL 159.896 9.603 2380.971 56.580 652.633 298.229

CAPITAL 158.506 11.684 2352.431 3056.319 515.039

TRANSPORT 2505.014 9.550 236.548 268.801 4618.214 2044.980

ELECTRIC 156.672 8.919 0.572 103.705 171.044 26.561

TOURISM 241.359 0.254 0.523 30.976 115.438 83.410

SERVICES 4224.293 175.279 740.709 160.301 6711.432 925.660

PUBLIC 230.276

*SOURCE: THESE TABLES ARE FROM NEPAL91.GMS FROM TIMOTHY BUEHRER, HARVARD UNIVERSITY AND

*FILIPPO DI MAURO OF ADB, MANILA.

TABLE IMA(I,J) Capital formation matrix ('91 million Nepal Rs)

	FOOD-CROP	CASH-CROP	FOOD-PROC	TEXTILES	CHEMICAL	CAPITAL
FOOD-CROP	364.405	208.046				
CASH-CROP	310.472	85.370	0.308	1.810	4.136	
CAPITAL	413.962	76.175	182.655	258.304	219.796	121.884
CONSTRUCT	1549.419	875.346	295.142	376.623	408.506	302.251

+	TRANSPORT	ELECTRIC	CONSTRUCT	TOURISM	SERVICES	PUBLIC
CAPITAL	1299.240	346.107	1049.805	158.560	144.980	256.837
CONSTRUCT	304.409	150.197	581.400	358.897	5394.889	2833.010

TABLE WAG(I,LC) Wage bill by sector and labor category ('91 million Nepal Rs)

	RURAL	URBAN
FOOD-CROP	10170.876	699.382
CASH-CROP	4400.109	104.336
FOOD-PROC	419.027	153.535
TEXTILES	406.733	683.136
CHEMICAL	639.521	170.218
CAPITAL	94.589	164.555
TRANSPORT	2388.523	270.712
ELECTRIC	0.152	283.535
CONSTRUCT	4815.254	738.678
TOURISM	84.991	348.908
SERVICES	974.731	1794.524
PUBLIC	5105.196	1459.128

* TABLE UPDATED ACCODRIN TO POPULATION CENSUS, 1991.

TABLE XLE(I,LC) Employment by sector and labor category (1000 persons)

	RURAL	URBAN
FOOD-CROP	5778.945	150.786
CASH-CROP	826.567	11.635
FOOD-PROC	48.149	9.308
TEXTILES	104.324	22.339
CHEMICAL	48.150	12.100
CAPITAL	48.149	9.308
TRANSPORT	256.797	21.408
ELECTRIC	.015	18.616
CONSTRUCT	353.097	49.331
TOURISM	24.075	13.031
SERVICES	320.997	94.009
PUBLIC	216.673	53.520

* The table below is somewhat special in that it contains both SAM data
* and data related to the parameters of the functions of the model. For
* instance the items called sigc and sigcm are parameters for the
* Armington functions used to calculate import demand.

TABLE ZZ(*,I) MISCELLANEOUS PARAMETERS AND INITIAL DATA

	FOOD-CROP	CASH-CROP	FOOD-PROC	TEXTILES	CHEMICAL	CAPITAL
M0	112.047	2180.373	1842.668	2069.570	1714.674	8506.668
MI0	906.736	601.761	691.503	804.708	2333.491	2432.801
E0	263.374	242.016	68.038	5246.832	1.029	81.211
IE0	574.869	363.380	246.923	453.168	33.271	26.489
DT0		241.935	234.490	302.076	194.229	1478.884
IDT0		12.305	21.923	26.889	69.318	173.150
QR0		98.784	178.534	80.900	392.782	
SALES0		99.291	72.239	66.874	19.104	338.220
SALESI0		16.720	8.415	49.144	33.584	146.408
ETDUTY	2.720	2.500	0.703	54.190	0.011	0.839
EITDUTY	5.937	3.753	2.550	4.680	0.344	0.274
ITN0	0.000	0.0093	0.0619	0.0085	0.050	0.000
XD0	53354.318	16622.235	8905.454	8224.082	6208.245	4368.751
K	80031	32746	14427	11267	10056	7077
DEP	424.000	973.281	163.364	218.539	409.220	119.130
SIGC	0.75	0.75	1.50	1.50	1.50	1.50
SIGCM	1.50	2.50	2.5	2.0	1.50	1.50
SIGT	0.75	0.75	1.50	1.50	1.50	1.50
SIGTE	1.50	2.50	2.5	2.0	1.50	1.50
TAX	196.153	178.020	415.791	495.265	282.318	348.535
EC0						
CONSU	2902.316	413.141	1110.546	438.612	662.899	544.646
CONSR	38788.426	3036.366	9081.676	4754.928	5701.839	5652.421
TCONS		232.874	236.502			
ID	572.451	402.097		4528.304		
DST	10.468	10.468	398.700	231.404	406.521	284.319

+	TRANSPORT	ELECTRIC	CONSTRUCT	TOURISM	SERVICES	PUBLIC
M0			895.911			
MI0	13.574		1016.896			
E0			1162.988			
IE0	3.100		600.251			
XD0	12338.092	1069.260	13429.089	3113.699	26820.871	11372.305
K	21590	2673	20144	3892	26821	17058
DEP	624.639	100.243	659.357	64.901	789.381	281.617
SIGC	0.75	0.75	0.75	0.75	1.50	0.75
SIGCM	0.75	2.50	0.75	0.75	2.50	0.75

SIGT	0.75	0.75	0.75	0.75	1.50	0.75
SIGTE	0.75	2.50	0.75	0.75	2.50	0.75
TAX	58.181	-14.681	6.825	3.306	658.587	
CONSU	268.546	43.064		138.115	4052.828	
CONSR	1209.435	416.194		658.410	8078.593	
TCONS	139.197		1842.212	848.715		
GD0				10486.000		
ID		13429.089				
DST			101.120 ;			

* THESE TABLE RELY ON ECONOMCI SURVEY, OF MINISTRY OF FINANCE, AND QUARTERLY BULLETINE OF NRB.

```
PARAMETER   M0(I,R)    Value of imports by sector and partner M. N.Rp
            X0(I,R)    Value of exports by sector and partner M. N.Rp
            SUPPLY(I,*) Additional output statistics
            ELAST(I,*) Elasticities of substitution and transformation
            MDUTY(I,R) Import duty collections M.N Rp
            RENT(I,R) Import quota rents M. N Rp
            MTAX(I,R) Import sales tax
            EDUTY(I,R) Export duty collections M.N Rp
            TARIFF(I,R) Tariff rate applied to Nepali exports
            D0(I,*) Components of final demand;
SUPPLY(I,"XD0") = ZZ("XD0",I);
SUPPLY(I,"K") = ZZ("K",I);
SUPPLY(I,"DEP") = ZZ("DEP",I);
SUPPLY(I,"TAX") = ZZ("TAX",I);

ELAST(I,"SIGC" ) = ZZ("SIGC",I);
ELAST(I,"SIGCM") = ZZ("SIGCM",I);
ELAST(I,"SIGT" ) = ZZ("SIGT",I);
ELAST(I,"SIGTE") = ZZ("SIGTE",I);

M0(I,"INDIA") = ZZ("M0",I);
M0(I,"ROW") = ZZ("MI0",I);

X0(I,"INDIA") = ZZ("E0",I);
X0(I,"ROW") = ZZ("IE0",I);

MDUTY(I,"INDIA") = ZZ("DT0",I);
MDUTY(I,"ROW") = ZZ("IDT0",I);
```

```
RENT(I,"ROW") = ZZ("QR0",I);

MTAX(I,"ROW") = ZZ("SALES0",I);
MTAX(I,"INDIA") = ZZ("SALESI0",I);

EDUTY(I,"INDIA") = ZZ("ETDUTY",I);
EDUTY(I,"ROW") = ZZ("EITDUTY",I);

TARIFF(I,"INDIA") = ZZ("ITN0",I);

D0(I,"URBAN") = ZZ("CONSU",I);
D0(I,"RURAL") = ZZ("CONSR",I);
D0(I,"GOVT") = ZZ("GD0",I);
D0(I,"TOURIST") = ZZ("TCONS",I);
D0(I,"INVEST") = ZZ("ID",I);
D0(I,"STOCK") = ZZ("DST",I);

* THERE APPEARS TO HAVE BEEN A MISTAKE IN SPECIFICATION OF X0.
* THIS SHOULD BE AT INTERNATIONAL PRICES:

DISPLAY M0,X0,SUPPLY,ELAST,MDUTY,RENT,MTAX,EDUTY,TARIFF,D0;

* Check supply-demand relations:

SET FD /GOVT, TOURIST, INVEST, STOCK/; FD(HH) = YES;

PARAMETER MKT Check of supply-demand balance;

MKT(I)  =  SUPPLY(I,"XD0")
        +  SUM(R, M0(I,R) + MDUTY(I,R) + MTAX(I,R) + RENT(I,R))
        -  SUM(R, X0(I,R)) + SUM(R, EDUTY(I,R))
        -  SUM(FD, D0(I,FD))
        -  SUM(J, IOF(I,J));

DISPLAY MKT;
MKT(I)$SUPPLY(I,"XD0") = ROUND(100 * MKT(I) / SUPPLY(I,"XD0"));
DISPLAY "Percentage deviation:", MKT;

*       Move imbalance into stock:

D0(I,"STOCK") = D0(I,"STOCK") - MKT(I);
PARAMETER LABMKT(LC) Labor payments - receipts balance;
LABMKT(LC) = ENDOW("L",LC) + INCTAX(LC) - SUM(I, WAG(I,LC));
DISPLAY LABMKT, INCTAX;
```

```
*    ADJUST FACTOR ENDOWMENTS:

ENDOW("L",LC) = SUM(I, WAG(I,LC)) - INCTAX(LC);
*    Fix tax payment to the public sector so that capital
*    earns a 10% rate of return:

SUPPLY("PUBLIC","TAX") = SUPPLY("PUBLIC","XD0")
                    - SUPPLY("PUBLIC","DEP")
                    - SUM(J, IOF(J,"PUBLIC"))
                    - SUM(LC, WAG("PUBLIC",LC))
                    - 0.1 * SUPPLY("PUBLIC","K");

PARAMETER PROFIT(I) Sectoral profits net depreciation;
PROFIT(I) = SUPPLY(I,"XD0") - SUPPLY(I,"TAX") - SUPPLY(I,"DEP")
                    - SUM(J, IOF(J,I)) - SUM(LC, WAG(I,LC));
DISPLAY PROFIT;

PARAMETER ROR(I) Net rate of return;
ROR(I) = NA;
ROR(I)$SUPPLY(I,"K") = PROFIT(I) / SUPPLY(I,"K");
DISPLAY ROR;

PARAMETER CAPMKT Capital earnings;
CAPMKT = SUM(I, PROFIT(I)) - TAXREV("CORP") - SUM(HH, ENDOW("K",HH));
DISPLAY CAPMKT;

* ADJUST CAPITAL ENDOWMENT EARNINGS TO CLEAR THIS MARKET:

ENDOW("K","URBAN") = ENDOW("K","URBAN") + CAPMKT;

PARAMETER SAVING(*) Benchmark savings;
SAVING(HH)      = SUM(R, REMIT(R,HH)*ER(R)) + SUM(F, ENDOW(F,HH))
                    - SUM(I, D0(I,HH)) - SUM(R,FTRN(HH,R)*ER(R))
                    - TAXREV(HH) - ER("ROW")*LOANS(HH);
DISPLAY SAVING;
SCALAR DEPR0;
DEPR0 = SUM(I, SUPPLY(I,"DEP"));
SAVING("GOVT") = SUM(I, D0(I,"INVEST")) - SUM(HH, SAVING(HH)) - DEPR0;

PARAMETER TINCBAL INCOME BALANCE FOR TOURIST;
TINCBAL = SUM(R, TY0(R)) - TAXREV("TOURIST") - SUM(I, D0(I,"TOURIST"));
DISPLAY TINCBAL;
```

```
PARAMETER FSAV IMPLICIT FOREIGN SAVINGS;

FSAV    = SUM((I,R), M0(I,R) - X0(I,R))
        - SUM(R, TY0(R))
        - ER("ROW")     * LOANS("GOVT")
        - ER("ROW")     * LOANS("AID")
        - ER("INDIA")   * LOANS("REFUND")
        - ER("ROW")     * SUM(HH,LOANS(HH))
        - SUM((R,HH), ER(R) * REMIT(R,HH))
        + SUM((HH,R), ER(R) * FTRN(HH,R));

DISPLAY FSAV;

PARAMETER
   IOC(I,J)     INPUT OUTPUT COEFFICIENT
    Y0(I)       BASE YEAR SECTORAL OUTPUT ..
    VX0(I)      VOLUE OF SECTORAL EXPORTS NET OF TAXES
    X0(I,R)     AMOUNT OF SECTORAL EXPORT TO INDIA AND ROW
    PX0(I,R)    SECTORAL EXPOR PRICES TO INDIA AND ROW
    S0(I)       SUPPLY OF COMPOSITE COMMODITY OF THE SECTOR I
    M0(I,R)     AMOUNT OF SECTORAL IMPORTS FROM INDIA ANR ROW
    PM0(I,R)    IMPORT PRICES FROM INDIA AND ROW
    IDTOT0      TOTAL INVESTEMENT DEMAND IN THE BASE YEAR
    ID0(I)      INVESTMENT BY ORIGIN
    D0(I,*)     COMPONENTS OF FINAL DEMAND

    TI(I)       INDIRECT TAX RATE
    TX(I,R)     INDIRECT TAX ON INTERNATIONAL TRADE
    TM(I,R)             TARIFFS
    VK0(I)      BASE YEAR RETURN TO CAPITAL GROSS DEPRECIATION
    TY(R)       INCOME OF INDIAN AND FOREIGN TOURISTS
    ETRNDX(I)   ELASTICITY OF TRANSFORMATION OF EXPORTS
    ETRNXX(I)
    SIGMADM(I)  ELASTICITY BETWEEN IMPORTS AND DOMESTIC
PRODUCTS
    SIGMAMM(I)  ELASTICITY OF SUBSTITUTION
  ALPHAK(I)  CAPITAL'S SHARE OF OUTPUT
  ALPHAL(I,HH)    LABOR'S SHARE IN OUTPUT;
   ETRNDX(I) = 2;
   ETRNXX(I) = 5;
```

```
        SIGMADM(I) = 4;
        SIGMAMM(I) = 8;

Y0(I) = SUPPLY(I,"XD0");
IOC(I,J)=(IOF(I,J))/Y0(J);
ALPHAL(I,HH) = WAG(I,HH)/Y0(I);
ALPHAK(I) = 1-SUM(HH,ALPHAL(I,HH));
VX0(I) = SUM(R, X0(I,R) - EDUTY(I,R));
TX(I,R)$X0(I,R) = EDUTY(I,R) / X0(I,R);
PX0(I,R) = 1 - TX(I,R);
TM(I,R)$M0(I,R) = (MDUTY(I,R) + MTAX(I,R) + RENT(I,R)) / M0(I,R);
PM0(I,R) = 1 + TM(I,R);
S0(I) = SUM(R, PM0(I,R)*M0(I,R)) + Y0(I) - VX0(I);
ID0(I) = D0(I,"INVEST");
IDTOT0 = SUM(I, ID0(I));
VK0(I) = PROFIT(I) + SUPPLY(I,"DEP");
TI(I) = SUPPLY(I,"TAX") / Y0(I);
TY(R) = TY0(R);

MKT(I) = S0(I) - SUM(J, IOF(I,J)) - ID0(I) - D0(I,"TOURIST")
        - D0(I,"GOVT") - SUM(HH, D0(I,HH)) - D0(I,"STOCK");
DISPLAY IOC,MKT, ALPHAL, ALPHAK;

SCALAR TTR; TTR = TAXREV("TOURIST") / SUM(I, D0(I,"TOURIST"));
```

APPENDIX III

A Simple Static CGE Model

```
$TITLE A Simple Static CGE Model for Nepal

$ONTEXT
$MODEL:STATIC
$COMMODITIES:
    P(I) ! SUPPLY PRICE
    PD(I) ! DOMESTIC OUTPUT PRICE
    PX(I)$VX0(I) ! EXPORT PRICE AGGREGATE
    RK(I) ! CAPITAL RENTAL RATE
    PL(LC) ! WAGE RATE
    PINV ! INVESTMENT PRICE
    RKA ! AGGREGATE RENTAL RATE
    PFX ! EXCHANGE RATE
    PG
    PT
    PU(HH)
$SECTORS:
    T
    G
    U(HH)
    Y(I) ! PRODUCTION
    X(I)$VX0(I) ! EXPORT
    A(I) ! ARMINGTON AGGREGATION
    INV ! INVESTMENT
    KA  ! AGGREGATE CAPITAL SUPPLY
```

```
$CONSUMERS:
    RA(HH) ! PRIVATE HOUSEHOLDS
    INVESTOR !
    GOVT ! GOVERNMENT
    TOURIST ! TOURISM DEMAND

$PROD:Y(I) s:0 t:ETRNDX(I) VA:1
    O:PD(I)        Q:(Y0(I)-VX0(I)) A:GOVT T:TI(I)
    O:PX(I)        Q:VX0(I) A:GOVT T:TI(I)
    I:P(J)         Q:IOF(J,I)
    I:PL(LC)       Q:WAG(I,LC)
    I:RK(I)        Q:K0(I)

$PROD:X(I)$VX0(I) t:ETRNXX(I)
    O:PFX#(R)      Q:X0(I,R) P:PX0(I,R) A:GOVT T:TX(I,R)
    I:PX(I)        Q:VX0(I)

$PROD:A(I) s:SIGMADM(I) m:SIGMAMM(I)
    O:P(I)         Q:S0(I)
    I:PD(I)        Q:(Y0(I)-VX0(I))
    I:PFX#(R)      Q:M0(I,R)          P:PM0(I,R) A:GOVT T:TM(I,R) M:
$PROD:INV
    O:PINV         Q:IDTOT0
    I:P(I)         Q:ID0(I)

$PROD:KA
    O:RK(I)        Q:K0(I)
    I:RKA          Q:(SUM(I,K0(I)))

$PROD:G
    O:PG           Q:(SUM(I,D0(I,"GOVT")))
    I:P(I)         Q:D0(I,"GOVT")

$PROD:U(HH) s:1
    O:PU(HH)       Q:(SUM(I,D0(I,HH)))
    I:P(I)                    Q:D0(I,HH)

$PROD:T
    O:PT           Q:(SUM(I,D0(I,"TOURIST"))+TAXREV("TOURIST"))
    I:P(I)         Q:D0(I,"TOURIST") A:GOVT T:TTR
```

```
$DEMAND:TOURIST
    E:PFX        Q:(SUM(R, TY(R)))
    D:PT

$DEMAND:GOVT s:1
    E:PFX        Q:FSAV
    E:PFX        Q:(ER("ROW")*(LOANS("AID")-LOANS("GOVT")))
    E:PFX        Q:(ER("INDIA")*LOANS("REFUND"))
    E:PL(LC)     Q:INCTAX(LC)
    E:P(I)       Q:(-D0(I,"STOCK"))
    E:PINV       Q:(-SAVING("GOVT"))
    E:PL(HH) Q:TAXREV(HH)
    E:RKA Q:TAXREV("CORP")
    D:PG

$DEMAND:INVESTOR
    E:RKA Q:DEPR0
    D:PINV Q:DEPR0

$DEMAND:RA(HH) s:1
    E:PINV Q:(-SAVING(HH))
    E:PL(HH) Q:ENDOW("L",HH)
    E:RKA Q:ENDOW("K",HH)
    E:PFX Q:(SUM(R,ER(R)*(REMIT(R,HH)-FTRN(HH,R))))
    E:PFX Q:(-ER("ROW")*LOANS(HH))
    E:PL(HH) Q:-TAXREV(HH)
    D:PU(HH)

$OFFTEXT
$SYSINCLUDE mpsgeset STATIC

STATIC.ITERLIM = 0;
$INCLUDE STATIC.GEN
SOLVE STATIC USING MCP;
```

APPENDIX IV

Data Sources on Value Added

Model Sectors	Principal Activities/Industries	NSIC & National Account Codes
1. Food Crop	food crops, rice milling	
2. Cash Crop	industrial crops, fisheries, livestock, forestry & mining	
3. Food-Proc	food manufacturing, beverages and tobacco industries	311, 312, 313, 314
4. Textiles	textiles, apparel, leather and footwear manufacturing	321, 322, 323, 324
5. Chemical	paper, printing, chemicals, rubber, plastic, glass & nonmetallic mineral products	341, 342, 352, 355, 356, 362, 369
6. Capital	wood, furniture, iron and steel, cutlery and tools, machinery, professional and other manufacturers	331, 332, 371, 381383, 385 and 390
8. Transport	internal transport, storage and communication	7
8. Electricity	electricity, water, gas	4
9. Construction	building construction services	5
10. Tourism	restaurants and hotels	6.2
11. Services	trade, financial and real estate, and other privateservices.	6.1, 8, and 9.3
12. Public Services	government services excluding productive enterprises	9.1

Activities Account

Account/ Variable	Data Source
Intermediate inputs	CBS I-O table adjusted with data form the manufacturing census plus agriculture sector own input consumption
Wages	CBS I-O table adjusted with data from the manufacturing census.
Operating surplus	CBS I-O table adjusted with data from the manufacturing census
Indirect taxes	CBS I-O table adjusted with data from the Tax Department Ministry of Finance

Commodities Account

Domestic Supplies	Derived as residuals by subtracting exports and tourist earnings from total supply
Rent from import controls	Derived from Department of Commerce, license auction prices
Tariff Revenue	Based upon statutory tariff rates weighted by import values from the Custom Department revenue collection data
Sales taxes on imports	Calculated from collection data from the sales tax department of the MOF, weighted by import value from Custom collection data
Imports of goods and NFS from India	Custom Department data plus data on invisible items from the Nepal Rastra Bank BOP department
Imports of goods and NFS from overseas	Custom Department data plus data on invisible item from the Nepal Rastra Bank BOP department

Income and Consumption Accounts

Labor incomeIncome tax	Wages from the CBS less income tax on salariesEconomic Survey Table 8.2
Net return on capital Corporate taxesDepreciation Households -Private consumption Private Savings Tourists - Consumption Tourist taxes	operating surplus from the CBS I-O table less corporate income taxEconomic Survey, Table 8.2CBS I-O table Economic Survey Table 1.3Derived as the difference between household income and consumption Total foreign exchange earning form tourism less taxes paid by touristsEconomic Survey Table 8.2; hotel and air flight tax
Government-Consumption	CBS I-O table
Subsidy	Economic Survey Table 1.3
Savings	Derived as difference between government expenditure and income

Data Sources on Capital Flows and International Transaction

Capital Flows

Capital Flows - Investment	CBS I-O table adjusted to the balance of capital and commodity accounts;
capital flows from India	Derived as balancing item from current account transaction with India
capital flows from other economies	Derived as balancing item for current account transactions with the rest of the world

International Transactions

INDIA Exports of goods and NFS to India Tourist Income from India	Custom Department data plus data on invisible items from the Nepal Rastra Bank BOP department Derived from Nepal Rastra Bank BOP department and Table 6.6 of Economic Survey
OTHER ECONOMIES Exports of goods and NFS to other economies Unrequited transfers (Gorkha remittances) Tourist income from the other economies Foreign Aid from other economies	Custom Department data plus data on invisible item from the Nepal Rastra Bank BOP departmentDerived from Nepal Rastra Bank BOP department and Table 6.6 of Economic SurveyDerived from Nepal Rastra Bank BOP department and Table 6.6 of Economic SurveyDerived from Nepal Rastra Bank BOP department and Table 6.6 of Economic Survey

APPENDIX V

Nepal SAM 1990/91

		Activities Food-Crop	Cash-Crop	Agro-Processing	Textiles	Activities Chemicals	Capital Goods	Transport	Activities Electricity/W/G	Construction	Hotels and Rest	Other Services	Public Services
ACTIVITIES	Food-Crop												
	Cash-Crop												
	Agro-Processing												
	Textiles												
	Chemicals												
	Capital Goods												
	Transport												
	Electricity/W/G												
	Construction												
	Hotels and Rest												
	Other Services												
	Public Services												
COMMODITIES	Food-Crop	5319.847	1011.540	3762.978	0.000	0.000	0.000	0.000	0.000	0.000	1170.105	6.384	0.000
	Cash-Crop	5648.229	314.546	347.228	4013.569	2691.578	1738.541	1.194	0.000	264.234	0.000	294.285	0.000
	Agro-Processing	0.000	4.879	2.833	1.986	60.261	6.696	35.898	0.263	0.000	48.868	27.940	783.223
	Textiles	0.000	2.195	0.683	107.094	11.928	6.708	51.078	0.390	0.000	0.057	112.593	130.203
	Chemicals	24.254	12.992	6.127	29.677	172.329	45.050	159.896	9.603	2380.971	56.580	652.633	297.229
	Capital Goods	21.930	3.406	1.341	8.933	10.325	343.970	158.506	11.684	2352.431	0.000	3056.319	515.039
	Transport	550.367	143.483	26.304	133.132	100.105	85.416	2505.014	9.550	236.548	267.801	4617.214	2044.980
	Electricity/W/G	0.360	3.103	4.972	50.936	68.010	25.623	156.672	8.919	0.572	103.705	171.044	26.561
	Construction	0.000	0.000	0.000	0.000	0.000	0.000	0.000	0.000	0.000	0.000	0.000	0.000
	Hotels and Rest	0.000	0.425	0.156	0.562	1.419	1.440	241.359	0.254	0.523	30.976	115.438	83.410
	Other Services	598.829	99.996	6.934	98.362	98.081	50.306	4224.293	175.279	740.709	160.301	6711.432	925.660
	Public Services	0.000	0.000	3.135	143.826	54.927	454.141	0.000	0.000	230.276	0.000	0.000	0.000
Factors	Lab-Rural	10170.876	4400.109	419.027	406.733	639.521	94.589	2387.523	0.152	4815.254	84.991	974.731	5105.196
	Lab-Urban	699.382	104.336	153.535	683.136	170.218	164.555	270.712	283.535	737.678	347.908	1794.524	1459.128
	Capital	30124.091	10344.205	3754.409	2050.871	1846.226	1004.180	2087.765	584.312	1663.069	839.100	7628.745	1.677
Households	Urban												
	Rural												
	Toursists												
	Government	196.153	177.020	415.791	495.265	282.318	347.535	57.181	-14.681	6.825	3.306	657.587	0.000
Capital Account	Phys. Cap.												
	Stocks												
External	India												
	Row												
Total		53354.318	16622.235	8905.453	8224.082	6207.246	4368.750	12337.091	1069.260	13429.090	3113.698	26820.869	11372.306

source: ADB SAM for Savings and Economic Survey Tables 6.6, 7.3, 7.1, 7.5, 8.10 and 8.11
Table 6.6: Foreign exchange reserve of banks; Table 7.1: Currency holding
Table 7.3: Total deposit; Table 8.10: Foreign Debt; Table 8.11: Internal Borrowing of Govt
Table 7.5 For assets of other financial institutions.

	Commodities Food-Crop	Cash-Crop	Agro-Processing	Textiles	Chemicals	Capital Goods	Commodities Transport	Electricity /W/G	Construction	Hotels and Rest	Commodities Other Services	Public Services	Lab-Rural	Factors Lab-Urban	Capital
Food-Crop	52524.732														
Cash-Crop		16023.091													
Agro-Processing			8593.747												
Textiles				2582.952											
Chemicals					6173.300										
Capital Goods						4262.163									
Transport							12337.092								
Electricity/W/G								1066.160							
Constructions									13429.089						
Hotels and Rest										3113.699					
Other Services											25057.631				
Public Services												11372.305			
Food-Crop															
Cash-Crop															
Agro-Processing															
Textiles															
Chemicals															
Capital Goods															
Transport															
Electricity/W/G															
Constructions															
Hotels and Rest															
Other Services															
Public Services															
Lab-Rural															
Lab-Urban															
Capital															
Urban														6337.347	7952.422
Rural													29498.703		48485.356
Toursists														531.300	663.200
Government	0.000	370.251	435.852	622.517	397.135	2528.444									4827.671
Phys.Cap.															
Stocks															
India	906.736	601.761	691.503	804.708	2333.491	2432.801		13.574			1016.896				
Row	112.047	2180.373	1842.668	2069.570	1714.674	8506.668					895.911				
	53543.515	19175.476	11563.770	6079.747	10618.600	17730.076	12337.092	1079.734	13429.089	3113.699	26970.438	11372.305	29498.703	6868.647	61928.649

		Households Urban	Rural	Toursists	Government	Capital Account Phys. Cap.	Stocks	External India	Row	Total
A	Food-Crop				-8.657			574.869	263.374	53354.318
C	Cash-Crop				-6.253			363.380	242.016	16622.234
T	Agro-Processing				-3.253			246.923	68.038	8905.455
I	Textiles				-58.870			453.168	5246.832	8224.082
V	Chemicals				-0.354			33.271	1.029	6207.246
I	Capital Goods				-1.112			26.489	81.211	4368.751
T	Transport									12337.092
I	Electricity/W/G							3.100		1069.260
E	Construction									13429.089
S	Hotels and Rest.									3113.699
	Other Services							600.251	1162.988	26820.870
	Public Services									11372.305
	Food-Crop	2902.316	38787.425			572.451	10.468			53543.514
C	Cash-Crop	413.141	3036.367			402.097	10.468			19175.477
O	Agro-Processing	1110.546	9081.676				398.700			11563.769
M	Textiles	437.612	4754.927	232.874			231.404			6079.746
M	Chemicals	662.899	5701.840				406.521			10618.601
O	Capital Goods	544.646	5652.421	236.502		4528.304	284.319			17730.076
D	Transport	268.546	1209.435	139.197						12337.092
I	Electricity/W/G	43.064	416.192							1079.733
T	Construction	0.000	0.000			13429.089				13429.089
I	Hotels and Rest.	137.115	658.408	1842.212						3113.697
E	Other Services	4052.828	8078.595	847.715			101.120			26970.440
S	Public Services				10486.000					11372.305
	Lab-Rural									29498.702
Factors	Lab-Urban									6868.647
	Capital									61928.650
	Urban							56.800	799.700	15146.269
House-	Rural							1578.700	549.600	80112.359
holds	Tourists							1593.800	1993.800	3587.600
	Government	312.731	1664.969	289.100		4398.500		211.600	8421.442	23471.341
Capital	Phys. Cap.	2295.024	1070.105		11977.342			3059.118	2816.482	26045.742
Account	Stocks									8801.470
External	India	1965.800			1086.500	1272.300				21646.511
	Row									
	Total	15146.268	80112.360	3587.600	23471.343	24602.741	1443.000	8801.469	21646.512	

CHAPTER-WISE SUMMARY OF DISSERTATION

The major argument advanced in this dissertation is that financial sector reforms in Nepal have released extra resources for investment by improving efficiency in resource allocation, and increased the volume of savings available for productive investment as spending was cut on unproductive assets to meet unseen contingencies in the future. It also argues that the Nepalese reform process has redistributed income from urban to rural households. Financial liberalization has increased the demand for rural labor to complement added capital stocks in rural-labor intensive sectors. Wage rates for rural labor increase more than that of the urban labor, leading to an increase in their welfare.

In Nepal the financial reform process started in mid 1980s and took major shape in 1992 under a new government. Before the 1992 reforms, the Nepalese financial sector was characterized by ceilings on interest rates, credit controls, high reserve requirement, tight regulations on entry and exit of financial institutions, controls on foreign exchange, uncontrolled budgetary deficits and underdeveloped capital markets. The financial repression from all these features resulted in higher transaction costs for borrowers, and often negative rates of interest for savers. High subsidies on credits to selected sectors coexisted with higher interest rates for other sectors. The distortionary effects of repression were wide ranging. Though the reform measures have removed many of the distortionary elements involved debate on efficiency and redistribution effects of further reforms continues.

Financial sector reforms have their main impacts on the volumes of saving and investment. However, economic theory alone cannot determine the magnitudes of changes in the volume of savings and investment concomitant to such reforms. Whether the volume of saving increases with financial liberalization or not, depends upon whether the income effect from a change in the rate of interest dominates the substitution effect. Saving will increase only if the substitution effect is stronger than the income effect. Thus the effect of financial sector reform on saving is ambiguous. Similarly, financial sector reform is often characterized by an increase in the real interest rate. Standard theory states that when the cost of investment funds increases, the amount of investment is likely to fall. The net effect of the reforms on investment, then, depends upon whether the reallocation of capital after the liberalization can compensate for the effect of an increase in the cost of funds after liberalization.

I consider the economy-wide long-run consequences of financial sector liberalization using a forward-looking multi-sectoral computable general equilibrium (CGE) model of the Nepalese economy with financial intermediation. The model is used to investigate efficiency, redistribution and welfare effects of financial sector reform as the economy evolves. In the model consumers are located in urban and rural areas. Their decisions between saving and consumption are studied under life-cycle behavior. There are 11 producers of goods and services. Investors' decisions regarding the allocation of the capital stock reflect inter-temporal profit maximization. They sell products both in domestic and foreign markets. The government collects revenues from taxes on income, consumption and international trade and spends all of these revenues. The laws of motion of capital and exogenous growth rate of the population determine the growth path of the economy.

The model is applied to study the effects of partial and complete economy wide reforms, as well as piecemeal reforms. A partial reform refers to a 50 percent reduction in the distortionary cost of financial transactions after the reform, while a complete liberalization means the elimination of all distortions across all sectors. Piecemeal liberalization is sector specific.

The major conclusions from the model analyses are following:

1. By equalizing rates of return across sectors, liberalization insures efficiency in the allocation of resources. Efficiency in resource allocation increases the capital usage in sectors that were more repressed before liberalization. It causes a reduction, or slower growth, of capital use in sectors that used to be subsidized before repression. Ultimately all sectors return to their output and capital use levels on a steady state growth. The expansion in the capital stock allows production to expand accordingly. Output expansion is greater in sectors that were repressed heavily before the liberalization.
2. The benefits of liberalization accrue more to the rural households than to the urban households. Following liberalization rural labor intensive sectors invest more in response to an increased access to financial institutions. More labor is required to complement additional capital. Demand for unskilled labor increases faster than the demand for skilled labor. This means increases in wage rates of rural labor is greater than the increases in the wages rates of the rural labor. Consequently welfare gains of rural households are larger in comparison to the welfare gains of urban households. In this sense, liberalization redistributes income from urban to rural households. The redistribution of welfare occurs by increasing wages of unskilled labor in comparison to the wages of skilled labor.

The impact of economic liberalization has been phenomenal in the growth of formal financial institutions. The number of banks and financial institutions and deposits mobilized from them have increased significantly, the cost of intermediation decreased, interest rates completely liberalized, an independent capital market developed. Control on budget deficit and public borrowing contributed to reduce inflation; reforms in the exchange rate system and convertibility of current accounts helped to build up the confidence of the investors in the domestic financial system. In spite to these achievements there are still many problems in the Nepalese financial system. The formal financial industry of Nepal that evolved from a monopoly during 1930-1960 to a duopoly in the 1960s, then to an oligopoly in the 1980s and finally to a monopolistic competition in the 1990s still possesses enough market power to control the interest rates in non-competitive basis. The size of the financial sector is very small because of the low level of the income of the households. Lack of infrastructure and widespread illiteracy add further problem in developing an efficient financial system. Commercial banks that predominate the formal financial system still are very conservative. They still emphasize on collateral while making loans. Informal financial sector plays a very important role in rural and only a negligible amount of rural borrowing flowing from informal sector is spent on investment activities. Finally, the political instability that started from the mid-1994 causes uncertainties regarding financial sector policies. A good general equilibrium model that includes these characteristics could be a right framework for studying the impact of liberalization in the Nepalese economy.

Three categories of model can be found in the literature on Nepalese economy: a simple econometric model used by the government of Nepal, Chris Elbers' multi-regional model for the Nepalese economy and Asian Development Bank's model for Nepal.

A simple econometric model though good for forecasting for a very short run do not take account of the general equilibrium effects required for more rigorous analysis of a policy designed to promote economic growth and welfare over the period. Chris Elbers' multi-regional multi-sectoral model and ADB's multi-sectoral models are very useful frameworks of analysis but they lack dynamic specification and analysis of the financial sector. These shortcomings are overcome by developing a fully specified forward looking multi-sectoral CGE model of the Nepalese economy in this dissertation.

A significant body of literature exist on the role of the financial sector in long run growth. The applicability of a particular model for policy analysis depended upon its structure. Models with single representative agent are good study long-run growth but are not appropriate to study income or welfare distribution issues among the households. One sector macro models are not appropriate to answer cross-sectoral impacts of liberalization. One period models are not suitable to study growth and development of an economy. Thus a choice of appropriate modeling environment is very important for policy analysis.

Various CGEs with financial sectors were developed in the late 1980s and early 1990s and show the possibility of general equilibrium analysis with a financial sector. These models focus on a relatively short period. The effect of financial sector variables in these models really depends upon the assumptions about the flexibility of wages, exchange rates, and other prices in the economy. In the short run, this is the key issue of debate among macro economists, classical and neo-classical, Keynesian, neo-Keynesian, rational expectations, new classical and new business cycle theories have their own interpretations of transmission mechanisms between the financial sector and the real side of the economy. For the long run opinions of these schools converge as there can be a perfect adjustment in portfolio allocation so that prices, wages, and exchange rates can change as dictated by long-run equilibrium. The contribution of the financial sector in the economy should be channeled through a reduction in the real cost of resources, such as intermediation cost, or elimination of monopoly mark-ups, and equalization of rates of returns across sectors. This is the approach taken in this dissertation. There has been a continuous improvement in theoretical and computational techniques to make studies more realistic. Improvement in computation technology has allowed models to capture more dimensions over time, sector and regions.

In the forward-looking CGE model of Nepalese economy developed in this dissertation, period by period static equilibria are embedded in a completely dynamic equilibrium of households and investors. Households maximize utility by allocating their life time income between consumption and saving over the model horizon. Investors maximize the rate of return from investing in projects generating the highest rate of return. The exogenous growth rate of labor force and the cost of capital between the periods drive the growth rate of the economy. The model economy is open for trade with India and the rest of the world. The government collects taxes and spends on public consumption. The basic model is an all purpose model and can be modified in order to answer specific questions relating to policies designed to improve the growth rates of income and welfare of households in the model economy. Impact of a partial, complete or piecemeal liberalization are studied under various model assumptions relating to constraints international borrowing and lending, leakage of savings to unproductive assets and non-steady state conditions.

In each period the supply process in this economy can be explained by ten types of nested production functions: composite labor from skilled and unskilled labor; capital accumulation and capital allocation functions; value added function; Leontief function between value added and intermediate inputs; constant elasticity of transformation (CET) export function between the Nepalese markets and the other economies; constant elasticity of transformation export (CET) function between domestic sales and exports to India ;constant elasticity of substitution (CES) function between domestically supplied goods and imports from India; constant elasticity of substitution (CES) between the Nepal-India market and the other economies; total absorption in the economy; and intermediate inputs. Finite discrete-time approximations to approximate the infinite horizon problem faced by consumers in the model economy.

The bench mark rate of return is calibrated assuming the non-distorted economy being in the steady state in the base year. Relation between one unit of investment this period and the corresponding unit of capital next period is used for calibration of dynamic component of the model. This means investment produces one unit of capital stock in period 2 (P_2^k) from one unit of output in the period one, P_1^k. The present value of one unit of capital in period two is equal to $(1-r)P_1^k$.

In a repressionary regime the cost of capital is distorted by a repressionary component of intermediation, t_j, so that price of capital is $P_1^k = r_1^k(1-\tau_i)+(1-\delta)(1-r)P_1^k$.

The distortionary element of repression is given by $\tau_j = 1 - \frac{\bar{r}_j^k}{\delta + g}\frac{I_j}{V_j}$, where $\bar{r}_j^k$ is the true cost of capital, r_1^k is the actual cost of capital, I_j is the level of investment, V_j is capital earnings, δ is the rate of depreciation, and g is the growth rate of the economy.

Saving decisions are influenced by the rate of interest prevailing in the economy and the time preference of individuals. Efficiency in the financial system will enhance the amount of saving available in the economy by reducing the wedge between the cost of capital to investors and gains received by the savers. Households keep their income in financial institutions to finance their transaction needs, or to fulfill precautionary demands or simply to store wealth in liquid forms. Efficient financial system even attracts deposits from foreign savers. Total of household savings, and government savings constitute the total savings of the economy, which ultimately depends on vector of relative prices, including the exchange rates, the interest rates, indirect taxes, and tariffs. Balance sheet conditions of financial institutions requires that total financial assets be equal to the total of capital stocks, debt outstanding of government and foreign reserves.

The leakage of resources in unproductive assets is incorporated in the BLKHOLE model. A certain portion of saving dissipates in the process of financial intermediation. Therefore the total investment in the economy is constrained by the savings net of intermediation costs. Moreover, additional resources may be available by liquidating the real unproductive assets (DRA)of the households and firms. Change in real assets, DRA, depends on perception of households on the return of financial assets. If it is negative, some of the funds saved during the current period may in fact turn in purchase of real assets.

Impact of international financial markets are studied by considering two different options to close the balance of payment account. The first rule is a strict rule of balance of payment, where imports should be paid by exports plus remittances and capital inflows do not exist to close the current account deficit. In the second rule, borrowing may be allowed to the tune of the trade gap for some periods, so that the present value of the imports and exports are equal to zero for the time horizon under consideration. When foreign capital market exists the foreign exchange rate is fixed leaving the trade balance to be determined endogenously. In the current model the period by period balance of payment constraint case is incorporated in BOPCON sub-model and the case where intertemporal borrowing and lending is permitted is explained by the CAPFLOW model.

The demand and supply equations generated from the optimization of households and firms' maximization problem are presented both in primal form and then in dual forms. Essentially solution of every primal problem has a dual counterpart: primal and duals are two sides of the same coin. While the primal form is more obvious among the economists a dual form is more compact for discussion and development of more complex solution algorithms.

A competitive equilibrium is a set of sequence of prices of composite commodities, $P_{i,t}$; domestic goods sold in domestic markets, $PD_{i,t}$; prices of exported commodities, $PX_{i,t}$; prices of capital goods, $P_{j,t}^{k}$; prices of terminal capital, $PTK_{j,t}$; wage rates for each categories of labor, $w_{h,t}$; prices of government services, PG_t ; prices of provisions for tourism, PT_t ; prices of transfer, PR_t ; prices of consumption, PU_t ; price of aggregate welfare, PW_t : price of foreign exchange, PFX_t , present value of foreign exchange, $PVPFX_t$; rental rate of capital for each sector, r_1^k : R+ ®R, and sequence of gross output, $Y_{i,t}$; total supply of commodities, $A_{i,t}$; sectoral capital stock, $K_{i,t}$; sectoral investment, $I_{i,t}$; exports, $X_{i,t}$; government services, GOV_t ; level of household utility from consumption, U_t ; and total welfare, W such that given these prices and commodities

(i) households solve intertemporal utility maximization problems,
(ii) investors and producers solve intertemporal profit maximization problem,
(iii) markets for goods and services, labor, capital clear,
(iv) government constraint is satisfied,
(v) balance of payments condition is fulfilled.

The closure rule of our model is income-expenditure balance over the life period based on perfect foresight of consumers. Capital accumulation is consistent with households optimization problems and growth rate of the economy. Higher income induces more saving as well as more demand for consumption goods.

A general equilibrium model is valid when a given set of parameter can replicate the base year quantities and prices of a model economy. In dynamic models the benchmark equilibrium is computed along the steady state reference path of the economy. In applied general equilibrium models parameters are calibrated using initial values of variables obtained from a social accounting matrix of the model economy.

There is a debate among economic policy analysts about the appropriate method of deriving model parameters. Some prefer econometric estimates; others can live with "point estimate" or calibration of the model parameters. Properly calibrated parameters in light of the intuition from economic theories produce sensible results over an intermediate or long-term period, they can stand out even if judged according to the mean absolute deviation(MAD) and mean square error (MSE) criteria. Therefore the calibration technique is widely used in applied general equilibrium models. After all, there is very little difference using calibrated parameters against econometrically estimated parameters. In theory any model that can be calibrated can be econometrically estimated but not vice versa. Benchmark replication is more challenging in dynamic models, as we do not yet have any realized information about the future of the economy. Modelers solve this problem by choosing a model horizon, a balanced growth rate and investment rate in the terminal year along with the intertemporal maximization problem to compute a benchmark equilibrium that serves as a reference path of the model. This essentially means looking at the time path of model variable over the model horizon assuming all sorts of policies and structure of economy be continued in the future.

I have calibrated parameters such as share of labor and capital income in total value added, rate of return to capital by sector, the distortion coefficient due to repression of financial system, wage rates, the share of spending on commodities in the consumer's budget, supply index of labor force in the economy from the base year data. Alternative estimates of parameters that drive the dynamics of the model such as utility discount factor, rate of depreciation, bench mark rate of return were set after studying the sensitivity of model outcomes to these parameters. The elasticity of substitution between domestic and imported products and the elasticity of transformation between domestic sales and foreign sales become the most crucial parameters in relating the volume of Nepal's imports and exports with the commodity prices in India and other economies. A higher degree of elasticity implies a large trade effect, while a small elasticity implies a small consequences in the trade balances when prices of exported and imported commodities change. The elasticity parameter depends upon the behavior of consumers and technical factors that hinder or promote trade in general.

The forward looking CGE model of Nepal discussed in chapter 3 is formulated in Mathematical Programming System for General Equilibrium (MPSGE: Rutherford 1993) and uses PATH (Ferris and Dirkse 1994) as the solution algorithm. MPSGE is the most useful, transparent and relatively painless way to write down and analyze the complicated system of nonlinear inequalities contained in a multi-sectoral model. Originally it was designed for solving Arrow-Debreu economic equilibrium models, allowing very concise specification of complicated non-linear models in four classes of variables namely, sectors, commodities, consumers and auxiliary, and nested CES or CET functions for preferences and technologies.

The model outcomes of the model very much depend upon the quality of data we have used for the base year. The limited amount of time and resources during this study did not permit us to refine the data more extensively. Refinement of the social and financial accounting matrix using macro- and micro-level data sources deserves a serious research.

The reporting framework is organized in terms of five models, i.e. (1) Base-line model; (2) CAPFLOW Model; (3) BOPCON model; (4) NON-SS model; (5) BLKHOLE model and two different major scenarios, i.e., (1) economy-wide liberalization, and (2) piecemeal liberalization. Economy-wide liberalization is further classified into partial and complete liberalization depending upon the amount of reduction in the spread under two model horizons. The piecemeal liberalization is considered for 9 different sectors. For this study, this model was solved for a 30 years horizon form 1990 to 2020. The turnpike properties of the model were insured by solving the model for 35 years' and 100 years' horizon starting 1990.

Comparing model results across different models I find that financial liberalization is more effective with complete liberalization than with partial or piecemeal liberalization. Liberalization works when markets are perfect but is ineffective when markets are subject to a period by period balance of payment constraints.

1. Liberalization favors rural households over urban households, as reflected in the higher welfare index for rural households in comparison to the welfare index of urban households. In this sense liberalization redistributes resources from urban to rural households. Urban household gain more than rural households in case of partial liberalization which still retains some of the distortionary elements of repression and when non-steady state growth rates are applied to urban labor.
2. The redistribution of welfare occurs through the effect of liberalization in wage increases. The wages of unskilled labor increase faster than the wages of skilled labor.
3. Liberalization equalizes the rates of return across the sectors. This insures efficiency in the allocation of resources.
4. The efficiency in allocation causes more increase in capital stock of the sectors that were more repressed before the liberalization started. It causes a reduction or a slower growth of capital stock in sectors that used to be subsidized before repression. Ultimately all sectors return to steady state growth rate of the economy.
5. The expansion in capital stock allows production to expand accordingly. Output expansion is greater in sectors that were repressed heavily before the liberalization.
6. The modeling exercise done in this dissertation shows that it is possible to develop a well disaggregated general equilibrium model by using inter-temporal behavior of households and producers and to study the effects of economy-wide and sector specific policy issues aimed at increasing efficiency and welfare in the economy.

The rich institutional structure contained in forward-looking CGE models allows one to experiment with many structural assumption characterizing the particular economy under investigation. Therefore this framework is definitely an improvement over the staples of growth models including the fixed coefficient Harrod-Domar growth model, neoclassical growth models, one sector endogenous growth models as well as static and sequential dynamic CGE models available in the literature. As such this new approach is an addition to the literature on financial repression and liberalization. It provides a theoretical framework and empirical tool to study long run growth and distribution in an inter-temporal and inter-sectoral framework of a decentralized economy. However, it should be noted that the use of the current model is only appropriate to track down the growth path of the economy along the steady state. It need to be further improved in order to study the dynamic adjustment process.

Applied to the Nepalese economy, this model is capable of evaluating alternative policies designed to enhance the long run growth. This represents a significant improvement over modeling exercises done so far. With improvement in the quality of information on model variables and parameters, this model can be used to study many policy issues under investigation.

The base-line model contained in this dissertation can be applied to analyze several other issues on Nepalese economy particularly related to public finance, international trade, human resource development, migration, regional and sectoral development, and parallel markets, with very few modifications. Some hints are listed below for some important issues that could not be covered in this paper, as guidelines for further research.

BIBLIOGRAPHY

Abel Andrew B. and Blanchard Oliver J. (1983), An Intertemporal Model of Saving and Investment, Econometrica Vol. 51, No. 3, May 1983.

Adelman Irma and Robinson Sherman (1978), Income Distribution Policy in Developing Countires: A Case of South Korea, Standford UP, Stanford, California.

Aghevli, Bijan B, Boughon, James, M, Montiel, Peter J., Villanueva, delano and Woglom Geoffrey (1990), The Role of National Saving in the World Economy: Recent Trends and Prospects, IMF Occasional Paper no.67, 1990.

Aghevli, Bijan B, and Khan, Mohsin S. (1991), Exchange Rate Policy in Developing Countries: Some Analytical Issues, IMF Occasional Paper no. 78, 1991.

Ahluwalia, Montek S. and Lysy, Frank J., Employment, Income Distribution, and Programs to Remedy Balance-of-Payments Difficulties.

Anand, Ritu and Wijnbergen, Sweder Van (1989), Inflation and the Financing of Government Expenditure: An Introductory Analysis wiht an Application to Turkey, World Bank Economic Review, Vol. 3, no.1: 17-38.

Ang James S. and Pradhan Radhe S. A. Comparison of Financial Management Practices in Nepal Among Government_owned, Publicly-Traded and Privately held Firms, Research in International Business and Finance, Volume 11B pp. 139-163, 1994.

Antzoulatos Angelos A. (1994), Credit Rationing and Rational Behavior, JMCB vol. 26, no. 2, 1994.

Armington, Paul S. (1969), A Theory of Demand for Products Distinguished by Place of Production, IMF Staff paper, 1969, pp. 159-199.

Arrau Patricio, Gregorio J. D. Reinhart C. M. and Wickham P. (1995), The Demand for Money in Developing Countries: Assessing the Role of Financial Innovation, JOEDC vol. 46 (1995) 317-340.

Asian Development Bank, Assessing Development Options: A Computable General Equilibruim Framework For Nepal, 1992, ADB Manila.

Azariadis Costas and Smith Bruce D. (1993), Private Information, Money and Growth: Intermediary, Fluctuations and the Mundell-Tobin Effects, manuscript, Federal Reserve Bank of Minneapolis.

Backus David K, and Kohoe, Patrick J. (1986), Notes on Models of Economic Growth, Federal Reserve Bank of Minneapolis, Research Department working paper.

Bacha,Edmar L. ———— (1992), External Debt, Net Transfers, and Growth in Developing Countries, World Development, 20:8, Aug. 1992, pp. 1183-1192.

—— (1990), A Three-Gap Model of foreign Transgers and the GDP Growth Rate in Developing Countries, JDE 32: (1990): 279-296, North-Holland.

—— (1987), IMF Conditionality: Conceptual Problems and Policy Alternatives, World Development, 15:12, Dec. 1987, 1457-1467.

Backus, David, Brainard, William C., Smith Garry, Tobin, James (1980), A Model of U. S. Financial and Nonfinancial Economic Behavior, JMCB, vol. 12, no. 2, May 1980.

Baltensperger, Ernst (1980), Alternative Approaches to the Theory of the Banking Firm, JME 6 (1980) 1-37.

Ball Laurence and Romer David, Real Rigidities and the Non-Neutrality of Money, Review of Economic Studies, 1990 57 183-203.

Ballard Charles L. (1983), Evaluation of the Consumption Tax with Dynamic General Equilibrium Models, Ph.D. Dissertation, Stanford University.

Ballard Charles L., Fullerton Don, Shoven John B. and Whalley John (1985), A General Equilibrium Model for Tax Policy Evaluation, University of Chicago Press, Chicago.

Bardhan, Pranab (1993), Economics of development and the Development of Economics, JEP, vol. 7, no. 2, Spring 1993, pp. 129-142.

Barro, Robert J. (1991), Economic Growth in a Cross Section of Countries, QJE, May 1991, pp. 407-443.

Barry Christopher B. and Horowitz Ira (1975), Risk and Economic Policy Decision, Public Finance, No. 2, 153-165.

Basu Susanto, Kimball Miles S., mankiw Gregory N, and Weil David N, Optimal Advide for Monetary Policy, JMCB, vol. 22, no. 1, 1990.

Bencivenga Valerie R. and Smith Bruce D. (1993), Some Consequences of Credit Rationing in an Endogenous Growth Model., JEDC, 17 (1-2, January-March) 97-122.

—— (1992), Deficit, Inflation and Banking System in Developing Countries: The Optimal Degree of Financial Repression., Oxford Economic Papers, 44 (4, October): 767-790.

—— (1991), Financial Intermediation and Endogenous Growth, Review of Econ. Studies, (1991) 58, 195-209.

Berger, A. N., Hancock D. and Humphrey D. B. (1993), Bank Efficiency Derived from Profit Function, *Journal of Banking and Finance*, 17:317-347.

Berger, A. N., Hunter W.C. and Timme S. G. 1993: The Efficiency of Financial Institutions: A Review and Preview of Research past, present, and future, JBF, 17 221-249.

Bernanke, Ben and Gertler Mark (1989), Agency Costs, Net Worth, and Business Fluctuations, AER, 14-31.

Berthelemy, Jean-Claude and Bourguignon, Francois (1994), North-South-OPEC Trade Relations in an Intertemporal Applied General Equilibrium Model, in Mercenier Jean and Srinivasan, T.N. ed. 1994: Applied General Equilibrium and Economic Development: Present Achievement and Future Trends, University of Michigan Press, Ann Arbor.

Bhattacharya, Sudipto (1993), Contemporary Banking Theory, Journal of Financial 'Intermediation, 3, 2-50 (1993).

Bhattarai Keshab R. (1990), The Role of Foreign Aid in Economic Development of Nepal: Policy Simulations Using Multi-sectoral Regionally Disaggregated General Equilibrium Model of Nepal, ISS, Hague, Netherlands.

Bird, Richard M. (1992), Taxing Tourism in Developing Countries, World Development vol. 20, no. 8, pp. 1145-1158.

Black Fisher (1995), Exploring General Equilibrium, MIT Press, Cambridge, MA.

Blejer, Mario I, and Cheasty Adrienne (1991), The Measurement of Fiscal Deficits: Analytical and Methodological Issues, JEL, vol. XXIX, Dec. 1991, pp. 1644-1678.

Blejer, Mario I, and Szapary Gyorgy (1991), The "Gulliver Effect" and the "Optimal ivergence" Approach to Trade Policies: The Case of Nepal, World Development, vol. 19, no. 2/3, pp. 255-262.

Blenman L.P., Cantrell R.S., Fennell, R.E., Parket D.F., Reneke J.A, Wang L.f.S. Womer, N. K. (1995), An Alternative Approach to Stochastic Calculus for Economic and Financial Models, JOEDC 19(1995) 533-568.

Blitzer Charles R, Clark Peter B. and Taylor Lance (1975), Economy-wide models and Development Planning, OUP.

Bolnick, Bruce R. (1989), The ABCs of CGEs: Computable General Equilibrium Models for Development Planning, HIID, DDP # 326, Cambridge, MA 02138.

——(1990 ?), Moneylenders and Informal Financial Markets in Malawi, World Development, pp. 57-68.

—— (1982), Concessional Creidit For Small Scale Enerprise in Indonesia: A Review and Analysis of KIK/KMKP, HIID, DDP, no. 130.

Bourguignon, Francois, Melo, Jaime de and Morrisson (1991), Poverty and Income Distribution During Adjustment: Issues and Evidence from OECD Project , World Development, Vol. 19, No. 11, pp. 1485-1508, 1991, Pergamon Press plc.

Bourguignon, Francois, Melo, Jaime de and Suwa Akiko (1991), Modeling the Effects of Adjustment Program on Income Distribution, World Development, Vol. 19, No. 11, pp. 1525-1543, 1991, Pergamon Press plc.

Bourguignon, Francois, Branson , William H. and Melo, Jaime de 1992: Adjustment and Income Distribution: A Micro-Macro Model for Counter Factual Analysis, JDE 38: (1992) 17-39, North Holland.

Boyd, John H. and Prescott, Edward C. (1986), Financial Intermediary-Coalitions, JET, 38: 211-232 (1986).

Boyd John D. and Smith, Bruce D. (1992), Intermediation and the Equilibrium Allocation of Investment Capital: Implications for Economic Development, JME, 30 409-432.

—— (1994), Capital Market Imperfections, International Credit Markets, and Nonconvergence, Research Department, Federal Reserve Bank of Minneapolis, Working Paper No. 522.

Boyd John D. and Smith, Bruce D. (1994), Capital Market Imperfections in Monetary Growth Models, Research Department, Federal Reserve Bank of Minneapolis, Working Paper No. 533.

Boyd John D. and Smith, Bruce D. (1994), The Use of Debt and Equity in Optimal Financial Contracts, Research Department, Federal Reserve Bank of Minneapolis, Working Paper No. 537.

Brainard, William and Nordhaus, S. (1991), Money, Macroeconomics and Economoc Policy: Essays in Honor of James Tobin, MIT Press, Cambridge, MA.

Braun Anton R. (1994), How large is the optimal inflation tax?, JME 34 (1994) 201-214, North Holland.

Brook, A. Kendrick D., Meeraus A. (1992), GAMS: Users's Guide, release 2.25, The Scientific Press, San Fransisco, CA.

Brunner, Karl and Meltzer, Allan H. (1976), The Phillips Curve and Labor Markets, North Holland, New York.

Bruno, Michael (1993), Inflation and Growth In An Integrated Approach, NBER, working paper no. 4422.

Buehrer Timothy S. and Mauro, Filippo di (1993), A Computable General Equilibrium Model of Nepal, manuscript.

Burgess, Robin, and Stern Nicholas (1993), Taxation and Development, JEL, vol. XXXI, 1993 pp. 762-830.

Cameron, Rondo, Olga Crisp, Hugh T. Patrick, and Richard Tilly (1967), Banking in the Early Stage of Industrialization: A Study in Comparative Economic History, OUP, New York.

Campbell, John Y. (1994), Inspecting the Mechanism: An Analytical Approach to the Stochastic Growth Model, JME 33 (1994) 463-506, North-Holland.

Capros P., Karadeloglou, P. and Mentzas, An Empirical Assessment of Macroeconometric and CGE Approaches in Policy Modeling, *Journal of Policy Modeling* 12(3): 557-585 (1990).

Caravani, P. (1995), On H¥ Criteria for Macroeconomic Policy Evaluation, JOEDC 19 (1995) 961-984.

Cass, David (1965), Optimum Growth in Aggregative Model of Capital Accumulation, *Review of Economic Studies*, 32: 233-240.

Central Bureau of Statistics, Manual of National Accounts of Nepal 1976-77, 1984, Kathmandu Nepal.

——Nepal in Figures (1994 and 1993), Kathmandu, Nepal.

——(1987), Population Monograph of Nepal, CBS, Kathmandu, Nepal.

Central Department of Economics, *The Economic Journal of Nepal* Vol. 16: 1993 and 17: 1994, T.U. Kathmandu, Nepal.

Claessens Stijn (1993), Alternative Forms of External Finance: A Survey, WBRO, Vol. 8, no. 1: 91-117, (Jan 1993).

Chechi, Daniele (1993), Creation of Financial Markets in (previously) Centrally Planned Economies, JBF, 17:819-847.

Chand, Sheetal K. (1989), Towards Growth Oriented Model of Financial Programming, World Development, vol. 17, no.4 pp. 437-490.

Chari V. V., Christiano<lowrence J, Kehoe Patrick J. (1991), Optimal Fiscal and Monetary Policy: Some Recent Results, JMCB, vol. 23, no.3 part 2.

Chemmanur, T. J., and Fulghieri, P. (1994), Investment Bank Reputation, Information Production, and Financial Intermediation, JOF Vol. XLIX, No. 1, March 1994.

Chenery Hollis B. (1986), Structural Transformation: A Program of Research, HIID, DDP no. 232, June 1986.

—— (1986), Industrialization and Growth: Alternative View of East Asia, HIID, DDP no. 217, June 1986.

Chris Elbers (1992), Spatial Disaggregation in General Equilibrium Models, VU University Press, Amsterdam 1992.

Christensen Garry (1993), The Limits to Informal Financial Intermediation, World Development vol. 21, No. 5 pp. 721-731, 1993.

Cole, David C, Slade BEtty F. (1991), Developemnt of Money Markets in Indonesia, HIID, DDP no. 371.

Cooley, Thomas F. and Smith Bruce D. (1995), Indivisible Assets, Equilibrium, and the Value of Intermediation, Journal of Finanical Intermediation 4, 48-76 (1995).

——(1991), Financial Markets, Specialization and Learning by Doing, The Rochester Center for Economic Research, Working Paper No. 276.

Cooley, Thomas F. and Hansen Gary D. (1989), Inflation Tax in a Real Business Cycle Model, AER, September 733-748.

Cordern, Max W. (1991), The Theory of Debt Relief: Sorting Out Some Issues, JDS, Vol. 27, no.3, pp.135-45.

Cover, James Perry (1992), Assymetric Effects of Positive and Negative Money-Supply Shocks, QJE, 1992 pp. 1261-1282.

Cowen, Tyler and Kroszner Randall (1990), Empirical Predictions of the New Monetary Economics: Perspectives on Velocity, JPM 12 (20:265-279 (1990).

Dahal, Madan K. Future of Nepalese Economy, 1993, NEFAS and FES, Kathmandu, Nepal.

De Gregorio, Jose (1992a), The Effect of Inflation on Economic Growth: Lessons from Latin America" European Economic Review, 36 (2-3, April): 417-425.

——(1992b), Liquidity Constraints, Human Capital Accumulation and Growth, IMF, Washington D.C., August.

——(1993c), Savings, Growth and Capital Market Imperfections: The Case of Borrowing Constraints" IMF, Washington D. C. December.

——(1993), Inflation, Taxation and Long Run Growth, JOME, 31(3, June): 271-198.

Deaton, Angus (1989), Saving in Developing Countries: Theory and Review, World Bank Annual Conference in Development Economics, 1989, Supplement to WBER, 61-108.

Decaluwe bernard and Matens Andre' (1988), CGE Modeling and Developing Economies: A Consise Empirical Survey of 73 Application to 26 Countries, *Journal of Policy Modeling* 10 (4): 529-568 (1988).

Defina Robert H. (1991), International Evidence on a New Keynesian Theory of the Output-Inflation Trade-off, JMCB vol. 23, no.3, 1991.

De Melo, J. and Roland-Holst, David (1994), Tariffs and Exorts Subsidies when Domestic Markets Are Oligopolistic: Korea, in Mercenier Jean and Srinivasan, T.N. ed. 1994:

Applied General Equilibrium and Economic Development: Present Achievement and Future Trends, University of Michigan Press, Ann Arbor.

Demirguc-Kunt, Asl and Huizinga Harry (1995), Barriers to Portfolio Investments in Emerging Stock Markets, JOEDC, vol. 47 (1995) 355-374.

Dervis, Kamal, De Melo Jaime, and Robinson, Sherman (1985), General Equilibrium Models for Development Policy, CUP, New York.

Devarajan, Shantayanan, De Melo Jaime (1987), Adjustment with a Fixed Exchange Rate:Cameroon, Cote d'Ivoire, and Senegal, WBER, Vol. 1, no. 3: 447-487.

Devarajan, Shantayanan and Go Delfin S. (1995), The Simplest Dynamic General Equilibrium Model of an Open Economy, manuscript, The World Bank.

Devarajan, Shantayanan, and Lewis Jeffrey D. (1990), Policy Lessons from Trade Focused Two-Sector Models, *Journal of Policy Modeling* 12(4):625-657 (1990).

—— (1991), Structural Adjustment and Economic Reform in Indonesia: Model Based Policies vs. Rules of Thumb. In Reforming Economic Systems in Developing Countires, ed. D. Perkins and M. Roemer, HUP, Cambridge, MA.

Devarajan, Shantayanan, and Lewis Jeffrey D., Robinson Sherman 1996: A Bibliography of Computable General Equilibrium Models Applied to Developing Countires, HIID, DDP No. 224.

Devarajan, Shantayanan and Offerdal Erik (1989), Capital Markets and Computable General Equilibrium Models: Comparative Statics Without Apology, *Journal of Policy Modeling* 11(2): pp.191-212.

Dewatripont, Mathias and Michel Gilles (1987), On Closure Rules, Homogeneity and Dynamics in Applied General Equilibrium Models, JDE 26 (1987) 65-76.

DFAMS, Main Report on National Farm Management Study Nepal, 1983-1985, MOA, DFAMS, 1986, Pulchowk Lalitpur.

Diamond, Douglas W. (1984), Financial Intermediation and Delegated Monitoring, RES, LI 393-414.

Diamond, Douglas W. and Dybvig, Philip H. (1983), Bank Runs, Deposit Insurance, and Liquidity, JPE, 401-419.

Diamond, Peter (1965), National Debt in Neoclassical Growth Model, AER, December 1965, 1127-56.

Dirkse Steve P. Ferris Michael C. (1994) A Pathsearch Damped Newton Method for Computing General Equilibria, Computer Sceince Department, University of Winsconsin, Winsconsin, Madison. Available from ftp://ftp.cs.wisc.edu/math-prog/tech-reports/.

Dirkse S.P., Ferris M.C., Preckel P.V. and Rutherford T. (1994), The GAMS Callable Program Library for Variational and Complementarity Solvers, Computer Sceince Department, University of Winsconsin, Winsconsin, Madison. Available from ftp://ftp.cs.wisc.edu/math-prog/tech-reports/.

Dixit Praveen M. (1995a), Economic Policy Making: The Nepal Experience, Working Paper No. 182, IRIS, 2105 Morrill Hall, College Park, MD 20742.

—— (1995b), Economic Reform in Nepal: A Cursory Assessment, Country Report No. 17, IRIS, 2105 Morrill Hall, College Park, MD 20742, e-mail: info@iris.econ.umd.edu.

Dixon Peter B. Parmenter B. R., Powell Alan A. and Wilcoxen Peter J. (1992), Notes and

Problems in Applied General Equilibrium Economics, North-Holland, Amsterdam.

Dornbush, Rudiger (1992), Lessons from Experiences with High Inflation, WBER, Vol. 6, no. 1:13-31.

—— (1991), Policies to Move from Stabilization to Growth, World Bank Annual Conference on Development Economics 1990, supplement to WBER, 19-58.

Dornbush, Rudiger and Fisher Stanley (1993), Moderate Inflation, WBER, Vol. 7 no.1:1-44.

Dornbusch, R. and Edwards, Shaw (1990), Macroeconomic Populism, JDE, 32:2 249-278.

Dornbusch R. and Reynoso, A. (1989), Financial Factors in Economic Development, NBER, working paper No. 2889.

Duesenberry, James S. and McPherson, Malcolm F. (1991), Monetary Management in Sub-Saharan Africa, HIID, DDP, no. 369, 1991.

Edwards Sebastian (1994), The Political Economy of Inflation and Stabilization in Developing Countires, EDCC, 42:2 (Jn. 1994), 235-266.

Easterly, William and Schmidt-Hebbel, Klaus (1993), Fiscal Deficits and Macroeconomic Performance in Developing Countires, WBEO, vol.8, no.2 (july 1993), pp. 211-37.

Eaton, Jonathan (1993), Sovereign Debt: A Primer, WBER, 7:2, May 1993, 137-172.

Economic Intelligence Unit, Report on Nepal and India, 1st quarter, 1995.

Elue Ronel (1995), Welfare Effects of Financial Innovation in Incomplete Markets Economies with Several Consumption Goods, Journal of Economic Theory 65, 43-78 (1995).

English M., Grosskipf S. and Hayes K. (1993), Output Allocative and Technical Efficiency of Banks, *Journal of Banking Finance* 17 349-366.

ESCAP, UN (1993), Policy Analysis Through Macro-Models: Issues, Techniques and Applications in Selected Developing Asian Countries, Development Papers No. 14, ESCAP, Bangkok.

Fair, Ray C. (1984), Specification, Estimation, and Analysis of Macroeconometric Models, HUP, Cambridge, MA.

——(1994), Testing Macroeconometric Models, HUP, Cambridge, MA.

Fair, Ray C. and Taylor, John B. (1983), Solution and Maximum Likelihood Estimation of Dynamic Nonlinear Rational Expectations Models, Econometrica, Vol. 51, no. 4 (July 1983).

Fama, Eugene F. (1980), Banking in Theory of Finance, JME, 6(1980) 39-57.

Fargeix, Andre and Sadoulet, Elisabeth (1994), A Financial Computable General Equilibrium Model for the Analysis of Stabilization Programs, in Mercenier Jean and Srinivasan, T.N. ed. 1994: Applied General Equilibrium and Economic Development: Present Achievement and Future Trends, University of Michigan Press, Ann Arbor.

Farmer, Roger E. A. (1984), A New Theory of Aggregate Supply, AER, Decemberm 920-930.

Feltenstein, Andrew (1986a), Money and Bonds in Disaggregated Open economy, in Scarf Herbert E and Shoven John B. 1986: Applied General Equilibrium Analysis, CUP.

——(1986b), An Intertemporal General Equilibrium Analysis of Financial Crowding Out, JPE, 31 79-104.

Feltenstein, Andrew and Shah Anwar (1995), General Equilibrium Effects of Investment Incentives in Mexico, JOEDC vol 46(1995)253-269.

Ferris M.C. and Pang J.S. (1995), Engineering and Economic Applications of Complementarity Problems, Computer Sceince Department, University of Winsconsin, Madison. Available from ftp://ftp.cs.wisc.edu/math-prog/tech-reports/.

Fisher, Eric O'N. (1992), Sustained Growth in the Models of Overlapping Generations, JET 56, pp. 77-92 (1992).

Fisher, Stanley (1977), Long-Term Contracts, Rational Expectations, and the Optimal Money Supply Rule, JPE. 1977, vol.85, no.1.

Fisher, Stanley and Easterly William (1990), The Economics of the Government Budget Constraint, WBRO, vol. 5, no.2, (July 1990) pp. 127-42.

FitzGerald, E.V. K. and Vos Rob (1989), Financing Economic Development: A Structural Approach to Monetary Policy, Gower, Brooksfied, USA.

Frenkel, Jacob A. and Razin, Assaf (1992), Fiscal Policies and the World Economy, MIT Press.

Friedmand, Benjamin, and Hahn Frank (1990), Handbook of Monetary Economics, Vol. 1 and 2, North-Holland.

Friedman, Milton (1968), The Role of Monetary Policy, AER, vol. LVIII, March 1968, no.1.

Fry, Maxwell J. (1995), Money, Interest, and Banking in Economic Development, 2nd editiion, The JHUP, Baltimore.

Galbis Vicente (1977), Financial Intermediation and Economic Growth in Less-Developed Countries: A Theoretical Approach, JDS, Jan 1977, pp. 58-72.

Gale Douglas (1991), Optimal Risk Sharing through Renegotiation of Simple Contracts, JOFI, 1 283-306.

Gertler, Mark (1988), Financial Structure and Aggregate Economic Activity: An Overview, JMCB, Vol. 20, no. 3, (Aug. 1988, Part 2).

Giminez, J.D., Prescott E.C., Fitzgerald, T., Alvarez, F. (1992), Banking in Computable General Equilibrium Economies, Staff Report 153 and 155, Federal Reserve Bank of Minneapolis.

Ginsburgh, Victor (1994), In the Cournot-Walras General Equilibrium Model, There May Be "More to Gain" by Changing the Numerair than by Eliminating Imperfections: A Two-Good Economy Examplem, in Mercenier Jean and Srinivasan, T.N. ed. 1994: Applied General Equilibrium and Economic Development: Present Achievement and Future Trends, University of Michigan Press, Ann Arbor.

Giovannini, Alberto, ed. (1993), Fince and Development: Issues and Experience, CUP.

Giovannini, Alberto, and De Melo, Martha (1993), Government Revenue from Financial Repression, AER, September, 953-963.

Go, Delfin S. (1993), External Shocks, Adjustment Policies and Investment in a Developing Economy: Illustrations from a forward-looking CGE model of the Philippines , JDE 44 (1994) 229-261

Go, Delfin S. (1988), Growth and Adjustment in the Philippines- A Dynamic General Equilibrium Analysis, Ph. D. dissertation, Harvard University, Cambridge, MA.

Goldsmith Raymond W. (1969), Financial Structure and Development, Yale UP, New Haven.

Gomme Paul (1991), Money and Growth Revisited: Measuring the Cost of Inflation in an Endogenous Growth Model, JME 33 51-77. gomme@uwovax.bitnet

Good, Richard (1984), Government Finance in Developing Countries, Brookings.

—— (1993), Tax Advice to Developing Countries:An Historical Survey, World Development, vol.21, no.1 pp.37-53.

Goulder, Lawrence H., and Summers Lawrence H. (1989), Tax Policy, Asset Prices, and Growth: A General Equilibrium Analysis, Journal of Public Economics, 38:265-296, North Holland.

Goyal Ashima (1994), Growth Dynamics in a General Equilibrium Macroeconomic Model for India, *Journal of Policy Modeling* 16(3): 256-289, 1994.

Grandmont, Jean M. and Laroque Guy (1975), On Money and Banking, Review of Economic Studies, Vol XLII(2) No. 130 pp. 207-36.

Graboswski, R., Rangan N. and Rezvanian (1993), Organizational Forms in Banking: An Empirical Investigation of Cost Efficeincy, Journal of Banking and Finance, 17 531-538.

Grindle Merilee S. and Toumi Francisco (1991), Muddling Towards Adjusstment: The Political Economy of Economic Policy Change in Ecuador, HIID, DDP, WP no. 375, 1991.

Greemwald Bruce C, and Stiglitz, Joseph E. (1993), QJE, Feb., 1993.

Fuerst Timothy S. (1994), Monetary Policy and Financial Intermediation, JMCB vol. 26, no. 3, 1994.

Greenwood Jeremy, Jovanovic Boyan (1990), Financial Development, Growth, and the Distribution of Income, JPE, vol. 98, no. 5, pt.1

Greenwood, Jeremy and Bruce D. Smith (1993), Financial Markets in Development and the Development of Financial Markets: Rochester, University of Rochester, March.

Grossman Gene M. and Helpman Elhanan (1991), Quality Ladders in th Theory of Growth, 1991, Rev. of econ. Studies, pp. 43-61.

—— (1991), Quality Ladders and Product Cycles, QJE, May 1991, pp. 557-586

Gurley John G. and Shaw Edward S. (1955), Financial Intermediaries and Saving-Investment Process, Journal of Finance, 1955 pp. 257-276.

Haaland, Jan I. Modelling General Equilibrium in a Small, Open Economy: A Norwegian Example 13(4): 571-594 (1991)

Hadji Ismail and Van Cuong Le: (1994), Convergence of Equilibria in an Intertemporal General Equilibrium Model : A Dynamical System Approach, JEDC 18 381-396.

Hannan, Timothy H. (1991), Foundationa of the Structure-Conduct- perforamce Paradigm in banking, JMCB,1991, vol. 23, no. 1 Feb. 1991.

Haque Nadeem Ul, Montiel Peter, and Symansky Steven (1991), A Forward-Looking Macroeconomic Simulation Model for a Developing Country, JPM, 13(1):41-65 (1991).

Hayashi Fumio (1982), Tobin's Marginal q and Average q: A Neoclassical Interpretaion, Econometrica vol 50, no.1 Jan 1982

Henkel, Robert L and Levi Maurice D. (1992), The Structure of International Banking, JIMAF, 11 251-272.

Hester, Donald D. and Tobin James, ed. (1967), Financial Markets and Economic Activity, Yale University Press, New Haven.

Hicks, J. R. (1937), Mr. Keynes and the "Classics"; A Suggested Interpretations, Econometrica 5: 1937.

Ho, Mun S. and Jorgenson Dale W. (1994), Trade Policy and U. S. Economic Growth, JPM 16(2): 119-146 (1994).

Hoover, Kevin D. The New Classical Macroeconomics: A Sceptical Inquiry (1989), Basil Blackwell, Cambridge, MA, USA.

IMF (1993), IMF Economic Reviews: NEPAL, IMF, 1993, Washington D.C.

IMF Institute (1992), Macroeconomic Adjustment: Policy Instruments and Issues, IMF, Washington D.C.

—— (1981), Government Financial Statistics, Financial Policy Workshop, pp. 55-96.

Ireland, Peter N. (1994), Supply Side Economics and Endogenous Growth, JME 33 (1994) 559-571, North Holland.

Imrohoroglu Selahattin (1994), A Recursive Forward Simulation Method for Solving Rational Expectations Models, JEDC, 18 1051-1068.

Isaac Ehrlich (1990), The Problem of Development: Introduction, JPE, 1990, Vol. 98, no. 5, pt. 21.

Ireland, Peter (1994), Money and Growth: An Alternative Approach, AER, March ,47-65.

James William and Quibria M.G., Improving Domestic Resource Mobilization Through Financial Development: NEPAL, 1988, Asian Development Bank, Manila, Philippines.

Jensen Henrik (1994), Sustaining policy cooperation between economie of different size, JIE, 36 (1994) 289-307, North Holland.

Jones, Larry E. and Manuelli Rodolfo E. (1995), Growth and the Effects of Inflation, JOEDC, 19 (1995) 1405-1428.

Jones, Larry E. and Sokey Nancy L. (1992), Introduction: Symposium on

Economic Growth, Theory and Computations, JET, 58 117-134(1992).

Jorgenson, Dale W. (1986), Econometric Methods for Applied General Equilibrium Analysis, in Scarf Herbert E and Shoven John B. ed. Applied General Equilibrium Analysis, CUP.

Kapur Basant K. (1992), Formal and Informal Financial Markets, and Neo-structuralist Critique of the financial liberalization strategy in less developed countries, JDE, 38: (1992) pp.63-77, North-Holland.

Keuschnigg, Christian and Kohler, Wilhelm (1994), Modeling Intertemporal General Equilibrium: An Application to Austrian Commercial Policy, Empirical Economics, 1994, pp. 131-164.

Khan, Moshin S., and Montiel, Peter J., ed. (1991), Macroeconomic Models for Adjustment in Developing Countries, IMF, Washington D.C.

Kimbell, Larry J. and Harrison Glen W. (1986), General Equilibrium Analysis of Regional Fiscal Incidence,in Scarf Herbert E and Shoven John B. 1986: Applied General Equilibrium Analysis, CUP.

King, Robert G. and Levine, Ross (1993), Finance and Growth: Shumpeter Might Be Right, QJE, Aug. 1993, pp.717-737.

King, Rober G. and Rebelo, Segio (1990), Public Policy and Economic Growth: Developing Neoclassical Implications, JPE vol. 98 no.5 pt.2.

King, robert G. and Levine Ross (1993a), Finance and Growth: Shumpeter Might be Right, QJE 108(3, August) 717-737.

——(1993b), Finance, Entreprenuership, and Growth: Theory and Evidence, JOME 32(3, December): 513-542.

—— (1993c), Financial Intermediation and Economic Growth . In Capital Markets and Financial Intermediation, Ed, by Colin Mayer and Xavier Vives, CUP, pp. 156-189.

Kitagawa, Hiroshi and Kurosawa, Yositataka (1994), Japan: Development and Structure of Financial System, in Patrick, Hugh T. and Park, Yung Chul ed. 1994: The Financial Development of Japan, Korea and Taiwan : Growth, Repression and Liberalization, OUP, New York.

Kreps, David M. (1990), A Course in Microeconomic Theory, Princeton University Press, Princeton, New Jersey.

Krugman, Paul (1993), International Finance and Economic Development, in Alberto Giovannini, ed., Finance and Development: Issues and Experience CUP, pp. 11-28.

Kydland, Finn E. and Prescott, Edward C. (1977), Rules Rather than Discretion: The Inconsistency of Optimal Plans, JPE vol. 85, no. 3, pp. 473-491.

Lapman Beverly J. (1995), A Dynamic General Equilibrium Analysis of Deviations from the Laws of one Price, JOEDC, 19(1995)1355-1389.

Larry, Jones E. and Manuelli Rodolfo E. (1993), Growth and Effects of Inflation, NEBR, working paper no. 4523.

Leeper, Eric M. and Sims, Christopher A. (1994), Towards a Modern Macroeconomic Model Usable for Policy Analysis, in NBER Macroeconomics Annual 1994, pp.81-139.

Leechor, Chad (1986), Tax Policy and Tax Reform in Semi-Industrial Countries, World Bank, pp. 1-35.

Leite, Sergio Pereira and Sundarajan V, (1990), Issues in Interest Rate Management, IMF Staff Papers, Vol. 37, No. 4, pp.735-752.

Lim, Suk S., Prescott, E. C. and Sunder Shyam (1994), Stationary Solutions to the verlapping Generations Model of Fiat Money: Experimental Evidence, Empirical onomics, 1994 pp. 255-277.

Lensink, Robert and Van Berbgeijk, A. G. (1991), Official Finance requirement in the 1990s, World Development, vol.19, no.5, pp. 497-510.

Lewis, Jeffrey D. (1994), Macroeconomic Stabilization and Adjustment Policies in General Equilibrium Model with Financial Markets: Turkey, in Mercenier Jean and Srinivasan, T.N. ed. 1994: Applied General Equilibrium and Economic Development: Present Achievement and Future Trends, University of Michigan Press, Ann Arbor..

—— (1991), A Computable General Equilibrium Model of Indonesia: HIID, DDP no. 378, 1991.

—— (1990), Macroeconomic Stabilization and Adjustment Policies In A General Equilibrium Model with Financial Markets, HIID, DDP no. 340, 1990.

—— (1985), Financial Liberalization and Price Rogidities in a General Equilibrium Model with Financial Markets, HIID, DDP no. 211.

—— (1989), The Macroeconomics of Policy reform Experiments With A CGE Model of Bangladesh, HIID, DDP no. 296, 1989.

——— (1986), Coping With Adjustment Turkey 1973-81, HIID, DDP no.233.

Lucas, Robert E. (1993), The Determinants of Direct Foreign Investment, World Development, March 1993, 21:3, 391-406.

Lucas, Robert Jr. (1980), Methods and Problems in Business Cycle Theory, JMCB, vol.12, no.4, 1980.

Lucas, Robert, Jr. (1980), Equilibrium in Pure Currency Economy, Economic Inquiry, Vol. XVIII, April 1980.

Lucas, Robert, Jr. (1988), On the Mechanics of Economic Development, JME 22(1988) 3-42 North-Holland.

Lucas, Robert Jr. and Sargent, After Keynesian Macroeconomics, Spring (1979), Federal Reserve Bank of Monneapolis Quarterly Review.

Mackie-Manson Jeffrey K. (1990), Do Taxes Affect Corporate Financing Decisions, Journal of Finance, Vol. XLV, no.5, Dec., 1990.

Mankiw, Gregory N., Romer, David, and Weil, David N. (1992), A Contribution to the Empirics of Economic Growth, QJE, 107, 407-438.

Mankiw Gregory N. (1985), Small Menu Costs and large Business Cycles: A macroeconomic Model of Monopoly, QJE, 1985, pp. 529-537.

Mankiw Gregory N, and Romer David, ed. New Keynesian Economics Vol. 1,2, 1993< MIT Press.

Mann A.S. and Rutherford T.F. (1991), A Long Term Model of Oil Markets, Economic Growth and Balance of Payment Constraints, EMPEC,16: 51-69.

Mansur, Ahsan and Whalley John (1986), Numerical Specification of Applied General Equilibrium Models: Estimation, Calibration and Data, in Scarf Herbert E and Shoven John B. 1986: Applied General Equilibrium Analysis, CUP.

Marcet Albert and Marinon Ramon (1992), Communication, Commitment and Growth, JET, 58, 219-249 (1992).

Matsuyama Kiminori (1992), Agricultural Productivity, Comparative Advantage, and Economic Growth, JET 58, 317-334, (1992).

Mathieson, Donald J. (1980), Financial Reforms and Stabilization Policy in a Developing Economy, JDE, 7(3, September): 359-395.

Mauer David C. and Trianstis, A. J. (1994), Interaction of Corporate Financing and Investment Decisions: A Dynamic Framework, JOF Vol. XLIX, no.4 Sept. 1994.

Maxwell Stamp Report: Assessing Development Options: A Computable General Equilibruim Framework For Nepal, 1992, ADB Manila.

Mayer, Colin and Vines Xavier (1993), Capital Markets and Financial Intermediation, CUP, 1993.

McAndrews James J. (1995), Banks, Payments, and Coordination, Journal of Financial Intermediation, 4, 305-327(1995).

McKinnon Ronald I. (1993), The order of Economic Liberalization: Financial Control in the Transition to a Market Economy, 1993, JHUP, Baltimore

—— (1973), Money and Capital in Economic Development, the Brookings Institution, Washington D. C.

Mercenier, Jean and Michel, Philippe (1994), Discrete-Time Finite Horizon Approximation of Infinite Horizon Optimization Problems with Steady-State Invariance, Econometrica, vol. 62, No. 3, (May 1994), 635-656.

Mercenier, Jean and Souza M. D. C. S. D. (1994), Structural Adjustment and Growth in Highly Indebted Market Economy: Brazil, in Mercenier Jean and Srinivasan, T.N. ed. 1994: Applied General Equilibrium and Economic Development: Present Achievement and Future Trends, University of Michigan Press, Ann Arbor.

Mercenier Jean and Srinivasan, T.N. ed. (1994), Applied General Equilibrium and Economic Development: Present Achievement and Future Trends, University of Michigan Press, Ann Arbor.

Miller Merton H. (1977), Debt and Taxes, the Journal of Finance, vol. XXXII, May 1977, no2.

Mills Cadman Atta and Nallari Raj (1992), Analytical Approaches to Stabilization and Adjustment Programs, The World Bank, EDI Seminar Paper no.44.

Modiogliani Franco, and Miller, Nerton H. (1958), The Cost of Capital, Corporation Finance and the Theory of Investment, AER, vol. XLVII, June 1958.

Montrucchio Luigi (1995), A Turnpike Theorem for Continuous-time Optimal Control Models, JOEDC 19(1995)599-619.

Morgan, Donald P. (1994), bank Credit Commitments, Credit Rationing, and Monetary Policy, JMCB Vol. 26 no.1, Feb. 1994

Milner Chris (1993), Country Size and Medium Term Growth Process: Some Cross-Country Evidence, 1993, vol. 21, no. 2 pp.203-211, 1993.

Ministry of Finance, Economy Survery 1990, to 1994, MOF, Kathmandu Nepal.

Montiel, Peter J. (1995), Financial Policies and Economic Growth: Country-Specific Experience from Sub-Saharan Africa, African Economic Research Council, Nairobi, 1995.

Montiel, Peter J. and Agenor Pierre-Richard and Haque Nadeem Ul, (1993), Informal financian Markets in Developing Countries: A Macroeconomic Analysis, Oxford: Basil Backwell.

Morisset, Jacques (1993), Does Financial Liberalization Really Improve Private Investment in Developing Countries, JDE, 40 (1993): 133-150, North-Holland.

Muth John F. (1961), Rational Expectations and the Theory of Price Movements, Vol. 29 no. 3 (July 1961).

Myers, Stewart C. (1984), The Capital Structure Puzzle, Journal of Finance, Vol. XXXIX, July 1984, no. 3.

Nagurney A. (1994), Variational Inequalities in the Analysis and Computation of Multi-sector, Multi-instrument Financial Equilibria, JEDC 18 161-184.

Nancy, Benjamin (1994), Investment, Expectations and Dutch Disease: A Comparative Study of Bolivia, Cameroon and Indonesia, in Mercenier Jean and Srinivasan, T.N. ed. 1994: Applied General Equilibrium and Economic Development: Present Achievement and Future Trends, University of Michigan Press, Ann Arbor.

Nepal Rastra Bank, Multi-Purpose Household Budget Survey: A Study on Income Distribution, Ejmployment and Consumption Patterns in Nepal, 1988, NRB, Kathmandu, Nepal.

——Agricultural Credit Review Survey Nepal: The Survey Report Volume I-III, 1981, NRB, kathmandu Nepal.

——Agricultural Credit Survey Nepal: The Survey Report Volume I-III, 1972.

—— Quarterly Bulletin.

Nashashibi, Karim, Gupta S., Luiksila C., Lorie H., and Mahler W. (1992), The Fiscal Dimension of Adjustment in Low-Income Countries, IMF Occasional Paper 95.

National Planning Commision, Eigth Plan (1992-1997), NPC, 1992, Singh Durbar, Kathmandu, Nepal.

NBER. (1994), Macroeconomics Annual 1994, MIT Press, Camb. MA.

OECD (1992), Banks Under Stress, OECD, Paris.

Oshikoya, Temitope W. (1994), Macroeconomic Determinants of Private Domestic Investment in Africa: An Empirical Analysis, EDCC, April 1994, 573-597.

Pagano, Marco (1993), Financial Markets and Growth: An Overview, European Economic Review, 37(2-3, April) 613-622.

Parente Stephen L. (1994), Technology Adoption, Learning-by-Doing, and Economic Growth, JET, 63, pp. 346-369.

——— (1994), Debt, Default and Development, manuscript, Northeastern University.

Parente Sthepen L.and Prescott Edward C. (1994), Barriers of Technology Adoption and Development, JPE 1994, vol. 102, no.2.

——— (1993), Changes in the Wealth of Nations, Federal Reserve Bank of Minneapolis Quarterly Review 17 (Sprint 1993) 3-16.

Park, Yung Chul (1994), Korea: Development and Structural Change of Financial System, in Patrick, Hugh T. and Park, Yung Chul ed. 1994: The Financial Development of Japan, Korea and Taiwan : Growth, Repression and Liberalization, OUP, New York.

Park, Yung Chul and Kim, Won Dong (1994), Korea: Development and Structural Change of the Banking System, in Patrick, Hugh T. and Park, Yung Chul ed. 1994: The Financial Development of Japan, Korea and Taiwan: Growth, Repression and Liberalization, OUP, New York.

Patinkin, Don (1989), Money, Interest, and Prices: An Integration of Monetary and Value Theory, 2nd ed., MIT Press, 1989.

Patrick, Hugh T. Comparison, Contrast, and Implications, in Patrick, Hugh T. and Park, Yung Chul ed. 1994: The Financial Development of Japan, Korea and Taiwan: Growth, Repression and Liberalization, OUP, New York.

Patrick, Hugh T. and Park, Yung Chul ed. (1994), The Financial Development of Japan, Korea and Taiwan : Growth, Repression and Liberalization, OUP, New York.

Pesaran Hashem M. and Samiei Hossein (1995), Limited-dependent Fational Expectations Models with Future Expectations, JOEDC, 19(1995)1325-1353.

Pesendorfer Wolfgang (1995), Financial Innovation in a General Equilibrium Model, JET, 65, 79-116(1995).

Phelps, Edmund S., Money-Wage Dynamics and Labor-market equilibrium, JPE..

Phillips, A. W. (1958), The Relation Between Unemployment and the Rate of Change of Money Wage Rates in the United Kingdom, 1861-1957, Economica, pp.283-299.

Pischke, Von, Adams W Dale, and Donald Gordon, Rural Financial Marketing in Developing Countries, 1983, JHUP, Baltimore.

Polak Jaques J. Financial Policies and Development, OECD Development Centre, 1989.

Ramakrishnan Ram T.S. and Thakor Anjan V. (1984), Information Reliability and a Theory of Financial Intermediation, RES LI 415-432.

Rebelo, Sergio (1991), Long-run Policy Analysis and Long-run Growth, JPE, 1991, vol. 99, no. 3.

Reffett Kevin L. (1995), Arbitrage Pricing and the Stochastic Inflation Tax in a Multisector Monetary Economy, JOEDC 19 (1995) 569-597.

Revera-Batiz Luis A and Romer Paul M. (1991), Economic Integration and Endogenous Growth, QJE, 531-555, 1991.

—— (1991), International Trade with Endogenous Technological Change, European Economic Review 35 (1991) 971-1004, North-Holland.

Restoy Fernando and Rockinger, Michael (1994), On Stock Market Returns and Returns on Investment, JOF Vol. XLIX , no. 2, June 1994.

Rhyne Elizabeth and Otero Maria (1992), Financial Services for Microenterprises:Principles and Institutions, World Development, vol. 20, no.11, pp.1561-1571.

Robinson, Sherman (1991), Macroeconomics, Financial Variables, and Computable General Equilibrium Models, World Development, vol. 19, no.11, pp.1509-1523, 1991, Pergamon Press plc.

Robinson, Sherman and Tyson D'Andrea (1986), Modeling Structural Adjustment: Micro and Macro Elements in a General Equilibrium Framework, in Scarf Herbert E and Shoven John B. 1986: Applied General Equilibrium Analysis, CUP.

Romer, Paul M., Capital Accumulation in the Theory of Long-Run Growth, in Barro Ed. Business Cycle Theory..........

——(1994), Idea Gaps and Object Gaps in Economic Development, JME, 32 543-573.

——(1994), New Goods, Old Theory, and Trade, JDE,

——(1990), Endogenous Technological Change, JPE vol. 98, no. 5, pt. 21.

—— (1993), Idea Gaps and Object Gaps in Economic Development, JOME, 32 543-573.

Rosensweig and Taylor 1990 in Taylor, Lance ed. 1990: Socially Relevant Policy Analysis: Structuralist Computable General Equilibrium Models for the Developing World, MIT Press, Cambridge 1990.

Roubini Nouriel and Sala-i-Martin (1992), A Growth Model of Inflation, Tax Evasion, and Financial Repression, NBER, working paper no. 4062.

—— (1991), Financial Repression and Economic Growth, JDE 39(July) 5-30 North Holland.

Rozelle Scott, Boisvert Richard N. (1995), Control in a Dynamic Village Economy: The Reforms and Unbalanced Development in China's Rural Economy, JOEDC vol. 46(1995)233-252.

Rutherford, Thomas F. (1995), Extension of GAMS for Complementary Problems Arising in applied Economic Analysis, Journal of Economic Dynamics and Control, 19 (1995) 1299-1324.

——(1995), Microeconomics of General Equilibrium: An Intermediate Level Introduction to MPSGE, a manuscript, Department of Economics, University of Colorado, Boulder.

—— (1995), Alternative Treatment of Capital Adjustment for EPPA: Formulation Strategies and Implications for Model Results, a manuscript ,MIT, 1995.

——(1994), The GAMS/MPSGE and GAMS/MILES User Notes, 1994.

Saint Paul, Gilles (1992a), Technological Choice, Financial Markets and Economic Development, European Economic Review, 36(4, May) 763-781.

——(1992b), Technological Dualism, Incomplete Financial Markets and economic Development JOITAED, 1 (1,June) 13-26.

Samuelson, Paul A. (1958), An Exact Consumption-loan Model of Interest with or without the Social Contrivance of Money, JPE, vol. LXVI, no.6 Dec. 1958.

Sargent Thomas J, Macroeconomic Theory, Academic Press Inc. 1987.

——(1987), Dynamic Macroeconomic Theory, HUP, Cambridge, MA.

Sargent, Thomas J. and Wallace, Neil (1975), "Rational" Expectations, the Optimal Monetary Instrument, and the Optimal Money Supply Rule, JPE, 1975, pp. 241-254.

Scarf, Herbert E. (1986), The Computation of Equilibrium Prices, in Scarf Herbert E and Shoven John B. 1986: Applied General Equilibrium Analysis, CUP.

Scarf Herbert E and Shoven John B. (1986), Applied General Equilibrium Analysis, CUP.

Schreft, Stacey L, Smith Bruce D. (1993), Money, Banking and Capital Formation, Manuscript, Federal Reserve Bank of Richmond and Minneapolis.

Scheinkman, Jose A. and Weiss Laurence (1986), Borrowing Constraints and Aggregate Economic Activity, Econometrica, Janaury 23-45.

Selowsky Marcelo and Van Der Tak H.G. (1986), The Debt Problem and Growth, World Development, 14:9 pp.1107-1124.

Serven Luis (1992), Private Investment and Macroeconomic Adjustment: A Survey, WBRO, vo. 7, no. 1, (jan 1992) pp.95-114.

Serven, Luis and Solimano, Andres (1993), Debt Crisis, Adjustment Policies and Capital Formation in Developing Countires: Where Do We Stand?, World Development, Vol. 21, no.1, pp.127-140, 1993.

Shaw, Edward S. (1973), Financial Deepening in Economic Development, OUP, New York.

Shea, Jia Dong: (1994), Taiwan: Development and Structural Change of the Financial System, in Patrick, Hugh T. and Park, Yung Chul ed. 1994: The Financial Development of Japan, Korea and Taiwan : Growth, Repression and Liberalization, OUP, New York.

Shoven John B. and Whalley John (1992), Applying General Equilibrium, CUP, 1992.

——(1984), Applied General-Equilibrium Models of Taxation and International Trade: An Introduction and Survey, JEL, vol. XXII, Sept, 1984, pp. 1007-1051.

Solow, Robert M. (1956), A Contribution to the Theory of Economic Growth, QJE, pp.65-95.

Stiglitz, Joseph E., (1993), The Role of States in Financial Markets,Proceedings of the World Bank Annual Conference in Development Economics 1993, pp. 19-61.

Stiglitz, Joseph E and Weiss Andrew (1981), Creit Rationing in Markets with Imperfect Competition, AER, June, 393-410.

Stokey, Nancy L. and Lucas Robert E.Jr. (1989), Recursive Methods in Economic Dynamics, HUP, Cambridge, MA.

Stokey, Nancy (1991), Human Capital, Product Quality, and Growth, QJE, 1991 pp.587-616.

Stokey, Nancy l., (1991), The Volume and Composition of Trade Between Rich and Poor Countires, Rev. of Economid Studies, (1991) 58: pp.63-80.

Stokey Nancy and Lucas Robert E., Recursive Methods in Economic Dynamics, 1989, HUP, Cambridge MA.

Storm, Servaas, (1994), The Macroeconomic Impact of Agricultural Polcy:A CGE Analysis for India, JPM 16(1):55-95 (1994).

Sussman Oren (1992), A Theory of Financial Developement, in Finance and Development: Issues and Experience ed. Alberto Fiovannini, CUP, 29-57.

Taylor, Lance ed. (1990), Socially Relevant Policy Analysis: Structuralist Computable General Equilibrium Models for the Developing World, MIT Press, Cambridge 1990.

Teranishi, Juro (1994), Japan: Development and Structural Change of the Financial System, in Patrick, Hugh T. and Park, Yung Chul ed. 1994: The Financial Development of Japan, Korea and Taiwan : Growth, Repression and Liberalization, OUP, New York.

Thorton John (1987), The Short-Run Impact of the May 1986 Interest Rate Liberalization in Nepal, Journal of Development Administration, Vol. 9, No. 2, Dec. 1987, pp. 13-22.

Tobin, James (1969), A general Equilibrium Approach to Monetary Theory, JMCB, 1969 pp. 15-29, 1969.

——(1965), Money and Economic Growth, Econometrica , Vol. 33, No. 4 Oct. 1965.

——(1968), Notes on Optimal Monetary Growth, JPE, 1968 pp. 833-59.

——(1968), A Dynamic Aggregative Model, JPE, 63:1955 pp. 103-15.

——(1981), Money and Finance in Macroeconomic Process: Nobel Lecture, 1981, JMCB vol. 14, no. 2, May 1982.

——(1956), The Interest Elasticity of Transaction Demand for Cash 1956, Rev of Eco. Stat. vol. XXXVIII, no. 3, Aug. 1956.

Todd, Michael J. (1986), Efficient Methods of Applied General Equilibria, in Scarf Herbert E and Shoven John B. 1986: Applied General Equilibrium Analysis, CUP.

Torstel Phillip A. (1993), The Effect of Taxation on Human Capital, JPE, 1993, vol. 101, no. 2

Towsend, Robert M. (1983), Financila Stucture and Economic Activity. AER, Dec. 1983, pp. 895-911.

Turtleboom, B. (1991), Interest Rate Liberalisation: Some Lessons from Africa, IMF Working Paper WP/91/121, December.

Uzawa, H. (1962), On a Two-Sector Model of Economic Growth, Review of Economic Studies, 29 (1962) pp. 40-47.

——(1964), Optimal Growth in a Two-Sector Model of Capital Accumulation, Review of Economic Studies, 31 (1964) pp.1-25.

Varian, Hal R. (1992), Microeconomic Analysis, 3rd edition, W.W. Norton and Company, New York.

Villanueva, Delano and Mirakhor Abbas (1990), Strategies for Financial Reforms: Interst Policies, Stabilization, and bank Supervision in Developing Countries, IMF Staff Paper Vol. 37 No. 3.

Walras, L. Elements of Pure Economics, Allen and Unwin, London, 1954.

Wanda, Tseng and Corker Rober, Financial Liberalization, Money Demand, and Monetary Policy in Asian Countries, 1991, IMF, Occasional Paper No. 84.

Wang, Ping and Yip Chong K. (1992), Alternative Approaches to Money and Growth, JMCB, 1992 vol. 24, no. 4, Nov., 1992.

Whalley, John (1985), Trade Liberalization Among Major World Trading Areas, MIT Press, Cambridge, 1985.

White, Howard, (1992), The Macroeconomic Impact of Development Aid: A Critical Survey, JDS, vol.28, Jan. 1992, pp.163-240.

Weiss, Laurence (1980), A Model of International Trade and Finance, QJE, Sept. 1980.

Wijnbergergen Sweder Van, (1991), Fiscal Deficits, Exchange Rate Crises and Inflation, Rev. of Econ. Studies, (1991) 58, pp.81-92.

Williamson Stephen D. (1986), Costly Monetaring, Financial Intermediation, and Equilibrium Credit Rationing, JME, 18 159-179.

Winton Andrew (1995), Delegated Monitoring and Banmk Structure in a Finite Economy, Journal of Financial Intermediation 4, 158-187(1995).

World Bank (1991), Lessons of Tax Reform, The World Bank, Washington D.C.

—— (1990), Making Adjustment Work for Poor: A Framework for Policy Reform in Africa; Washington D.C.

——Nepal: Poverty and Incomes (1991), A Joint Study of World Bank and UNDP, Washington D.C.

—— (1994), Nepal Fiscal Restructuring and Public Resource Management in the Nineties vol. I , II, Washington, D. C.

——(1975), Economy-wide models and development planning, OUP.

Yadav S., Otsuka K., and David C.C. (1992), Segmentation in Rural Financial Markets:The Case of Nepal, World Development, vol. 20 no.3, pp. 423-436.

Yang, Ya-Hwei (1994), Taiwan: Development and Structural Change of the Banking System, in Patrick, Hugh T. and Park, Yung Chul ed. 1994: The Financial Development of Japan, Korea and Taiwan : Growth, Repression and Liberalization, OUP, New York.

Young Alwyn (1991), Learning by Doing and the Dynamic Effects of International Trade, QJE, 1991 pp. 369-405.